UNCOMMON COURAGE

The yachtsmen volunteers of World War Two

Julia Jones

**ADLARD
COLES**

LONDON · OXFORD · NEW YORK · NEW DELHI · SYDNEY

ADLARD COLES
Bloomsbury Publishing Plc
50 Bedford Square, London, WC1B 3DP, UK
29 Earlsfort Terrace, Dublin 2, Ireland

BLOOMSBURY, ADLARD COLES and the Adlard Coles logo are trademarks of
Bloomsbury Publishing Plc

First published in 2022

A catalogue record for this book is available from the British Library

Library of Congress Cataloguing-in-Publication data has been applied for

ISBN: HB: 978-1-4729-8710-5; ePub: 978-1-4729-8708-2; ePDF: 978-1-4729-8709-9

2 4 6 8 10 9 7 5 3 1

Typeset by Deanta Global Publishing Services, Chennai, India
Printed and bound in Great Britain by CPI Group (UK) Ltd, Croydon CR0 4YY

To find out more about our authors and books visit www.bloomsbury.com and sign up
for our newsletters

Contents

Introduction

A riddle in the attic

I came to this story by accident. I was searching a far corner of the attic for something else entirely. Our family yacht, *Peter Duck,* built for writer Arthur Ransome immediately after WWII, was almost wrecked when she circumnavigated Britain in 1991. Someone had asked me for the logbook. Instead, I found a blue HM stationery office folder containing an account by my father, George Jones, of a trip to the Baltic in August 1939. Dimly, guiltily, I remembered him showing it to me and my brother years ago, when we were teenagers, and mentioning that he'd gone through the Kiel Canal. When he had returned – on 2 September 1939 – he found that his naval call-up papers had been waiting for a week. He put on his new uniform and left immediately for Scotland. There, he was to join HMS *Forth*, depot ship of the 2nd Submarine Flotilla. He had become Probationary Temporary Paymaster Sub-Lieutenant Jones RNVR.

Later, he would receive his commission – the formal document 'Charging and Commanding [him] to observe and execute the King's Regulations and Admiralty Instructions for the Government of His Majesty's Naval Service […] and likewise Charging and Commanding Officers and Men subordinate to you according to the said Regulations, Instructions or Orders to behave themselves with all due Respect and Obedience to you their Superior Officer.' This was a new, highly ordered world of duty and hierarchy, entered voluntarily at a time of national emergency on the basis of his personal passion for messing around in boats. I'm sorry, now, that I didn't show more interest.

My father was 21 years old in 1939 and would remain in uniform for the next six years. The course of his life would be in the hands of others, its outcome unguessable. The account I'd found was stored in a suitcase of miscellaneous diaries, a few photos and some papers from his wartime service, including his commission. I gave up my search for the logbook, settled down (not very comfortably), and began to read. It wasn't long before the tears were streaming down my face as I began to feel the impact of this prequel to the person I had loved. He was so young, so uncertain...

I discovered that, earlier in 1939, my father had been accepted by the Royal Naval Volunteer Supplementary Reserve (RNVSR), an organisation of which I knew nothing. They had arranged a summer cruise with four other men, on *Naromis*, a small, modern, 38ft motor-yacht. Dad's diary revealed that he'd paid the organiser 9 guineas and thought he was going to Danzig. *Danzig*? In August 1939?! They didn't get there. When *Naromis* had reached Kiel, my father and his shipmate Bill (RNVSR member William Archibald Fuller KC, not his normal social circle) wandered around the harbour taking photographs of warships. They already had pictures of merchant shipping in the Scheldt and the Royal Netherlands Navy cruiser *Van Tromp* spotted in Den Helder. They'd seen type 740 U-boats waiting to lock out at Brunsbüttel and had scurried to the edge of the Nord-Ostsee-Kanal to avoid collision with two of Germany's latest destroyers, *Karl Galster* and *Eric Giese*. They'd dipped their ensign; the Germans had returned their salute and waved.

As *Naromis* arrived in the Kieler Fjord on 16 August, her crew glimpsed the heavy cruiser *Admiral Hipper* in the twilight. The following morning, she was gone, but the cruisers *Leipzig*, *Nürnberg*, *Königsberg* and *Köln* were there, along with the *Gneisenau,* pride of the German Navy. More photographs were taken. Then, the official attitude changed. Where they'd initially been welcomed to the Yacht Club of Germany and found themselves exchanging slightly surprised 'Heil Hitlers' with officers of the Kriegsmarine, now they were told that they must go. This was effectively enforced: there would be no more fuel available to them while they remained in German waters.

On the morning they left Kiel (18 August), my father had walked into the town to buy milk and bread. 'I was treated to the sight of the citizens of Kiel lining up for their gas mask at what seemed to me an extraordinary hour, seven o'clock in the morning. Things must be pretty serious for them to be issued at all. My mind rushed back to the September crisis of a year before. I got the milk and bread and hurried back to the ship.'[1] The skipper recognised it was time for his daughter, Iris, to depart Berlin.

Naromis was owned by a banker, WJ Clutton, a WWI veteran working for Schröders, a company with substantial – and problematic – business interests in Germany. She was a Gentleman's yacht powered by two hefty Dorman diesel engines with only a scrap of sail. Clutton's plan to meet his daughter at their next stop, Warnemünde (still heading east towards Danzig), had to be cancelled. Instead, *Naromis* set her course north for Denmark, firmly escorted out of German waters by a minesweeper. The fjord that morning was alive with naval vessels: a minelayer, small U-boats practising their diving, a torpedo boat that raced past upsetting their washing up, a gunnery school tender that opened fire as if they were the target. The Kelsnor lighthouse in Langeland was a welcome sight. They would wait for Iris in Copenhagen. My father felt relieved.

Photography continued as they cruised north through Denmark and Sweden. They refuelled at Farsund in Norway before crossing the oddly empty North Sea to arrive in Aberdeen on 30 August. Bill Fuller and my father were not recording warships as they explored Scandinavia. The list I found in Dad's attic suitcase detailed bridges, shipyards and oil tanks. He had sent them all to the Admiralty's Naval Intelligence Department (NID). The photographs of warships had been despatched as soon as he had reached HMS *Forth*; the topographical features followed later, in December 1941. I found letters of acknowledgements from the NID. To me, then, 'naval intelligence' sounded like secret service – James Bond and all that. Was my father some sort of spy?

I began to investigate the organisation he had joined, the RNVSR. It was not large: at most it claimed 2,000 names, though I have not been able to trace as many. Socially, it ranged from earls to Birmingham clerks (my father). All of them were male; all were British; all were yachtsmen, though that term included men like Adrian Seligman, who'd spent two years exploring the Pacific in his three-masted barquentine, the *Cap Pilar*; competitors from the prestigious Fastnet Race, such as the barrister Ewen Montagu; international dinghy racers like the ornithologist Peter Scott;

weekend sailors and 'social' yachtsmen like Arthur Prideaux, who claimed to have called in for a gin and ended up commanding a destroyer. There were accountants, solicitors, teachers, typesetters, vicars' sons and advertising agents.

My father was a tenant farmer's son who'd learned to sail on the River Deben in Suffolk. His father had died in an accident and the farm had been sold. He was indeed a passionate small boat sailor but one who was more likely to be found sleeping on floorboards up a creek or trawling under sail for flatfish than wearing a blazer at Cowes. In 1939, he and his brother Jack were both living in Birmingham. My father had completed his articles with a somewhat rackety stockbroker and was uncertain whether he wanted to be a currency dealer, a bargeman or a poet. His characteristic expenditure was measured in shillings and pence. Nevertheless, he had celebrated his acceptance into the RNVSR by writing to the naval outfitters Gieves, to order a silk tie. 'I tell everyone I am an officer,' he wrote in his diary, 'but nothing about the probationary, temporary bit.'

I don't remember him ever mentioning the RNVSR, though I now know he had remained a member long after the war was over. All it had been, initially, was a list of 'gentlemen, who are interested in yachting or similar pursuits'[2] who were aged between 18 and 39 and would be prepared to serve as naval officers in case of an 'Emergency'. They had to be physically fit, resident in the UK and the son of natural-born or naturalised British parents. In the years before WWII, they were neither paid nor (officially) trained. If they managed to inveigle themselves on board a destroyer for a week, they stumped up their own expenses. As soon as RNVSR members were called up for wartime service, they became part of the Royal Naval Volunteer Reserve (RNVR), always retaining the prefix 'Temporary'.

The 'regular' RNVR had been in existence since 1903, established by an Act of Parliament, and was able to offer its volunteers expenses-paid training, an orderly progression of courses and promotions and a uniform allowance. It comprised both officers and men, sometimes with specialist functions such as wireless operators or electricians. Social background wasn't necessarily an issue, nor was an interest in small boat sailing. As war drew closer, the Admiralty made use of the RNVR 'Special' branch, a designation for men who hadn't done any naval training, wouldn't be expected to go to sea, but had some desirable skill. This might be something tangible such as meteorology; pre-war, it was more likely to be the networking ability, charm and possible lack of scruple that might qualify someone as an 'assistant naval attaché'. An RNVR uniform provided a convenient camouflage for an increasingly eclectic range of potentially useful individuals. When clergymen or doctors offered their professional skills, they too became part of the RNVR.

In 1939, the Navy's professional reservists were the officers and men of the Royal Naval Reserve (RNR). They were seamen – merchant navy, fishermen, paid yacht crew – who undertook regular specialist training courses that qualified them to serve with the Royal Navy (RN) in times of crisis. A number of these men had started their careers in the Navy but had been dismissed as surplus to requirements in the post-WWI depression. There was a retired list where ageing officers dawdled on half-pay. When war began, entire crews of merchant ships or fishing vessels were offered the choice of signing up via a T124 agreement or losing their jobs. Later, men were conscripted as 'Hostilities Only' ratings. More openings were advertised for 'elderly yachtsmen' as the manpower shortage intensified. It wasn't always easy for these volunteers to adapt to the Nelsonian mould. Perhaps it wasn't always desirable.

The Navy was a profoundly hierarchical institution, both in its systems and social outlook. In the early war years, the gulf between officers and men was very difficult to cross – even for 'petty officers' (those with ranks and responsibilities but without commissions). Casual prejudice was expressed through the saying that 'RNVR officers were gentlemen trying to be sailors: RNR were sailors trying to be gentlemen and the RN were neither, trying to be both.' The RNVSR formed a subset within subsets. They were gentlemen by official definition, sailors by choice and would only ever be temporary. What did this mean to them as they cast off from their families and from the careers that (aged 18–39) they were perhaps only commencing or were already well established? Was there something in the ethos of yachting that predisposed them to volunteer for such an ill-defined experience? 'Throw off the bowlines. Sail away from the safe harbor. Catch the trade winds in your sails. Explore. Dream. Discover.'[3] 'Grab a Chance and you won't be sorry for a might have been.'[4] But this was war, not exploration. Within my father's book collection I found Peter Scott writing in 1945 about the 'strain, discomfort and boredom, which are the three predominant features in modern warfare'[5] and Robert Hichens' *We Fought Them in Gunboats* published in February 1944, by which time Hichens (b. 1909) was dead.

Yachting is a way of life with a literary habit. People write up their logbooks as a duty, then go a little further and offer their adventure to a Club Journal or a magazine. Although, like so many of their wartime generation, the yachtsmen volunteers tended not to talk about their experiences, many of them wrote. Some, such as Nicholas Monsarrat, Nevil Shute, Ludovic Kennedy, Robert Hichens and Peter Scott, wrote contemporaneously; others after some years had passed – Denys Rayner, Iain Rutherford, Robin Balfour, Ewen Montagu, Edward Young, David Howarth, Francis Brooks Richards, Adrian Seligman, Fredman Ashe Lincoln, Patrick Dalzel-Job, Arthur Bennett, Edward Terrell, Stewart Platt, Rozelle Pierrepont. Not all of them were published: Eric Newell, Kenneth Jacob and Peter Cooper left typescripts with their families and I'm willing to bet that there are others tucked away in the far corners of attics, in sturdy leather suitcases, still waiting for their readers.

I looked at the evidence of my father's photographs – not the warships or the topography but the few black-and-white head-and-shoulders uniform snaps – and began my belated attempt to understand what this period had meant to him, and to the hundreds of other yachtsmen who'd put their lives on hold as they volunteered to serve 'for the duration'.

'There must be hundreds of chaps like me'[1]
1903–1918: The formation of RNVR and WWI

When I told friends about my discovery of my father's typescript and my surprise at his activities, several people commented 'It's like *The Riddle of the Sands*!' For those who haven't read Erskine Childers' yachting masterpiece (his only novel, published in 1903), it tells the tale of two young men, not naturally congenial, who get over snobbery and social awkwardness to search the sands and creeks of the Frisian Islands. Davies and Carruthers show bravery, physical endurance, meticulous chart work, independence and imagination. They steer a careful course between reconnaissance and spying, and in doing so, foil plans for a German invasion of England. Childers' style is not that of the action-packed thriller. Some readers might share Carruthers' feelings as he reads *Dulcibella*'s logbook: 'The bulk dealt with channels and shoals with weird and depressing names [...] "Kedging-off" appeared to be a frequent diversion; "running aground", an almost daily occurrence. It was not easy reading.'[2] The central action of the novel is the day-to-day practical challenge of handling a small, relatively comfortless yacht in shallow waters and bad weather. It's enlivened by the interplay of character, an indefinable tension and the central mystery.

Erskine Childers (1870–1922) surprised his colleagues in the House of Commons clerks' department when they discovered his enthusiasm for the muddy creeks of the English East Coast or for blowing across to France in an 18ft semi-open boat with a tent. He was a member of the Royal Cruising Club (RCC) and had spent three months during 1897 exploring the Baltic in *Vixen* (aka *Dulcibella*), a converted ship's lifeboat. His time in Kiel and nearby Flensburg had alerted him to significant developments in the Imperial German Navy and the potential threat these posed to Britain. He wrote up his cruise for the RCC *Journal*, as well as for *Yachting Monthly* magazine. The resulting novel, *The Riddle of the Sands*, was both a warning against Germany at a time when she was not thought to be Britain's natural enemy, and an advocacy of irregular small boat warfare with a plea for the special skills of yachtsmen. Childers sets out an invasion scenario in which precise knowledge of coasts and depths is crucial for an amphibious landing. He imagines defensive tactics involving a swarm of shallow-draught boats. Specialist knowledge – and the right type of person – would be essential for success: 'Reckless pluck is abundant in the British Navy but expert knowledge of the tides and shoals in these waters is utterly lacking. The British charts are of no value and there is no evidence that the subject has been studied in any way by the British Admiralty.'[3]

This is where Childers' hero, Arthur Davies, small boat sailor and amateur hydrographer, sees an opportunity. In early youth, he had failed to gain acceptance into the Navy: 'And I can't settle down to anything else,' he said. 'I read no end about it and yet I am a useless outsider. All I've been able to do is to potter about in small boats, but it's all been wasted until this chance came.' Carruthers is sympathetic: 'There ought to be chances for chaps like you,' I said, 'without the accident of a job such as this.'[4]

Davies insists he's just one of many: 'There must be hundreds of chaps like me – I know a good many myself – who know our coasts like a book – shoals, creeks, tides, rocks; there's nothing in it, it's only practice. They ought to make some use of us as a naval reserve.'

On 4 March 1903, the Naval Forces Bill was introduced 'to provide for the Constitution of a Royal Naval Volunteer Reserve'. *The Riddle of the Sands* was published in May. The Bill became law in June. Plenty of campaigners then and since have pinned their hopes on government guidance, only to experience disillusion as officialdom crushes the spirit of the enterprise. And so it was with the RNVR in the years before WWI: it bore little resemblance to Davies' (or Childers') concept of expertise and individual initiative. Early volunteers were drilled on military lines and rarely got to sea. Their dedication ensured that they made impressive progress against establishment prejudice but Davies wouldn't have wanted to join. It was not until the formation of the RNVSR in 1936 that 'chaps like him' would be welcomed for their specific skills as yachtsmen.

Nevertheless, *The Riddle of the Sands* was immediately influential on publication. It also inspired plenty of young men with 'reckless pluck' to turn their cruises into reconnaissance trips. Maldwin Drummond quotes a tongue-in-cheek article that calls for its suppression: 'Too many young men of patriotic instincts in whom the love of adventure is strong have chartered small boats and cruised stealthily among the islands in question to the great scandal of the authorities of the Fatherland in whose blood the microbe of spy-mania flourishes exceedingly.' The yachtsmen get arrested, sales of the book go up, more young men are inspired to set out and the writer foresees a time when 'the key of a German prison will turn on the last able-bodied Englishman, and when our country, defended only by women, infants and invalids, will be at the mercy of any unneighbourly neighbour who may choose to attack it.'[5]

Gordon Shepherd (b. 1885) was just such an enthusiast. Erskine and Molly Childers invited him sailing on their Colin Archer-designed yacht *Asgard* (a wedding present from Molly's wealthy father) and Shepherd was soon hooked. In 1912, he explained his position to the First Lord of the Admiralty, Winston Churchill:

I am a yachtsman of much experience and have during the past few years made extended trips in a twelve-ton sailing yacht along the German coast and in the Baltic. As I am an officer in the Regular Army, a friend of mine who is an officer in the Naval Intelligence Department at the Admiralty suggested to me that any information I could procure regarding coast defences and channels in foreign waters would be of great service [...] During my last trip I had the misfortune to be arrested at Emden, but I had carried out investigations in a sufficiently prudent manner to prevent the German authorities having any grounds for taking legal proceedings, and after four days' detention I was released.[6]

Lieutenant Vivian Brandon RN and Captain Bernard Trench (Royal Marines) were less fortunate. In 1909, they had both been in Kiel serving on the training ship HMS *Cornwall*, where they had successfully assisted Captain Reginald Hall with some undercover photography. They had changed out of their uniforms, borrowed a private motorboat, then sped round the harbour, 'breaking down' at the site that Captain Hall wanted to investigate. Subsequently, however, the two young men used their own initiative to go on a yachting holiday to the Frisian Islands. Brandon was arrested far too close to a coastal battery on Borkum, and photographs of coastal areas and defence installations were discovered under the mattress in Trench's hotel room in Emden. They were both charged with spying. At their trial in Leipzig, the prosecution waved a copy of *The Riddle of the Sands* at them. 'Yes,' said Lieutenant Brandon, 'I've read it. I've read it three times.'[7] They were sentenced to four years in prison. The Admiralty refused to make any contribution to their legal fees, or the cost of prison subsistence, until 1914 when their former captain, now admiral, 'Blinker' Hall, became the Director of Naval Intelligence (DNI). Brandon and Trench then joined his unorthodox and successful Room 40 team, which made a significant contribution to victory in WWI.

In the months immediately before WWII, Admiral Hall came out of retirement to give the new DNI, Admiral John Godfrey, the benefit of his advice. One of his recommendations was that Godfrey should appoint a 'fixer' – someone with contacts, imagination and unofficial unscrupulousness who would be effective at getting things done. He suggested that the City of London might be a good place to look. In July 1939, Godfrey appointed Ian Fleming, then a stockbroker, giving him a Special Branch commission in the RNVR. Fleming wasn't a yachtsman but he often made use of the amateur sailors' skills in ways Childers would have approved. As I had sorted through my father's attic suitcase, I had felt puzzled by the different timescales with which his and Bill's *Naromis* photographs were accepted by the NID. I didn't guess that the creator of James Bond would provide the answer.

In 1906, with the Anglo–German naval arms race intensifying, Childers had become more interested in the possibility of Britain occupying the Frisian Islands than in Germany invading England. He sent a discussion paper, 'Remarks on the German North Sea Coast in its Relation to War between Great Britain and Germany',[8] to a friend, Sir George Clarke, then secretary for the Committee for Imperial Defence. Though little came of this, the idea would be picked up again in the early months of WWI.

Meanwhile, Childers had demonstrated 'the innate subversiveness of small boat sailing'[9] in a much more controversial manner through his involvement with the Howth gun-running. In July 1914, Childers and Gordon Shepherd, with Childers' wife Molly and his Irish cousin Mary Spring Rice, had used *Asgard* to deliver 1,500 rifles and ammunition to the Irish Volunteers. Part of the load was carried by yachtsman Conor O'Brien, another Spring Rice cousin, on his yacht *Kelpie*.

In August 1914, Childers was recalled to London by the Admiralty and given a commission in the RNVR and the task of looking again at plans for the invasion and occupation of Borkum and Juist. He accepted gladly. It appears, however, this was an official stitch-up: a means of diverting the over-enthusiastic First Lord of the Admiralty, Winston Churchill, who had put the idea forward at a Cabinet meeting. Childers was set to work with no professional support. When he produced his report, Captain Herbert Richmond, the Assistant Director of Naval Operations, who had requested it, wrote: 'It is quite mad. The reasons for capturing it are NIL, the possibilities about the same. I have never read such an idiotic, amateur piece of work as this outline in my life.'[10] Childers had attached a personal note to his report: 'The writer ventures to hope that he may have the honour of being employed, if the service permits, whether in aeroplane work or in any other capacity if any of the operations sketched in this memo are undertaken.'

He was seconded to the Royal Naval Air Service and despatched to HMS *Engadine*, a former cross-Channel railway ferry. She had been modified to carry seaplanes and was being sent to Harwich. On 4 August, the first night of the war, the former Hamburg–Heligoland excursion boat, *Königin Luise*, had left her home port of Emden and headed for the English coast. She began laying her mines at dawn. These were the moored variety, lying concealed below the surface, some of them about 30 miles from Orford Ness off the Suffolk coast. Next day, destroyer leader HMS *Amphion* and the 3rd Flotilla left Harwich Harbour to patrol across to the Dutch Island of Terschelling and discovered her at work. They attacked and sank her, managing to rescue most of her crew. Returning from patrol the following morning, however, the Harwich destroyers crossed the minefield. HMS *Amphion* struck a mine and sank with the loss of 169 people, including the 18 German prisoners rescued earlier.

HMS *Engadine's* task was to use her three seaplanes to try to spot mines, with Childers helping to identify likely areas and instruct the Royal Naval Air Station (RNAS) pilots in navigation. He resurrected the North Sea charts that he'd been annotating and correcting since his first cruises in *Vixen*, together with the photographs and coastal postcards that he'd also been collecting. He flew with the pilots as often as he could, though this was not part of his job spec. On one occasion, bobbing 20 miles off the coast with engine failure, dusk approaching and no real hope of rescue, he felt impelled to write Molly a letter of apology for these unnecessary forays into danger: 'You must forgive me if I was wrong to fly. You must trust me that I decided it was my duty as the only way of making real use of myself.'[11]

The 'regular' RNVR volunteers, meanwhile, who had conscientiously committed their free time and hard-earned money to weekly drill, often subsidising their own equipment and premises, had been formed into the Royal Naval Division and marched away to land-based warfare. The London Division, feeling betrayed, ceremonially interred a marlinspike and a copy of the *Admiralty Manual of Seamanship* next to their headquarters as a symbol of their lost ambitions.

On Christmas Day 1914, Childers flew as an observer on the Cuxhaven Raid. This was seen as a new type of warfare; a pre-emptive strike by air and sea against suspected Zeppelin sheds near the mouth of the Elbe, with the additional motive of luring the German High Seas fleet out to an old-style naval battle. Although the raid itself was unsuccessful, Childers' contribution to the navigation planning was appreciated by the expedition commander, Roger Keyes. A copy of *The Riddle of the Sands* was sent to every ship in the fleet.

By the spring of 1916, Childers was back in England, where he and Molly learned, with shock and distress, that the weapons they had landed in Howth in 1914 had been used by Sinn Féin extremists as they proclaimed a republic in Dublin on Easter Monday.

The schoolboy Nevil Shute Norway (b. 1899) was in Dublin then. His elder brother Fred had died in France the previous year and their father, director of the postal service, had decided to store his son's most precious personal relics in the General Post Office for safekeeping. The building became the headquarters of the leaders of the Rising and was later destroyed by fire. Seventeen-year-old

Nevil, meanwhile, volunteered with the first aid services and dashed around the city. News from his mother made its way back to his prep school, Lynams in Oxford.

> *30/4/16. This week has been a wonderful week for Nevil, never before has a boy of seventeen had such an experience. Yesterday morning he was at the Automobile Club, filling cans of petrol from casks for the Red Cross Ambulances. In the afternoon he went round in an ambulance with the Lord Mayor collecting food for forty starving refugees harboured in the Mansion House, and then went out for wounded, and brought in an old man of 78 shot through the body. He was quite cheery and asked Nevil if he thought he would get over it? So Nevil said, 'Good Lord, yes! Why not?' and bucked the old man up.*

The headmaster (*Blue Dragon* yachtsman CC Lynam) commented: 'You might wonder at Nevil's pluck, but nowadays at the Public Schools the Officer Training Corps are preparing the boys for war and Nevil will have had two years of training, so that he was in readiness for such events as occurred in Dublin.'[12]

Childers, meanwhile, was making unsuccessful attempts to learn to fly so he could undertake additional reconnaissance for the new fast motorboat raids that were being planned. A new 'small ship' Navy was developing as trawlers, drifters, paddle steamers and other shallow-draught vessels were requisitioned in an attempt to clear the minefields and also to counter the threat from submarines. These brought belated opportunities for amateurs. Conor O'Brien was serving on a minesweeper. Edinburgh-born surgeon Sir Morton Smart, an enthusiast for fast motorboats, had been co-opted by Churchill to establish the Royal Naval Motor Boat Reserve (RNMBR). Small powerboats were chartered and their owners given temporary commissions in the RNVR. They enrolled their own crews and made themselves available 'for patrol and despatch work or such duties as the Admiralty may from time to time direct'.[13]

As the U-boat danger became more acute, larger private yachts were requisitioned, armed and sent on more wide-ranging patrols. Many of these were the rich men's yachts on which Carruthers would have enjoyed sitting under an awning in his snow-white ducks, sipping a drink and watching a regatta. Continuous patrolling into the North Sea winter was hard on these vessels 'and when their guns were fired parts of them were liable to drop off'.[14] By 1916, purpose-built motor launches (MLs) were being delivered from the USA via Canada, and new British-built coastal motorboats (CMBs) were being added to the fleet. These, finally, were the 'mosquitoes with stings' that Davies had dreamed of. 'They'd get wiped out often, but what matter? There'd be no lack of the right sort of men for them, if the thing was organised. But where are the men?'[15]

By 1916, the 'right sort of men' had very largely been dispersed elsewhere. New RNVR recruits from all backgrounds were being given their preliminary training at the Crystal Palace in London then sent either to the Royal Naval Division in the trenches or HMS *Hermione* for an eight-week course in navigation and ship handling to qualify them for command of the new MLs and CMBs. Childers had been posted to Dunkirk in the early months of 1917 to support them when he was abruptly sent back to Ireland to attend the Imperial Convention. He therefore missed the brave and violent raids on Zeebrugge and Ostend in which the RNVR played such an essential part.

His final posting was to King's Lynn, where his navigation skills were to be used by the new RAF long-range bombers. Their primary objective was Berlin. Childers had briefed his teams on 10 November 1918 when the operation was postponed due to bad weather. It was rescheduled for the afternoon of the following day but by then Britain and Germany were no longer at war. Until the next time.

2

'I happened to look around and he was gone'[1]

1918–1940: Growing up, sailing for pleasure

Though Childers had been relatively old when he served with the RNVR and RNAS during WWI, he was relatively young when he died, executed aged 52 by a military court of the Irish Free State in November 1922. The charge was derisory – possession of an ornamental pistol given to him by his former friend Michael Collins – but Childers was by this time hated and distrusted on all sides. Churchill described him as a murderous renegade. The night before he died, Childers summoned his 16-year-old son to his cell and made him promise to shake the hands of all those who had signed his death warrant. That promise was kept.

Although Childers' legacy to yachting literature remained secure, in the intermission between the two world wars almost everything that he'd urged and exemplified about the best practical use of amateur sailors' skills for national advantage was forgotten, together with the value of a small ships' navy.

Part of the amnesia may have come from a lack of communication between the generations. With 10 per cent of the British male population under 45 dead at the end of WWI, many fathers had not returned. Patrick Dalzel-Job (b. 1913) never forgot the day his mother told him that his father had died at the Battle of the Somme. She was looking away from him, brushing her hair; he was playing with a toy on the floor. Although he was only three years old, he understood at once what had happened. He stared at her back; she continued her brushing. He returned to his toy.

Dalzel-Job, who would later join the RNVSR and become one of Ian Fleming's 'intelligence commandos', describes their relative poverty and his mother's pride as she determined to survive on her widow's pension and refused to accept help from her family. Every meal 'was a matter of careful thought' and undernourished Patrick was often unwell. Eventually, his mother decided to take him away from school. They lived economically by a lake in the Jura mountains, where Patrick learned to ski, to speak a Swiss-French patois, and to explore. When he was attracted by the flat-bottomed local boats, his mother borrowed a sewing machine to help him make a lugsail. He began to study navigation by correspondence courses. In 1931, they returned to England and bought an elderly converted lifeboat on the Isle of Wight. Eventually, they moved to Loch Tarbert in Scotland, where Patrick spent a year building a schooner. The local boatyard needed to keep their skilled men employed so fashioned the hulls and spars 'for a ridiculously small sum'.

This schooner, *Mary Fortune,* then became their home. They spent two years wandering the coasts of the British Isles before crossing to Norway in the summer of 1937. Patrick learned the language, discovered how to make *Mary Fortune's* cabin snug in winter, and began to explore the intricate coastline, charmed by the friendliness of the local people. Soon he became so intrigued by the military possibilities of the Norwegian Inner Leads that he took ship for England and made contact with the Admiralty. 'I said I was likely to be at least two years exploring all of the coast as far as the Arctic Russian border and I offered to make detailed plans of all the places where small craft might hide in time of War.'[2] The Admiralty didn't seem very interested but Dalzel-Job went ahead anyway.

One of the strengths of Arthur Ransome's post-war novel *Swallows and Amazons* (1930) may have been its reassurance that youngsters were resilient and could cope. The period immediately following the Great War was a hard time to enter adulthood. Writer Margery Allingham (b. 1904) felt the lack of the immediately older generation, a need to take responsibility early and a pervasive sense of uncertainty: 'To most of our elders – and they were considerably our elders – this was a passing phase, a temporary lack of faith in humanity, a time of exhaustion after great trial; but to those of us who were green and rather frightened, as all people are at that age, there was nothing but broken planks wherever we trod.'[3]

Ransome's youngsters learn confidence. Yachting historian Mike Bender suggests that one of the achievements of the series is to give his readers a vision of England that was worth fighting and dying for – an unwelcome success (if indeed Ransome ever considered it) given that it would be his own young 'web-footed' readers who would be volunteering to make that potential sacrifice.

***

At the end of WWI, Nevil Shute was surprised to find that he was still alive. His school days had been overcast by the ever-growing Roll of Honour as younger schoolmasters and older contemporaries died. Before the war, he'd been lucky in his prep school, Lynams – a school marked by the personality of the headmaster, the 'Skipper', where pupils might enjoy boating on the Cherwell or answering exam questions on *The Riddle of the Sands*. During the time Shute was a pupil, 'Skipper' Lynam took the summer term of 1912 off in order to cruise to the North Cape in his 43ft yawl *Blue Dragon II*. (At school and in his non-literary life Nevil was known by his true surname 'Norway'. In this book I usually use his chosen literary surname 'Shute'.) In his autobiography *Slide Rule*, Nevil Shute claimed that this had helped inculcate the idea that it was 'very good for the character to engage in sports which put one's life in danger from time to time'.[4]

From 1914, however, Shute had moved on from Lynams to Shrewsbury School and wrote that 'the remainder of my time at school was mostly spent in preparation for war till finally my own turn came and I left school and went to war myself'.[5] As a 17-year-old, hampered by a stammer, he struggled to gain entry to the Royal Military Academy in Woolwich for training as a gunner with the Royal Flying Corps. In the summer of 1918, he admitted defeat and joined the Suffolk Regiment as a private. 'I had grown to accept the fact that in a very short time I should probably be dead.' In fact, his battalion was never sent overseas. Instead, he spent the last months of 1918 in Kent, helping to provide funeral parties for the large numbers of returning soldiers who were dying of Spanish flu, while mentally readjusting his own ideas to the fact 'that there was a strange stuff called fun to be got out of life'.

Sailing was fun. Shute returned to Oxford to study engineering, then spent his first long vacation crewing a 28-ton yawl for an elderly solicitor who could no longer afford a pre-war crew of paid hands so had advertised in *The Times* for undergraduates. The yawl, *Aeolia,* was moored on the Hamble. She was engineless and unhandy:

> *Running on the mud and kedging off was normal and collisions with other boats moored in the river were so frequent that it was the usual practice for the owner to keep a supply of visiting cards handy near the cockpit. When you collided with another yacht and carried away his crosstrees or his forestay, you would apologise politely for what was an everyday occurrence and hand your card to the owner or his paid hand, requesting him to send you in the bill and go bumping on your way to sea.*[6]

Robert ('Robin') Balfour (b. 1901), son of a Sheffield steel manufacturer, also answered an advertisement to act as a volunteer crew member for an elderly yachtsman whom he later dubbed 'the Mad Major' and thanked for teaching him so much about what not to do. There was just one paid 'hand', a Breton fisherman who was a wonderful seaman – when he wasn't drunk.

★★★

Sailing began to broaden its appeal. The titanic yacht racing where kings and emperors arrived at Cowes to compete in immense and beautiful J-class yachts continued, but on a reduced scale – King George V had inherited his father's *Britannia* but Kaiser Wilhelm II had been forced to abdicate and Tsar Nicholas II was murdered. Imperial ostentation was no longer in tune with the times. This was more the age of the weekend sailor, enthusiastic young men (and a few women) without very much money. 'The war to end all wars had ended but a land fit for heroes to live in was failing to provide a living for many of them. [...] The length of the working week included working until 12:00pm (noon) on Saturdays while any study was in your own time which made leisure and hobbies pretty limited.'[7]

Robin Balfour was learning his trade in his father's steelworks but still found time to build a 10ft cruising dinghy on which he hoped to be able to sleep on board with a friend. They had a primus, a paraffin lamp, a galvanised bucket for their creature comforts and a tent over the boom for shelter at night. One memorable expedition was the circumnavigation of Lincolnshire – 250 miles achieved in three weekends, with disproportionate effort and discomfort. Some friends chose not to sign on again but overall, Balfour was proud of his achievement.

Yachting on a Small Income (1925) by Maurice Griffiths was one of the publishing successes of the period. Griffiths was born in East London in 1902 but grew up in Ipswich, Suffolk. His salesman father had not fought in WWI but had not prospered either. His son needed to make his own way. When he lost his first job in the early 1920s' slump, he began developing his enthusiasm for yachts into a sales agency, run from his bedroom. In 1924, his father died, suddenly and almost bankrupt. Griffiths sold his own tiny yacht and began to think of ways to extend his business. He was already writing the evocative weekend adventures that would later be published as *Magic of the Swatchways* but this first book aimed to develop a commercial market for vessels 'other than those expensive white things that fluttered about the Solent and cost someone hundreds a year to run'.[8] It was sold on station bookstalls and was picked up by an entrepreneur who appointed Griffiths editor of a commercial news sheet, *Yacht Sales and Charters*. In 1927, this led to the editorship of *Yachting Monthly*, which gave him the platform he needed, not only to sell second-hand yachts but also to develop a concept of affordable small boat cruising that suited the ethos of the time – as well as its economics. *Magic of the Swatchways* (1932) and *Ten Small Yachts* (1933) brought the thrill of voyaging and self-reliance within reach of people who could not set off for months in the Baltic as they had only Friday evening (or Saturday lunchtime) until first thing Monday morning.

'Griff' became an authoritative figure, losing any vestige of social uncertainty and becoming much respected for his editorial pronouncements (whether right or wrong) and for his generous encouragement of others. Outdoor adventure was a way to prove oneself – as well as being fun.

Sailing clubs (usually less socially exclusive than yacht clubs) began to proliferate. The International 12 design was developed to try to reduce the cost of competitive dinghy racing from the established International 14, which cost more than a new car. Older professionals, such as bargemen put out of work by the economic depression, found themselves in demand to teach excited young dinghy sailors to manage their craft. Occasionally, one can glimpse these 'owd boys' as fulfilling an emotional need in the outwardly sophisticated, inwardly uncertain youngsters. On my own river, the Deben, barge skipper Jimmy Quantrill took my father and uncle under his care in the absence of their own father.

In 1931, Edward Stanley (b. 1907) succeeded his father as Baron Stanley of Alderley but dodged the tradition of successful public service until he joined the RNVSR. Instead, he acquired a gambling habit, drank too much, failed as a husband, and was eventually forced to sell the family estate. Yacht cruising, either alone or with a friend, brought him challenge and peace. In 1937, Stanley met Mr Parsons, the perfect 'paid hand'.

> *His advent began an association, and indeed a friendship, which was to last until the war put a stop to sailing [...] Parsons came from Brixham and had served many years in trawlers before taking to yachting. [...] A man who was at once both simple and robust, dependable and devoted, it can never be known what I owe him both for seamanship and friendship.*[9]

Some impecunious young couples discovered the practical appeal of boats as floating homes: AS Bennett had bought his first boat in 1925 with school prize money intended to be spent on books. In 1933, he and his wife Dorothy purchased one of many redundant sailing barges and converted her to a liveaboard, writing about the process and selling the resulting book as *June of Rochester* (1939). He based *June* in Kent then commuted to work in the City.

Advertising agent Eric Newell (b. 1902) and his wife Gladys lived first on the barge yacht *Nancibelle* (later a Dunkirk 'little ship'), then on *Fortis,* a 60ft ketch 'with every modern convenience throughout' – as *Yachting World* described her. They usually wintered afloat in Teddington but during the sailing season Newell had negotiated a rail pass that enabled him to commute from any port in the Southern Railways area to work at the SH Benson advertising agency in London.

Yachting Monthly's longest-serving correspondent (since 1906), Percy Woodcock (b. 1884), had consistently failed the medical inspections when he had attempted to join up during WWI. At first, he recalled, the other volunteers in line looked at him with sympathy: later, when he presented himself every six months as required by the conscription scheme, he was 'a lucky devil'. Woodcock had married, continued writing for *Yachting Monthly* under a variety of pseudonyms as well as his own name, and carefully persuaded his wife Ellie that she loved sailing almost as much as he did. The family's current yacht was usually their home and their son Samuel was their only child. Woodcock was inspired to write a series of 11 sailing adventure stories for his son and when Samuel was accepted into the Navy, it was a matter of great pride for his parents.

Those young men who had lost their fathers in WWI or whose relationships had been broken by wartime absence had more complex journeys into adulthood. Major Valentine Fleming MP was killed in 1917 when his oldest son Peter was ten years old, his second son Ian was nine, and his younger sons Richard and Michael were aged six and four respectively. Nicholas Rankin includes the detail that Major Fleming's *The Times* obituary, written by his friend Winston Churchill, hung on Ian's bedroom wall all his life. For the fictional character James Bond, 'M' (head of the secret service) is something of a father figure; for Lieutenant Commander Ian Fleming RNVR, Admiral John Godfrey, head of NID, may have filled a similar need. *Moonraker*, the 1955 novel that offers glimpses of Bond undertaking departmental paperwork (as Fleming did, unglamorously), expresses Bond/Fleming's affection for the admiral, describing 'the weatherbeaten face he knew so well and which held so much of his loyalty'.

The Navy itself was a patriarchal institution, inspiring loyalty and conferring – but also withdrawing – status. In the years after WWI, the regular Navy was drastically reduced, having an immediate impact on individuals and their families. 'There is a school of naval officers,' wrote Acting Sub-Lieutenant LHC Kennedy RNVR, 'who are embittered at an institution which has no use for their service as senior officers. Their bitterness is understandable. When you have devoted the best years of your life to a service which equips you for no other calling and flings you out when it is done with you, you are entitled to a complaint.' Kennedy believed this had been the case with his own father, Captain Edward Coverley Kennedy, who had been placed in the retired list in 1923. 'He could never altogether escape the weight of the blow. Meeting old Navy friends, hearing Navy talk from past shipmates, any incident which brought him in touch with the Navy, during the post-war years, reminded him with a pang of his yearning for the sea.'[10]

Many years later, Ludovic Kennedy (b. 1919) would discover that the circumstances of his father's final years in the Navy had not been straightforward. (Captain Kennedy had been court-martialled for leniency when sent to maintain order among strikers in a Depression area.) All his son knew, as he grew up, was that he loved his father deeply but Captain EC Kennedy (retired) was not always easy to get on with: 'To argue with my father was like arguing with a brick wall; there was no matter on earth on which he did not hold a precise and definite opinion. As he had held the same opinions for the past forty years there was no likelihood that my immature opinions would alter them.'[11]

Nicholas Monsarrat (b. 1910) remembered the wartime absence of his father Keith, a surgeon and a member of a territorial unit who had served principally in Salonika. He remembered his empty armchair and the lack of male control within their household. This came to feel normal: 'since nearly everyone we knew had the same story to tell, the same hollow space where a man had once been, and would return to, or *might* return to, or never would again.'[12] Although Keith Monsarrat did return, and continued his successful professional practice, his was a permanent emotional absence from his family, an unknowability as he sealed off that period of his life. His son described it later as a 'fierce' privacy.

Nicholas rebelled against what he saw as his parents' values – conservatism, imperialism, financial responsibility, the class structure. He indignantly denied his mother's assertion that every Englishman had salt water in his veins. She had been dressing him in sailor suits since earliest childhood; family holidays had been spent in the sailing haven of Trearddur Bay, Anglesey, where his elder brother Toby had died and been buried. He did very much enjoy being part of the sailing club and then venturing further as navigator when his friends bought yachts, but uniforms, militarism and the Navy were beyond the pale. He was a committed pacifist.

Monsarrat didn't put his name forward as a naval volunteer either before the war or in its early months. Instead, he served as a

London ambulance driver – when there were no casualties – and an ARP organiser, before there were air raids. Then, in April 1940, his father sent him an advertisement from *The Times*. 'Gentlemen with yachting experience' were invited to apply for commissions as temporary probationary sub-lieutenants in the RNVR. Monsarrat capitulated, filled in the application form and relished the irony that he discovered himself immediately endorsing all the parental values he'd spent his life so far denying. All the other young men in this chapter had already done the same.

3

'They ought to make some use of us'[1]

1936: The formation of the RNVSR

When Lieutenant Commander DA Rayner (b. 1908), from the 'regular' RNVR, said goodbye to his wife Elizabeth in September 1939, he told her he was glad that 'his' war had come. Both his father and hers had been machine gunners in WWI. They had participated in many of the major actions and were lucky to have survived. Perhaps they'd inculcated a feeling of inferiority? It wouldn't have been uncommon. Robert Hichens wrote that he had often thought about his father's wartime experience and wanted to test himself to see if he could keep cool under fire. When Patrick Dalzel-Job was in a post-D-Day Normandy field, surrounded by wounded and dying, he reminded himself that however bad things were for him, it had been worse for his father on the Somme. Tony Hugill, one of his companions in Fleming's 30AU, noticed Dalzel-Job's occasional compulsion to put himself in situations where he would be seriously frightened. Perhaps he was still testing himself?

Rayner had been obsessed by ships and the Navy since he was at prep school and was bitterly disappointed when he failed to gain acceptance into the service. The reason given was his flat feet but it was also at a time when harsh cutbacks were being implemented and new entrants were correspondingly unwelcome. His enthusiasm was rekindled by a representation of the Zeebrugge Raid in the British Empire Exhibition at Crystal Palace (April 1924–October 1925) and he began applying to his local RNVR division as soon as he left school. Within its limited role, the RNVR had won respect and admiration during WWI. It was inexpensive, so was not being reduced in the same proportion as the regular Navy. Its numbers were limited, however: there could be only 484 officers and 5,000 men throughout the country. Rayner called at HMS *Eaglet*, headquarters ship for the Mersey Division, in the first week of every month for five months until he was finally accepted as a probationary midshipman in July 1925. 'Throughout all those pre-war years I had to attend drill on at least one night of every week, and preferably on both the drill nights. I had to give up first one month and then fourteen days of my yearly holiday to service with the Navy.'[2] It was harder once he was married and he thanked Elizabeth for her 'forbearance'. Fourteen years later, it had finally been worth it.

Few committed yachtsmen joined the RNVR during this period – its requirements took too much time away from sailing. Rayner was an exception. He had used the *Yachting Monthly* advice pages to help him design his own small yacht, *Robinetta,* and accepted financial support from his father to have her built at Birkenhead.

Owing to the small capital available, and the need for economy in upkeep, the smallest possible sailing vessel is required to accommodate a young married man and his wife, or three young men. The vessel must be capable of open water cruising and must carry sufficient stores and water to be entirely independent from the shore for fourteen days.[3]

Rayner worked for the camera company Kershaw's, but that was just a job. His ambition was focused on promotion as an officer within the RNVR, despite the regular discouragement from the Mersey Division Captain Elgood. Almost all the volunteer officers chose specialist courses in gunnery, though signals, torpedo and navigation were also available options. Rayner, growing adventurous as a yachtsman, asked Elgood for permission to take the specialist navigator's course. His captain did his best to refuse, telling Rayner that the Navy would never allow a ship to be navigated by an RNVR officer, and that if he wanted to spend the whole of the next war correcting charts, he was going the right way about it. Rayner persisted and passed the exams with such high marks that the admiral commanding reserves sent a message of congratulation to Mersey Division.

As the possibility of war grew closer, yet more specialised courses began to be offered to the regular RNVR. Rayner became determined to qualify for responsibility on an anti-submarine vessel. He knew there was a big construction programme underway and guessed they might eventually be short of suitably skilled commanding officers. Once again, his captain was discouraging: 'You'll never get a command, Rayner – the Navy won't give RNVRs command of a ship, no matter how long the war lasts.'[4]

Augustine Courtauld (b. 1904) would have understood Rayner's initial disappointment at being rejected by the Navy. Born into an increasingly wealthy textile family (black crepe for Victorian mourning had been their first big success; 20th-century rayon followed), WWI had dominated his childhood until he became determined to make his career at sea. Although the Courtaulds had no direct naval tradition, August's father's first cousin was Captain Savill of HMS *Hampshire*, the cruiser that had gone down in June 1916 with Lord Kitchener on board. August, a determined child, had learned the names of all the ships in the Navy and their armaments and all the lighthouses round the British Isles. Aged 13, still at prep school, he had been summoned to the Admiralty, passed the medical and then been asked to write an essay:

> *When I saw the subject I was supposed to write about, I shook with horror; it was 'The Public School System'. Before I could think of a thing to say I was summoned into the dreaded interview. I found myself confronted by a number of elderly gentlemen, some of them probably Admirals. They asked me, I remember, about Mesopotamia and what crops were grown in Essex. They also seemed interested in how the* Hampshire *was lost. I said 'Mine' which I think was right and having got out of that I went back to my essay but the paper – a complete blank – had been taken away. So it was not surprising when a few weeks later old Browne [headmaster] came into my form and handed me a curt notice from the Admiralty that Their Lordships had no use for my services. I'm afraid I burst into tears.*[5]

He, too, tried for the RNVR but was rejected and did not persevere. As a Cambridge undergraduate, he went beagling and wildfowling and joined a cavalry squadron to drill on hired horses before breakfast. His father bought him a 24ft racing yacht to compete at Burnham-on-Crouch on Saturday afternoons and he had a West Solent-class yawl built at Lymington. He began travelling and taking part in scientific and geographical explorations, the most significant of which was the 1930–1931 British Arctic Air Route expedition to Greenland. This was organised by the charismatic Gino Watkins and funded to a significant extent by the Courtaulds. Its scientific (and potentially military) aim was to survey a great circular air route to Canada. Fourteen young men, 50 dogs and two Gypsy Moth aeroplanes were transported by Shackleton's former vessel *Quest* and lived in Greenland for a year.

One of their activities involved establishing a weather station on the ice cap and taking turns to man it. First volunteers were Quintin Riley (b. 1905), the expedition's meteorologist, and Martin Lindsay (b. 1905), already an Army officer. Courtauld survived there alone from 6 December 1930 to 5 May 1931 – 150 days in vicious winter weather. For the final eight weeks, he was entombed under deep snow. Afterwards, he explained that he had spent much of his solitude singing Gilbert and Sullivan, thinking about his fiancée, Mollie Montgomerie, and fantasising about the design of his ideal yacht. By the time his companions arrived and dug down to find him, all his supplies were exhausted. Watkins had brought a prayer book, expecting to hold a service over Courtauld's grave.

Participating in such expeditions was a means by which some of these interwar, indefinably dissatisfied young men chose to test themselves. Peter Fleming (b. 1907), oldest son of the dead Major Valentine Fleming, undertook gruelling journeys to Brazil and from Moscow to Peking, writing about them in *Brazilian Adventure* and *News From Tartary*. In 1933, five young naval officers, led by Robert ('Red') Ryder, sailed the engineless ketch *Tai-mo-Shan* 16,217 miles from Hong Kong to Dartmouth, via the Kurile and Aleutian islands. Although the subsequent book *The Voyage of the Tai-mo-Shan* (1935) by Lieutenant Martyn Sherwood focused only on their sailing adventures, they were also 'yachting with a purpose' in post-Childers style, investigating the military potential of the Kurile islands, a volcanic island archipelago stretching 700 miles north-east from Japan. On his planning notes for the voyage, Ryder had offered to supply the NID with 'Intelligence Report on all places visited . . . Observing any possibilities advanced base for submarine operations, or as a W/T [wireless transmitter] or W/T F [wireless interception] in the event of hostilities against Japan or between Japan and America.'[6]

From 1934 to 1937, Ryder captained the schooner *Penola*, which transported more young explorers on the British Graham Land Expedition in Antarctica. The adventurers formed strong friendship bonds; Martin Lindsay apparently believed it was because of their shared background – only three of the 14 members of the 1930–1931 Greenland expedition hadn't been to public schools.

Ian Fleming (b. 1908), Peter's younger brother, had followed Peter to Eton but was not a 'team player'. He'd missed out university, been expelled from Sandhurst and had been effectively banished, by his mother, to the Alps. Like the ex-Wykehamist Monsarrat, his preferred style of adventure was literary and sexual. When Fleming came to work for the NID, however, the explorer networks provided a fertile recruiting ground for irregular operations, often bringing the participants into the RNVR Special Branch – if they had not already signed up via the RNVSR.

August Courtauld was one of the first to propose this volunteer route for yachtsmen. He was among many people who were alarmed by the Abyssinian Crisis in 1935 and sent a suggestion to the Admiralty:

> *It seemed to me that men who know a bit about the sea ought to be allowed to give a hand in the Navy. I got out a scheme whereby we might help, using our own ships, and went to see the Admiral Commanding Reserves. He did not sound at all hopeful but said he would consult the 'powers that be' in the Admiralty. Sometime later he asked me to come and see him. He explained that he had consulted all the Staff Departments they had all said that there would be no small craft in the next war. The only way the Admiralty thought we could help was by sitting in the bowels of a trawler listening in to headphones. He told me that this was the great secret of the Navy called 'Asdic'. It seemed the Navy wanted, for this purpose, men who would not be seasick all the time.[7]*

★★★

In that same year, 1935, Stanley Baldwin's government, still talking the language of disarmament, waved through Hitler's plan to expand the Kriegsmarine beyond the limits allowed by the Treaty of Versailles. In particular, Germany was to be allowed parity in submarines. During 1936, however, the government began to realise how far the Navy had fallen behind either the one- or the two-power standard (ability to match the combined strength of two other nations' fleets – the German and Japanese, for instance). An expensive programme of new building and ship modernisation was thus put in place and the corollary faced that these ships would need skilled personnel, which the Navy had not got: too many officers had been axed and too few were being promoted from the ranks. The RNR and the RN (retired) list were finite and the likely contribution from the existing RNVR was a known, but limited, quantity.

The Naval Estimates for 1936–1937 represented the largest expenditure ever proposed in peacetime. Any cost-free initiative to increase the potential officer pool was likely to find welcome. The legend of the 1936 creation of the RNVSR is that the First Lord of the Admiralty was at a loss for something positive to announce in a debate on Naval Estimates so helped himself to an idea that had been lying on the desk of the Admiral Commanding Reserves. Could this have been Courtauld's proposal? The secretary to the Royal Cruising Club had also written a letter along similar lines:

> *The Board of Admiralty decided that a new Reserve, to be called the Royal Naval Volunteer Supplementary Reserve (RNVSR), would be formed and consist of 'Gentlemen interested in yachting and similar pursuits, desirous of being earmarked for training as executive officers in the event of war'. They would have no rank, no uniform, no pay and no training. The First Sea Lord announced the formation of the RNVSR on the 27th October 1936 and, by the end of that year, there were over a thousand members.[8]*

Many voluntary training schemes sprang up. In Devon, volunteers in groups and yacht clubs at Exmouth, Topsham, Starcross and Lympstone decided to link together in an association called the Exeter Flotilla, helping all members to improve their efficiency at simple navigation, seamanship and signalling. In London, Royal Ocean Racing Club (RORC) members Henry Chisholm and Henry Trefusis bought a redundant naval steam pinnace and moored it to the RNVR London Division headquarters, HMS *President*, to provide powerboat experience. Also on the Thames, the Little Ship Club (founded in 1926 by Maurice Griffiths and others) offered such a range of courses to help members and non-members gain their Yachtmaster qualifications that they were granted permission to 'deface' their ensign. (Non-flag etiquette buffs may like to know that this means adding what we'd now call their logo to the blue flag flown at the back of their yachts.) Also in London, Master Mariner Captain OM Watts offered courses leading to the Yachtmaster (Coastal) certificate.

In Dublin, yachtsmen took special courses at Tom Walsh's merchant marine training school to fast-track themselves into the RNVR, despite Ireland's official status of neutrality. And in East Anglia, Courtauld and his friend Frank Carr (owner of the Bristol pilot cutter *Cariad*) offered classes in seamanship, signalling and navigation. They had both signed up for the RNVSR as soon as the scheme was available and had entered themselves for the Board of Trade exams. Courtauld took fellow RNVSR members sailing on *Duet*, the yacht he had dreamed about in his days beneath the Greenland ice cap. 'As a seaman he was fearless and undefeated and frequently frightened his friends,' wrote Freddie Chapman, a fellow member of that expedition.[9] Future art historian Richard Walker, then a student at the Courtauld Institute (founded by August's uncle), agreed: 'August Courtauld, though a highly competent yachtsman, was a terrifying skipper. He would go out in all weathers, crowd on the maximum of sail and, with the Courtauld millions behind him, did not mind in the least if they were torn to shreds; he just ordered a new set.'[10] Later, when Walker was posted to the German-built anti-submarine trawler HMS *Northern Reward*, patrolling off the north of Scotland through the exceptionally rough winter of 1939–1940, he decided this had been very good experience.

Advertising agent Eric Newell was one of many who joined the RNVSR and attended the Little Ship Club lectures. Their regular instructor was Higley Halliday, a well-known naval architect who had worked with TOM Sopwith on designs for the fast CMBs in WWI and specialised in motor craft of all kinds – including the small yacht *Naromis*. Once WWII had been declared, Halliday was brought into the Special Branch of the RNVR and continued his successful training courses. For Newell, in 1937, the Little Ship Club lectures were just an enjoyable way to spend an evening:

A series of lectures on naval affairs and the Admiralty's requirement for a naval officer were given once a week at the Hudson Bay Company's fur sale room in the City of London known as Beaver Hall. It was a large semi-circular hall, each seat being equipped with a writing desk for the fur traders to make their notes. I and many of my friends attended these lectures on, as far as I remember, a Wednesday evening. We regarded it as rather a lark especially as very good draught beer was served to all who wanted it. At that time we did not really believe that we would be required to become naval officers; to us it was a good excuse for an evening out. It was entertaining to listen to retired N.O.s on life in the Navy. It was only a few years later that I realised how wrong I was.[11]

In 1937, Newell was offered a week on the destroyer HMS *Winchelsea*, then based in Harwich. Unlike the regular RNVR members, who were obliged to go to sea for longer periods, and were paid and provided with uniforms, RNVSR yachtsmen wore their own clothes and paid their own bills. Newell and his companion wore their double-breasted yachting jackets with Royal Corinthian Yacht Club (RCYC) buttons and their yachting caps with an RCYC badge. They were expected to dress for dinner so had brought dinner jackets with black tie. It wasn't long before seagoing reality asserted itself:

The day after we joined it started to blow and the Winchelsea *being Duty Destroyer was ordered to sea. By the time we cleared Harwich harbour it was blowing a full gale. Spritsail barges were racing down channel before it, some having lost their top masts. We had to stand by a coastal steamer whose cargo had shifted giving her a dangerous list. It was my first experience of being hove-to in a destroyer in a gale of wind. The way she rolled was quite unbelievable.[12]*

Robert Hichens was another yachtsman who'd tried and failed to join the regular RNVR. Living in Cornwall, the apparently inflexible requirement that he should attend weekly drills at HMS *Flying Fox* in Bristol, three hours away, was too much for him. He had written to the Admiralty pointing out that there were many more men like him who would be potentially useful volunteers but could not manage this commitment. Hichens was a keen motor racer and competitive sailor, both in dinghies and yachts, and had already gained a commission in his local Territorial Army (TA). His father, like Monsarrat's, had served in the Royal Army Medical Corps and had experienced major battles, including the Battle of the Somme in 1916.

Peverell Hichens had run a number of casualty clearing stations and a major field hospital near Calais. In 1922, however, he had to retire from work as a consulting physician at Northampton General Hospital due to brain disease. His grandson, Antony, believes this to have been encephalitis lethargica (as profiled by Oliver Sacks in his 1973 book *Awakenings*), which reached epidemic proportions around the world between 1915 and 1926. Peverell Hichens died in 1931, an event that Antony considers affected Robert profoundly, hastening his early maturity. It didn't, however, stop Hichens from risking his own life frequently in sporting events – this was part of his philosophy. He raced at Le Mans three times, crewed in the Fastnet and Channel races and was a keen competitor in International 14 dinghy racing events, as well as being a member of the RORC. He was one of the first yachtsmen accepted into the RNVSR, on 3 December 1936.

Quintin Riley joined the RNVSR in October 1937, as soon as he returned from the British Graham Land expedition. He gave his profession as 'gentleman' and was one of very few people entitled to wear a Polar Medal with both Arctic and Antarctic clasps. Riley was an amateur sailor but also an experienced meteorologist and quartermaster, and a devout high churchman. Launcelot Fleming, a geologist who had been the chaplain on some of the expeditions, described Riley as 'short in stature, dapper in appearance and with a high regard for his creature comforts. On the face of it he would not have seemed the kind of man to indulge in polar exploration.'[13] Perhaps it was this regard for 'creature comforts' that made him so efficient in his logistics role, together with a clear analytical approach. 'A healthy man can adapt to this 124 degrees of frost, a sick or starved man feels cold even in a warm room. I have experienced -62°F and only noticed it from the thermometer yet have felt cold and miserable in Suffolk.'[14]

Riley's particular contribution to Gino Watkins' 1932–1933 expedition had been his sturdy clinker-built motor launch *Stella Polaris*. She was used for ferrying equipment or people, undertaking reconnaissance and towing the seaplane or the main expedition ship through awkward channels in the ice. Later, Riley would specialise in teaching small boat handling skills to commando units. Launcelot Fleming also joined the RNVR (though not as a yachtsman) and would serve as chaplain on the battleship *Queen Elizabeth*.

A combination of profound religious faith, cultural conviction and romantic attraction to the Royal Navy motivated Fredman Ashe Lincoln (b. 1907) to sign up early for the RNVSR. Lincoln was a Jewish lawyer and activist who had been involved in the anti-Nazi protest meetings and East End boycotts in the early 1930s and would be listed in Hitler's 'Black Book' because of his work as chairman of the Anglo-Ukrainian committee. He had been born in Bradford but his parents had moved to Plymouth when he was young and he'd attended Hoe Grammar School, where he'd developed an intense love of sailing. As he saw war growing nearer, he became determined to serve with the Navy. He tried to join the RNVR but discovered he was over their age limit. As soon as he heard about the RNVSR scheme, he put his name forward and began studying with Captain OM Watts. 'In 1938 I reported to the Board of Trade and sat for my ticket, acquiring Yacht Master's certificate number 70. [...] And it was all done with one goal in mind: to serve at sea in the Royal Navy when war came.'[15]

Lincoln would never finally achieve his goal of direct sea service but these were the initial steps in an extraordinary career.

4

'Are there many like you in England?'[1]

1938–1939: The Munich crisis to the outbreak of WWII

The wind died to nothing, and as night fell the grey mist rose from the river and seemed to gather us in. [...] Autumn was upon the land; the night air was damp and soft against our faces. We reached the East India Docks, from which we had set out exactly two years before, waving like heroes to a large crowd. Now we came sneaking back to London in the dead of night with not a soul to welcome us. By 3 a.m. on the 24th of September we were safely berthed. We spent the remainder of that day in cutting down the sails and making all snug for the winter. In the evening we all gathered at Stone's chop house, Piccadilly, for a farewell supper. The low oak-panelled room became thick with smoke and the smell of fried onions and beer. Everyone made speeches. We insisted that nothing could take from us the memories of all that we had seen and done together. We made plans to meet again each year. Out in the street the newsboys were waving special editions of the evening papers. Next day the whole world shouted, "War and Disaster!" Hastily we wound up our affairs and went our separate ways.[2]

Adrian and Jane Seligman and the crew of the *Cap Pilar* had returned from two years' adventure round the world. They had left in 1936, newly married and having spent the £3,500 given to Adrian (b. 1909) for a house on purchasing and restoring the three-masted engineless barquentine *Cap Pilar*. Jane's schoolteacher brother, George Batterbury, and Lars Paersch, a former merchant seaman, were the initial members of the crew, which had been supplemented by an advertisement in

The Times offering places for a voyage to the South Seas to six young men prepared to contribute £100 each to expenses. This caught the public imagination and applications (mostly unsuitable) had poured in. They had finally set sail with nine volunteers aged 18–31: an ex-RN paymaster, a builder's labourer, a newly qualified solicitor, a ventilation engineer, a prep-school teacher, a biologist, a newly qualified doctor, a refugee photographer, a university student. None of them, apart from Adrian and Lars, had any previous seafaring experience. Some stayed the full two years, others left, new volunteers had joined, and baby Jessica had been born in New Zealand.

Almost their first stop, in October 1936, had been Tenerife, where they had seen evidence of the imposition of Fascism and mass executions. Meanwhile, the Nuremberg rallies in September had celebrated the occupation and remilitarisation of the Rhineland. In October, there was Fascism in London, with Mosley's Blackshirts in the East End; a Hunger March set out from Jarrow; volunteers for the International Brigades began arriving in Alicante; the Condor Legion was founded – and so was the RNVSR. The *Cap Pilar* had sailed away from the nascent battlelines of European politics to Tristan da Cunha, Cape Town, the Southern Ocean, Pacific Islands, Panama, New York and Newfoundland. Now she and her crew were home: it was September 1938, the Munich crisis. 'Two years ago we had looked on our voyage as a gesture of defiance in a gloomy world. Now that gesture had assumed more the appearance of a facetious grimace.'[3]

Adrian Seligman joined the RNVSR on 1 November. Harrow and Cambridge-educated, son of a metallurgist and a sculptor, Seligman had previously worked as an ordinary seaman in merchant ships. He had failed his Cambridge exams, been dumped by his girlfriend and was in trouble with both his bank manager and his father. In the Depression years of 1930–1931, he'd slept in the Red Ensign club, Dock Street E1, at 9d per night, and stood in a queue of the unemployed until he finally landed a job as a mess room steward in a tramp ship (a ship with no fixed itinerary or routing). He'd spent three years working his way round the world in trading sailing ships. His father, he discovered later, had left the small side door of the family home open for him every night, just in case.

★★★

Alfred Duff Cooper, First Lord of the Admiralty, began the mobilisation of the Royal Navy on 27 September 1938 and it was made official by Buckingham Palace on 28 September. This show of determination had persuaded Hitler to extend his ultimatum to Czechoslovakia for a few more days and propose a new meeting with Neville Chamberlain. Antiquated, understrength and undermanned, the British fleet was still an impressive sight. Coming up the Channel in his yacht *Merlin* shortly after midnight earlier in the month, Edward Stanley had seen 'the whole horizon ahead of us, dotted with an immense number of lights'. The Home Fleet was at sea:

> *As we approached the line, a Fishery Protection Cruiser detached itself from the formation and circled round us two or three times, focusing a searchlight on us. However she appeared convinced of our innocent intentions, and we proceeded unmolested. The Fleet made a magnificent spectacle of silent efficiency as one by one they crossed our bows, standing on their course westwards. It is a sight that anyone who has seen it on a moonlit night would certainly never forget.* [4]

After Chamberlain had signed the Munich Agreement for 'Peace in our Time', Hitler began the process of repudiating the 1935 Anglo-German Naval Agreement. By January 1939, he had announced Plan Z, a colossal increase in German naval forces aimed at direct confrontation. Fortunately, most of these ships were never built. Meanwhile, Duff Cooper had resigned. Speaking on 3 October 1938, immediately in advance of Chamberlain's House of Commons statement, he said:

> *The Prime Minister has believed in addressing Herr Hitler through the language of sweet reasonableness. I have believed that he was more open to the language of the mailed fist. [...] I have forfeited a great deal. I have given up an office that I loved, work in which I was deeply interested and a staff of which any man might be proud. [...] I have ruined, perhaps, my political career. But that is a little matter; I have retained something which is to me of great value – I can still walk about the world with my head erect.* [5]

Duff Cooper's successor, the 7th Earl Stanhope, would later be fingered by Cato (Michael Foot, Frank Owen and Peter Howard) as one of the Guilty Men denounced for their collective failure to re-arm Britain and stand up to Hitler. He was in office for less than a year before he was replaced by Churchill in September 1939 and seems to have slipped through without touching the sides.

Some lessons were being learned, however. The Flower-class corvettes and the Hunt-class destroyers were put into production and plans were developed for the Operational Intelligence Centre (OIC) at the Admiralty to reach war readiness, and for the merchant fleet to be brought under Admiralty control as soon as this was necessary. Minelaying and blockade plans began to be drawn up. There was still no thought for Childers' 'mosquitoes with stings' – the small, fast, heavily armed motorboats that had proved effective towards the end of the previous war and that had become especially associated with the RNVR. Journalists such as Maurice Griffiths, as well as campaigners like August Courtauld, were told categorically that these would not be needed. Technological problems, such as the shortage of suitable engines, were not therefore addressed.

The worst material shortages were in the air and that was where the main fears were focused. The cruising recollections of both Robin Balfour and Edward Stanley that summer testify to the impact that the bombing of Guernica had on people's imagination, as well as their observation of the physical impact of civil war in Spain. When Stanley and a friend moored off the casino at San Sebastián, they found it pockmarked with bullet holes and noticed how many of the men in uniform walking the streets had been wounded. They were unpleasantly impressed by the thoroughness of the air raid precautions: shelters were conspicuously marked, there were posters everywhere and loudspeakers had been installed on the lamp posts in all the principal streets. They didn't stay long.

The crisis in the Munich negotiation was made shocking for the British public by the issuing of gas masks, plans for the mass evacuation of cities and a hurried spate of lectures on air raid precautions and first aid. Nevil Shute's novel *What Happened to the Corbetts* (1939) is a vivid, period-specific tale, written as a warning. As Nevil Norway, he had enjoyed a busy, inventive entrepreneurial career in the aviation industry. This had included employment with Vickers, involvement with the development of the R100 airship and the foundation of his own company, Airspeed, in 1931. Writing fiction and sailing his Estonian-built gaff cutter *Skeardmore* had been leisure activities. In April 1938, however, he had been paid off from Airspeed and was living at Southsea, near Portsmouth, preparing for his new career as a full-time novelist. Profits from the sale of film rights to *Ruined City*, meanwhile, were being spent on a new 40ft yacht, *Runagate*, being designed and built by David Hillyard at Littlehampton.

During the Munich crisis, Shute's wife Frances, a doctor, was being deluged with anti-gas leaflets, whereas he was certain that high-explosive precision bombing of civilian targets was the real danger. In *What Happened to the Corbetts?* he imagines this being inflicted on Southampton in the first days of an undeclared war. As well as the direct casualties, bomb damage to the city's sewer system causes outbreaks of typhus and cholera. The protagonists, Peter and Joan, take refuge on their elderly smack yacht *Sonia*. Then, when the bombing becomes less precisely targeted and the Hamble begins to feel unsafe, they sail for the Isle of Wight, where they are refused landing due to quarantine regulations.

What Happened to the Corbetts? presents the Navy as a source of strength but also reveals it as dangerously out of touch with civilian problems. In the book, when Peter Corbett is interviewed by the Admiral, he's questioned about his yacht, his sailing experience, his peacetime profession and, yes, whether he had been to public school. (He had.) 'The Admiral crossed to his desk and sat down. "We need fellows like you for our auxiliary craft." He stared Corbett in the eyes. "I should like to recommend you for a commission as a sub-lieutenant in the Volunteer Reserve. Would you take it?"'

The Fleet had already been in battle and two capital ships had been lost, but Peter and Joan know nothing about this. Peter answers the Admiral angrily:

My home is a ruin and a wreck. There's no glass in any of the windows. The ground floor and the garden are flooded with sewage. There's no water to drink but polluted water running in the gutters of the road. There's no milk for my baby. There's no fresh meat for the children. It's in a cholera district. It's bombed to hell every night – for all I know it may have been

hit by now. That's my home, sir. And if you think I'm going to send my
wife and children back to that while I join the Navy, you can bloody well
think again.[6]

Frank talking on both sides achieves understanding. Peter and Joan set out and sail for Brest, where they wait out a period of quarantine before Joan and the children can take ship for Canada. *Sonia* is laid up and Peter returns to accept his RNVR commission.

Edward Stanley had joined the RNVSR in November 1936, as soon as the scheme was announced. His brother Lyulph joined the following year; Balfour signed up in the summer of 1938, possibly not long after he had been elected to the RCC, whose members joined en masse. The yachting establishment (men like Adlard Coles, Maurice Griffiths and Frank Carr) had mostly joined early unless they had military commitments elsewhere or fell outside the required age range. The overall level of response had been so unexpected that the Admiralty bureaucracy was finding it hard to cope. Some volunteers would not discover that they didn't meet the fitness or eyesight criteria until they were finally sent for their official training in the autumn of 1939.

The RNVSR was not mobilised at the time of the Munich crisis but the regular RNVR was. Denys Rayner received a telegram ordering him to report to the Naval Officer in Charge at Kirkwall 'with all despatch'. He reached Inverness, expecting to continue to Thurso and thence to Orkney via a fleet minesweeper. But at Inverness, all was chaos. He joined forces with two other officers who had also been ordered to Kirkwall and continued by local railway to Helmsdale, where they missed a connection with an ammunition train. The driver of the local train was persuaded to take the three men onwards as far as Wick, where the line divided and the train stopped. There was a phone call for the senior officer, taken, apprehensively, by Rayner. It was the movements officer from Thurso, under the impression that Rayner and his Special train was conveying 200 troops. The three men continued their haphazard journey with Rayner wondering whether he would be facing the first court martial of the war. By the time they finally reached Kirkwall, the crisis was over and their presence was no longer required. He was depressed to discover that his posting would have been as a boarding officer within a contraband control system. This was not what he'd worked towards for so many years.

Similar muddles had occurred across the country and many felt it was fortunate that this had been only a dress rehearsal. New vacancies were immediately created for administrative volunteers in the RNVR Writer and Supply branches and more efforts made to involve the RNVSR members with the regular divisions, where they might receive some formal training. Rayner found himself doing additional evenings at Mersey Division to help with the Supplementaries. 'Often I went down to the ship three nights in a week [...] Now there was an urgency about our preparations that had been lacking before.'[7]

Figures for enrolment in both the RNVR and RNVSR rose sharply, though there was still a lack of capacity to accept all who put themselves forwards. Acceptance could seem quite random: lawyer Arthur Guyon Prideaux, who was accepted on 28 September 1938, portrays himself as simply strolling along to HMS *President,* drinking a gin with the commanding officer, discovering mutual friends and being accepted despite his absolute lack of sailing knowledge. Experienced, well-qualified yachtsman John Miller, however, was so shocked by the Admiralty's rejection of his services that he replied immediately, suggesting he had been sent the wrong-numbered form. At this point, he was accepted and scurried away to training before anyone could change their mind. (Prideaux would later command a destroyer and Miller earned a George Cross in mine disposal.) Artist and naturalist Peter Scott (son of 'Scott of the Antarctic') had been in America as captain of an International 14 dinghy racing team. 'I arrived back in England just before Christmas 1938. War with Germany was threatening but the slogan on everybody's lips was "Peace in our time". I felt it would be wise to get my name on a reserve list and I was accepted onto the Royal Naval Volunteer Supplementary Reserve.'[8]

While there would never have been a problem accepting a volunteer like Peter Scott, my father, George Jones, needed the post-Munich reorganisation of the logistical services to gain his RNVSR opportunity. He was aged 21, working as a small-scale currency trader on the Birmingham Stock Exchange. His 1939 diary, clearly written as an exercise in self-analysis, shows how aware he was of the international situation and how very much he didn't want to go and fight. His father had been a modestly successful tenant farmer in Suffolk but had died in an accident in 1933 – hard times for agriculture. George, the youngest son, had left Ipswich School, where he'd been a day boy, to go to work for £1 a week, first in Woolworths, then for a paint factory. It was a puzzling and unhappy period from which he was rescued by two unmarried aunts. They ran a girls' school in Felixstowe and helped him complete his education to school certificate level. The kindness of a more distant relative had gained him this financial apprenticeship in Birmingham.

On the night of his 21st birthday, 5 January 1939, he was in a self-consciously poetic mode. 'I am wondering tonight whether the arrows will be flying in the frontiers before the snow is gone from the mountains.' As midnight approached, he settled to read WE Henley. Would he have chosen Henley's famous poem 'Invictus' – 'I am the master of my fate / I am the captain of my soul'? Because it wouldn't have been true. His diary shows he was deeply uncertain, afraid of being afraid and ashamed of his private vacillations.

He made enquiries about joining the RNVR in February but was discouraged by the medical requirements. 'The Admiralty don't want yachtsmen with defective eyesight.' He set out to attend a National Service rally held by Anthony Eden but went to a hotel and got drunk instead. On 15 March, news came that the German occupation of Czechoslovakia was complete. He records that the currency markets were tumbling and the phones were out of order so he couldn't cut his trading losses. On Thursday 16 March, he notes, 'Hitler in Prague. Hungary in Ruthenia.' Then, on Friday 17 March, 'I am not likely to forget today in a hurry. I lost £15 in one fell swoop and had to close. Black Friday with rumours and counter rumours. Chamberlain makes a fighting speech in Birmingham town hall. Broadcast to the world.'

The Prime Minister was making this speech in his home city. He defended his actions at Munich, condemned Hitler and pledged himself (and everyone else) to resist any further territorial expansion by Germany. 'The Government, as always, must bear the main responsibility but I know that all individuals will wish to review their own position and consider again if they have done all they can to offer their service to the state.'[9]

The remainder of March and April 1939 was a miserable period for my father as he felt ever more indecisive: 'The veil of war is heavy over us.' He was only happy at the weekends when he managed to go sailing, either in a racing dinghy with the Severn Sailing Club, or home to Suffolk to his beloved open boat *Hustler* on the River Deben. The spring countryside seemed so intensely beautiful; the prospect of leaving it, unbearable. Then Chamberlain announced plans for the conscription of 20- and 21-year-old males. Dad finally decided he must drive to Bristol and volunteer for the RNVR. But first he spent some time sitting alone in the Birmingham Oratory, looking at the lamps and candles, and the gleam of the setting sun:

Across Edgbaston came the bells of the Old Church rising and falling, now hidden by a house, now clear and tumbling over each other. In the sky there was a plane curling and diving. It seemed synonymous. Here were two things – the culture we loved and believed and the death that perhaps awaited us. Already we were leading a different life among the recruiting offices. [10]

But would the RNVR accept him? Though he had been sailing since childhood, he wasn't, strictly speaking, a yachtsman or even technically a 'gentleman' – though he was doing his best to shore up his social position where possible. He belonged to a sailing club, not a yachting club, and his seagoing experience was limited. Dad decided he would accept anything he was offered in the RNVR; it didn't have to be a commission. It was Saturday 29 April by the time he reached HMS *Flying Fox*, the drill ship for the RNVR Severn Division, and the commanding officer wasn't there. Luckily, the duty officer turned out to be from Suffolk. My father was allowed to look round the ship, 'fondle' the guns and make his commitment. Nothing would alter the fact that he knew he would fail a sight test.

Just five days later, on 4 May 1939, the Navy extended its criteria for acceptance into the RNVSR to welcome volunteers with accountancy qualifications. Eyesight would not matter. There had been criticism, in Parliamentary debate, of the Admiralty's antiquated accounting methods and a suggestion that civilian expertise might help. Many of the expenses of those who had mobilised in September remained unpaid eight months later. 'The Admiralty creates a Special

Reserve for me!' Dad wrote jubilantly. By 5 July 1939, all formalities were complete and he was a 'Probationary Temporary Paymaster Sub-Lieutenant RNVR'. Soon he found himself recruited to 'pay 9 gns and go to Danzig'. He was helped to organise his passport and by 10 August he was on his way to join *Naromis* and her unknown crew: WJ Clutton, the banker; 'Jock', a stockbroker who was in the Territorials; 'Mike', a medical student about to join the RNVR; 'Bill' Fuller RNVSR; and himself. 'I can't see that I'm going to be much use to them,' he wrote. He didn't know that the 'Paymaster' branch, in which he was enrolled, had historically close links with intelligence, as did the City of London financial institutions. My father would be in uniform before any of *Naromis*' crew – even 'Jock', who crossed to France with the British Expeditionary Force (BEF).

★★★

August Courtauld's wife Mollie recalls that they too went 'yachting with a purpose' in the summer of 1939: 'I don't now remember if the request came from the Foreign Office or the Admiralty but the idea was for owners of yachts to cruise the coast of Europe from western France to the north of Norway, apparently on holiday, but in reality collecting as much evidence as they could of the size of piers, capability of ports, positions of nearby factories, and to collect picture postcards of the areas, in readiness for the coming hostilities.'[11] Their friend Michael Spender (elder brother of Stephen and Humphrey) sailed with them on this trip. Michael was a surveyor and explorer who became an expert in photo reconnaissance. Like Childers' friend Gordon Shepherd in the first war, Spender joined the RAF and died in an air accident not long before it was over. Mollie played innocent, pretending not to notice as the men of the party strolled 'nonchalantly' along piers, pacing out their length. She couldn't miss the atmosphere, however: 'I remember going ashore at Andalasnes and seeing the stark word "Krieg" in a newspaper headline. It cast a shadow over that beautiful little harbour with thoughts of what lay ahead.'[12]

Immediately before the war, and in its early months, Courtauld had connections with Major Lawrence Grand of Section D, the Secret Intelligence Service/MI6 (SIS) organisation that had been set up in March 1938 to investigate future opportunities for sabotage. Courtauld was uncomfortable about this and called them 'the crooked people'. RCC member Gerry Holdsworth was similarly recruited by Section D to investigate the Norwegian coast in his Bristol pilot cutter *Mischief*. When war began, Holdsworth was given a short training course in explosives and sent back to Norway to be part of the group investigating ways to disrupt Germany's iron ore supplies. In the end, he would be fortunate to escape back to England, via Sweden and Finland.

Other yachtsmen enjoyed less complex, though bittersweet, memories of sailing in that last summer before the war. For Peter Scott, the annual Prince of Wales Cup for International 14 dinghies was a regular event in his life. In 1938, he and his partner John Kift Winter had caused a sensation by using a trapeze. These days, it's a fairly standard piece of equipment but then, it was revolutionary. Local competitor Robert Hichens was ahead of Scott and Winter when he looked round, and was staggered. 'For a critical ten seconds Robert sailed his boat "off the wind", which allowed us to luff across his wake and get our wind clear [...] we rounded the weather mark a full 30 seconds ahead.'[13] It was a thrilling victory – though, predictably, it caused a row. In the 1939 summer, the atmosphere felt very different:

> I remember leading the fleet home at the end of one race and looking back into the afternoon sun and the silver brightness of the sea. A dozen dinghies were following us with spinnakers set on the run up the coast from Pakefield past the Claremont Pier. The nearest was more than fifty yards astern. As we approached the finish line it should have been a moment of triumph. Instead I felt a sudden fierce sadness. Not only was this the end of the sailing season but the end of an era, for nothing now could stop the war. Perhaps we should never sail dinghies again.[14]

Many people would remember their final 1939 cruises or races with similar vividness. In the lean years ahead, *Yachting Monthly* would fill issue after issue with memories from those last few months of peace. If there was little excitement around the 1939 Prince of Wales competition, however, there were headlines when two young British naval officers scooped the Hindenburg Cup in German home waters at Kiel. The 22-year-old helmsman, Lieutenant Samuel Woodcock, was the only son of sailing author Percy Woodcock and his wife Ellie. His victory in Kiel was almost a *Boy's Own* triumph. Later that summer, the Kriegsmarine got their revenge in the Fastnet race. Their yacht *Nordwind* was the largest in the fleet and took line honours with a record that would stand for 24 years. She was one of the fleet of yachts (the *Seefahrtkreuzer Klassen*) built up during the 1930s for the nautical training of German officers.

After the war, Maurice Griffiths would write of the 'thorough training in seamanship and navigation' that the future U-boat commanders and the Luftwaffe pilots received on board these fine yachts. Occasional commentators have wondered whether the Navy-crewed yachts who came over to compete in British regattas were taking the opportunity to have a good look round our coastline – as we were arguably doing elsewhere.

This fellowship of the sea was a human bond. My father records an incident in Copenhagen when *Naromis* found herself berthed between a Polish and a German yacht. They were making wry jokes about implementing the government's pledge to protect Poland when the skipper of the German yacht received his message to return home. 'He said how sorry he was that the situation looked so bad and he trusted it would soon be alright.'[15] That was the day that news broke of the Soviet–German non-aggression pact. In its edition of Friday 8 September 1939, the editor of *Yachting World* wrote:

> *In past seasons we have made many friends with the country with whom we are now at war, and they have shown themselves good seamen and good friends. How can we feel enmity against them? As Mr Chamberlain has stated, in terms as definite as could be desired we have no enmity against the people of Germany but only against their government. With that eliminated we can and will live at peace, sailing and racing against them in friendly rivalry as before.*[16]

In fact, at the war's end the Allies would confiscate most of those lovely German yachts as 'reparations'.

Jewish barrister Ewen Montagu (b. 1901) had crewed on board the legendary William Fife yacht *Latifa* in the 1939 Fastnet. He had served briefly at the end of WWI as a gunnery instructor and claimed he had chosen to sign up for the RNVSR to avoid the prospect of 'drowning in mud', which had been the fate of too many of his contemporaries. After the Fastnet, he swapped on to his own yacht *John Dory* and collected his family to enjoy a cruise in Brittany. It was only then that he turned on the radio. War was imminent and all Britons were advised to leave France. 'What was to turn out to be my last sail for seven years was a heart-warming fast run up Channel, hard on the wind, in glorious weather and escorted for over an hour by porpoises playing round our bow – scraping into the Solent on the last of the tide just before midnight on the Friday-Saturday night before war was declared.'[17]

Fellow lawyer Edward Terrell and his wife had been pottering about the creeks and swatches of the River Blackwater in their shallow-draught barge-yacht *Swan*. They'd left their child in London and crept up Bradwell Creek to the Green Man pub as planes from the local aerodrome 'buzzed all day like angry bees'. That evening, they found themselves talking to the commander of the airfield, who told them: '"War is very near." And he gazed with troubled eyes over the calm waters, intensely blue from the reflected light of the setting sun.'[18] Terrell and his wife cut short their holiday and hurried back to London.

The weekend of 26–27 August would be the last that Arthur and Dorothy Bennett would ever sail *June of Rochester*. They were already laying her up as Arthur was in the RNVSR and expected to be summoned by telegram as soon as war was declared. Their weekend began in the bight of the River Medway close under Cockham Woods. They were away downriver past Gillingham 'with a sparkle in the water and a nip in the air'; then rounding the Ness and beating up Faversham Creek past Harty Ferry to the East Swale, where they anchored outside Conyer Creek.

That night I turned out once. It was low water and dark banks of mud showed on either side of us but June *lay quietly and the riding light burnt brightly. It was a beautiful starlit night with dawn not so very far away. For a few minutes I stood in the hatchway listening to the marsh birds [...] Next morning we were underway in good time and stood across for the eastern end of Fowley Island. Our huffler was waiting in his boat and together we worked* June *up the narrow winding gut* to berth at Conyer Quay. It was Sunday morning, the last Sunday in August 1939.[19]

Edward Stanley's final glimpse of his yacht, *Our Boy*, was from the bridge deck of a destroyer. The date was 1 September and he sighted her off Portland Bill:

With Parsons at the wheel single-handed, bound to the westward and to Brixham where they were both born. It was a moment of heartbreaking longing as I watched her, and then 'Echo bearing green four five, one thousand yards, closing' for we were doing anti-submarine exercises. The whole complex mechanism of the destroyer clicked smoothly into gear. I had my small part to play in that organisation which left no room for thinking of my beloved ship and the seas we had sailed. A curtain came down in my mind which was not to be lifted for 6 long years.[20]

5

'Do you think you'll like this sort of thing?'[1]

September–December 1939: Initial experiences and training

Although the first air raid siren of the war was a false alarm, and the bombing of cities did not materialise as soon as expected, there was no 'Phoney War' period at sea. It was not (yet) a confrontation of the big battleships – though their whereabouts was always a matter of the keenest interest. The immediate focus was on protecting British trade and supply lines via the convoy system, while attempting to impose an economic blockade on the enemy. Inflicting starvation on Germany had been an effective tactic in WWI. It was unlikely to work equally well this time because of the different pattern of alliances, but Britain still hurried to cut off the entrances to the North Sea both via the Channel and (a much more difficult challenge) round the north of Scotland, beyond Shetland to the Faroe Islands and Iceland.

Merchant shipping and the fishing fleets were placed under Admiralty control on 26 August, and the first convoy sailed on 2 September. Four days later, the regular series of East Coast convoys began. Initially, one passed in each direction every other day. The Thames Estuary was the busiest waterway in the world and the English East Coast was immediately open to attack as it faced Germany across the North Sea. A protective mine barricade was laid and the 'working classes' of the Navy – patrol boats, escorts, minesweepers, anti-submarine trawlers, boom defence units – began six years of activity. Essential chores such as sweeping the convoy channels to ensure they were clear of mines had to be carried out every day. Hundreds of small vessels were needed, and thousands of men. They were based in ports such as Harwich, Lowestoft, Hull, Grimsby, Blyth, Newcastle and Dundee, all the way to Rosyth.

Despite the Depression, those ports were still dedicated maritime communities. When the miscellaneous local vessels were taken over for war work, most of their skippers and crews came too.

In May 1939, 15,000 reservists had been called up to get the older warships ready for sea. Ludovic Kennedy's father, Edward, was overjoyed to be brought back from the retired list and given command of the armed merchant cruiser HMS *Rawalpindi* (a former ocean liner with some guns added).

I had never seen him so happy; he was like a child who has been given a new toy. In his cabin, a luxurious room behind the bridge, he kept jumping up to discuss with dockyard officials alterations they were making to the ship's structure; or one of his officers would come to him with a batch of papers for scrutiny and signature. Afterwards he took me round the ship. [...] His enthusiasm was unbounded, his pride immense. I knew then that the disappointments which had been rankling for the past 18 years had vanished. They were forgotten in his passionate interest and pride in his new command.[2]

That was the last time the 19-year-old saw his father.

Every small vessel, every area of responsibility needed to have an officer in charge. For Probationary Temporary Paymaster Sub-Lieutenant Jones hurrying north in his new uniform to join the depot ship HMS *Forth*, already late and with no previous training, this may have felt somewhat daunting. For Lieutenant Commander Denys Rayner, suitcase packed, yacht laid up, wife and family fondly farewelled, this could not come too soon. Four days before war was declared, he was on his way to the Sparrow's Nest trawler base in Lowestoft 'for disposal' as a unit commander. Disconcertingly, the taxi driver only knew the address as a park with a Pierrot show. When Rayner finally arrived, there was just one other officer and the captain expected later:

We had twenty-four hours to get the base working. I dumped my bags in the house and we walked together down the road to the tree-lined park. Passing inside the gates we came to a large concert hall. Sounds of music and singing could be heard. We went round to the stage end of the building and came across some of the artists sunning themselves in deck chairs and

drinking coffee. Others were on the stage rehearsing. Gently but firmly we
told them that there would be no show that night.[3]

Rayner relates how he and the others laboured to create a working
base. When the first draft of men arrived to be posted to their ships
on the evening of the second day, HMS *Pembroke X* (later HMS
Europa) was ready for them. Because everyone in the Navy must
be appointed to a ship, these shore establishments, known as 'stone
frigates', were all named as if they were about to vault the seawall
and sail away. Rayner and his newly met colleague, Lieutenant Lord
Churston RNVR, found themselves working as drafting officers,
putting people together with their actual vessels. For a week, they
drafted crews to vessels until they'd accommodated more than 600
Patrol Service ratings on to 80 minesweeping trawlers.

As the conversion of the largest anti-submarine warfare (ASW)
trawlers neared completion, Rayner and Churston began to identify
the skippers and crews they personally wanted to work with. They
then asked the skippers their advice on the best and soundest vessels.
Their plan was to choose their ships, their skippers and their men,
then draft them all together. 'After all, we had come to fight a war,
not to be Drafting Officer and Assistant Drafting Officer of the
Royal Naval Patrol Service Base Lowestoft.'[4]

Rayner, with his 12 years' RNVR training, and Churston with his
social position, had the confidence to act in this way. 'The discipline
of the Court Martial means nothing to us,' Rayner's captain at HMS
Eaglet had complained. 'If you were dismissed the service tomorrow,
Elizabeth and your kids would not starve, you'd just go back to
your shoreside job. Now with the RN it's entirely different. A severe
reprimand will lose them the chance of promotion and an RNR
could lose his Board of Trade certificate.'[5] RNVR officers were
bound by *The King's Regulations and Admiralty Instructions (KR&AI)*
equally with the other branches. Although they were enthusiastic
and eager to do right, they were not necessarily conformist.

In the wardroom of HMS *Forth*, my father is unlikely to have felt
such confidence. I wonder what those first few weeks were like for
him. HMS *Forth* was the depot ship for the 2nd Submarine Flotilla.
She was an 8,600-ton floating factory, designed for her role and with
a complement of almost 1,200 people. She possessed torpedo and

engineering workshops, accommodation, stores, training facilities and an operations room. Depot ships travelled with their flotillas, offering rest and recuperation, personnel services, medical treatment, debriefing and entertainment as well as the necessary maintenance to keep vessels and equipment functioning efficiently. As a supply officer on a depot ship, my father was involved with pay and logistics but also with communications and human resources. By January 1940, he had become cypher officer and confidential books (CBs) officer – a position he held for the next two years. These were routine jobs but ones that required meticulous attention to detail and also discretion and responsibility. He must have known what orders had been issued and what reports made, been aware of truths that must not be made public, and been involved in the administrative processes around loss and death.

When a submarine was not in service, her confidential books (containing code information and instruction manuals) would be taken off her, checked, signed for and stored securely, then returned when she was ready to go back to sea. On HMS *Forth*, this would have been my father's responsibility. At sea, it would also have been a designated duty. When a ship went down it was imperative that her CBs be destroyed, usually sunk in a lead-lined bag. If this hadn't happened and it looked as if the vessel might continue to float after the survivors had been taken off, an escort would be required to sink her with gunfire or a torpedo. Though torpedoes were expensive, this was easily outweighed by the potential danger of the enemy being able to collect both the latest codes and the technical manuals for the vessel's equipment. (The entire British war effort would later benefit from the acquisition of a set of Enigma rotor wheels and code books salvaged from the sinking armed trawler *Krebs* during Operation *Claymore*, the 1941 raid on the Lofoten Islands, off north Norway.)

In September 1939, the 2nd Submarine Flotilla had 12 boats, based at HMS *Forth*. Four of these – *Seahorse, Sturgeon, Swordfish* and *Spearfish* – had already been out patrolling the Scandinavian and German North Sea coasts when *Naromis* was scurrying home from Farsund on 29–30 August across an apparently empty sea. 'The fishing fleets were all in port by government order and we were very much alone.' Eight of the 12 were S-class submarines: the other four in that class would soon return from the Mediterranean. Only three of the total 12 S-class submarines would survive the first year of war.

The first casualty from the 2nd Submarine Flotilla, however, would be HMS *Oxley*, torpedoed in error off the Norwegian coast on 10 September by fellow flotilla member HMS *Triton*. *Triton* picked up three survivors but 53 people died. Hers must have been an extraordinarily difficult return to the depot ship. The official explanation given was that *Oxley* had suffered an 'explosion'. Her dead are commemorated on the Dundee War Memorial but the full facts were not told until the 1950s. Initially, as a very junior officer, perhaps my father didn't know the detail of such incidents; very soon, as a cypher officer and certainly once he began acting as a captain's secretary, there would have been many uncomfortable truths that he knew but could not share.

There were other difficult incidents. When HMS *Sturgeon* had set out on 13 September 1939 for her second war patrol, she fired three torpedoes at HMS *Swordfish*, who was returning from her patrol off the Norwegian coast near Stavanger. Fortunately, all three torpedoes missed. *Sturgeon* herself had already been bombed in error by a British aircraft when returning to Dundee on 4 September. *Snapper* was bombed when entering Harwich on 3 December. (This incident may have provided the basis for Shute's 1940 novel *Landfall.*[6]) Coastal aircraft were understandably so jumpy in the early days that it was unwise for a patrolling submarine to show herself on the surface without an escort.

Then there was enemy action. HMS *Spearfish* endured a terrible pounding by hostile warships off Horns Reef (west of Denmark) on 24 September and was in Rosyth for several months before she could go out on patrol again. Percy and Ellie Woodcock's son Samuel, as a regular RN lieutenant, was serving on board HMS *Salmon*, usually based in Harwich, though also often in Rosyth. On her second war patrol in December 1939 she torpedoed and sank a German U-boat (*U-36*), attempted to halt the liner *Bremen*, torpedoed and damaged the destroyer *Nürnberg* and the cruiser *Leipzig*, then survived a four-hour depth-charge attack when she lay on the seabed with explosions happening all round her. If Percy and Ellie Woodcock had known anything about HMS *Salmon*'s ordeal, they might reasonably have felt relieved when Samuel was transferred out of submarines and on to the surface warship HMS *Barham*.

In July 1940, *Salmon* left HMS *Forth* on her ninth war patrol and was lost with her entire crew when she ran into a German minefield. In that same month, HMS *Shark*, commanded by Nicholas Monsarrat's Trearddur Sailing Club friend Lieutenant Commander Peter Buckley RN, had set out to patrol off Skudenes, Norway. On 6 July, a message was received that she had been depth-charged by German anti-submarine trawlers and was so badly damaged she could not dive. Although ships from the Home Fleet were sent out from Scapa Flow in a rescue attempt, *Shark* was captured and sunk. Buckley and his crew spent the rest of the war as prisoners.

RNVR personnel were not permitted to volunteer for service in submarines at the outbreak of war. As a member of the HMS *Forth* wardroom, my father helped entertain at least four people who would go on to win VCs, two of them losing their lives in the process, as well as many other extraordinarily brave officers of his own age. Although he was using his best efforts on their behalf, it must have been a humbling experience to remain behind as they set off, knowing as the cypher officer what instructions they had been given, what reports were coming in, and presumably being involved in amending the personnel records and financial arrangements when they did not return. In 1941, he persuaded the captain of HMS *Forth* to send a memo to Admiral Max Horton: 'Many keen seamen have been compelled through poor eyesight to join the service as officers of the Accountant branch of either the RNR or the RNVR. It is suggested that such officers could be employed to advantage as Liaison officers in Allied submarines where it would not be essential for them to have technical knowledge but where their knowledge of cypher would be particularly valuable.' The Admiral's office replied: 'This suggestion is appreciated but there is no requirement at present for officers referred to in paragraph 1 of minute One. A number of RNVR Executive officers have volunteered for liaison duties in submarines and have been trained for the duty at Fort Blockhouse.'[7]

The disparity of esteem between 'executive' and 'supply' branches of the Navy was just one of the complex discriminations that characterised this new life. When Ewen Montagu KC received his commission and became 'Probationary Temporary

Acting-Sub-Lieutenant Montagu RNVR', he commented: 'I couldn't but admire the cautious way in which the Admiralty kept its options open – three ways of getting rid of one!'[8] Montagu was one of the first of the RNVSR members to be sent to the training centre at HMS *King Alfred*. There, he would begin to acquire necessary familiarity with *KR&AI* while being unobtrusively scrutinised for his 'Officer Like Qualities' (OLQs). It would transpire that Montagu would never be permitted to go to sea yet he clung to his 'executive' (seagoing) status. Even when he was working deep in the Admiralty Citadel, he refused to become a 'green-striper' (RNVR Special Branch) even though it cost him promotions. Tony Hugill witnessed an angry exchange between Dunstan Curtis (an 'executive' officer) and Ian Fleming (Special Branch) when Fleming was told to 'forget that bloody green stripe'. Curtis hoped Fleming would find himself 'in the drink' one day and prophesied that would make him think differently.[9]

★★★

During the first months of war, other amateur sailors, who had not volunteered to fight at sea, were struggling to stay true to their personal ideals while supporting the national effort. Nicholas Monsarrat, still a socialist and pacifist, was working as an air raid warden in London. Like many people, he had expected obliterating bombing to begin immediately so had assumed he would be putting himself in direct personal danger. Naval architect George O'Brien Kennedy's wife had joined the Peace Pledge Union. Sunday 3 September 1939 had felt like a watershed moment when O'Brien Kennedy (b. 1912) delivered a newly built International 14-footer to a customer at Edgbaston Sailing Club. They had a short sail then went into the clubhouse to hear Chamberlain's announcement. When they came out, there were already barrage balloons filling the air about Birmingham.

It is hard now to recall one's feelings at a time like that. At Trent [the author's school] the then so-called Great War had been close to us with the school's roll of honour, and there had been a propeller from one hero's plane on the wall of our dining room. The school library was full of bound copies of The Illustrated London News *of the First World War period, and this had brought home to us the horror and destruction and carnage of war... and now it was to start all over again. One had a dreadful sick feeling, a sense of unbelief, and a sense of fear too.*[10]

Throughout his apprenticeship as a naval architect and in his early years of employment, O'Brien Kennedy had worked on military projects: destroyers, a river gunboat, a corvette and several fast harbour launches for JI Thornycroft at Southampton. He'd drawn sections of the first production Spitfire for Vickers Supermarine. Looking back, he reflected:

I sometimes wonder how people can bring themselves to work on the design of better, more efficient, more lethal weapons systems, whether nuclear or conventional in time of peace: and yet in my younger days I was doing that without a thought — just interesting problems — one did not really give any actual thought to the practical effect for which they were designed.[11]

In September 1939, O'Brien Kennedy went straight to the Labour Exchange and volunteered for whatever non-combatant work was required. He also joined the Communist Party (CP). At first, he was sent to make air raid shelters. Then a dinghy-sailing friend, John Coste (an RNVSR member), introduced him to a naval architect who was designing motor launches to be built by Fairmile Marine. Kennedy took the job but soon found himself in disagreement with his new employer over both the design details and personal politics. He transferred to the Ministry of Shipping as a surveyor and was sent to tour London's docklands, making notes of the condition of the tugs, lighters and miscellaneous small vessels that were being requisitioned into government service.

His status as a CP member began to tell against him. When the call came for volunteers experienced in handling small boats (for Dunkirk), he offered immediately but was rejected and was then dismissed from his work as a surveyor. For the remainder of the period that Hitler and Stalin were in alliance, he found it increasingly difficult to get employment — he would be hired, then fired half an hour later. But because he was in a reserved occupation as a naval architect, he was not allowed to take any unrelated task. His wife had returned to neutral Ireland but it never occurred to him to do the same. Instead, he struggled not to starve. Eventually (June 1941), Hitler invaded the Soviet Union, Stalin became Britain's ally and 'I was apparently a good guy again'. Kennedy went back to work for Vospers, first in Portsmouth, assembling steering gear and gun control for motor torpedo boats (MTBs), and then in Glasgow, supervising the powerful vessels on their trial runs and keeping the performance records.

Before the war, the impecunious O'Brien Kennedy had needed to beg transport to be able to sail an International 14 of his own design in the prestigious Prince of Wales Cup at Falmouth. The men at the front of the fleet, such as Stewart Morris, Uffa Fox, Peter Scott, John Winter and Robert Hichens, may have experienced fewer difficulties directing their competitive instincts into the war effort. Indeed, Scott had no hesitation: 'When war comes to a country there is only one course for its people to take, and that is to fight as hard as they can until the war is won ... or lost.' He and his dinghy-sailing partner John Winter had joined the RNVSR and expected to be called up at once. On 3 September, Scott wrote to the Admiralty stating his readiness for service:

> *I soon discovered that my impatience to start a new life with the Navy was most unpopular with the authorities. When I wrote to the Admiralty I had no reply for about three weeks and when an answer did come it was to inform me that I was on no account to write to them again about being called up and that I was not wanted now, and quite possibly never would be wanted at all. About a week later I was called up.*[12]

Ludovic Kennedy had also written to the Admiralty on 3 September. 'The reply came four months later (when I had been in naval uniform for nine weeks) regretting that there were at present no vacancies and advising me to try again in six months.'[13] Kennedy had found an alternative way into the RNVR through the Joint Universities Recruiting Board, his enthusiasm undampened by the snub.

He wrote later of his joy and pride at joining this historic institution; the 'family' that had included Nelson and Drake, as well as his own father.

Clyde yachtsman Iain Rutherford's office colleagues nicknamed the RNVSR 'the forgotten legion' as he waited for his orders. Still others waited patiently for letters that never arrived. Adlard Coles, editor of *The Yachtsman*, was one of them:

> *A year before the war (at the time of the Munich crisis) I had applied for membership of the supplementary RNVR and had been accepted, so, when hostilities broke out, I expected to receive a commission and go to the* King Alfred *naval establishment for training like most of my friends. The disability which had developed in the meantime* [Coles had been diagnosed with diabetes] *ruled me out of active service but there were other branches for which I might have been eligible. Time passed without hearing anything from the Admiralty so I remained in accountancy practice with my firm.*[14]

Coles became the county accountant for the Ministry of Food and volunteered for service in the Home Guard and as an air raid warden. It wasn't until 1942 that he came 'nearer to the navy' (in his words) when he was appointed to the RNVR Special Branch and asked to take charge of the Fareham and Gosport unit of the Sea Cadets. He hastily passed editorship of *The Yachtsman* on to Eric Hiscock, one of his regular contributors who had been pushed in the opposite direction. Hiscock had poor eyesight so had got himself taken on at the outbreak of war as an engineer, where his eyesight would not be significant. He served two years at sea so successfully that he was recommended for a commission. At that point, his defective eyesight was rediscovered and he was dismissed, even as an engineer. He tried to describe his pre-war sailing experience: 'I had cruised in small yachts and other craft; had piloted my own vessels 20,000 miles in safety; was something of a navigator; knew intimately much of the Continental coast; had written books of sailing directions', but was disbelieved and discharged 'as a danger to the service'.[15]

Maurice Griffiths at *Yachting Monthly* had been summoned early and was directed to HMS *Vernon*, the mine and torpedo school. The magazine's advertising manager, Norman Clackson, was also an RNVSR member and was soon despatched for action in the Mediterranean. That left only the office manager, Kathleen Palmer, who moved the magazine out of central London to her home in High Barnet and acted as editor for the next six years without feeling the need to reveal either her name or her gender. Susan Hiscock managed similarly at *The Yachtsman* when Eric eventually discovered a way of returning to sea as part of the Admiralty Ferry Service.

Though there had been no official pre-war training for RNVSR members, most of them were required to attend HMS *King Alfred*, a municipal leisure centre in Hove, Sussex, which had been requisitioned as a 'stone frigate'. Arthur Bennett remembers the general atmosphere of keenness as he 'jumped to it' and doubled round the obsolete guns. Navigation the Navy way was clearly going to be somewhat different from his habits on board the barge. 'I had to work in degrees now instead of points. No longer was it permissible to lay off a course with the edge of a book, nor could I hold her up a couple of points for leeway and a bit for tide.'[16]

RNVSR enthusiast Fredman Ashe Lincoln had been anxious about missing Rosh Hashanah and the Jewish New Year ('How like Hitler, I thought, to start a war in such a week!') but was relieved to discover that established Admiralty orders already provided for automatic leave for Jewish personnel for the New Year and the Day of Atonement. Fellow yachtsman and lawyer Ewen Montagu was differently surprised by the religious arrangements:

Our very first experience, after reporting back from our billets on the day after our arrival, was morning Divisions, our first Parade. After the roll-call came the first order, 'Fall out the Roman Catholics'. I thought there would be a further order applying to others who were not Church of England, including Jews like myself. But not a bit of it. Next came the lovely Naval Prayer: 'Oh Eternal Lord God who alone spreadest out the heavens and rulest the raging of the sea [...]' at that moment, with a group of us dedicating ourselves together to a common effort in anticipation of unknown dangers, saying that prayer together was exactly right and a most moving experience.[17]

Accommodation at HMS *King Alfred* could be very limited and Lincoln was initially anxious that his fellow officers would think he was odd. However, he explained what he was doing as he prayed and found there was no difficulty. Many men had to learn respect for one another's beliefs when they were living at close quarters on a vessel. When RCC member Iain Rutherford was given command of a former herring drifter manned by Peterhead fishermen, he discovered that they expected grace to be said before meals: 'On the few occasions that I forgot the grace I felt like someone who has committed a dreadful *faux pas* at a public dinner.'[18]

There's some disparity between the list of yachtsmen who'd been accepted into the RNVSR from November 1936 and those who were commissioned into the RNVR active service list in 1939–1940. Some, like Peter Scott's dinghy-sailing partner John Winter, were judged ineligible to serve as their shore employment was more significant. Others were diverted into the Special Branch. A further 10 per cent failed their medical on arrival at HMS *King Alfred*. 'I shall never forget the look of abject misery on the face of one of my friends when he was failed on his eyesight,' wrote Rutherford.[19]

One officer who probably should have been turned away was Peter Beatty, younger son of Earl Beatty (b. 1871), a WWI admiral so famous that he had been given a state funeral and is buried in the crypt of St Paul's Cathedral. Peter Beatty and his brother had walked behind their father's coffin ahead of the Duke of York, who was now King George VI. Their mother had been a somewhat scandalous American heiress who had left them extremely rich. Peter Beatty was a racehorse owner whose horse, Bois Roussel, had won the 1938 Derby. Ludovic Kennedy remembered that Beatty brought his chauffeur and valet to HMS *King Alfred*. He was delivered every morning in his Rolls-Royce and the chauffeur would be waiting each evening for his return.

Kennedy recounts this as illustrating his wealth and eccentricity, though it could have a different interpretation. Beatty had a serious eye disease, contracted at birth (probably from either gonorrhoea or chlamydia in the birth canal), which worsened throughout his life and also affected his personality. Perhaps he therefore needed the chauffeur and valet to guide him through the unfamiliar surroundings. Out of respect for his father, the RNVR kept him on the Navy list for as long as possible, usually in shore-based positions, until he was 'honourably discharged'. By 1949, he could only find his way with his valet's support and committed suicide by throwing himself from the sixth floor of The Ritz.

For some yachtsmen, this training period at HMS *King Alfred* may have felt a little like joining the Army via a Pals battalion. Iain Rutherford was delighted to find an RCC friend, David Kemsley, in his group of trainees. Both men's wives had come along with them and they managed to share lodgings together. Ludovic Kennedy bonded with fellow old Etonian Bill Richmond. There may have been an occasional unappealing note of public-school snobbery and cliquiness on display. Kennedy tells an anecdote of Peter Beatty, who had been paired with a slightly older man from Aberdeen in the fish and chip business in a semaphore group. At lunch, Kennedy asked Beatty how he had fared: Beatty replied that his partner had been unable to decipher his message. It transpired he had been signalling Bois Roussel – the name of his Derby-winning horse.[20]

Robert Hichens joined HMS *King Alfred* in October with his friend and fellow RORC member Henry Trefusis (he who had bought the steam pinnace for training in London). Hichens, an impatient personality, had found waiting for the Admiralty letter extremely trying and had finally threatened to rejoin the TA if his commission was delayed any further.

Ultimately, at least four of the August 1939 Fastnet competitors were among the first *King Alfred* trainees. The International 12 dinghy sailors had been on the penultimate day of their annual championship at Torbay when Hitler invaded Poland. Already, 34 of the 73 potential entrants had been prevented from qualifying on account of military service obligations. Three of the 18 who sailed in the hastily rearranged final were RNVSR members who soon met again in Hove; architects, archivists, adventurers, accountants and impresarios, all united by their love of yachting and willingness to volunteer. During the summer of 1940, former Antarctic explorer the Rev Launcelot Fleming acted as *King Alfred* chaplain for a few months and preached sermons on courage, attempting to reassure his listeners that 'God has not lost control of this crazy world'. It can't have been an easy task.

Judy Middleton, historian of HMS *King Alfred*, reports that some of the experienced RNVSR yachtsmen in these first batches of trainees did not hesitate to correct their instructors on matters of navigation and seamanship. Others stayed quiet. Iain Rutherford remembered an instructor complimenting Adrian Seligman on his tying of a bowline: '"You seem to know your knots well, I suppose you have done a bit of small boat sailing." "Yes sir," replied Seligman, omitting to add that he'd sailed his own square-rigger round the world.'[21]

All of them were instructed into the Navy mindset. John Miller (the volunteer who had bluffed the Admiralty by suggesting he'd been sent the wrong form) wrote:

> *It is odd to consider how extremely little a man in the modern world —* *even a yachtsman — knew about naval life. I had shot rabbits and* *shot at birds for years but knew nothing about explosives. I had dined* *frequently with my naval brother in the barracks at Portsmouth but had* *never considered distinctions of rank or supposed that anybody under* *the level of an admiral was a person of much consequence. I had never* *bled so much as a pint. Entering* King Alfred, *mercifully in civilian* *clothes, I responded to the officer-in-charge and was told to find my* *'class captain'. I should have no difficulty as he would be wearing a* *DSO. I realised with a shock that I had not the faintest notion what* *a DSO ribbon looked like. In this place it appeared that a Lieutenant* *Commander was a high functionary. A Captain was a God.*[22]

Lay ignorance of this second fact got Lincoln into trouble. He had been sent on from *King Alfred* to HMS *Vernon*. Always punctilious, he felt he should inform the local Jewish chaplaincy of his new whereabouts. Lincoln, still a probationary temporary acting-sub-lieutenant, was horrified to receive an answering letter from the chaplaincy addressing him as Captain Lincoln. He was summoned by HMS *Vernon*'s commanding officer, Captain Boyd, and ordered to explain himself. Two months later, he wondered whether this insignificant encounter had altered the course of his naval career.

6

'I hardened to the life'[1]

1939–1940: Early assignments: patrolling and minesweeping

The Royal Naval Patrol Service (RNPS) memorial in Lowestoft bears 2,397 names of men who died during WWII and have 'no known grave but the sea'. The RNPS, whose central depot was HMS *Europa* (formerly Sparrow's Nest), was known as 'Harry Tate's Navy' – a nickname that was applied in derision but adopted with pride. It was the Navy for the 'Minor War Vessels' – the trawlers, drifters, paddle steamers, whalers, motor minesweepers, tugs, launches and converted yachts that patrolled the coast, cleared the channels and did the innumerable dull and dangerous sea–jobs that enabled the warships and the merchant fleets to function. When SS *Athenia* was torpedoed and sunk by Oberleutnant Fritz Julius Lemp (*U-30*) in the Western Approaches on 3 September 1939, Churchill, who was appointed First Lord of the Admiralty that same day, promised the nation that 80 ASW trawlers would be on station within a fortnight. Rayner, Churston and their carefully chosen group hurried away from Lowestoft to take up their position guarding the entrance to the Firth of Forth.

> *Patrol, patrol and more patrol. Up and down the line. Ping, ping, ping on the Asdic* [an early form of sonar] *for days without number until you knew every aspect of the coast bordering your beat. In fog it had peered at you dimly and sometimes unexpectedly close. At night it would recede until you longed to catch a glimpse of landmarks which by day you hated because of their familiarity.*[2]

Urgent orders soon sent the trawlers further north. Korvettenkapitän Günther Prien in *U-47* had slipped into the Home Fleet anchorage at Scapa Flow on the night of 14–15 October and sunk HMS *Royal Oak* with the loss of 835 lives. The small ASW flotilla then patrolled the turbulent waters of the Pentland Firth through one of the hardest winters in living memory. Wind, tide and weather were their determined enemies but the time spent at anchor, guarding against potential intruders, was generally felt to be even worse than the patrols at sea. The holding ground was poor and the trawlers dragged their anchors or yawed and snubbed to their cables until, by March 1940, Rayner felt they were all 'going round the bend'. He found himself having serious problems with his vision and was prescribed three weeks' rest – of which he took only a week before hurrying back to rejoin his ship as the Norway crisis developed.

Sub-Lieutenant Geoffrey Darlow's name is at the top left-hand corner of the first panel on the Lowestoft memorial, the first to be inscribed there. Born in 1911, he was from Wanstead in Essex and was a member of the Little Ship Club. He'd joined the RNVSR in October 1937 when he was 26. As well as sailing in the club yachts, Darlow had attended the training courses and obtained his Board of Trade Yachtmaster certificate. This ensured he was one of the first to be called up. He was commissioned a sub-lieutenant on 11 September and posted to HMT *Northern Rover*, an ASW trawler operating out of Kirkwall in Orkney. His time at *King Alfred* must have been brief, if indeed he was there at all, given that he already had his Board of Trade certificate and the need for ASW trawlers was urgent.

Northern Rover had been built in Bremerhaven in 1936 and was owned by Northern Trawlers Ltd of Grimsby. When my father had arrived in Grimsby on 2 September, he had commented, 'The port was a hive of industry busy commissioning some ninety fishing vessels as minesweepers, A/S [anti-submarine] and patrol vessels. There was an air of urgency.'[3] *Northern Rover* was likely to have been among them. Her deck frames would have been strengthened to enable her to carry at least one gun, plus racks of depth charges. She would have been fitted with ASDIC equipment to help her detect and track submarines. Internal modifications would enable her to ship a larger crew.

The fish-hold became the main ship's company mess deck with wooden mess tables and stools. Above in this confined and cramped area, hung hammocks on special hooks on the beams in any available space. Sometimes the stokers (often nicknamed the black gang), had a separate mess. Usually below the mess deck and in a specially constructed magazine, was stored the ammunition for the ship's guns. The officers' quarters were situated below the wheelhouse and contained a couple of bunks along with some basic furniture, a cupboard and a safe for confidential books etc. Lastly a small galley was included, where one cook had the impossible task of keeping an entire crew happy with the sparsest of wartime provisions.[4]

As soon as her refit was complete, Northern Rover was sent to join the Northern Patrol, keeping lookout across the sea area Orkney and Shetland to the Faroes and Iceland. This was the gap through which German warships would need to pass if heading for the Atlantic – although, in those final weeks of August, the *Graf Spee* and the *Deutschland* had already slipped by. In the period between the Munich crisis and the declaration of war, the Ministry of Economic Warfare (as they were termed from 3 September) had been gathering quantities of information about trading ships, their routes and cargoes in order to impose a blockade on Germany. Kirkwall had been designated a Contraband Control Port (the others were Weymouth in Dorset and The Downs off the coast of Kent). All neutral merchant ships were required to stop in these ports for cargo inspection. *Northern Rover* was to act as an armed boarding vessel, one small cog in the organisation that was going to translate this policy into action.

Her crew of 27 came from all four countries of the UK as well as from Grimsby itself. The majority were Royal Naval Reservists. *Northern Rover*'s commanding officer, Lieutenant Martin Hugh Macpherson RNR, had started his career in the RN. He had served in WWI as a midshipman, then when he had been 'retired' in 1922 he had continued his seagoing career in the merchant navy. Some specialist crew members such as the signalman and telegraphist and the first lieutenant had been provided by the 'regular' RNVR together with Sub-Lieutenant Darlow, the yachtsman volunteer from the Little Ship Club. The remainder of the crew – the engineers and firemen who kept the trawler's coal-fired engines running, the stewards who were responsible for domestic well-being – were Naval Auxiliary Personnel, pre-war seamen who had been offered the choice of signing on for 12 months under the T124 agreement or losing their jobs.

'Harry Tate's Navy' prided itself on a refusal to wear regulation uniform or run its ships according to 'pusser' routines. Geoffrey Darlow, in his newly tailored uniform, would have found himself among men whose rigs 'varied from the weird to the wonderful – seamen's jerseys and bell-bottoms, overalls, windcheaters, oilskins, duffle coats and kapok suits, topped by balaclavas, pom–pom and tea-cosy caps and even trilbies'. Arthur Bennett, sent north after only a fortnight at King Alfred to take command of a former herring drifter based in Dundee, remembers 'jerseys and slouch caps were the order of the day as I stepped aboard in all the glory of my new gold braid'.[5] As winter set in, the need for warmth was paramount. Denys Rayner set members of his crew to unravel all the ill-fitting 'comforts' they had been given, then sent the wool back down to London for Elizabeth's aunts to reknit into more useful protections against the bitter cold.

HMT *Northern Rover* didn't last long enough to need any extra woollies. Among the variety of vessels gathered in the Kieler Fjord in August, the crew of *Naromis* had noticed a small, local variety of submarine: 250-ton U-boats of the type called 'North Sea Ducks'. As my father recalled, 'There was no apparent escort for these two submarines who were carrying out independent diving exercises. This seemed to me a somewhat hazardous operation in such a crowded area but I suppose the Germans knew what they were doing.'[6] It seems that they did. These 'North Sea Ducks' were Type IIc submarines, eight of which had recently been built in Kiel. They were intended to be used as school-ships but in the autumn and winter of 1939–1940, when boats were scarce, they were formed into an active service flotilla. This was named in honour of a WWI U-boat commander, Oberleutnant Emsmann, who had died on 28 October 1918 while attempting to break into the British Home Fleet anchorage in Scapa Flow. Almost 21 years later, this feat had been achieved.

On 21 October 1939, Günther Prien was given a hero's welcome on his return to Kiel. Then, on 23 and 25 October, the first four boats of the Emsmann Flotilla (numbers 56–59) went on the hunt in the Orkney and Shetland areas. On 30 October, *U-56* fired three torpedoes at the Home Fleet flagship HMS *Nelson*. All the torpedoes misfired (and fortunately these small submarines only carried five). There's a persistent legend that Churchill was on board HMS *Nelson* that day. In fact, it was on 31 October that he and Sir Dudley Pound, the First Sea Lord, met Admiral of the Fleet Sir Charles Forbes for a conference on the flagship. A hit from *U-56* then could have changed world history.

On the same day and in the same sea area (north of Orkney and 100 miles west of Shetland), *U-59*, commanded by Kapitänleutnant Harald Jürst, torpedoed and sank HMT *Northern Rover*. *U-59* had already sunk two Hull fishing boats, *St Nidan* and *Lynx II*. Although Jürst's subsequent record suggests a tendency to fire first and check later, on this occasion he had behaved correctly, following the Prize Rules and ordering the fishing boat crews to abandon their vessels before he scuttled them. The crews were later rescued. There was no such mercy for the men of *Northern Rover*.

Months later, when *Yachting Monthly* named Sub-Lieutenant Darlow as the first RNVSR member on its yachtsman's Roll of Honour, it was only able to say that *Northern Rover* was 'presumed to have been lost with all hands as she was so long overdue'.[7] This was possibly genuine uncertainty or it may have been that the Admiralty were reluctant to ascribe yet another success to the U-boats. This absence of information was likely to have been an additional burden for Geoffrey Darlow's parents, Andrew and Agnes, and for all the families of the 27 men from *Northern Rover* who had no grave but the sea. Commanding Officer Martin Hugh Macpherson's widow, Florence, joined the recently re-formed Women's Royal Naval Service (WRNS or 'Wrens'), setting herself on course for a similar fate.

There had been no absence of information when Ludovic Kennedy's father died commanding the *Rawalpindi* in November 1939. Kennedy, still only 19, was on a training course in Bedford when he heard the news on the radio: '"The secretary of the Admiralty [...] regrets to announce the loss of the armed merchant cruiser *Rawalpindi*. HMS *Rawalpindi* was an ex-P&O liner of 17,000 tons…" The voice drifted on but I did not listen for I knew then that my father was dead.'[8]

Rawalpindi had also been on the Northern Patrol, keeping watch for enemy activity and intercepting merchant ships. Captain Kennedy was running her as if she were a warship. He led his crew in exercise every morning and ensured her gun crews put in as many practice shoots as the weather allowed. Vice-Admiral Max Horton described her as 'outstanding'. None of this helped, however, when *Rawalpindi* encountered two real warships, *Scharnhorst* and *Gneisenau,* in poor visibility north of the Faroe Islands. Captain Kennedy refused to heave-to when commanded. As *Rawalpindi's* guns were obsolete and she had no armour plating, the *Scharnhorst's* weaponry reduced her to a blazing wreck in less than half an hour, and 238 crewmen died. Approximately one-third of them were Naval Auxiliary Personnel – that is, her former P&O crew who had been asked to sign T124 agreements to transfer across to naval service. Much later in his life Ludovic Kennedy commented that if the *Rawalpindi* had still been a merchant ship, flying the red ensign, she could have scuttled or surrendered. Under the white ensign of the Royal Navy her only option was to fight as if she were a major warship.

This was one of those disasters that are somehow turned into triumphs. The fact that the *Rawalpindi* hadn't stood a chance brought her (apparently) within 'the highest traditions of the Royal Navy'. Ten of the survivors were filmed marching down Whitehall to be greeted by the Second Sea Lord and one can find no fewer than three Pathé newsreels on YouTube, celebrating her gallantry. Churchill had set the tone with his House of Commons tribute:

> *They must have known as soon as they sighted the enemy that there was no chance for them but they had no thought of surrender. They fought their guns till they could be fought no more. They then – many of them – went to their deaths and thereby carried on the great traditions of the Royal Navy. The example will be an inspiration to those who come after them.*[9]

Margery Allingham wrote hyperbolically that 'To come from the same village as a man on the *Rawalpindi* is a fine thing, as good as having had a great-great-uncle who had served on the *Victory*.'[10] She was, however, shrewd enough to notice that the media was short of inspiring material just then.

★★★

Through the winter of 1939–1940, the sea news was both depressing and alarming. Although the Type IIc North Sea Ducks of the Emsmann Flotilla had only five torpedoes, they also carried 12 mines. On *U-59*'s next patrol, early in December, she laid these close to the Norfolk coast, destroying HMS *Washington*, a steam trawler on her way for conversion to ASW status, and *Marwick Head*, a small merchant vessel. These were magnetic mines against which, at this time, British vessels had no defence. In January 1940, *U-56* used her magnetic mines to sink two merchant vessels off Smith's Knoll, the outer edge of Haisborough Sands, east of Cromer. U-boats often chose warlike emblems for themselves (British submarines frequently flew the skull and crossbones and recorded their kills on their conning towers). Harald Jürst and the crew of *U-59* displayed a scorpion grasping Britain in its claws.

Patrolling and minesweeping were immediate postings for several of the RNVSR yachtsmen. Arthur Bennett, Peter Tritton and Iain Rutherford were sent north as a group to take command of three small diesel drifters – *Venture, Viola* and *Suilven* – and to patrol the entrance to the River Tay. Adrian Seligman was also posted nearby. The drifters were 70ft long and retained their skippers and crews.

Temporary Probationary Acting-Sub-Lieutenant Iain Rutherford felt acutely aware of his personal inexperience and the fact that, as an RNVR officer, he was being given command of a vessel that already had her own skipper. He was relieved to discover that Skipper Foreman, from Peterhead, was 'quite one of the finest men I have ever come across. Apart from being a magnificent seaman who had been one of the most successful drifter skippers in peacetime fishing, he was also positively saint-like in character.' It was a reassuring example of the unexpected learning from and about others that many people affirm as part of their wartime experience. Rutherford, who had lived in Scotland all his life, admitted that the North East dialect of the Peterhead crew was so strong that he wasn't always confident in understanding them 'and to my wife, who is English, they seemed to speak an unknown foreign language, particularly when talking among themselves.'[11]

The group's duty was to maintain a continuous day and night patrol in the Firth of Tay. This was another challenging location, with strong tides, a dangerous bar and the unusually severe 1939–1940 winter weather:

Sometimes blizzards swept over the Firth reducing visibility to a few yards, and when this happened at night it made pilotage in these tide-ridden waters a nightmare. It was on such occasions that Foreman was such a tower of strength for he was always there to check my course, a thing he did without ever looking at the chart. These experienced fishing skippers have a sort of sixth sense which allows them to work out a course in their head which allows for tide and wind in an amazingly accurate way. Foreman carried all his courses in his head and could tell me the course, let us say, from Cape Wrath to Stornaway, without any trouble at all.[12]

Arthur Bennett was particularly grateful for the support he was given by Jock Hay, the engineer on board *Venture*. Several years of experience working on board Thames barges and sailing *June of Rochester*, in addition to his day job as a shipping agent on the Baltic Exchange, had not provided Bennett with any experience handling boats under power. When he arrived to take command at Dundee, he'd scarcely had time to stow his gear before *Venture* was required to get underway within the crowded harbour. Bennett and the *Venture*'s skipper eyed each other diffidently.

The Chief saw how matters lay. 'Ach, I ken her fine,' he murmured with a disarming grin. He jammed in the gears, worked ahead and astern, shouted a few completely unintelligible commands to the deckhands, and gradually the solid phalanx of craft opened up and we backed out into the dock. Then we turned short round and nosed up to the Quay. I watched him carefully to see how it was done, for all this was new to me. He turned to me with a smile and whispered confidentially. 'She's a bonnie wee ship we'll do fine.'[13]

Hay's tuition must have been effective because Bennett's next posting, in the spring of 1941, was to Coastal Forces, where he became an instructor in a motor launch (ML) training flotilla. However, although these newly made RNVR commanding officers got on well with their crews, they didn't find social relationships with the RN base staff so harmonious. Rutherford was angered by what he saw as the snobbery displayed towards *Suilven*'s admirable fishermen. Bennett found they quibbled at providing his T124 hands with the daily tot of rum everyone else enjoyed.

Through the winter of 1939–1940, the drifters spent four days patrolling at sea and two in harbour. Though it was physically demanding, it didn't seem quite like war, until early in the spring when the enemy started seeding magnetic mines around this northern section of the coast. Michael Richey, later well known for his solo crossings of the Atlantic, was not then a yachtsman. He was a Catholic who had considered becoming a monk but had chosen instead to work in the artist studio of Eric Gill. Despite his pacifist beliefs, he'd joined the RNPS and was serving on a drifter off the Yorkshire coast when she was blown up by a mine. Richey described the trauma of the experience in a 1941 short story that could not immediately be published in Britain, but which later won the first John Llewellyn Rhys Prize for young writers.

> *There came simultaneously a crack like that of a pistol shot going off in both ears and a lifting up of my whole body.*
>
> *The crack – there was nothing muffled about it as in a bomb explosion – was all-embracing, stunning, terrifying.*
>
> *It was followed by this bodily upward lift, rather like the up-going of a swing, with a second of silence that was impressive and merciful. It was, at least, a sign to your stunned consciousness that you were alive, even if a second later you might not be. We all knew in that silence that we had been mined. Perhaps a preparedness, a dull expectation of it somewhere at the back of one's brain was exploded in the open.*[14]

Though Richey and the rest of the crew survived, seeing their ship go down had been 'like seeing a man drown'.

★★★

Back on that August 1939 day in the Kieler Fjord, the crew of *Naromis* had observed a minelayer 'with a load of black, sinister-looking mines' and had surmised she might be on her way to block the Little Belt Channel, one of the three straits that connect the Baltic to the North Sea via the Kattegatt.

Britain, too, had been quick to begin minelaying immediately on the outbreak of war. A protective barricade of moored contact mines was established off the East Coast from the North Kent buoy to Scotland. It was a vast undertaking for which there were very few suitable vessels available. Charts of the dangerous areas (as required by international law) were adapted to make the minefields look larger than was actually the case. Dummy mines, which would be visible, as if by accident, at half-tide, were also laid. The barricade included gaps to allow vessels access to the major ports. These were an obvious temptation to hostile minelayers. Submarines, destroyers, aircraft and (a little later) fast E-boats ('E' standing for 'enemy') might cross the North Sea by night and lay their cargoes in the access channels. Minesweeping was a continuous requirement from the first days of the war until months after its end.

Maurice Griffiths, writing as 'Lone Gull', described the tension and the monotony of daily sweeping but also the occasional glimpses of beauty.

Soon the Young Bert would be over the bar and already her slab-sided bow was beginning to curtsy to the North Sea. From nowhere, it seemed, a swell suddenly lumped up ahead like a jade-green hill lifted by a magician's wand, while the little drifter climbed its smooth face and fell with a sidelong roll into the trough. The Lieutenant braced himself to the gyrations of his bridge and looked aft to see the Silver Harvest appear over the same mountain of water – her bridge, her wheelhouse, her bow and finally her stern, as she tumbled forward over the crest to disappear once more until only her funnel and her masts could be seen.

[…] Squinting across the bowl of the standard compass, the Lieutenant made a rough fix. Twenty years of coastal cruising in small ships may have unfitted him for the more precise methods of naval ships, nevertheless from long practice with far less convenient compasses his fix was quite good enough. They were near enough, he reckoned, to the position of the enemy's most recent laying.

He bent over the speaking tube.

'Wheelhouse?'

'Sir,' the voice came back muffled and metallic like that of an early phonograph.

'Half speed and close in on Silver Harvest's *port quarter.'*

Rolling steeply the two little ships edged over towards one another until it looked as if their wireless aerials might touch if they got any closer. Then the heaving line was passed over to the Harvest's *crew and the end of the trawl sweep shackled on and paid out. The apparent confusion of sweep wires and net and bottle green pellets was sorted out by dexterous hands and pushed willy-nilly over the low rail. The voices of the crew punctuated their work with cheery good humour.*[15]

The lieutenant sees three black specks 'no bigger than dragonflies' that turn out to be Spitfires returning from a mission 'over there'. They might equally easily have been Heinkel bombers, against which the minesweepers had only a Lewis gun to defend themselves. He cannot relax: at any moment there might be a shattering upheaval. He reflects that perhaps it was this subconscious bracing of oneself that became so tiring after every spell of sweeping.

Everything published in *Yachting Monthly* was subject to censorship yet the understanding of propaganda during WWII seems to have been more subtle than in previous conflicts. The amount of officially sanctioned writing (and also art and film) published from within operational situations appears quite startling – which leaves the unspoken and suppressed even more significant.

Many of the yachtsmen volunteers kept diaries, with or without permission. In *Gunboat Command* (2007), his biography of his father, Antony Hichens has included some telling extracts from Robert Hichens' diary made during his early weeks on minesweeping duty, as he faced up to seasickness, monotony and fear. Hichens had been posted to HMS *Halcyon*, a purpose-built Admiralty minesweeper, based in Harwich. She was the lead ship of a class of 21 commissioned between 1934 and 1939 – ten of which would have been sunk by the end of 1944. Hichens' diary entries offer an insight into the mindset of a solicitor-sportsman who developed into a hero. They also, sometimes, provide an inside story; in this case, to the events surrounding the loss of the minesweeper HMS *Sphinx*.

The entry below Geoffrey Darlow's, in the *Yachting Monthly* Roll of Honour, reads:

Also a Little Ship Club member and one of the first to join the RNVSR, Sub-Lieut. John Comfort often sailed aboard Sieglinda, *owned by Bernard Blaser. In the early days of the war he was engaged upon contraband control, but later joined HMS* Sphinx *for minesweeping duties. HMS* Sphinx *was attacked by enemy aeroplanes on February 3ʳᵈ and capsized when the tow parted in heavy weather as she was being taken into port. John Comfort's name was among the missing presumed to be dead.[16]*

Sphinx had been sweeping off the Scottish coast when she had been bombed from the air. Hichens' diary, however, reveals that it was not the bombing but a mismanaged rescue that had caused the majority of the deaths. HMS *Sphinx* had earlier been *Halcyon's* flotilla leader: 'so we all knew her very well and the officers on board.' Initially, he was inclined to assume *Sphinx's* crew had been insufficiently vigilant with her anti-aircraft gun. Two days later, he learned the full facts: the captain and four crew members had been killed in the initial explosion but then the remainder of the ship's company had been left on board when she was taken in tow. She turned turtle in heavy seas and a further 51 lives were lost.

'A terrible thing after the comparatively light casualty list resulting from the bombing,' wrote Hichens. A terrible thing – and an avoidable one. Not a story to spread at the time. Hichens records two other horrifying (and secret) tales, then comments:

People ashore don't realise what a grim war we are waging at sea with the Germans. A cold-blooded war, in a way I think requiring the maximum of bravery from the men of both sides in the long run, as it is so ceaseless and intangible. You just don't know whether the next moment will be your last, and it's surprising how untroubled by it most people manage to be.[17]

'So casual and quiet in the extraordinary things that you do'[1]

November 1939–September 1940: Rendering mines safe

From the first week of the war there were sinkings close to the English East and South coasts: on 10 September, the *Magdapur* went down off Aldeburgh and the *Goodwood* off Bridlington; on 14 September, the Belgian *Alex Van Opstal* off Weymouth; on 16 September, the *City of Paris* off Aldeburgh; on 24 September, the French *Phryne* off Aldeburgh, once again. Through October and November, the situation worsened: on 13 November, the destroyer HMS *Blanche* exploded and sank north of Margate when she was trying to rescue the damaged minelaying cruiser *Adventure;* the cargo ships *Ponzano* and *Matra* sank in the same area on the same day. Five days later, the Dutch liner *Simon Bolivar* carrying 397 passengers, mainly civilians bound for the West Indies to escape the war, went down near the Sunk Lightvessel off Harwich with the loss of 102 lives, many of them children.

The Netherlands was a neutral country. Initially, the Amsterdam press stayed quiet and there were attempts in Germany to deny responsibility – or even to suggest it was a British plot. Nevertheless, the horrific stories from this sinking were soon widely publicised: there were photos of the oil-covered survivors being cared for in Harwich, and Queen Wilhelmina spoke out, expressing her concern. Over the next five days, six more ships went down, including a large Japanese passenger liner. The new Town-class cruiser, HMS *Belfast,* was seriously damaged off the Firth of Forth. Then, on the evening of 21 November, the destroyer HMS *Gypsy* exploded and sank almost within Harwich Harbour itself. *Gypsy*'s captain and 30 crew members died in the explosion. *Gypsy* had only recently come south from Rosyth to join the Harwich destroyer flotilla. On 18 November, she had rescued survivors from the mined cargo ship *Blackhill* and from *Grazia* on 19 November. Earlier on that day that she herself was sunk, she had picked up three German airmen and brought them back into port. There was outrage when it was discovered that the German seaplanes (suspected of dropping the mines) had been spotted only two hours previously but that no effective action had been taken. This brought a furious Churchill to Harwich and the port commander resigned. All traffic in and out of the Thames was stopped, all navigation lights extinguished, and East Coast convoys were suspended or diverted. The country's economy could not hold out for long in this situation.

On 17 November, Acting-Lieutenant Lincoln, serving on the minelayer *M1* at HMS *Vernon*, had received an unexpected summons to the Admiralty. He found himself being interviewed together with a professional RN officer, Lieutenant Commander Dick Ryan, by Admiral Wake-Walker, a torpedo specialist who had been recalled from his seagoing command to deal with this crisis. Lincoln felt puzzled by his inclusion in such high-ranking company but soon discovered it was his legal training that was wanted. Could he help sift the evidence? Once he discovered that Captain Denis Boyd, the commanding officer of HMS *Vernon*, was also part of Admiral Wake-Walker's new unit, he guessed Boyd must have remembered him from the slightly ludicrous episode when Lincoln had been sent a letter addressing him as 'captain' and had been summoned to explain himself.

It seemed obvious that the weapon must be a mine. But what type? How was it triggered? How might it be countered? All the effort Lincoln had put into improving his navigation skills and studying for his Yachtmaster certificate was disregarded – it was his barrister brain that the Navy needed. He found himself in a roomful of gold braid listening to Admiral Wake-Walker telling Churchill that the new unit included a lawyer.

'Lawyer?' said Churchill, glaring over his spectacles. 'Where is he?'

I rose from my seat at the back of the room to come under the scrutiny of the entire gathering. Churchill gave what sounded suspiciously like a grunt, then returned to the business of the conference. I thankfully sat down again. When the meeting ended, Ryan and I set to work. It was then that I realised my role was to be that of a detective.[2]

Lincoln was reassigned to the minelaying department of the Admiralty and was given a sheaf of reports, mainly from survivors who had been asked to try to recall anything they had heard or seen immediately prior to the explosions. In addition, he was given details of the ships that had been damaged but not sunk. This was the evidence that should help him deduce the nature of the weapon and the way it worked.

Elsewhere, other HMS *Vernon* experts were doing their best to find ways of making the shipping lanes safe. Two common factors had been identified from most of the recent sinkings: first, that the mines had been laid in relatively shallow water; and second, that they were not mines of the 'contact' type. A contact mine would blow a definite hole in a ship, usually in the area of the bows. If the damage had been caused by a torpedo, there would be a similarly definite area of impact. These new weapons, by contrast, usually caused damage amidships or from below. They might blow the ship out of the water or break her back, but there never seemed to be any massive ripping away of plates. Any holes were usually quite small. This suggested that they were 'influence' mines, triggered by something other than a direct collision.

On the same day (18 November 1939) that the *Simon Bolivar* had gone down, the Esso tanker *James J Maguire*, carrying 15,000 tons of aviation fuel from New Jersey, was also damaged. She was towed into Tilbury for repair and a dent 140ft long was discovered in her hull. Lincoln recorded his feeling of excitement. He'd learned at HMS *Vernon* that underwater explosions acted in a predictable manner as water could not be compressed. The force of an explosion would take the form of a cone with a right angle at its apex. Lincoln used the length of the dent to represent the base of a triangle and thus suggest the likely depth of water. When this depth was confirmed by the ship's master, it offered conclusive proof that the mine had not been moored but had been lying on the seabed. It explained why they had been unable to bring one to the surface through routine sweeping. So much coastal navigation consists of drawing triangles – perhaps Lincoln's pre-war studies hadn't been entirely wasted.

Conventional contact mines could be cleared using the trawlers already requisitioned from the fishing fleet, but ground-lying mines were very much harder to retrieve or to detonate safely. On 20 November, an attempt to trawl one up using a specially designed non-magnetic net ended in tragedy when the converted ASW trawler HMT *Mastiff* blew up with six crew members killed and a further eight wounded. The commanding officer, Lieutenant Commander AAC Ouvry RN, recalled:

> *There was a sudden thud – no real noise, and I found myself about halfway to heaven, somersaulting through the air and No. 1 doing likewise. I don't remember going down again or hitting the water but, some way under I swam up and was pleasantly surprised to find I had reached the surface before my breath ran out [...] The poor old ship was in a bad way – both masts gone – motorboat completely smashed – skiff entirely blown away and the stern already awash. The boiler had burst and was blowing off great clouds of steam with a continuous roar. She only lasted about 5 minutes and then heeled over and sank [...] It is a very sad loss, as I was very fond of the ship and much regret the six good chaps who did not survive.*[3]

The loss of HMT *Mastiff* convinced the HMS *Vernon* experts that they needed to look for more of the older drifters with wooden hulls, as alternatives to the strong steel-hulled trawlers they had already requisitioned. Two RNVSR officers were selected to assist with this search: Robert Selby Armitage and Maurice Griffiths. Griffiths remembered being given his instructions from HMS *Vernon*'s Commander Hamond. He was to go to Aberdeen, Buckie and Peterhead to assess whether four elderly drifters were in good enough condition to withstand the pull of the trawl gear. Griffiths selected three of the four; the last was too far gone, 'even for expendable duties' – a somewhat chilling phrase. When their conversion was complete, he was put in charge of a small group, designated the 3rd Mine Recovery Flotilla, and sent to investigate the mouth of the River Tay. The small vessels pulled heavy nets made of bronze wire and their orders were not to destroy but attempt to recover the unknown mines so they could be examined.

On the third day of seeking a heavy object was caught in the net being dragged between them by Scottish Thistle *and* Achievable. *With excitement mounting on each of the two little ships, they slowly hauled the object out of the ship channel, shuddering under the maximum power of their engines, towards the sandy beach. But alas! In the shallows of Buddon Ness there was suddenly a mighty roar, a mountain of dirty water astern, and all hopes of a retrieved specimen had gone.*[4]

By 22 November 1939, the day after the loss of HMS *Gypsy*, all Thames Estuary defence forces were on heightened alert. At Southend, sailors with machine guns were stationed on the pier and sent out to patrol in small motorboats as they guarded the mouth of the Thames. They heard a plane − or planes − and opened fire. A few miles further down the coast, at Shoeburyness, an Army officer of the 518 Coast Artillery Regiment did the same. Griffiths describes what happened next:

Soon after dawn when the ebb tide had drawn all the water off the foreshore a black cylindrical object was sighted, lying partially embedded in the wet sand. A short distance away the sodden folds of a dark green parachute lay draped like some grotesque seaweed. The military authorities at nearby Shoebury fort were alerted and as the object was evidently some type of sea mine and below the highwater mark, the Naval Officer in Command (NOIC) Southend was informed.

At once a special Vernon *party was despatched [...] with orders to get to Southend at all speed and to recover the mine 'at all costs'. And by the time they arrived at Shoeburyness a second object, similar in every detail to the first, had been discovered rather more deeply buried in the sand, about 300 yards nearer the lowwater mark.*[5]

A photographer was identified and sworn to secrecy in order that photographs could be taken, before the tide rose again, and rushed to the Admiralty. An impression of the fuse plate was taken so that a brass screwdriver of the correct size could be made to open what seemed to be the primer pocket. Both the mines were secured to keep them immobile under water and the local ordnance depot began making suitable non-magnetic tools while the recovery team took the chance to have some breakfast. The second phase of the operation could at least take place in daylight, once the tide was ebbing. More photographs were taken at every stage and detailed records were made. One team of experts (Ouvry and Baldwin) worked while the other (Lewis and Vearncombe) observed. Wherever possible, this would become part of the routine in the months ahead – for the pragmatic reason that if the mine exploded and the person defusing it was killed, it would be possible to know what stage he'd reached or what particular movement had triggered the tragedy. Usually, the teams were two people: an officer and a trained rating. It was the 'etiquette of the job' to keep the rating out of the danger area 'until the real fang of the job, the bomb fuse, had been drawn'. John Miller explains:

In the beginning and later with any unfamiliar mine, our method was to station our sailor at least a hundred yards away behind some cover – a rise in the ground or a broken wall. He carried a notebook and a pencil. Then, taking a selection of tools, we started work, shouting to the sailor before each move and explaining as precisely as possible what we were going to do. We would call, for example, 'I am now going to cut a blue lead.' The sailor would write this down in his book and raise his hand when he had finished. If the mine exploded, he could return to the Admiralty, show his notes and say, 'Next gentleman must not cut a blue lead'.[6]

On this first occasion – the first attempt to defuse this unknown type of mine – the lead operator was a professional. Lieutenant Commander JDG Ouvry, a 43-year-old former RN officer from HMS *Vernon*, had served in WWI, ending it as the Navy's youngest torpedo officer. He was first cousin to Lieutenant Commander AAC Ouvry, recently of HMT *Mastiff*. John Ouvry was a vicar's son who described himself self-deprecatingly as 'not pretty, intelligent or brave but blessed with steady nerves and strong hands'. It's hard to disagree with the comment made in Ouvry's obituary that 'these qualities are not much use unless they are controlled by a brave mind'. He set to work:

The next two sweaty hours brought Ouvry and his team into history. He did not know, he could not tell, how the mine was armed, and until he found out, nobody else could be any the wiser. [...] The measures taken to

protect ships, the development of the Rendering Mines Safe Section and
then of the Land Incidents Section all derived from Ouvry's courage.[7]

Initially, the mines had been laid by U-boats (such as Harald Jürst's
U-59) and by small groups of destroyers. Since they sank immediately
to the seabed, they would have remained very hard to retrieve
and study. Fortunately, perhaps, departmental rivalry between the
Kriegsmarine and the Luftwaffe had prompted the use of aircraft
to lay mines by parachute. This was very demanding for pilots,
who needed to fly low and in the dark over the surface of the sea
and could therefore become disorientated – hence the mislaying
at Shoeburyness, which had provided the first specimens. During
the Battle of Britain and the Blitz period in 1940–1941, however,
the Luftwaffe would drop these parachute mines on land as large,
destructive bombs. They didn't always explode on landing and,
because the weapons had originated at sea, it remained the Navy's job
to attempt to make them safe. This was undertaken by the volunteers
of the RNVR, usually trained by Commander John Ouvry.

The immediate problems were not over. The aeroplane (or planes)
flying over Southend and Shoeburyness during the night of 22
November 1939 had been busy: over the next few days a further
three mines exploded in the area – one apparently spontaneously, the
other two detonated by fishermen, both of whom escaped unhurt.
The RAF raided the islands of Borkum and Sylt, where the planes
were thought to be based, but with little effect. The naval authorities
had to accept that there were already an incalculable number of
mines, sowed more conventionally by destroyers and submarines,
lying in wait in coastal waters and still no effective way of either
locating them or rendering them safe.

The rate of sinkings showed no signs of slowing. The cargo
ship *Hookwood* (Convoy FS 40) struck a mine off the Tongue and
went down on 23 November; the *Mandalay* off Spurn Head on 24
November; on 27 November it was the Dutch cargo ship *Spaarndam*
in the Tongue minefield; then the *Rubishaw* (same minefield) on 28
November. On 29 November, *Ionian*, travelling in Convoy FN 43,
went down off the Norfolk coast; on 30 November, the Norwegian
tanker *Realf* off Flamborough Head and the British cargo ship *Sheaf
Crest* off Margate. Lives were lost in all but one case.

Many more minesweepers were brought into service, including elegant paddle steamers dating from the 1890s and more recently used as excursion vessels. Edward Stanley found himself appointed third officer on HMS *Kellett*, one of the WWI minesweepers that were known as the 'Smokey Joes' because of the quantities of black smoke that poured from their funnels. Yet success during this period was negligible. In the absence of any fail-safe way of locating and removing the mines, the Admiralty began to ask whether there was any way of protecting the ships themselves: 'Is it possible,' asked Admiral Wake-Walker, 'to de-magnetize a ship?' Lincoln was instructed to ring HMS *Vernon* and was told they were already working on the idea.

★★★

Lieutenant Commander Charles Goodeve RNVR was the son of an Anglican clergyman in Canada. Money had always been short but when Rev Goodeve was appointed to a church on Lake Winnipeg, Charles and one of his brothers had refurbished an old boat and acquired a deep love of sailing. University was a financial struggle but, while he was there, Goodeve joined the Royal Canadian Navy Volunteer Reserve to gain further nautical training and some seagoing experience. He took all the opportunities available and when his career as a scientist brought him to University College London, he applied to the regular RNVR and began attending its training courses. This included a torpedo course and training in naval electrics.

On the outbreak of war, he was immediately appointed to HMS *Vernon* as a lieutenant commander. Goodeve used Canoe Lake at Southsea, a popular site for model boats, to begin experimenting with a new Double-L minesweeping method that finally proved successful in clearing magnetic mines. He also developed techniques of 'degaussing' (installing electrically charged coils around ships to reduce their magnetic signatures) and 'wiping' (undertaking the same process on a temporary basis) to gain immediate protection for the greatest possible number of vessels of all sizes. At the time of the Dunkirk evacuation, 400 ships would be wiped in four days.

Lincoln, meanwhile, was discovering that there was no standstill in the new variations of mine warfare. The sinking of the tanker *Inverlane* on 14 December 1939 and damage to other ships in the northbound Convoy FN 54 (the Thames to the Firth of Forth), together with the destroyer HMS *Kelly*, which had been escorting the rescue tugs, did not conform to the pattern of destruction by magnetic mine and prompted him to travel to Tyneside, inspect the damage and interview survivors. These included HMS *Kelly*'s captain, Lord Louis Mountbatten. Mountbatten took him to inspect the damage to the *Kelly*'s stern. A search by torchlight revealed part of the horn of a contact mine embedded in the ship's plating. Minesweepers were despatched to the site of the sinking and 140 mines from a previously unsuspected field were swept up and destroyed. One was recovered intact, investigated and made safe by Lieutenant Robert Selby Armitage RNVR, a specialist from HMS *Vernon*.

Selby Armitage (b. 1905), aged 34, was, like John Ouvry and Charles Goodeve, the son of a vicar. His father had held the living of Nettlebed in Oxfordshire from 1908 to 1920 and had known the Fleming family well. Ian Fleming's first biographer, John Pearson, records that when Fleming approached Selby Armitage to join 30AU (the intelligence commando unit), Armitage refused 'with a mistrust of all Fleming's schemes that dated back to childhood'. Tantalisingly, no more details are offered but it was evidently a friendship that endured as Fleming's subsequent biographer, Andrew Lycett, has Armitage and Fleming playing golf together late into Fleming's life.

Armitage had attended Rugby School, read Classics at Cambridge, worked as a stockbroker and qualified for the Bar just before the outbreak of war. He owned a Breton-built cutter called *Penboch*, which he kept in Southampton, and had joined the RNVSR London Division in March 1937. Like Maurice Griffiths, he was almost immediately deployed to join HMS *Vernon*.

King George VI had honoured the courage of Ouvry, Lewis, Glenny, Baldwin and Vearncombe at a special ceremony on HMS *Vernon*'s parade ground on 19 December 1939. The medals presented then were the familiar DSO, DSC, DSM; they were the first Royal Navy decorations of WWII. Some people suggested that a VC would have been appropriate for the courage displayed in that initial defusing on the beach at Shoeburyness but VCs must technically be earned 'in the face of the enemy'. The author of John Ouvry's obituary in the *Independent* commented:

There are still those who think that it is unrealistic to distinguish between the human and the mechanical presence of the enemy, that several hundredweight of fused explosive deliberately delivered is a palpable manifestation of his literal presence, and that it is metaphysical nonsense to pretend otherwise.[8]

In September 1940, a new honour, the George Cross, with its associated George Medal, was instituted to recognise 'acts of the greatest heroism or for most conspicuous courage in circumstances of extreme danger not in the presence of the enemy' by members of the British armed forces or British civilians. On 27 December 1940, Robert Selby Armitage became the first of the yachtsmen volunteers to be gazetted for this award. With him were RNVR officers John Herbert Babington (a teacher) and Richard Valentine Moore (who had previously worked for the London Electricity supply company). Over the following five years, a further 13 RNVR officers would earn the George Cross and many more (including Griffiths and Armitage) the George Medal.[9]

The previous week, a George Cross had been announced for Lincoln's RN colleague Lieutenant Commander Dick Ryan, together with his assistant Chief Petty Officer Reg Ellingworth. Sadly, both were posthumous.

'I couldn't help noticing that it wasn't quite what you expected'[1]

January–June 1940: Action in Norway

Much of the naval activity during the first months of the war was precautionary or defensive. There were also moments of traditional battle, as when the cruisers HMSs *Exeter, Ajax* and *Achilles* forced the *Graf Spee* to retreat at the Battle of the River Plate on 13 December 1939. On 17 December, there was drama when Captain Philip Vian of HMS *Cossack* sent a boarding party with revolvers and (allegedly) drawn cutlasses on to the *Graf Spee's* former supply ship, the *Altmark*, to rescue 299 British merchant seamen imprisoned below decks. Their shout 'The Navy's here!' became a catchphrase. It was unfortunate that this incident took place in Norwegian territorial waters and was thus a violation of international law.

In the Admiralty, Norway may have been a sensitive topic. Ever since Churchill had taken over from Lord Stanhope as First Lord of the Admiralty on 3 September 1939, he'd been pressing for action. One of his favourite ideas (Operation *Catherine*) was to send an armoured squadron into the Baltic to establish British supremacy and persuade the neutral Scandinavian countries (especially Sweden, a crucial source of iron ore) to enter the war on the British side. The First Sea Lord, Dudley Pound, and others were playing him along, appearing to agree while bringing up a succession of practical objections. Perhaps it was a little like the early days of WWI when Childers had been delegated to draw up a plan for the invasion of the Frisian Islands to keep Churchill happy – while being set up to fail in practical terms. It was a powerful dream: Ian Fleming later admitted that he'd been inspired by *The Riddle of the Sands* to dream of setting up a two-man observation post in the Islands where agents would live on shellfish and report the activities of German U-boats by wireless.

★★★

Patrick Dalzel-Job, meanwhile, had been continuing to survey the Norwegian coast and collect charts and pilotage information as he'd promised when he had offered his assistance to the Admiralty in 1937. On 12 September 1939, he and his mother finished packing up their home on the schooner *Mary Fortune*. They moored her safe in Tromsø, said goodbye to their friends the Bangsunds and left for England. Despite his lukewarm reception by the Admiralty, Dalzel-Job had remained convinced that this vast and complex area would be a battleground for small fast boats in time of war. (He may not have realised how few such boats the Navy possessed in 1939.)

For two years, he'd been working steadily up towards the Arctic weathering storms, learning Norwegian, making friends and finally passing the North Cape to reach Arctic Finland and the Petsamo inlet, where no one seemed ever to have seen a British vessel before. His 'fisherman's Norwegian' was good enough for him to be accepted as a North Norwegian if he was in the Westland, or as a Westlander in northern Norway. Later, he discovered that he could pass as Norwegian in other Scandinavian countries or as Danish if in Norway.

On their journey south from the Arctic, Dalzel-Job had been taken in twice for questioning and ordered to report all his movements to the Norwegian police. When he finally arrived in London, however, no one seemed interested in the specialist knowledge he had brought.

August Courtauld likewise didn't believe that any of the information he and Michael Spender and other yachtsmen had gathered that summer was ever used by the Admiralty. Some years later, he discovered that an invaluable set of charts, donated in 1939 by a Norwegian ship's captain, had been stuffed behind a filing cabinet. Dalzel-Job called it negligence. To Courtauld, it was ignorance: 'The ignorance of the NID was fantastic,' he wrote.[2]

Courtauld, who retained his contacts with 'the crooked people' (Lawrence Grand's Section D) in the early months of the war, also spent some weeks in Admiral Godfrey and Ian Fleming's NID

Room 39 (nicknamed 'The Zoo'), where he was miserable. He was then transferred to the Balkans section, though his expertise was in Scandinavia. When he was shifted to the German section (which included Scandinavia), he discovered it was being run by an expert on Egypt. Senior officials simply didn't want to hear the sort of information that he and other yachtsmen (such as Gerry Holdsworth) had collected – or that Frank Carr had been able to glean from Grimsby trawler skippers. News that there was a navigable channel through the pack ice in the Denmark Strait in all but the hardest winters was met by hostility. 'How the devil do you think I'm going to find the cruisers to do all that?' barked Captain Harcourt (Director of Operations (Home)). The navigability of the Norwegian Inner Leads – by iron ore carriers, for instance – was similarly not credited. Courtauld's complaints about the quality and availability of charts in the Admiralty are reminiscent of Childers' comments more than three decades earlier.

When Dalzel-Job finally received his RNVR sub-lieutenant's commission, he was posted as navigating officer on board a tug. Next, he was given command of a steam drifter working as a patrol vessel out of Scapa Flow. He was probably part of the auxiliary anti-submarine patrol described (somewhat patronisingly) by Denys Rayner:

> small drifters officered by the RNVSR and manned by 'hostilities only' ratings. The drifters were equipped with an immature asdic and were employed to steam back and forth between the booms. They intrepidly strapped a couple of depth charges to their sterns and we wondered what would happen if they ever had to fire one.

Dalzel-Job enjoyed navigation but his heart was in Norway. He began to feel that he was almost alone in believing that the war would eventually reach into the Norwegian Inner Leads.

He wasn't quite alone, but the situation was complicated. As well as his enthusiasm for Operation *Catherine*, Churchill had been agitating since late September for mines to be laid by the Royal Navy in Norwegian waters (Operation *Wilfred*) – an obvious violation of neutrality to which the Norwegian government objected strongly. When ice closed the more direct route via the Gulf of Bothnia, the Norwegian port of Narvik was used to ship essential iron ore from

Swedish mines to Germany. Churchill wanted to despatch destroyers to sink any such ore-carrying vessels. While Rear-Admiral Victor Danckwerts, the Naval Director of Plans, lost his job for the directness of his opposition, everyone else around Churchill worked more subtly.

On 30 November 1939, Russia invaded Finland: Allied indecision increased. Churchill pushed again in January 1940 for the mining of the Inner Leads: neutral countries' objections remained. By March 1940, when the British Navy was ready to take action and use the Finnish situation as a pretext for sending an expeditionary force to Narvik, the Finns had been defeated. The expeditionary force was stood down.

This was a disappointment, and a possible waste of expertise for polar explorer and RNVSR member Quintin Riley. In the first months of the war, Riley, like so many other RNVSR members, had been directed to an anti-submarine yacht. In January 1940, he had written to *The Times* warning that, without expert advice, people organising expeditions to cold climates might waste money and endanger lives by buying unsuitable equipment. He suggested input from the Scott Polar Research Institute in Cambridge. Later in that same month, when he heard of the intention to equip the Scots Guards reserves to fight in Norway, Riley left his anti-submarine yacht (possibly without permission) and offered his experience as a polar quartermaster. Three others of the pre-war explorer group joined him, including his friend Andrew Croft, whose sister Riley would later marry. They were busy at once collecting suitable equipment: Nansen sledges, sealskin boots and reversible Grenfell wind jackets (white on one side, fawn on the other) for the intended specialist troops. Riley's biographer and cousin Jonathon Riley (a career soldier) comments:

> *Nowadays one is used to the idea of certain battalions and Royal Marines commandos being trained as formed bodies for Arctic warfare, but this idea did not find favour in 1940. Instead the War Office put out a call for volunteers by telegram to all parts of the world. [...] some could not shoot, some were in uniform for the first time, but all were experienced skiers.*[3]

Riley was soon lecturing the volunteers on loading sledges, camping in snow and avoiding frostbite. He ensured that each man had properly fitted kit. Then they all spent a happy, if faintly confusing, fortnight training in Chamonix. On 14 March, a hurried recall to Glasgow en route for action in Norway ended there. The Finns had surrendered: the specialists were disbanded. Riley, who had accepted the rank of colour sergeant to enable him to serve in the Scots Guards, found that the Navy did not approve this arrangement. Eventually, he was judged to have taken 'special leave without pay' and was officially reinstated in the RNVR.

After the defeat of Finland there was further indecision, delay and intelligence failure. Reports of German preparations were routinely discounted if they didn't fit in with the current intelligence preconceptions. These focused on economic warfare and the Atlantic trade routes and didn't include a German occupation of Norway. The Norwegians may have been complacent, too. The British minelaying force Operation *Wilfred* finally set off on 7 April 1940, just two days before the Germans invaded.

The invasion operation (*Weserübung*) was a gamble for the Germans, especially for those troop ships and supply vessels heading furthest north to Narvik and Trondheim. They were led by the *Gneisenau* together with the *Scharnhorst* and the heavy cruiser *Admiral Hipper*, but knew their forces were potentially inferior to the full strength of the Royal Navy. Most of the British fleet, however, were steering north-east from Scapa Flow, obsessed with stopping the Germans breaking through into the Atlantic. Only the battleship HMS *Renown* and a small force of destroyers were nearing Narvik, their task to support the Operation *Wilfred* minelayers.

On 8 April, HMS *Glowworm,* one of *Renown*'s destroyer escort group, had lost a man overboard and stayed behind, searching for him. As she journeyed to rejoin her sister ships, she encountered two German destroyers and began to fire at them. They lured her on, through fog, until she met the *Admiral Hipper*, ten times her size and with heavy, radar-directed guns. HMS *Glowworm* was soon on fire and hopelessly outnumbered, yet she was still nimble. Her captain, Lieutenant Commander GB Roope, turned towards the *Hipper* at high speed, ripping off 150ft of side plating as he rammed her. *Glowworm*'s bow was torn away. She disengaged and managed a few more shots before she finally blew up and sank. In all, 118 of her 145 crew died, including Roope. *Yachting Monthly* added another name to its Roll of Honour:

John Kennedy joined the RNVSR two years ago and was called up for active service last August. After preliminary training he was posted to HMS Glowworm *which was lost on the eve of the first battle of Narvik. He was a member of the RORC and was well known in cruising circles as an excellent crew and dependable comrade. His friendship was a happy quality shared by many yachtsmen around the South and East Coasts.*[4]

Kennedy (aged 23), together with Ordinary Seamen Robert Weir and George Pugh (aged 19), were the only RNVR personnel on board *Glowworm* – three people among the ship's complement of 145. Few RNVR officers were posted to warships at this stage, though many dreamed of it. Neither John Kennedy's nor George Pugh's parents nor Roope's wife, nor any of the other relatives, would know exactly how they had died until the war ended. *Glowworm* had been on her own. The *Admiral Hipper* picked up the few survivors then returned to Germany, where she was repaired and the rescued men sent to prisoner-of-war (POW) camps, where they would remain for the next five years. On their release in 1945, the only surviving officer, Lieutenant R Ramsey, was finally able to describe their action. Unusually, however, the captain of the *Admiral Hipper,* Vice-Admiral Hellmuth Heye, had sent a message via the International Red Cross praising the courage of the *Glowworm* and recommending her captain for a decoration. Roope was posthumously awarded a VC.[5]

News of the *Weserübung* caused shock in the UK. Chamberlain's ill-advised comment on 4 April that Hitler had 'missed the bus' prompted any number of bitter press retorts: 'yes but he caught the workman's' (workmen's buses and trains offered cheaper tickets and left considerably earlier in the morning than regular services). A flotilla of five H-class destroyers steamed up the Ofotfjord to Narvik to attack larger German destroyers already there. They sank two, damaged two and fired at the invading land forces. As they left, they met five more large, hostile destroyers. HMS *Hardy* and *Hunter* were lost and *Hotspur* was badly damaged. To RNVSR's Peter Scott, still stuck in training courses and holding out for his own appointment to a destroyer, this dash and gallantry inspired envy. There was a second Battle of Narvik a few days later in which heavier British forces destroyed a further eight German ships with only minor losses. It was poor planning and co-ordination and a crucial lack of air power that would bring defeat, not a lack of initiative or bravery.

Finally, Dalzel-Job was recalled from his drifter and given orders to report aboard the cruiser HMS *Southampton*, which was carrying an advance party of Scots Guards to Norway on 11 April. He assumed it was because of his knowledge of the language, then realised that he was the only person with any knowledge of the country or ideas about winter warfare. Evidently none of the learning from Quintin Riley's group had yet been shared across. No one had expected there would be snow in northern Norway at this time of year: 'The Expeditionary Force was well supplied with motor cars and bicycles but there were no skis or snowshoes – nor any men trained to use them. There was no winter camouflage and (as would become distressingly clear later) there were no anti-aircraft guns.'[6]

Joint leadership of Rupertforce – to which Dalzel-Job was attached – was shared between Admiral the Earl of Orrery in HMS *Aurora* and Major-General Mackesy in HMS *Southampton*. Theirs was not a united command. Captain Maund, the naval chief of staff on board HMS *Southampton*, asked Dalzel-Job whether there were any boats on the coast that could be used for landing troops. He explained that there would be hundreds of *skøyter*, sturdy, well-built craft, with heavy single-cylinder, semi-diesel engines, dispersed through every inlet and anchorage. Maund told him it would be his job to collect sufficient boats to land the Expeditionary Force but when Dalzel-Job was rash enough to ask the general how many men this would be, he was slapped down.

> 'But, Sir, how am I to tell how many boats to get?'
> 'That's your affair,' said the General.
> I went away and made enquiries at a lower level – as perhaps I should have done in the first place.[7]

Dalzel-Job collected sufficient *skøyter* (immediately renamed 'puffers') to disembark Rupertforce but 'blunder followed blunder'. He found himself astounded at the lack of attention paid to camouflage. When German bombers attacked unexpectedly, there was a tendency to blame Norwegian 'fifth columnists': Dalzel-Job was certain that in almost every case it was because someone had been negligent about leaving equipment lying around in the snow, so easily spotted from the air. He also found it 'tragic' that the commanders could not understand how much safer it was to be in small craft using narrow inshore channels than in big ships on the main shipping routes. He formed the *skøyter* into a flotilla of about 30 vessels working in groups of three, as far as possible from the same village and following certain simple codes. Later, he estimated they had moved as many as 15,000 soldiers and 4,000 refugees, in heavily bombed waters, without losing a single person.

Twenty-six-year-old Dalzel-Job grew increasingly confident in backing his own judgement and ignoring senior officers. In the last days of May 1940, as the military expedition failed and the German forces advanced, he had begun a civilian evacuation from Narvik. He was instructed to cease but took no notice. His boats were removed on the orders of Allied Force Headquarters but he persisted: 'By cunning or force I recovered some boats and in the next two days I sent away 2,000–2,500 women, children and old men, including all the inhabitants of an old people's home, some of whom had not walked for years.'[8] He expected that he would be stripped of his RNVR commission for ignoring orders; the Mayor of Narvik assured him he would immediately be welcomed into the Royal Norwegian Navy. When the first heavy bombing raid came and fire swept through the wooden-built town, the majority of the 10,000 inhabitants had already been evacuated. 'When the Mayor and I left the harbour quay in my last fishing boat, late on Friday evening 7 June, there were probably not more than 100 people in the town.'[9] Only three people had lost their lives.

By this time, the theatre of war had moved decisively to the Channel coast. Germany had invaded the Netherlands, Belgium and France and there had been the much greater evacuation from Dunkirk. Chamberlain's government had fallen and Winston Churchill was prime minister. Dalzel-Job had hoped to stay behind when the Allied Expeditionary Force left Norway but when he arrived in Harstad early in the morning of 8 June, HMS *Southampton* was still there. He had no further excuse to disobey orders. He was still an RNVR officer, though he describes himself as 'disillusioned, ashamed and resentful'. King Haakon of Norway, who had to leave his country at that same time, sent him a personal message of thanks via the Admiralty, and would later award him the Knight's Cross of St Olav. Dalzel-Job retained his RNVR commission but was posted to a converted merchant ship, HMS *Corinthian*, and sent to the South Atlantic, where he remained for the next two years.

Sub-Lieutenant Ludovic Kennedy RNVR was serving on a Tribal-class destroyer, HMS *Tartar*. Known as 'lucky' *Tartar*, she was one of only four out of the 16 in her class to survive beyond 1942. HMS *Gurkha* had been the first to go, lost to air attack on 9 April 1940 as she headed to Norway with the Home Fleet. Her RNVR doctor, along with an RNVR sub-lieutenant and an RNVR seaman, were among those who died. Doctors, like stokers, were especially vulnerable when ships went down as their work often kept them deep below decks. HMS *Afridi* was sunk on 2 May 1940, also by bombing. On board HMS *Tartar*, however, 20-year-old Kennedy described his excitement as he streamed to sea with the Home Fleet:

> We had joined the rest of the Fleet; ahead and on either beam were destroyers – line upon line of destroyers, each keeping perfect station with its next ahead. [...] Just before I came off watch at twelve-thirty the Commander-in-Chief ordered a turn of 180 degrees. It was a wonderful sight to watch the leaders of each column swing round together to starboard when the executive signal was hauled down, the destroyers astern following in succession in their wake. To an inexperienced officer this would have been a tricky manoeuvre, but to the Captain it was child's play.[10]

Later that day, HMS *Tartar* was detached to accompany a convoy back to England. She spent the next two months almost continuously on escort duty, apparently immune from the air attacks that were sinking her sisters. Towards the end of April, *Tartar* was sent to Molde, a small town on the Romsdal Peninsula that Kennedy had previously visited on holiday with his parents. It was a horrifying sight. 'Not a house had escaped the German bombers; every building was either in flames or so gutted that there was nothing left to burn.'[11] He was sent to the woods above the town to offer the defeated General Ruge and his officers passage to England. He found them staring down at the burning town with despair in their eyes. They refused his offer and he carried away a vivid impression of them in their grey-blue cloaks and peaked caps standing, as in a tableau, lit up by the glow of the fires, their suitcases beside them in the snow.

★★★

Quintin Riley's Norwegian service was almost accidental. He was reinstated as a temporary lieutenant in the RNVR (after his brief incarnation as a Guards colour sergeant) but was not then sent back to routine duties. Instead, he became part of Colonel Colin Gubbins' Scissorforce, which was an early experiment in commando tactics. Gubbins – soon to be a founder of the Special Operations Executive (SOE) – was a WWI veteran who had earned a Military Cross at the Battle of the Somme. Subsequently, he had served in the Anglo-Irish war, where he became keenly interested in the potential of guerrilla activity. In the months immediately before the outbreak of WWII, he was closely connected with Section D (destruction). This was part of the SIS and had been set up in 1938 by Major Lawrence Grand of the Royal Engineers with a remit to plan clandestine sabotage and propaganda operations to undermine the German economy since 1938. Both August Courtauld and Gerry Holdsworth had links with Section D. Mollie Courtauld remembered Grand coming to stay at their house in Essex and upsetting the housemaid by leaving his revolver under his pillow.

Gubbins was also involved with unit MI(R) (Army research), writing manuals on irregular warfare and resistance tactics. He was central to the WWII development of 'ungentlemanly warfare', for which he had been supplied with a list of public school chaps. These were then sifted by his socially adept secretary, Joan Bright, a likely model for Ian Fleming's Miss Moneypenny (she dated him briefly). Adventurer Peter Fleming was one of Bright's first picks, soon followed by *Rogue Male* author Geoffrey Household. Explorers, mountaineers, people who had lived in distant parts of the world (as Bright herself had) were invited to inexplicable lunches in London clubs and mysterious interviews in the then MI(R) offices in Caxton Street.

In April 1940, Gubbins was given permission to raise Independent Companies to support the Norwegian campaign. As well as requesting Indian Army officers with experience of the North-West Frontier, he recruited explorer Andrew Croft. Croft had been trapped in Norway for the first fortnight of invasion: he had helped deliver the belated aid of arms to Finland then had hitched his way home on the destroyer HMS *Ashanti* before joining Gubbins. According to the MI(R) War Diary, Riley came to Gubbins' office to say goodbye to Croft, and 'was fired with enthusiasm and left with them four hours later'.[12] Riley (Navy) and Croft (Army) formed Gubbins' HQ team, together with Kermit Roosevelt (second son of former US President Theodore Roosevelt, explorer, shipowner and friend of Winston Churchill). Their task was to impede the German advance and they eventually established themselves outside Bodø, approximately 200 miles south of Narvik.

Lieutenant Commander Bill Fell RN, a WWI veteran, had been ordered to commandeer five Scottish trawlers, man them with 100 fishermen (whom he describes as being in 'a hungry, unpaid and semi-mutinous state') from Sparrow's Nest in Lowestoft, and sail to their support. Fell had initially been instructed to take his elderly trawlers 1,000 miles from Scapa Flow to the Lofoten Islands, where he would receive further orders. No orders were available so he headed for Narvik, where there was a battle in progress. As the impromptu flotilla neared Harstad, they were bombed by a flight of six Junkers 88s. 'This was my first taste of modern warfare and dive-bombing – the first taste of what was in store, and it was extremely unpleasant. The trawlers were utterly defenceless, unwieldy, slow and vulnerable to anyone who thought us worth a burst of cannon fire or a small bomb.'[13]

Fell was glad to exchange these deep-draught British vessels for some smaller and more manoeuvrable Norwegian 'puffers' – even if his new command did smell of decaying walrus. When he finally reached Bodø, his lines were taken by a tall Army officer and a short RNVR lieutenant – Croft and Riley. 'As the noise of our engine died away into a blessed silence, they jumped on board and joined me in a most curious conference, sitting on the sealskins in our stinking hold.'[14]

Planning for the Scissorforce expedition had been hasty and many men were equipped with little more than holiday brochures by way of maps. Fell, astutely, had collected a set of large-scale charts in Harstad, as well as his puffers and Norwegian engineers to keep them running. Soon, Riley had taken over two of these boats and Croft had embarked with Fell.

I set off on the first of many adventures up the fjords to supply the Gubbins force with the bare necessities to carry on their good work. We split up into two groups often working independently and landing our stores in different fjords, all of which reached up into the mountains of the mainland like the fingers of a score of hands.[15]

Andrew Croft remembers setting out on sabotage missions.

With Bill at the helm we would travel 50 miles south to land in the short hours of darkness behind the enemy lines, creep up on a sentry guarding a bridge, dig, position and tamp down our explosives and creep back to watch the resulting explosion from a safe distance, hoping to God that Bill would reappear and take us off.[16]

Although Scissorforce's irregular tactics could occasionally slow the German advance, it could not halt it. And very soon, events in Holland, Belgium and France prompted the evacuation of British troops from Norway. Bodø had been heavily bombed and Gubbins' HQ destroyed. During the short hours of darkness, Riley and Croft did their best to help Fell embark 4,000 troops on to the three destroyers that were all that could be spared for their evacuation. They also destroyed equipment and fuel. Fell hadn't believed they would succeed. He'd made plans to escape on foot into Sweden and had begun reconnoitering the path he would need to take.

It must have been about 3am and broad daylight when the last soldier embarked and the destroyer slipped away. My puffer lay chugging where the destroyer had been, waiting for Andrew and Quentin, who were still ashore destroying documents. Soon they came running down, their steps echoing in the silent ruins of loveliest Bodø. They jumped on board and we puffed off into the silent, empty fjord.[17]

Riley and Croft undertook yet more acts of sabotage as they paused at islands where diesel or petrol was stored, opened the valves and let the fuel drain into the sea. A luckless fishing boat steamed into the flooding petrol and went up in an inferno.

Back in Harstad, Fell was reunited with his Scottish trawlers and the withdrawal continued: 'It was a harassing business with hundreds of tons of urgently-needed stores to be destroyed and wastage such as I had never believed possible.'

Fell was exhausted and (as it turned out later) in the early stages of appendicitis but he remembered Croft and Riley as 'indomitable', driving the loading of the troop ships and the destruction of whatever could not be taken back to Britain. Again, they were the last to leave. 'On 17th June we steamed into Aberdeen – a battered and bedraggled fleet of five old trawlers, with all hands thankful beyond belief to be back in Scotland.'[18]

Scissorforce was disbanded but Gubbins wrote to Riley:'I am most grateful for all you did in Norway under very difficult conditions and, I am afraid, very little help from me. [...] Depend on it that, if ever I am lucky enough ever again to have a Naval Officer in my Establishment, I shall send you a wire.'[19]

It wasn't long in coming.

9

'He helped me out of a bit of a mess'[1]

May–June 1940: The siege of Calais and the evacuation from Dunkirk

Before the evacuation from Dunkirk had come the siege of Calais, from which evacuation was briefly promised but finally denied. As the German Panzer divisions approached, the town had been reinforced from England on 21 May 1940 amid much confusion. Over the next few days, a variety of vessels was used to deliver supplies and take off the wounded and the 'useless mouths', the support services that had been travelling with the BEF. At 3:00am on 24 May, Brigadier Claude Nicholson of the 30th Brigade was instructed to prepare for evacuation of his troops; three hours later, he was asked to hold on a little longer.

The French commander in the town complained to his superior that the English were preparing to leave; this complaint was escalated and by that evening Nicholson was told that there would be no evacuation 'for the sake of Allied solidarity' and no reinforcements. A French naval contingent, meanwhile, spiked their guns and ran for their departing ship. A few turned back and volunteered to remain.

On 25 May, the destroyers HMSs *Greyhound* and *Grafton* were ordered to help the land forces by bombarding German shore batteries from the sea. During the previous day, they had been patrolling off Calais with five other destroyers. All had been heavily dive-bombed: HMS *Wessex* was sunk (six RN stokers and a signalman died) and the Polish destroyer ORP *Burza* was badly damaged. At that stage of the war, there was little destroyers could do to protect themselves against dive-bombing as most of their guns hadn't sufficient elevation to be effective against aircraft.

Temporary Lieutenant Sir Marmaduke Blennerhassett (b. 1902) was *Greyhound*'s third officer. The Anglo-Irish engineer, amateur racing driver and Little Ship Club member had joined the RNVSR as soon as the scheme was announced and had achieved his posting to the destroyer in December 1939. Since that time, *Greyhound* had supported Operation *Wilfred* (mining the Inner Leads) off Norway, briefly engaged the *Scharnhorst* and *Gneisenau*, evacuated British forces after the Battle of Narvik and had been damaged by air attack. She had just been released from the dockyard when she was ordered to Calais. As she was beginning the bombardment on 25 May, a single hit from a battery east of Sangatte killed Sir Marmaduke and another crew member, wounding three more (one of whom later died). *Greyhound* and her sister ship HMS *Grafton* continued firing at the coast until it was too dark to continue, then returned to Dover, where Sir Marmaduke was buried. He never knew that he had become a father that same day.

Overnight 25–26 May, Vice-Admiral Bertram Ramsey at Dover sent a flotilla of small craft (seven trawlers, two drifters and three yachts) to lie off Calais in case official instructions changed, and to evacuate the wounded if possible. One of them, the requisitioned yacht *Conidaw* (built 1939 on the Clyde and now being used as a naval echo sounding vessel) carried yet another message ordering the soldiers to hold on. (Landline communications had been cut, though there was still wireless.) Probationary Temporary Sub-Lieutenant HP Granlund RNVR describes *Conidaw* entering the harbour, running aground and lying there for several hours. She eventually left, carrying 165 wounded. Five days later, she would rescue 80 soldiers from Dunkirk.

Meanwhile, Churchill had sent a further message to Brigadier Nicholson, who had retreated to the Citadel in the Old Town and was steadfastly refusing to surrender:

> *Every hour you continue to exist is of the greatest help to the BEF. Government has therefore decided that you must continue to fight. Have greatest possible admiration for your splendid stand. Evacuation will not (repeat not) take place, and craft required for above purpose are to return to Dover.*[2]

Churchill later wrote that he had felt physically sick as he sat down to dinner afterwards. He believed that the sacrifice of Calais had been materially significant. On 4 June, he told Parliament:

Their sacrifice was not however in vain. At least two armoured divisions, which otherwise would have been turned against the British Expeditionary Force, had to be sent to overcome them. They have added another page to the glories of the Light Division and the time gained enabled the Gravelines waterlines to be flooded and to be held by French troops; and thus it was that the port of Dunkirk was kept open.[3]

The German General Heinz Guderian put it on record that he did not agree with Churchill's analysis.

Calais fell on 26 May 1940 and most of the troops, including Brigadier Nicholson, were taken prisoner. One of them, Airey Neave, serving with the 1st Searchlight Regiment, Royal Artillery, later became the first British officer to escape from Colditz Castle (Oflag 4-C). Brigadier Nicholson suffered from depression and committed suicide while in captivity.

The last boat to leave Calais Harbour in the early hours of 27 May was the elegant motor yacht *Gulzar*. Built in 1934 for Mediterranean pleasure cruising, she was owned by the Armenian Zaret Couyoumdjian, a member of the Paris-based Greek Syndicate, one of the most successful gambling syndicates of all time. In July 1938, the Duke and Duchess of Windsor had enjoyed a Mediterranean cruise on board *Gulzar*. Now, she was working as an RN auxiliary patrol vessel, a danlayer (a boat that followed behind minesweepers laying markers, or dans, that demarcated the clear channels) for the minesweeping forces. On this occasion, she had been painted overnight with red crosses to emphasise her status as a hospital ship.

Gulzar entered Calais Harbour late in the evening of 26 May when the guns of Nicholson's defence had fallen silent. Did she stop and search for survivors or was she fired on immediately? Details vary, but the essential moment of rescue happened as she was leaving, in the very early hours of 27 May. The yacht was spotted by 47 survivors, hidden on the eastern breakwater: 'Some had no clothes or weapons; none had any ammunition and many were in the last stages of exhaustion'. [...][4] *Gulzar* pulled along the breakwater as slowly as she dared and, while German guns from around the harbour opened up on her, every one of the exhausted 47 managed to leap on board without injury. *Gulzar*, who had slowed, not halted, to take the men, then revved up and headed for home. She was in Britain by dawn.

Among these last evacuees was artist George Lambourn of Mousehole in Cornwall, who had joined the Red Cross and was working in France with an ambulance unit attached to the BEF. Lambourn himself was severely wounded but survived to paint the bleak 'Calais, 26 May, 1940. Died of Wounds', now in the Imperial War Museum. *Gulzar* went on immediately to serve at Dunkirk.

★★★

The sacrifice of Calais had bought time for Dunkirk. There had already been other evacuations along the coast, including troops from Boulogne on 24 May. Personnel carriers and storeships had been going in and out of Dunkirk Harbour regularly, even before the official start of Operation *Dynamo* in the evening of Sunday 26 May; 27,000 people had already been taken off. Once Calais and Gravelines were in German hands, however, hostile bombardment from the shore made the shortest cross-Channel route (Route Z) home to Dover unusable – at least in daylight. On 27 May, Dunkirk town and port suffered serious damage: the quays were no longer accessible so the evacuation from the beaches began.

The whalers and ships' boats carried by the destroyers and other larger ships were not well designed for beachwork, being relatively deep draught. In consequence, only 7,669 men arrived home on 27 May, followed by 17,804 on 28 May. The call for small vessels had already gone out on 26 May but their collection and organisation took precious time. The realisation late on 27 May that ships could come alongside the East Mole was a major factor for success (200,000 people were taken off from there); the other ingredient, small boats and dexterity handling them, would enable a further 138,000 to leave from the beaches.

This was an amphibious operation and every coastal sailor knows how tricky the apparently simple manoeuvre of getting passengers from shore to ship via a dinghy can be if there is any sort of sea running. Extracts from Robert Hichens' diary offer a vivid account of difficulties, some successes and the intense effort required to get other people to co-operate with his plans. Hichens was serving on HMS *Niger*, another Halcyon-class minesweeper, based in Harwich. She'd been undergoing repairs following a fire and he'd snatched some leave in Cornwall. Returning via a day in London with his wife Catherine (they went to see *Gone with the Wind*), he met *Niger's* captain at Liverpool Street, also returning, and heard news of the evacuation. It made leave-taking especially poignant.

Arrival off Dunkirk early on the morning of 31 May was grim. As they steamed up eastwards towards La Panne, Hichens was struck by the fires ashore, the damage to buildings, the thud of gunfire and most of all by the wreckage: there were wrecks about every quarter of a mile and the water was full of flotsam – including bodies. When *Niger* was anchored in her allocated position, he expected that boats would begin ferrying troops from the shore. None came. They sent their own boats in where a jetty had been constructed of Army lorries. There was a fresh breeze whipping up the surf. Hichens could see that *Niger's* sailors were failing to persuade the soldiers to embark. When they did, the whaler capsized, tipping the rescued men and their equipment into the sea. Hichens went ashore to take charge. 'For the first time in my life I had found my ability to act quickly and surely in small boats, a quality I have developed in myself since I was six years old, of great value in saving the lives of others. It was a most satisfactory and exhilarating feeling.'[5]

The soldiers were struggling. They were tired and demoralised and weighed down by their equipment, yet Hichens felt a profound admiration for their discipline as they waited in line. It was often hard to persuade them to embark if they didn't believe it was their turn. As the wind and tide strengthened, rowing away from the beach grew almost impossible. Hichens' idea was to take ropes to some of the small motor yachts that were cruising nearby and get them to anchor so that the soldiers and boats' crews could pull themselves off. He hurried back to *Niger* to get help putting his arrangement into operation, only to find his ship had been recalled to Dover. Hichens was horrified – he had promised the soldiers that he would return. *Niger* could not ignore her instructions, but he at least could have permission to remain behind. 'It was a grim thought being left on the beaches in the same position as the soldiers [...] But I had promised the soldiers that I would be back and they so pathetically needed a seaman ashore there.'[6]

Hichens had been a TA volunteer before he'd joined the RNVSR. Now, at Dunkirk, 'jumping about like a monkey getting boats alongside, getting them filled, getting them off, shouting to the soldiers to pull here, or shove there, or sit still or get in', he probably didn't have time to reflect that he might have been queuing with the BEF. Instead, he felt angry with the lack of shoreside organisation – there seemed to be no beachmasters in his area – and also with what he saw as the pusillanimity of some of the civilian skippers (reading Hichens is a good corrective for too much 'Little Ship' veneration). He learned to look out for other RNVR personnel who might share his can-do approach. That day, he was fortunate to find *Chico*, a 73ft Gentleman's motor yacht originally built for Sir Malcolm Campbell but now, like HMS *Conidaw*, requisitioned by the Navy to serve with the Dover Patrol. *Chico*'s commanding officer was Sub-Lieutenant Jack Mason RNVR. On the previous day, 30 May, *Chico* had embarked 217 soldiers from the beaches to waiting ships. On 31 May, she ferried 1,000 – despite having been built for ten passengers and two crew. She finally returned to Dover that night with an additional 100 on board, including Hichens, who needed to rejoin HMS *Niger*.

One of my mother's older brothers, a TA officer, was evacuated from Dunkirk on 30 May. Pat Scott was a stockbroker in peacetime and a keen sportsman, though his passions were polo and skiing rather than dinghy- and motor-racing. He was part of the Queen's Own Royal West Kent Regiment and had left for war early, as Hichens had been impatient to do. His experience may have been typical of many – if there was a 'typical' experience in those confused and often horrifying days of the Battle of France. His company had been engaged with the enemy or on the march for nine days with little food or sleep, then strafed by machine guns while they waited on the beach. Two of his companions had been killed beside him. He didn't speak of his emotions, though his daughter wonders whether he experienced survivor's guilt. The relationship between the Army and the Navy is a complex one. Many soldiers felt a mix of profound gratitude and trust towards the Navy but also some humiliation and a sense of failure.

Uncle Pat was brought home in the Liverpool cargo ship *Dorrien Star* and then billeted at Aston Villa football ground as there was little space available for the unplanned return of so many troops. Perhaps his response to his experience was best expressed by his actions. On 6 June, Churchill began outlining his appeal for troops 'of the hunter class' to begin training for retaliatory action against enemy-occupied coasts. Pat Scott was one of the earliest commando volunteers – as I'm certain Robert Hichens would have been, had their experiences been reversed.

Niger had run another trip during Hichens' absence and would run two more, bringing her total of men returned to England to 1,245. She had started later than some of her sister ships. The 5th Flotilla Harwich minesweepers, almost all of whom had former RNVSR yachtsmen among their officers, had been among the first to be sent. Edward Stanley on the 'Smokey Joe' HMS *Kellett* sailed from Harwich at 12:30pm on 28 May in the company of *Albury, Ross, Lydd, Pangbourne* and *Leda*. They were led by HMS *Gossamer* with former RNVSR member Bernard Wright as her first lieutenant. Once they reached the beaches, every ship had her own story. By the end of the evacuation, *Gossamer, Leda* and *Albury* had done six trips each, landing totals between 1,500 and 3,000 men; the rest had done three to five trips with numbers in proportion, and some turns of minesweeping duty as well. Lieutenant Commander Ross, of *Gossamer,* described the particular strain imposed by 'the belief that each trip was the last':

> *Again there were the long hours off the beaches in momentary expectation of the arrival of enemy aircraft (an expectation which was seldom disappointed). Then the six-hour passage home with constant report of the presence of enemy MTBs on the route and the knowledge that we had six or seven hundred souls on board and no boats whatsoever.*[7]

After the fourth trip, which had been especially harrowing, Ross – a senior gunnery instructor officer – burst into tears in the staff office at Sheerness where he had gone to replenish ammunition for the machine guns with which they had been trying to fight off the dive-bombers. Fortunately, 'It was too late to send us back that night and sleep did much to restore us.'

Experienced Yorkshire yachtsman Ronald Gresham, a timber importer who later sailed regularly with Robin Balfour on *Bluebird of Thorne*, was first lieutenant of HMS *Lydd* when she returned via the Kwinte Buoy at 2:00am on 29 May to find two halves of the destroyer HMS *Wakeful* visible above the water, with survivors clinging to the wreckage. *Lydd* lowered her whaler and two carley floats in an attempt to assist. HMS *Gossamer*, who was also trying to pick up survivors, appeared briefly and told *Lydd* to put out her lights. One of the survivors said he thought that *Wakeful* had been torpedoed by an MTB. The destroyer HMS *Grafton*, who had been returning in company with *Wakeful*, asked *Lydd* to circle round while she continued rescuing men from the water. Suddenly, *Grafton* too was hit. The men aboard *Lydd* saw a dark object turning away. Assuming it was the enemy MTB, they opened fire. *Grafton* also managed to open fire. *Lydd*, still firing, charged the darkened vessel and rammed her. She then set her course for home.

Only later did they discover that there had been no MTB. The real enemy had been *U-62*, lying in wait and unseen. The dark object had been the drifter HMS *Comfort*, who was also trying to rescue men from HMS *Wakeful*. Her RNPS crew of six were all killed. *Grafton*, with about 900 troops on board, was now sinking but such was the traffic on that route that she was able to transfer all her soldiers into other ships before she finally went down. HMS *Lydd* continued regular evacuation duties until the end of Operation *Dynamo*. In 1942, her first lieutenant, yachtsman Ronald Gresham, became a commanding officer. He was twice mentioned in despatches and won a DSC, leading US minesweepers in Assault Force U on D-Day.

The vessels involved in the tragic misunderstanding were travelling the night-time route Y, which went from Bray-Dunes via the Kwinte Buoy and the North Goodwin Lightvessel (LV), round the Goodwin Sands to the English coast. It was twice as long as the initial route Z, which had become impossibly dangerous after the fall of Calais. There was also route X, which could only be used in daylight as it involved a complex course through sandbanks and minefields. It, too, passed the North Goodwin LV. George Carter from Aldeburgh, who was serving there, remembered:

> *Day and night now, a non-stop fleet of every class of craft, from motor launch to destroyer were passing us. Huge billows of smoke were rising from burning oil dumps near Boulogne. The ships passed us empty and returned packed with haggard men in khaki [...] The sea was vile, polluted with the dead.*[8]

Admiral Ramsey's organisation in Dover had produced and issued almost a thousand sets of charts and route instructions as well as arranging for the provisioning and degaussing of this extraordinary, miscellaneous fleet. There were strict instructions that these chartlets must not fall into enemy hands. The commanding officer's report from the sinking HMS *Grafton* makes careful reference to the disposal of all their charts and confidential information over the side in the regulation weighted bag.

RNVSR yachtsman Eric Bellamy failed either to hand in or to destroy his instructions. In May 1940, he had been on a training course at HMS *Boscawen*, the naval police training school in Portland, Dorset. The 1916 steam drifter HMS *Thrifty* was also in Portland, undergoing repairs. She already had a skipper – George Corney RNR (perhaps her original fishing skipper?) – but Bellamy was given temporary command and instructed to take her to Dover and thence Dunkirk. His orders were marked 'SECRET' and 'TO BE DESTROYED BY FIRE WHEN COMPLIED WITH AND ON NO ACCOUNT TO BE ALLOWED TO FALL INTO THE HANDS OF THE ENEMY'. They included the details of Route X. It's likely that the RNVSR yachtsman had been ordered to supplement the fisherman skipper because of his up-to-date navigation training. Route X picked its way through the dangerous Goodwin Sands and also through British-laid minefields. Bellamy's orders instructed him to follow a sequence of half a dozen navigation buoys until he reached a position five cables 270° from the North Goodwin LV, thence via the Ruytingen Pass to Dunkirk Roads.

HMS *Thrifty* arrived at Dunkirk on 2 June and was employed ferrying men from the beaches. At some stage, Bellamy transferred to the drifter HMS *Kindred Star*, which was bombed while towing several smaller boats full of soldiers. The ship was severely damaged and Bellamy was blown overboard. He suffered concussion but, despite this, managed to reach Portland before finally going to hospital in Bath. His nephew Tony Ledger has a letter that Bellamy wrote to his mother after the event. The young officer's handwriting is said to be like a child's, totally different from normal. This probably explains why he forgot to destroy his secret documents.

The practice of putting an RNVR officer on board where possible – even if they were still in training – seems to have been widespread. Robert Harling (though not necessarily a reliable narrator) offers an account of being plucked from a navigation class with Captain

OM Watts, then towed across in open boats with a number of other trainee officers, in order to take their turn ferrying from the beaches. At HMS *King Alfred*, a special request was put out for any volunteers skilled with diesel engines. Temporary Lieutenant Reginald Mead (owner of the Scottish-built 11-ton cutter *Talisman*, which he kept in Southampton) was doing a course at the naval gunnery school HMS *Excellent* when he was sent to take over *E.M.E.D.*, a lifeboat usually stationed at Walton-on-the-Naze in Essex.

The first lifeboats to be sent were manned by their own crews. A famous survivor in my part of the world is *Trimilia*, formerly the Ramsgate lifeboat *Prudential*. Her new name was given in acknowledgement of the number of lives that she is estimated to have saved in her career. *Trimilia/Prudential* set off for Dunkirk on 30 May 1940, with her regular crew, all of whom had volunteered. She towed a ship's boat and eight wherries, loaded with water for the waiting troops and ropes to help them off the shore. The lifeboat had left Ramsgate in the early afternoon. It was dark when she arrived off the beach. This scrap of dialogue was recorded in the Coxswain Harold Knight's record of service:

> *'I cannot see who you are. Are you a naval party?'*
> *'No Sir, we are men of the crew of the Ramsgate lifeboat.'*
> *'Thank you and thank God for such good men as you have on this night proved to be. There is a party of fifty Highlanders coming next.'*

Prudential, drawing almost 4ft, anchored as close as possible to the shore, then the ship's boat towed the wherries and the drinking water to the beach and returned full of men. Gradually, the lifeboat was filled to capacity – 160 men crammed on board the 48ft 6in boat – and took the men, plus eight soldiers in each of her wherries, out to the bigger ships for transport back to England.

> *She saved some 800 men that first night. Shelling and bombing increased and a swell was making which resulted in the loss of many small boats. Prudential lost five of her wherries on the first night but despite suffering shell, shrapnel and bullet damage she continued her rescue work throughout the following day and night when the last of her wherries was lost. Into the third day and the Prudential had helped rescue 2800 men, both British*

and French. She sailed for Ramsgate at 1.30pm on the Saturday having worked on the beaches, under fire, for a continuous thirty of the forty hours she'd been away from home.[9]

Becky Cannon, who joined today's Ramsgate lifeboat aged 17, is the fourth generation of her family to serve since *Prudential* set off for Dunkirk. Around the UK coast, there are many such families for whom rescue at sea is an accepted occupation. 'We are proud to be fellow-countrymen of such men', as the CO of HMS *Icarus* wrote to the crew of the Margate lifeboat, *Lord Southborough*.[10] The story of Dunkirk celebrates this volunteer spirit – so famously evidenced by the arrival of the many 'Little Ships' – but it was also an Admiralty-run operation. After a difficult first day, when there were disagreements between independent, experienced lifeboat crew and the naval authorities, most later lifeboats were requisitioned and put under naval command – or, at least, under the command of those new RNVR officers who were being trained in *KR&AI*.

E.M.E.D's regular crew had brought her to Ramsgate, then were stood down and responsibility was given to the yachtsman Lieutenant Mead. Visibility was poor and the crossing was difficult but *E.M.E.D.* eventually arrived off Dunkirk on 31 May in the company of the London tug *Sun IV*. It's not entirely clear what happened next but all agree that the lifeboat got a rope round her propeller; Lieutenant Mead was hit by shrapnel and eventually died of his wounds. *Sun IV* then towed *E.M.E.D.* back to Dover, where Mead's body was removed and the lifeboat made fit for service again. She returned once more to Dunkirk and rescued 39 soldiers.

★★★

The requisitioning of miscellaneous vessels for service had been taking place since the beginning of the war. Some were donated by their owners, as *Naromis* had been. Most sailing vessels were laid up for the duration, though others, like August Courtauld's *Duet*, had the dubious honour of serving as 'obstructions', remaining on their moorings to prevent seaplanes landing. Nigel Sharp, whose father Philip was an RNVSR member, begins his study of WWII leisure-boating with four consecutive entries from his father's logbook.

27th August 1939 – Went out in JTQ in the afternoon. Wind southerly mod. Went out in the bay towards Helford.

    7th September 1939 – JTQ towed over to Little Falmouth yard to lay up.

    1st April 1946 – JTQ relaunched.

    3rd April 1946 – had our first sail in JTQ at 15:45.[11]

On 14 May 1940, a new level of compulsion was introduced when the Admiralty Small Vessels Pool required every seaworthy private motorboat over 30ft to be registered. Late in the evening of 20 May, Churchill gave the order for a force of small vessels to be assembled and by 26 May, officers were hurrying round the boatyards of the Thames Estuary and the upper reaches of the Thames to collect suitable craft. (Robin Balfour was amused to discover later that his yacht *Bluebird* had been rejected as her twin keel design was considered too bizarre.)

The RNVSR yachtsmen volunteers who took part in Operation *Dynamo* were there as part of the Navy, not in their own vessels. Their boat-handling expertise in shallow waters and close quarters may have been especially valuable. The paddle steamer HMS *Marmion* had come down from the Clyde with a largely Scottish crew, including yachtsman James McFarlane Black from Glasgow, who owned a 21ft sloop *Westra* (built Dumbarton 1899). He had joined the RNVSR in April 1937 (as had William Balfour, who was also serving on *Marmion*). Black was in charge of the paddle steamer's starboard lifeboat and the captain's report makes special mention of his skill in handling her in swell.

Yachtsman Leonard Jolly, who had joined the Mersey RNVSR in the wake of the Munich crisis, had been posted to the paddle steamer *Medway Queen* in October 1939. She was an excursion vessel whose first job had been to assist with the evacuation of London children to the countryside to escape the anticipated bombing raids. She was then converted to minesweeping and became part of the 10th Minesweeping Flotilla, helping keep the Thames Estuary clear.

Medway Queen was sent to Dunkirk on 27 May 1940 and from then made seven trips picking up from either the harbour or the beaches and bringing men home to Dover or to Ramsgate. Jolly was her navigator and gained this tribute from the first lieutenant, RN Reservist Jack Graves: 'He was quite the best small boat pilot

I ever met and how he kept *Medway Queen* moving backwards and forwards for ten long days and nights no-one will ever know. He did all the navigation although I, as the only other officer with watch-keeping experience, did relieve him from time to time.' Graves also appreciated Jolly's practical boat-handling skills:

Undoubtedly what saved the situation on many occasions was Medway Queen's *bow rudder. Jolly and I evolved a drill by which I, in the windlass flat forward, and he up on the bridge, connected up the bow rudder at the same time as disengaging the after rudder. It may sound simple but there were heavy pressures on all concerned when there was way on the vessel and additionally I often had to almost fight my way to the bow through crowds of soldiers. The net effect was that with a bow rudder* Medway Queen *could simply steer off the Mole and go backwards down the fairway instead of canting off with a back spring, turning and going ahead on standard rudder. As the rudder of a paddle steamer does not operate in propeller wash but in dead water, the bow rudder gave us an incalculable advantage and was, in my opinion the sole reason that we were able to negotiate that madhouse of a harbour on equal terms with the very latest destroyers or cross channel steamers.* [12]

Perhaps this language of 'bow rudders', 'canting off' and 'propeller wash' is jargon to the non-sailing reader but that carries its own message: a yachtsman like Jolly was quickly able to adapt his existing knowledge and work successfully alongside a professional, like Graves, from a different maritime background.

Despite their *KR&AI* training there may have been a certain RNVR independence of attitude, not only as demonstrated by Robert Hichens. *Oriole* was a paddle minesweeper from Scotland offered by the RNVR. When her skipper had assessed the problem of surf preventing embarkation from his section of the beach, he simply ran the minesweeper aground, used her as a pier to enable the soldiers to reach small ships further out, then filled his own space and waited for the flood to float her off again. David Divine quotes his signal later sent to the MOT:

Submit ref KR&A I 1167. Deliberately grounded HMS Oriole *Belgian coast dawn 29 May on own initiative objective speedy evacuation of troops.*

Refloated dusk same day no apparent damage. Will complete S.232 when operations permit meantime am again proceeding Belgian coast and will again run aground if such course seems desirable.[13]

Martin Solomon (b. 1915) had enrolled in the RNVSR at the time of the Munich crisis, when he was just 23. His father, a lawyer, was also a retired lieutenant colonel who had won the Military Cross and owned a converted Cornish fishing boat. Robert Solomon was active in the Jewish community and would serve immediately after the war as an adviser in the British Zone of Germany. In 1939, Martin had been working as a theatrical impresario and producer; by May 1940, he was one of a group of temporary lieutenants training to handle motor launches at HMS *Wildfire*, Sheerness.[14]

Martin Solomon was later characterised as someone who was always dashing off to help friends in distress. During Operation *Dynamo*, he took command of the tug *Fossa* on 31 May, towing the contingent of six cockle-boats from Leigh-on-Sea in Essex that formed part of the 'Little Ship's' 'armada'. Next, he transferred to manage the motorboat *Thetis* with a petty officer and two sea scouts from Mortlake.

On 2 June, Solomon discovered his command of French could be useful to assist officers on the Mole explaining arrangements to French troops. He returned to Dover on that night's last destroyer together with pier master James Campbell Clouston, who was reporting to Admiral Ramsey. On 3 June, he and Clouston were crossing for the last time to Dunkirk in two RAF motorboats. Six miles from Gravelines, they were attacked from the air with bombs and machine guns. Their boat was sunk and survivors left clinging to the wreckage. Clouston and Solomon tried to swim together to retrieve an abandoned cutter but Clouston found himself too weak. He returned to the wreck 'to chat, encourage and white lie to the end'.[15] Solomon reached the cutter but was unable to do anything more. Though he was eventually rescued, all but one of the people on the wreck had died. Commander Clouston's body was eventually discovered floating to the mouth of the Elbe.

All too soon, a long, weary stream of prisoners would be walking that way.

'The last strongholds were battered, stormed and overwhelmed'[1]

June–July 1940: Further evacuations from France

While the paddle minesweeper HMS *Oriole* lay grounded on the beach at La Panne, waiting for the tide, Temporary Sub-Lieutenant JR Crosby (b. 1918), son of a Glasgow bookseller, went ashore. La Panne (De Panne) is in Belgium, a country that had surrendered to the Germans just a few days earlier. There were local people looking on at the evacuation. 'The sight of a man with his hands in his pockets, idly watching this historic scene as if it was a cricket match, seemed grotesque.' Crosby went into the town and to a cafe, where he met a major in the RAMC.

> *He gave us his wife's address and asked us to drop her a line when we got back to Blighty and explain he was taken prisoner and wouldn't see her till after the war, but she wasn't to worry. Just like that, completely stoical about the whole thing. He said he must stay with the wounded and hadn't a dog's chance of getting off.*[2]

A few canines had attached themselves to the soldiers and been rescued; Robert Hichens saw one desperately swimming and pulled it aboard. Many more had been shot to avoid them dying of starvation in the ruins of the town. The shooting of army horses and mules was a particularly painful experience for their handlers. Many people were left behind: for every seven soldiers rescued, one became a prisoner of war and many others died. Captain Michael Fleming (b. 1913), for instance, Peter and Ian's youngest brother – an Eton-educated stockbroker who had joined the TA. He had arrived in Belgium in January with the 4th Battalion of the Oxford and Buckinghamshire light infantry. They had almost been ordered to

Calais on 24 May but instead were sent to Cassel to defend the area south of Dunkirk while the evacuation was in process. By 29 May, there was little more they could do. They were marching for Dunkirk when Fleming was seriously wounded. He was taken prisoner and eventually transferred to the British General Hospital at Lille, where he and other wounded POWs were cared for by British doctors and French civilian nursing staff. He died on 1 October 1940.

At the end of Operation *Dynamo*, 100,000 British servicemen were still in France, as were some servicewomen (ATS and nurses). 'Wars are not won by evacuations,' said Churchill to the House of Commons on 4 June, but there were a great deal more people and things to be retrieved if, as seemed likely, France was facing defeat.

Operation *Alphabet*, the evacuation from Norway, was taking place at the same time as the evacuations from northern France and Belgium. Late in the afternoon of 8 June, the Royal Navy suffered a devastating blow when HMS *Glorious*, one of Britain's largest and fastest aircraft carriers, encountered the German battlecruisers *Scharnhorst* and *Gneisenau* and was sunk along with her escorting destroyers HMS *Ardent* and HMS *Acasta*. The death toll of 1,519 put this among the major British naval disasters of the war and it was also significant material loss. When *Glorious* went down, two RAF fighter squadrons, returning home for the defence of Britain, were lost with her.

An Admiralty Board of Enquiry was held within days of the few survivors returning to Britain: its findings then sealed, only to be opened in 2041. In 1997, however, a *Secret History* TV documentary eventually prompted a Parliamentary debate at which some difficult questions were posed. Did the Admiralty fail to heed warnings from Bletchley Park? Had no one grasped the extent to which the German B-Dienst, under the brilliant cryptanalyst Wilhelm Tranow, was reading the naval cypher traffic? And, perhaps most controversially, did HMS *Devonshire*, nearby, pick up HMS *Glorious'* distress signal and choose to ignore it? Did she, in fact, put on all speed and hurry away? HMS *Devonshire* was carrying the Norwegian King Haakon, members of his government and the country's gold reserves. She would have stood little chance against the *Scharnhorst* and *Gneisenau* – but the absence of potential rescuers left 900 men from *Glorious, Acasta* and *Ardent* dying in the water.

Temporary Lieutenant Peter Scott RNVR could have been one of them. During his initial course at HMS *King Alfred*, he had persuaded the authorities (Scott was very persuasive) that he should be assigned to destroyers. This ambition had taken a while to achieve, but finally he had been sent for training as a torpedo control officer (Scott's famous father had also been 'a torpedo-man'.) Towards the end of his course, Scott was informed he was to be posted to HMS *Acasta*. She was then based in Plymouth. Typically, Scott discovered that her first lieutenant, 27-year-old Charles Robinson, was a sailing friend from Norfolk. He wangled an invitation to tea, met the captain, Commander CE Glasfurd, was shown the cabin that he would occupy and began to make friends with the other officers with whom he would serve. The following morning he woke with a sore throat and a high temperature: completion of his course was delayed and he missed his berth.

Acasta's end came after another of those suicidally brave actions as she attacked and damaged the *Scharnhorst*: 'The very severely damaged destroyer [...] fought on in a hopeless situation with her far inferior armament against the battleships,' said Admiral Schubert, first officer of the *Scharnhorst*, interviewed after the war.[3] After three days in the Arctic Sea, with no rescue mission, only 45 men from the three ships remained alive to tell the story that was then so urgently suppressed. Having missed *Acasta*, Scott was posted to the older destroyer HMS *Broke*, where he struggled with debilitating seasickness and an attack of jaundice. He was sent ashore for a month to recover from the jaundice, then, on his return to *Broke*, he found himself feeling sick again. 'There were a number of ratings working on the quarter deck. I was sure they could see how green I looked and the more I thought about it the greener I felt. At last I was overcome and had to rush to the rail.'[4] The swell that day was so slight that Scott was able to convince himself that it must be 'purely psychological' and thus learned to cope in the future.

On 9 June, when the loss of *Glorious* and her destroyers was not yet known, HMS *Broke* was directed to be part of Operation *Cycle*, the next stage of evacuation from France. More troops were still being sent out as last hopes remained that the French could continue fighting. The 51st Highland Division was fragmented around the Seine-Maritime department, trying to hold an unreasonably long front while being subjected to political manoeuvrings and misinformation. When HMS *Broke* entered Le Havre in the early morning of 10 June, there was no one for her to collect. Later that day, she came briefly under bomb attack. Scott was relieved to discover that although he had been intensely frightened, he had also, somehow, felt exhilarated. That night they observed fierce fighting at Fécamp, then were directed further east to the beleaguered small port of St-Valery-en-Caux. At 2:30am, Scott was sent ashore in *Broke's* motorboat to organise a preliminary evacuation of wounded troops. Having waved his pistol 'without much conviction' at a sentry, Scott found himself greeted with a cheer by the injured men of the 51st Highland Division. He organised sufficient small boats to take 120 men, many of them on stretchers, out to *Broke* then left, promising that *Broke* would return. When they reached England, however, orders were issued that no more destroyers were to be risked on the French coast. Their trip to St-Valery was cancelled. 'It was a terrible blow not to be allowed to keep our promise to the Highland division and we felt it sharply.'[5]

Thames estuary yachtsman Kenneth Jacob, an older RNVSR member (b. 1897), was in training at HMS *King Alfred*. He was enjoying the experience of having his mind free of business worries (Jacob was an engineer) and being able to concentrate on this new learning. He was not among those who were sent to assist Operation *Dynamo*. Those who returned described their experience as gruelling. Jacob's experience as part of Operation *Cycle* was closer to tedious.

About a week later on June 9th I joined the party to take a number of motor cruisers round from Shoreham to Newhaven. I had a 30-foot river type motor cruiser and with two civilians we left Shoreham at midnight and anchored off Newhaven about 0230 and entered the harbour in the morning. We spent that day getting fuel and stores on board and I was given a crew of two naval ratings, ordinary seamen who had very little experience. We were now told that we would be towed across to the French coast to try and rescue some of the 53rd [sic] Brigade from St-Valery-en-Caux.

We were towing all night with frequent stops as the tow ropes kept breaking and bollards pulling out etc. We arrived off the French coast north of Le Havre at 1430 hours on the 11th, but the destroyers with whom we were to rendezvous were not there. We saw a lot of aerial activity over Le

Havre. As it appeared we could do nothing, we turned round to tow back. A German aircraft came to have a look at us but fortunately we found a bank of fog. We eventually anchored off Newhaven at about 0330 and could get a bit of sleep. Fortunately the weather was fine and calm or it would have been chaos.[6]

Scott had spent 12 June doing nothing in Plymouth.

On the following morning The Times *reported a German claim that 20,000 prisoners were taken at St Valery-en-Caux. The BBC news said that 6000 British troops had capitulated there. It was explained that fog had delayed the evacuation and there were no extensive beaches as at Dunkirk [...] We felt very bitter about it. Our little operation had succeeded in its small-scale object but failed miserably on the major issue.*[7]

Operation *Cycle* was over. Scott and *Broke* spent most of the remainder of the summer on anti-invasion patrol. Kenneth Jacob finished his training and was sent to assist with the defence of the Thames oil refineries.

I was drafted to HMS Pembroke on 15th July 1940 and found myself at Thames Haven where I was in charge of a small party managing six torpedo tubes on one of the Thames Haven jetties. I was now a Lieutenant RNVR and I had with me another officer, one CPO and eight ratings. We were all living in an old house immediately behind the seawall near the Thames Haven station and in a very isolated position as the nearest village of any size was Stanford-le-Hope five miles away with a very sketchy bus service.[8]

There were still evacuations to be undertaken, however. Operation *Aerial* ran from 14 to 25 June as the German Army entered Paris and marched westwards. There were two BEF divisions trapped south of the Somme and significant material assets to be salvaged, including ships. In his pre-war life, Temporary Lieutenant Eric Newell RNVR had been employed in the marketing department of the SH Benson advertising agency. This was the firm where Dorothy L Sayers had worked and that she'd used as the basis for her mystery novel *Murder Must Advertise* (1933). Philip Benson, the owner of the agency, was a keen sailing man. While in business he appeared reticent and somewhat lonely, in his sailing life he was confident and cheerful. He had been an outstanding commodore of the Royal Corinthian Yacht Club in Burnham. Newell had been his sailing master and was a shareholder in the agency. He had enjoyed his sociable RNVSR evenings at the Little Ship Club and expected to spend a month or so at HMS *King Alfred*. As soon as he arrived, however, he was sent on to help manage a Naval Control Centre in November 1939 without any further training at all. He became part of the organisation responsible for convoy mustering, the examination service, harbour tugs and berthing, marine rescue and salvage. RNVSR member Christopher Holt had a comparable experience. He worte to his mother:

> *At divisions this morning all Subs who arrived at Hove on Wednesday were told to fall out – then those without uniforms were eliminated – then those with complete uniforms were mustered – I was one, or at least I had two pairs of trousers [...] We are an amusing selection. When we were asked our jobs they were stockbroker (me), nothing (sailing a yacht), steel ring maker and theatrical manager. Four of us were chosen and here we are.*[9]

Newell and five other former RNVSR members spent several anxious months managing the Naval Control Office at Gravesend: their job being to plot any observations of magnetic mines and intercept passing vessels to give instructions as to safe, swept, QZ routes. They were allocated no boats in which to do this, communications were poor, ships were 'going down like ninepins' and their morale was correspondingly low. Therefore, when a request arrived from Ramsgate, late in December, asking for an officer to be appointed to the Naval Patrol Station, HMS *Fervent*, Newell had no hesitation in appointing himself. By June 1940, he had spent several months as part of the North Goodwin patrol working with an RNR lieutenant commander called Ramus, a Kent sheep farmer whose passion was riding to hounds. Together, they encountered more magnetic mines; examined, and sometimes piloted cargo ships; shot up drifting contact mines; and listened to the increasing noise of guns across the Channel. They had experienced air attack and assisted refugees in all types of craft escaping from Holland and Belgium. During the period of evacuations from Dunkirk, they had been continuously busy: towing in vessels that had got into difficulty, transferring troops from sinking ships, giving out sailing instructions. Then it had all gone quiet:

> *Few ships were now coming up the Channel and through the Straits of Dover owing to the occupation of Calais and Dunkirk by German troops. Ships were now reaching London by way of the Pentland Firth and the East Coast. It now felt lonely on the North Goodwin patrol [...] There seemed to be nothing between the Germans on the French coast and England but our little tug* Doria *with our armament of one Lewis gun and five 303 rifles.*[10]

On 13 June, a message arrived in Ramsgate for Newell to report to the Admiralty with Party X. There were ten of them, including Peter Cooper, an old friend from Burnham who was also at HMS *Fervent,* and an RNR officer, Lieutenant Commander Beeching. They were instructed to pack overnight bags and told they would be flying somewhere. 'We were each issued with a Webley revolver and ammunition [...] What made us feel that we certainly were on a suicide mission was that Captain Phillimore RN and his staff came to the station to see us off and just as the train was pulling out handed a bottle of Scotch into the carriage.' Once they reached London, Party X discovered that they were destined for the French west coast: 'No one knew whether France was going to capitulate or fight on, and if their decision was capitulation, our job was to sail every ship we could lay our hands on to England.'[11]

Newell and Beeching were sent to Nantes. Although there was nominally an office there with a direct line to the Admiralty, this had been cut and the veteran RN resident was in a state of bewilderment. Newell and his companion swung into action:

> *It was obvious to Beeching and me that the French had no intention of continuing the war. The port was full of ships, some of them neutral such as Norwegian, Swedish and Dutch. We called a conference of all the captains and told them that, unless they wanted to be prisoners for the rest of the war, they had to get their ships out and sail for England.*[12]

The French harbour tugs and the Loire pilots refused to co-operate. Once Newell and Beeching had persuaded the captains that they would have to get their ships away unaided, they set to work to fill a British ship with troops and civilian refugees. When the time came for that vessel to leave, the Nantes dock master refused to open the gates. 'Beeching and I rushed down to the dock and ordered him to open the gate. Since we had our hands on our Webley revolvers, he thought better of it and opened the gate. The British ship sailed and by the evening we had routed all available ships for England.'

The following day, they made their own getaway on a 25ft yacht with an auxiliary engine but no mast or sails. They'd been issued with Admiralty code books, but they burned and sank these for safety. As they hurried down the Loire, Newell found himself remembering Horatio Hornblower's fictional escape in Forester's novel *Flying Colours* (1938). '[He] was befriended by a beautiful widow who hid him in her house on the banks of the Loire – there was no such prospect for me.' Instead, he found himself alone on the little yacht when Beeching was needed on board a tanker that was having trouble turning. The tow rope Newell had been trying to attach slipped from him into the river, then the yacht's engine failed.

The sky was clear and conditions calm as he drifted helplessly into the Bay of Biscay and witnessed the dive-bombing and destruction of HM troopship *Lancastria,* which had been evacuating troops and civilians. He watched as at least 3,000 people died. 'Within the next few moments she had turned over on her side and plunged to the bottom. It was a terrible sight. Where she had sunk, the sea was covered in a huge oil slick, in which I could discern hundreds of heads.'[13] The sinking of the *Lancastria* remains Britain's greatest maritime loss of life (more died from the *Lancastria* than from the *Titanic* and *Lusitania* combined) and was the subject of an immediate media blackout. 'The British people have had enough bad news for one day,' said Churchill. Unfortunately, he forgot to lift the embargo at any suitable later date. Despite a simple memorial erected 70 years later in the grounds of the Golden Jubilee hospital in Clydebank, some families continue to feel a sense of grievance and cover-up.

Once Newell had finally managed to leave his yacht and get ashore, he found St-Nazaire crowded with troops. He was soon back at work helping organise the ferrying of troops out to waiting transports. The German advance guard was expected imminently. When an unexpected detachment of Polish troops arrived, the language barrier was such that Newell wondered whether he might inadvertently be embarking the first of the invasion forces. He found his own passage home on HMS *Winchelsea* – the destroyer on which he'd had his initial experience, three years previously.

R A 'Bobby' Bevan, a colleague at the SH Benson agency, had also been sent to Nantes. Bevan was one of the firm's senior copywriters, and the inspiration for Sayers' 'Mr Ingleby'. He was an Oxford-educated man-about-town, the child of two artists and the high society friend of novelists like Anthony Powell. Janet Rushbury remembers him coming to her parents' Chelsea home when she was a child in the 1930s and showing her how to rig and manage a model ketch. There was no one else in her family with the slightest interest in sailing. Bevan was a keen ocean-racing yachtsman, part owner with Harold Paton of the yacht *Phryna*, a Fastnet competitor. They had both joined the London Division of the RNVSR. Whereas Paton, a barrister, was swiftly sent to sea in command of a minesweeper, the Navy was more interested in Bevan's talents as a wordsmith. Within the agency, Bevan had created slogans such as 'Guinness is good for you' and campaigns such as the Colman's Mustard Club, and in 1939 he was appointed to the Ministry of Information. During Operation *Aerial*, however, he was sent to France as a liaison officer, charged with getting vessels out of the country.

The *Commandant Dominé* was a newly built minesweeping sloop, commissioned in April 1940 and lying at Nantes. Following the French surrender on 22 June, her commanding officer was about to scuttle her when Bevan, too, drew his gun. He forced the *Commandant Dominé* to sail for Plymouth where, on 3 July, she was incorporated into the Free French Navy. Bevan continued as her liaison officer. Soon, the sloop gained a new commanding officer, the brave yet wayward Jacquelin de la Porte des Vaux, whose former ship *Jaguar* had been lost at Dunkirk.

After that, *Commandant Dominé* was fleetingly involved in the Battle of Dakar, General de Gaulle's attempt in September 1940 to persuade the Vichy fleet to join him. Bevan may be presumed to have been on board when she entered Dakar Harbour ahead of the main force under a white flag in an attempt to incite the crew of the battleship *Richelieu* to change sides. Propaganda leaflets should have been distributed in advance but the crew was shocked to find themselves shot at immediately. The sloop turned to flee but discovered she was directly below the *Richelieu's* guns, which were being lowered to blow her out of the water. The story goes that quick-thinking Jacquelin de la Porte des Vaux ordered his bugler to play *garde-à-vous* (stand to attention). The sloop and the battleship were so close that the big ship gunners were apparently confused into thinking that the order was coming from their own vessel. By the time they realised their mistake, the *Commandant Dominé* was gone. Bevan remained with her until spring 1941, when he was awarded an OBE 'for enterprise' and returned to his land-based information duties. *Commandant Dominé* was subsequently used on convoy escort duty.

Robin Balfour was also at the Battle of Dakar (Operation *Menace*). He was an accidental staff officer on board HMS *Ark Royal*. Balfour later wrote that he began to envisage the system of wartime personnel arrangements:

> *like a vast shunting yard with innumerable ramifications in which trains were being made up for almost infinite destinations, the trucks rolling constantly down a slope into the yard were dealt with by a team of half-mad men pulling levers to direct them. Some got through, some were lost, some forgotten at the end of the line, but somehow quite a lot of trains were assembled and chugged off for various destinations.*[14]

The berth on *Ark Royal* wouldn't be the first apparently random appointment in his wartime career, yet he seemed to have a happy knack of making the most of them. On board *Ark Royal,* for instance, although he was in the staff office, he managed to go out on patrol in one of the Swordfish aeroplanes. It was both thrilling and primitive; 'there you were, sitting in an aircraft with an open cockpit, with a plotting board on your knee, with a pair of dividers and parallel rulers, just as if you had been in a small yacht'. He was underwhelmed by the Battle of Dakar, which he saw as an unnecessary failure, mainly due to the arrogance of General de Gaulle. The Free French pilots who had taken off from *Ark Royal* into Dakar were imprisoned, and the British fleet retired with nothing achieved but disasters and further evidence of the irreconcilable divide between De Gaulle's forces and the Vichy French. Balfour concluded: 'I think one of the reasons the French Admirals wouldn't surrender to us was that they dreaded being under the orders of De Gaulle.'[15]

When my father reported on a little informal socialising with Vichy French junior officers based in West Africa in February 1943, he found that 'The Fighting French are unmentionable and are regarded practically as traitors. The subject was avoided through the whole evening.' These deep divides were created during the desperate events of summer 1940 and the decisions that were taken then, particularly of course the attack on the French Navy at Mers-el-Kébir on 3 July, in which the British bombardment sank a battleship, damaged five other ships and killed 1,297 French servicemen.

Wearing his trademark black wide-brimmed fedora, Charles Henry Howard, 20th Earl of Suffolk, was perhaps more Indiana Jones than Peter Wimsey or Horatio Hornblower. 'Mad Jack' was not a member of the RNVSR – though his younger brother, future St Ives MP Greville Howard, was. He'd left (or been expelled from) the Royal Naval College Osborne as a teenager but had made a working passage to Australia on the clipper ship *Mount Stewart*. He'd been a jackaroo, a ranch owner, an Edinburgh undergraduate, member of the House of Lords and country gentleman, research chemist, Stage Door Johnny, husband and father. In the spring and early summer of 1940, his job for the Ministry of Supply was to identify people and materials who might be of use to the Allied war effort. This meant scientists (particularly those working on France's nuclear programme), technicians (particularly those on armaments programmes), bankers and jewellers (particularly those holding significant deposits of diamonds).

A specific objective was to ensure that the current European supply of heavy water did not fall into German hands. French intelligence officer François Allier had already arranged for this to be moved to Paris from the Norwegian Norsk Hydro plant. As the enemy came closer, Suffolk had directed many vital scientists towards French west and south-west coasts. When he and his secretary Beryl Morden left Paris on 10 June, in a car loaded with diamonds, technical designs and armament specifications, Allier ensured that the heavy water was moved on to Bordeaux, where Suffolk would arrange its transport to Britain. Harold Macmillan was the undersecretary on duty at the Ministry of Supply when Suffolk arrived in the early hours of 23 June. He was confused, impressed and then persuaded to support Suffolk's demand that the Admiralty send a destroyer to collect another group of scientists and a supply of radium, hidden further south near Bayonne. Most of the heavy water was stored in Windsor Castle, with the Crown Jewels: the remainder was kept by MI5 in HM Prison Wormwood Scrubs.

Peter Cooper, an Essex-based architect, who sailed from pre-war Burnham, had also been despatched with Party X. He and his companion, Major Lawrence from the Royal Marines, were sent to Bayonne and St-Jean-de-Luz. The intention was that they should salvage shipping; in reality, they found themselves besieged by desperate refugees. The British Consul (who was not British) soon vanished, leaving Lawrence and Cooper to persuade merchant captains to load up with refugees and sail for Britain – as well as trying to persuade the French authorities to facilitate this. They needed to check credentials and issue passports while keeping the ever-growing number of refugees relatively calm. The Spanish border was closed; the Germans were approaching; people knew that if they could not get a passage out very soon, they faced internment. Two ships had already been forced to leave without passengers before Cooper and Lawrence achieved success with a Dutch vessel, the *Koningin Emma*, normal complement 500 people, evacuating 2,000.

Major Lawrence sailed with her, hoping to make contact with the Admiralty and explain their desperate situation. Cooper was fortunately joined by the British military attaché together with two more RNVR sub-lieutenants, Patrick Whinney and Steven Mackenzie. All of them had been working at the British Embassy in Paris so had considerably more understanding of a British Consul's role in a crisis. Cooper, however, still found himself responsible for attempting to check people's bona fides. One group whom he turned away were a dozen men dressed as priests who claimed to be British and to have come from Palestine to fight for their country, but when the men were searched, they were discovered to be carrying German-made revolvers beneath their cassocks.

This was not at all the type of service that Cooper had envisaged when he had volunteered for the RNVR as a yachtsman. Despite his anxiety about fifth columnists, he developed an admiration for the spirit and courage of people as they waited for embarkation. 'It was especially noticeable among the women and children who were silent but determined,' he wrote later.[16] Major Lawrence's mission to the Admiralty produced results: two Canadian destroyers and three small coasters arrived, enabling Cooper, Whinney and Mackenzie to carry on loading refugees until 25 June, when they were advised that the German arrival was imminent and they must leave. 'The scene from the quayside as we departed was an unforgettable sight; piles of abandoned luggage everywhere, jettisoned motor vehicles and groups of disconsolate people who had to be left behind.'

Figures are given of 191,870 military personnel and 30,000–40,000 civilians evacuated from France during Operation *Aerial*. For many, this represented a massive dislocation in human lives and relationships. Nevil Shute's novel *Pied Piper* (1942) tells the story of an old man who has lost his only son. He has rescued a heterogeneous collection of the children of others but when he leaves France, he knows it is a permanent farewell. He is leaving the girl his son has loved, standing on the quayside among German officers. 'The stretch of dark water that separated them from France grew to a yard, to five yards wide. The old man stood motionless, stricken with grief, with longing to be back upon the quay, with the bitter loneliness of old age.'[17]

Arrival in England is brisk and comic. The old man collapses on the quay and listens to the clucking of the ladies who are taking the situation in hand:

> There was an exclamation of concern. 'I had no idea! But they are in such a state! Have you seen the poor little heads? My dear they're lousy, every one of them.' There was a shocked pause. 'That horrible old man, I wonder how he came to be in charge of them?'
>
> The old man closed his eyes, smiling a little. This was the England that he knew and understood. This was peace.[18]

'I sign articles'[1]

Spring–autumn 1940: New ways to volunteer

Many people attest to the change of mood, the new sense of individual commitment experienced when Winston Churchill became prime minister, offering 'blood, toil, tears and sweat' (13 May) and pledging, 'We shall defend our island, whatever the cost may be. We shall fight on the beaches, we shall fight on the landing grounds, we shall fight in the fields and in the streets, we shall fight in the hills; we shall never surrender' (4 June). Margery Allingham, writing from her Essex village, said 'the reaction to the defeat was everywhere the same, it hardened everybody up at once'.[2] The Local Defence Volunteers became the Home Guard and beyond them were the covert Auxiliary Units being developed by some of the men with intelligence connections as 'stay behind' units, or the basis of a British resistance. In Kent and the South East this was led by Peter Fleming; in Essex and East Anglia by Kelvedon vicar's son, Andrew Croft. Likely civilians were recruited, sworn to secrecy under the Official Secrets Act, then given general training in guerrila tactics and the use of explosives. If invasion came, their duty was to gather in their secret hideouts and harass enemy communications with small acts of terrorism and sabotage.

Colin Gubbins, returned from Norway with his reputation enhanced, was given overall responsibility for these activities, attempting to find actual equipment (everyone wanted rifles) and smooth over awkward incidents, such as when Peter Fleming's recruits mounted a rather-too-successful practice attack on General Montgomery's HQ at Steyning. Gubbins, still with MI(R) and soon to become a prime mover with the SOE, worked closely with other subversive units, such as Section D, and ensured their contributions of sticky bombs, Molotov cocktails, time pencils and plastic explosives were efficiently distributed. Training for the Auxiliary Units, which was initially ad hoc and local, began to include weekend courses. At the same time, the much more significant structure of Combined Operations was being set up. This was led by Admiral Roger Keyes and would operate, in part, via the Commandos. They were natural successors to the Independent Companies that had operated in Norway. It's not therefore surprising to find Quintin Riley, seconded once again from the RNVR, in Newlyn, equipped with a selection of naval cutters and whalers, helping to train the new recruits in the surprisingly tricky arts of landing and disembarking:

I have concentrated on watermanship [...] it sounds simple enough to shove the cutter off after the shore party has disembarked, anchor the boat and return when ordered to the beach; but it takes much practice even to carry out a simple manoeuvre such as this, the importance of which is obvious if a raiding party is to be successfully withdrawn [...] In all the companies the men are beginning to understand the meaning of silence and to realise the need for the strictest discipline, but they have a long way to go before a landing and retirement is made without a word being spoken.[3]

All over the country, men and women were volunteering for service. *Yachting Monthly*'s June issue had included a new round of opportunities for yachtsmen:

The Admiralty announce that a limited number of temporary commissions in the Executive Branch of the Royal Naval Volunteer Reserve are available for experienced yachtsmen between the ages of 30 and 40. Candidates are required to possess a knowledge of navigation equal to that required for the Board of Trade Yacht Master's (Coastal) certificate. Where candidates are in actual possession of the certificate they may apply if they are of the age of 27 upwards.

The Admiralty are prepared also to consider applications from men between the ages of 40 and 45 with great experience of yachting [...][4]

Nevil Shute, who was 41 and had just completed the novel *Landfall* (1940), applied as an 'elderly yachtsman', expecting to be put in charge of a drifter or a motor minesweeper. He persuaded Frances to take their daughters to Canada, then presented himself at HMS *King Alfred*. He had only been there for two days when he was pulled out of training and sent to the Admiralty to be interviewed by Charles Goodeve. Shute was furious. Believing that the country was in peril of invasion, he had abandoned research for action. Now he was threatened with more of the same – and perhaps worse. He was not impressed by Goodeve: 'In my time I have met many cranks and this man bore all the external hallmarks.'[5]

Shute soon discovered he was wrong about Goodeve – and anyway he had no choice. He was put in charge of the Engineering section of the 'Wheezers and Dodgers', as Goodeve's Department of Miscellaneous Weapon Development was nicknamed. He lived most of the time in London 'and only went to sea to see my things go wrong'. He and his new boss became friends. It was, apparently, on a long train journey to Wales that Shute told Goodeve the story that became *Pied Piper* (1942). Goodeve then gave him three days off to dictate it and referred to it as 'one of the DMWD's most successful by-products'. That novel, though a heart-warmer, is not blind to the atrocities of war. A Gestapo officer accuses the English of shooting his brother, treacherously, after setting his tank alight: 'My brother threw the hatch up to get out, and the English shot him down before he could surrender. But he had already surrendered, and they knew it. No man would go on fighting in a blazing tank.'[6] Shute had already shown, in *Landfall*, how aware he was of the horrors as well as the potency of new weapons. He would return to the theme in *Most Secret* (completed in 1942 but censored until 1945).

Meanwhile, in the innovative summer of 1940, Shute and other members of the Wheezers and Dodgers embarked on an extraordinary range of projects, a significant number of which were focused on increased safety and defensive capability for merchant ships. Donald Currie, who had also entered the RNVR under the 'elderly yachtsman' scheme, worked with Peter Scott on HMS *Broke* to develop new approaches to camouflage. Currie, who had served in the WWI Navy but left as he 'found the regulations so boring', was a watercolour painter who had been rejected for WWII service until the new scheme offered him a chance. Like Nevil Shute, Currie was exceedingly disappointed that he wouldn't be going to sea. Instead, he spent a great deal of time in aeroplanes, looking down on various forms of shipping to see how they might best be merged into their environment. Scott, drawing on his pre-war wildfowling, challenged the WWI idea of breaking up a ship's outline by using dazzle paints. Instead, he developed colour schemes that would enable HMS *Broke* to merge into the background – with such success that in 1941 she was rammed by a trawler while at anchor in the Foyle and by HMS *Verity* in the Atlantic. On both occasions, the other captains protested that she was invisible.

Although Scott's success with *Broke* had been to blur her outline from the view of other ships, in this war camouflage from above was still more essential, as Patrick Dalzel-Job had realised. Currie's experiments with netting and colour would eventually provide reversible camouflage suggesting either rocks and vegetation, or snow. These would be used to conceal vessels on missions to Norway from the Shetland Islands. Later in the war, Adrian Seligman, when organising the Levant Schooner Flotilla, worked with Maurice Green, an art specialist, devising variegated nets that would merge with the different geographical characteristics of islands in the Aegean.

Edward Terrell joined the RNVR on 18 June 1940. He was the Recorder (circuit judge) of Newbury, a keen cricketer, spare-time inventor and weekend sailor. He wasn't overconfident in his abilities as a navigator as he seemed to spend much of his time running aground, so after Munich he had chosen to volunteer for Civil Defence rather than attempt to join the RNVSR. Like Monsarrat, however, he had become discouraged by inactivity. He wondered whether he might find his way into the Navy by offering a legal human resources service to take care of sailors' problems while they were away. This got him an interview but not a job. He filled in the RNVR forms and it was discovered that his father had been an expert in patent law and he himself enjoyed a little amateur chemistry. Charles Goodeve, who was establishing his department in the Admiralty, asked Terrell to walk down from his chambers in the Temple to see whether he'd be willing to develop an information section. He would do very much more. 'I returned to the Strand upon the important mission of ordering from my tailor the uniform of an officer in His Majesty's Royal Naval Volunteer reserve. I was no longer Mr Terrell, but Lieutenant Terrell and perhaps as a result I held my head a little higher.'[7]

Within a month, Terrell was visiting *King Alfred* feeling like a one-man press gang. He interviewed and selected eight volunteers, escorted them on to the London train next morning 'and kept them under close guard till they were all in our office – signed, sealed and delivered'.[8] Terrell had been asked to analyse intelligence reports on the effects of air attack on shipping, particularly the operations of the dive-bombers, a type of aircraft that Britain didn't possess but that had wreaked havoc at Dunkirk. Nevil Shute's aeronautical experience was invaluable. Terrell also worked with LHM Lane, a tree culture expert whom he'd met in Civil Defence and recruited to the RNVR. Lane highlighted a detail in a Dunkirk report, where asphalt-type caulking had seemed to reduce splintering when struck by a shell. By 22 August 1940, working from this tiny clue, Terrell and his team had invented 'plastic armour' to protect merchant shipping.

There was then a bitter row with the Department of Naval Construction and others. All too often, the innovative thinking for which civilians were recruited into the RNVR caused conflict with established procedures. Novelist and industrial psychologist Nigel Balchin (promoter of 'Black Magic' chocolates), who worked at the Ministry of Food during WWII, dramatised similar interdepartmental conflicts in *Darkness Falls from the Air* (1942) and *The Small Back Room* (1943). Within the Department of Miscellaneous Weapon Development, the flouting of correct procedures became known as 'doing a Norway' as Shute was such a persistent offender. Edward Terrell was more skilled at dealing with figures of authority. Backed by Goodeve, he was eventually successful in ensuring that his plastic armour (tactfully renamed 'plastic protective plating') was adopted instead of the Admiralty alternative of concrete cladding. By the time of the D-Day landings, 10,000 ships had been thus equipped. Terrell's achievement is commemorated in the Imperial War Museum and he successfully took action to achieve a promised payout after the war.

★★★

In the summer of 1940, actively patrolling the South and East coasts of England seemed imperative. There had been voluntary enterprise since September 1939 as older yachtsmen took to the water with or without official sanction. Independent MP Alan Herbert (b. 1890), who had served in the WWI RNVR, had enrolled his yacht *Water Gypsy* as part of the River Emergency Service in November 1938 and patrolled as regularly as his other duties allowed, occasionally anchoring off the Speaker's Steps. He refused both a commission and a place in the War Cabinet, taking pride in being the House of Commons' only non-commissioned officer.

A group of 'old and bold' yachtsmen (in their late 50s and 60s) patrolled the Western Channel assiduously in *Campeador V*. Initially, the yacht's owner, Lieutenant VW MacAndrew, had provided her crew from his own resources but from February 1940 she had been 'hired' by the Navy at £60 a month and her crew supplemented from RN Patrol Service in Lowestoft. On 22 June, she hit a mine and sank with the loss of all but two of her company.

Young David Cobb (b. 1921) had been a naval cadet at Pangbourne until a serious rugby injury had disabled him. By 1939, aged 18, he considered himself totally recovered but the Navy wouldn't take him back. He felt he had no alternative but to start an undergraduate degree. The national call for volunteers in May 1940 for anyone experienced in small craft had him on a train for Chichester within an hour. At Itchenor, he found two RNVR officers commandeering motor yachts. He was asked whether he knew any of the vessels. 'All of them. Every single one,' Cobb replied confidently. Asked which was ready for sea, Cobb picked the 45ft Gentleman's motor yacht *Iere*. He was then asked whether he could ferry her round to the Patrol Service depot at Hamble. Cobb didn't hesitate: 'It was a dizzy prospect. The immaculate, best-built and-engined yacht of her size in Chichester Harbour, delivered within seconds into the care of David Cobb. I was skipper, mate and engineer.'[9]

Cobb painted her naval grey, flew the white ensign with immense pride and formed part of the chain of little ships that kept watch nightly from Dover and Ramsgate. Each ship was armed with a WWI rifle and Hotchkiss machine gun, plus six large rockets, which it was their duty to fire should they sight the invasion fleet. Later, Cobb reflected that people like him – sea fencibles 'equally ill-prepared and expendable' – would have been keeping a similar watch against Napoleon. He would never return to university. When the invasion danger had receded and the additional patrols were withdrawn, he was commissioned as a temporary midshipman in the RNVR and sent to Commander Stephenson at Tobermory to take charge of a 115-ton diesel yacht, *Martinetta,* until he was finally old enough to become a sub-lieutenant (age 20) and join the Atlantic convoy escorts.

David Howarth (b. 1912) also joined the Patrol Service in those early June days. Before the war, he had been developing BBC radio outside broadcasts with his friend Richard Dimbleby. When Chamberlain made his announcement on 3 September, Howarth had been in the newsroom at Broadcasting House. Afterwards, he, Dimbleby and Harvey Sarney, an engineer, had purchased Army uniforms (paid for by the BBC) and headed for France, where Dimbleby had already organised them a car with recording equipment and pots of camouflage paint. 'We were the first radio war correspondents there had ever been. [...] Senior executives shook our hands with tears in their eyes. They fully expected we would be the first to die for broadcasting and the BBC. We fully expected it too.'[10]

They then spent the first seven months of war hunting for a battle. 'It was very hard indeed to believe that war had been declared and nobody, anywhere on land, was fighting it.' They also discovered the problems of censorship and the lure of propaganda. 'Brought up in the BBC we still cherished the truth but we found how little truth you can tell in wartime.'[11] By the spring of 1940, they were fed up. In April, Dimbleby was sent to Egypt and Howarth applied for leave. When the events they had been waiting for in France actually happened, he was away climbing mountains in the Isle of Skye. His decision to volunteer for active service was not long in coming. 'I did know how to handle a boat and the Navy had shown at Dunkirk it was not too proud to use amateurs. [...] "Fine," they said. "Report to the naval base in Lowestoft tomorrow morning" – and to my surprise they gave me a free railway ticket.'

Howarth's sailing had only been on inland waters so he bought a book of maritime 'rules of the road' and read it on the train journey to Suffolk. When the Patrol Service officers at Lowestoft asked whether any of that day's recruits could navigate, he answered yes with a neophyte's confidence. The following day, he was sent to Brightlingsea in Essex as a petty officer and flotilla leader to bring a small group of recently requisitioned patrol vessels up the coast to

Lowestoft. 'So I had been all of thirty six hours in the Navy, entirely bewildered, before I was sent to sea in charge of not one of his Majesty's ships, but seven of them.'[12]

Through the rest of that summer and into late autumn, Howarth patrolled his section of the Suffolk coastline, armed with a rifle, a revolver and a rocket and proud to be flying the white ensign. He also studied navigation assiduously. When the invasion threat receded, he and a friend obtained permission to run a sea rescue service searching for downed airmen. They were never successful though they found themselves useful transporting mine-disposal experts to tow floating mines out to sea, where they could be detonated safely – or relatively so. They discovered an urgent need to keep moving when towing a mine to ensure it didn't catch up with them. They were meant to attempt detonation at sea, by gunfire, but if this failed they had to bring the mines ashore. Howarth noticed how quickly people cleared out of their way when they were flying their red warning flag.

As the winter weather worsened, however, there was less and less they could usefully do with their lightweight patrol boat. Howarth applied for an RNVR commission, attended HMS *King Alfred* and was sent north as a flag lieutenant to Scapa Flow.

> The navy must have chosen me for this appointment by wartime logic which by normal logic is well-known to be back to front and upside down. I had done the usual two months training of a sub-lieutenant RNVR. I think I passed top of my division, or nearly top, in seamanship and navigation and I know that I was bottom in OLQs or Officer Like Qualities. [...] On the basis of that debacle, the Navy gave me a job which needed no navigation or seamanship whatever but all the OLQs in the world.[13]

He spent the next few months as personal assistant to Admiral Sir Hugh Binney, the Admiral Commanding, Orkneys and Shetlands. He changed his clean white shirt twice a day and carried ceremonial aiguillettes with him as they travelled to Iceland and the Faroe Islands and entertained distinguished visitors at Scapa Flow. Finally, in 1941, he was recruited for the SIS, to develop the clandestine operation known as the 'Shetland Bus'. This was his ideal assignment:

'boats, Norway, individuality and independence, yet with the status of a naval officer.'[14]

★★★

In the early autumn of 1940, a group of RNVR officer trainees at HMS *King Alfred* were asked to volunteer for a secret mission ... bomb disposal. Why did I volunteer, family solicitor Jack Easton asked himself later? 'I volunteered not because I am by nature courageous but because I am of mind curious, and anything at that moment seemed preferable to sitting at a desk working out navigational problems with the aid of a brain that would never cope with even the most elementary mathematics.'[15] Easton (b. 1906) may have been overly self-deprecating. He was a keen amateur sailor who, like David Cobb, had attended Pangbourne Nautical College (in the days when pupils still slept in hammocks) and had obtained his 'Master's Ticket' before the outbreak of war in preparation for service with the RNVR.

The bombing of Britain had begun in earnest during the summer of 1940, when the German occupation of Belgium, the Netherlands and France reduced the distances their aircraft needed to fly. At first, the focus was on the Channel convoys and on RAF airfields, then, from 6 September, Hitler's attention switched to London and other major cities. Many of the bombs dropped were the former magnetic mines that had caused such havoc among shipping during the winter of 1939–1940. Minesweeping had become more effective with Charles Goodeve's invention of the LL sweep and ships were better protected by the processes of wiping and degaussing. Vigilance had increased with the assiduous patrolling.

As underused mine stocks began to accumulate in German factories, Goering realised that they could equally be dropped on land. Responsibility for rendering them safe if they had failed to explode remained with the Navy. Maurice Griffiths was taken away from his minesweeping flotilla in September 1940 and put in charge of a naval diver and his team to deal with mines that had fallen by night into the London Docks. He remembered the scene that greeted them each morning as they threaded their way through the East End:

Streets that the diving party had driven through the previous day were now avenues of smoking rubble [...] In places groups of people with drawn faces lined the pavements but when they caught sight of the dark blue Navy truck hurrying through, their expressions lit up and they usually gave a cheer with Churchill's victory sign.

Increasing numbers of RMS (Rendering Mines Safe) parties were needed to deal with this increasing problem. 'Fledgling sub-lieutenants emerging from HMS *King Alfred*, the RNVR training school, were given the necessary instruction, issued with a standard kit of non-magnetic tools, and sent out with one of the experienced officers for instruction in the front line.'[16]

That was the theory at least. John Miller was one of these 'fledglings'.

I was by then myself a class captain and had just paraded my squad for a period of drill outside in the yard when a secret signal was brought up by an orderly. The first heavy air raid on London had taken place the night before. The signal stated that twelve volunteers were required from the Fleet to attempt to dismantle a number of German magnetic mines which had been dropped on London by parachute. [...] I reported that all my squad wished to go but asked that I, as class captain, might be allowed preference. I was handed a railway warrant and told to go immediately to HMS Vernon, the headquarters of the torpedo and mining department in Portsmouth. [...] In the train for Portsmouth, as we slipped along in the September sunshine beneath Arundel Castle, it was borne upon me that I might not have much longer to live.[17]

Miller and his 11 companions duly reported to HMS *Vernon*, remained there 48 hours, were introduced to a few tools and were given some brief instruction from Lieutenant Commander Ouvry. They were then sent on to the Admiralty with the assurance that they would be going out with an expert. At the Admiralty, Miller and his companions were issued with sheaves of papers showing addresses, dates and times.

We exchanged anxious glances. 'But who is taking us, sir?' I asked.

'TAKING YOU?' said the Captain, 'You're taking yourselves. Get out! But before you go pick up a set of tools from the table and choose a sailor from that row there against the wall.'[18]

John Miller chose Able Seaman Stephen Tuckwell, 'the finest fellow who ever put in eighteen years' service with the Royal Navy'. They were supplied with a large grey Humber car by the War Office and sent on their way with their lists. 'I saw to my delight that my "parish" was the area lying between the Thames and King's Lynn. A heavy proportion of the mines were down in Essex and my headquarters was to be Great Dunmow.' The new officers soon discovered, however, that the mines to be rendered safe were not laid out neat and clean as they had been at HMS *Vernon*, they were half buried in earth, stuck through roofs, blocking narrow passageways, in shallow tidal creeks.

Miller was a devout Anglo-Catholic. His post-war (1951) memoir intersperses his spiritual journey with his RNVR experience, arranged, as he disarmingly explains, in alternate chapters 'so that those who care only for the adventures with the parachute mines can more easily skip the adventures with the saints'.[19] For his first three days of service, he and Able Seaman Tuckwell had to return each night to the Admiralty confessing that, although he had ingeniously rendered some of the Essex mines safe, he had not actually succeeded in opening any of them.

The RNVR volunteers had been given instructions that the work 'was to be done only by officers' but unsurprisingly the varied demands of each task made this almost impossible to comply with. One night, before what he knew would be a particularly dangerous and awkward job defusing a mine half buried in the soft mud of Barking Creek, Miller was so certain that he was about to die that he asked Tuckwell to spend a few last hours with him in his family home in Northamptonshire. The following day, they returned to Essex, collected a canoe that they had borrowed from the borough engineer and paddled together up the creek to a point where one of the London sewers was 'discharging a cascade of yellow foam' and the tail of the mine could just be observed with the upper part of the main fuse showing.

At this point I regained, with an effort, an official manner and asked Tuckwell to withdraw. I said he had better take cover on the bank opposite the mine and make the usual notes. He said he thought it should hardly be necessary for him to point out that it would take him at least two hours to reach the place that I had indicated. Besides I should have to work under about a foot of water and would need somebody to hand me the tools. I should have to stand over the mine all the time – we could hardly drag our feet through the soft going at this point – and it would be quite impossible in the time available to get away to do anything from a distance. In short, if my number was up, he would like to be with me. The tide was showing signs of slackening. There was no time to lose. I smiled and we got to work.[20]

The George Crosses and George Medals awarded for this work represent a tiny fraction of the everyday stories of bravery from this group of amateur sailors. Over the winter of 1940–1941, the bombs they were required to tackle could be anywhere other than at sea. Temporary Lieutenant Harold Newgass (b. 1899) was sent to defuse a mine that had fallen into a Liverpool gasometer. It was swinging in the gas from its parachute, which was caught in the roof. The gasometer was adjacent to a munitions factory. Newgass had himself fitted into a diving suit so that he could be lowered in to swing beside the mine as he worked to remove the fuse and primer.

Newgass, owner of a 26ft auxiliary cutter named *Ondina*, which he kept in Falmouth, was already over 40 when he volunteered so had been drafted immediately into the Special Branch and directed to RMS duties. Defusing the mine in the Gaston gasworks took him almost two days as he had to keep returning to renew his oxygen supplies – and the more strain he felt, the more oxygen he used. By the time he reached his sixth cylinder he was close to exhaustion, but the mine was finally rendered harmless. 'We must forever salute his achievement and I shall always feel proud to have known him,' wrote Lincoln, celebrating Newgass as a fellow Jew.[21]

Amateur sailor Jack Easton was fortunate to survive this period, though his companion, Able Seaman Bennett Southwell, did not. They were in Hoxton in East London in a working-class street from which everyone had been evacuated. The parachute had caught round a chimney pot and the unexploded mine was dangling through a hole in the ceiling, 6in above the parlour floor. As Easton started work the chimney pot collapsed, the bomb slipped on to the floor and its mechanism began to whir. They had 12 seconds. Southwell ran down the street; Easton dived for the nearest air raid shelter.

I heard no explosion. It has since been explained to me that if you are near enough to an explosion of such force unconsciousness is upon you before any sound it makes reaches you, which is a merciful thing. I was blinded by the flash that comes split seconds before the explosion, but that was all I experienced.

I do not know what time passed before I became conscious. When I did, I knew I was buried deep beneath bricks and mortar and was being suffocated. My head was between my legs, and I guessed my back was broken but could not move an inch. I was held, imbedded.

Men dug me out eventually. To this day I do not know how long I was held in my grave. Most of that time I was unconscious. The conscious moments are of horror and utter helplessness.[22]

Easton had suffered a fractured skull, broken back, broken pelvis and two broken legs. He took six months to recover then served the rest of the war at sea, mainly in minesweepers.

I2

'Small things sidled out of dark hiding places'[1]

Autumn 1940: The first RNVR officer in the submarine service; the first to command a corvette

In October 1940, Edward Young, pre-war design director at Penguin Books, became the first executive RNVR officer accepted into the submarine service. After the Munich crisis, 27-year-old Young, a keen weekend sailor, had begun studying for his Master Mariner's certificate and joined the London River Fire Brigade. By the spring of 1940, he'd almost completed his initial three weeks' training at HMS *King Alfred* and had heard that the Admiralty had decided to risk the experiment of introducing RNVR officers into the submarine service. They only wanted two volunteers and already had them. Young was envious; the chosen ones were going to be promoted to the astro-navigation course that he wanted to take. He persuaded the commander to allow him to join the course and to put his name forward as an additional volunteer. Young spent the summer months as a probationary sub-lieutenant in the destroyer HMS *Atherton*, before he was sent to Fort Blockhouse for the six weeks' specialist training for submarines. By this time, the two other volunteers had withdrawn or been rejected.

Once he'd completed his training, Young's initial posting was to HMS *H28*, the oldest submarine in the British fleet and the only one to have undertaken war patrols in both world wars. He travelled to Harwich with two other recently qualified sub-lieutenants: Lionel Dearden RN and Jock Tait RNR. Dearden was immediately sent to sea in HMS *H49*, while Tait and Young waited for *H28*. These small 26-person submarines were patrolling off the coast of occupied Holland. When Dearden returned, looking weather-beaten and tired, the other two were eager to hear about his experience. They found, however, that there was now a gulf between them as Dearden had completed a war patrol and they had not. On their own first patrol, Tait and Young experienced a depth-charge attack and were machine-gunned from the air. Young described being 'lightly' depth-charged: 'A sharp crack, as of a giant hammer, struck the pressure hull, followed by a frightful reverberating roar which seemed to echo through all the subterranean ocean caves of the world. [...] there was a second mighty crack, and again that thundering rumbling aftermath.' The captain reassured the two new officers that this was not close. They also experienced being 'pinged' by hostile ASDIC: 'a faint slow regular knocking, as though someone was tapping gently on the outside of the hull. I thought of Pew's stick tapping along the road in *Treasure Island*. It was like being shut up in a dark room, with a blind maniac reaching out sinister fingers to find you.'[2]

They returned to the news that *H49* was missing. Later, everyone in the Harwich base was called together to hear the bad news: *H49* must be presumed lost. Young and Tait went off for a long walk, though they hardly spoke. Young felt 'cold and dead inside'. He remembered Dearden 'smiling again that same tired smile with which he had greeted us on his last return to harbour'.[3] Once more, their friend had crossed a gulf ahead of them.

They learned later that *H49* had been caught by a flotilla of five anti-submarine trawlers off Texel Island. Her crew had endured two hours of continuous depth-charging before the submarine's pressure hull ruptured and 26 crew members died. One man reached the surface and was taken prisoner. After this loss, the elderly *H28* was withdrawn from active duty and redeployed as a training boat off the Scottish west coast.

★★★

Nicholas Monsarrat had not intended his non-combatant war work – first as a stretcher-party driver, then as organiser of an ARP depot – to be 'shameful or cowardly'. He shared the general expectation 'that London at least would be bombed and burned to cinders from the first evening of day one'.[4] During the 1930s, he had become a pacifist and this type of war service was, initially, as far as he felt he could go. Months of inaction in London, followed

by the military disasters of spring 1940, changed him. He answered
an advertisement for 'gentlemen with yachting experience', sent by
his father, and by the autumn was a temporary sub-lieutenant on the
Flower-class corvette HMS *Campanula*, undertaking Atlantic convoy
escort duty. His captain, Richard Case, was a lieutenant commander
RNR, who had already won a DSC as commanding officer of the
A/S Trawler *Stella Cappella*.

In Monsarrat's great post-war novel *The Cruel Sea* (1951), the
commanding officer of HMS *Compass Rose*, George Ericson, is a
heroic figure who wins the devotion of his first lieutenant, Keith
Lockhart (aka Monsarrat). This was not the situation on *Campanula*.
Monsarrat wrote later that:

> *The Captain [...] thought nothing, less than nothing of us, the pink-
> cheeked amateurs: and the various ways he made this clear, no less than
> 17 times a day, ensured that the feeling was mutual. It stemmed no doubt
> from the traditional stupid and childish feud between the Royal Naval
> Reserve and the Royal Naval Volunteer Reserve.[5]*

It might also have stemmed from Monsarrat's own complex attitude
to authority or, more simply, to incompatible characters pitched into
an extremely uncomfortable vessel in a challenging environment.
The Flower-class corvettes had not originally been designed for
Atlantic service: they were slow, wet and spartan, with little off-duty
comfort and generally poor food. During their first winter of service
(1940–1941), the corvettes had only three watch-keeping officers
undertaking the constant vigilance necessary for station-keeping, as
well as looking out for attack and following the orders of the convoy's
senior officer, who was usually on a destroyer. Monsarrat was given a
list of jobs in addition to his watch-keeping duties: correspondence
officer, censoring officer, officer in charge of Sunday divisions.
The one he hated the most, which Case gave to him as soon as
he arrived, knowing that he was the son of Liverpool surgeon Sir
Keith Monsarrat, was ship's medical officer. Once *Campanula* was in
action, rescuing torpedoed survivors from the oil-soaked Atlantic,
the responsibility was truly horrific.

> *If anyone had told me, when I answered that* Times *advertisement for
> gentlemen with yachting experience, that as a result I would soon be*

*stitching up a gashed throat without benefit of anesthetics, or trying to coax
a dangling eyeball back into its socket; or if I had known that a man with
a deep stomach wound, spread-eagled on what seemed like the very rack
of Christ, could actually smell so awful, like an open drain, I might well
have kept my yachting experience as secret as the grave, and settled for the
Army Pay Corps or for prison or for shameful defeat itself.*[6]

Monsarrat's description of survivors climbing on board with gasping
lungs, terminally poisoned by corrosive fuel oil, 'coughing up their
guts until they died', or screaming with the pain of deep hopeless
burns, is excruciating. On *Campanula,* Monsarrat read the funeral
service so often that he knew it by heart as he supervised bodies
being tipped over the side and noted them in the ship's log as
'discharged dead'.

As 1940 became 1941, the ever-increasing losses among Atlantic
merchant shipping were fuelled by the relocation of Admiral Dönitz's
U-boat fleet from the relatively distant Kiel and Wilhelmshaven,
first to the Norwegian ports of Bergen, Narvik and Trondheim in
April 1940 then, from September 1940, to Lorient, St-Nazaire and
Brest on the French Atlantic coast. The Germans used forced labour
(Organisation Todt) to build reinforced concrete pens, which shielded
their U-boats from air attack. In 1941, these new, convenient ports
and the increasing numbers of boats being produced by German
yards facilitated the deployment of the wolf-pack tactics that Dönitz
had consistently advocated. The U-boat commanders later referred
to this period as their 'Happy Time'.

Even before wolf-pack strategies were fully operational, the
combination of German strength in the air, plus the activities of
their surface raiders (such as *Scharnhorst* and *Gneisenau*) were
beginning to cause serious alarm. Though the film director Pen
Tennyson attended HMS *King Alfred* as an RNVR trainee in the
summer of 1940 before directing the successful film *Convoy*, there
was little public understanding of the nature of this 'private war' and
the extraordinary heroism of the merchant navy.

Monsarrat was already a published novelist and began writing
notes on his experience as soon as he joined up. He described his
feeling of urgency − that he had something to say about the Battle
of the Atlantic and must say it while he could. 'It was a battle we had

to win if we were to exist at all – and that was something we *did* know at the time.' He was also worried he might die before he'd said what he needed to say. *HM Corvette*, his sanitised account of life on HMS *Campanula*, was published in 1942. Monsarrat keeps his true opinion of her captain to himself, deflecting the unpleasantness on to a fictional first lieutenant. He adds more officers than *Campanula* possessed (at least to start with) and gives her a moment of glory she probably never achieved. He holds nothing back, however, from his description of discomfort of life on board, taking the often-repeated saying that 'a corvette would roll on wet grass' and elevating this into a riff of anguish.

Apart from the noise it produces, rolling has a maddening rhythm that is one of the minor tortures of rough weather. It never stops or misses a beat, it cannot be escaped anywhere. If you go through a doorway, it hits you hard: if you sit down, you fall over; you get hurt, knocked about continuously, and it makes for extreme and childish anger. When you drink, liquid rises towards you and slops over: at meals the food spills off your plate, the cutlery will not stay in place. Things roll about, and bang, and slide away crazily: and then come back and hurt you again. [...] sometimes at worst height of a gale you may be hove to in this sort of fury for days on end, and all the time you can't forget you are no nearer shelter than you were 24 hours before.[7]

When he read letters complaining about petrol rationing, for instance, Monsarrat thought of torpedoed tankers ablaze at sea: 'That's your extra ten gallons of petrol, sir and madam: that's last week's little wangle with the garage on the corner. You might remember what you're burning, now and then: its real basic coupon is a corpse-strewn Atlantic.'[8]

In August 1941, HMS *Campanula* was part of Convoy OG 71 from Liverpool (OG stands for 'Outward for Gibraltar'). Twenty-three merchant ships set out on 13 August with a minimal escort of a Norwegian Navy destroyer, a sloop and the corvette HMS *Zinnia*. The convoy commodore was on board the passenger liner SS *Aguila*, which was ferrying a large number of naval personnel to the Mediterranean, including the first group of WRNS embarked on foreign service. Among them was 35-year-old Florence Macpherson, widow of Hugh Macpherson from *Northern Rover*. HMS *Campanula* and four other Flower-class corvettes joined the escort on 15 August but so, unfortunately, did a German reconnaissance plane that spent the day circling, just out of range, reporting their position. OG 71 was then attacked using the new '*rudeltaktik*' (wolf-pack) strategy. HNoMS *Bath* from the Royal Norwegian Navy, which had fallen behind the main convoy while attempting to attack a sonar contact, was the first to be sunk (88 men died). Corvette HMS *Hydrangea* went to rescue her survivors, therefore depleting protection. Cargo ship *Alva* in the main convoy was next, her survivors being rescued by *Campanula* and the Irish merchant ship *Clonlara* – which was herself sunk on 22 August.

Torpedoes hit the cargo ship *Ciscar* and SS *Aguila*. The *Aguila* caught fire and sank in 90 seconds, killing 152 people, including Florence Macpherson. Ten survivors were picked up by HMS *Wallflower* and a further six by the tugboat *Empire Oak*, who also had 11 *Alva* survivors on board. When the *Empire Oak* was herself torpedoed, on 22 August, the six *Aguila* survivors died, together with nine from the *Alva* and 14 from the *Empire Oak*. The *Empire Oak* survivors were picked up by *Campanula*, who completed her service by rescuing the survivors from the torpedoed merchant ship *Aldergrove* on 23 August. Merchant ships *Stork* and *Spind* were sunk that day, as was the corvette HMS *Zinnia* (68 died). This loss of a 'chummy ship' was especially painful for Monsarrat and the crew of *Campanula*. Though five more destroyers had belatedly joined the escort on 20 August, eight of the 23 ships carrying supplies to Gibralter had been lost. A further ten cargo ships retreated to neutral Portugal and went no further. Monsarrat might reasonably have felt he had become a seaborne stretcher-bearer.

'What do the escorts actually do?' Churchill is rumoured to have asked. If he had, it would have been a very good question. There was little tactical retaliation against the wolfpacks until 1942, when the Western Approaches Tactical Unit run by Gilbert Roberts and his team of WRNS developed a wargaming approach to train escort commanders. This proved so effective that there was said to be a photo of Roberts pinned up in the U-boat HQ in Flensburg captioned 'This is your Enemy'. From April 1943 – more than three years after the outbreak of war – the Navy began to develop increasingly sophisticated and aggressive interventions by trained support groups, most notably Captain FJ Walker of the 2nd Escort Group. Historian Martin Middlebrook suggests that 'the high quality of the RNRs' seamanship and the enthusiasm of the RNVRs should not be allowed to cloud the fact that the Battle of the Atlantic would have been fought better if the Navy had made available even a few more of its skilled regular officers in the early years of the war.'[9]

When Monsarrat was serving on *Campanula*, escorts might be asked to pick up survivors after an attack, as the convoy steamed on; to stand by another vessel that might be experiencing mechanical trouble; or to leave the convoy to chase after a raider. It wasn't easy to catch up again as corvettes were not very fast. Meanwhile, protection for the main convoy was depleted. The corvettes were equipped with sonic listening devices (ASDIC) and depth charges, which could be set to explode at different levels against U-boats. On *Campanula*, these were Monsarrat's responsibility. He wrote that he found them easier to harmonise with his remaining humanitarian principles as it was not like directing a gun at a fellow human being. It was perhaps fortunate for his peace of mind that he had not shared Edward Young's underwater experiences.

Still stationed in Lyness (Orkney) with his flotilla of ASW trawlers, Denys Rayner had begun lobbying for command of one of the Flower-class corvettes as soon as they began coming into commission. The initial commands were all going to RNR officers, such as Lieutenant Commander Case, and Captain Elgood from HMS *Eaglet* continued to assert his conviction that the Navy would never give such responsibility to volunteers. Rayner was perhaps fortunate that there was now an RNVR officer working in the Admiralty Drafting Office. In late autumn, he received a letter appointing him commanding officer of the corvette HMS *Violet*, but saying the date to take up this appointment would follow later. Rayner didn't wait: he handed over his current vessel and left Orkney that same night. When he arrived in Middlesbrough, he discovered that HMS *Violet* wouldn't be ready for months. He noticed, however, that she had a sister ship, HMS *Verbena*, much closer to completion – and with no captain. Rayner dashed back to the local Navy office to phone his friend at the Admiralty. The appointment was changed. He had his ship.

I hurried down to her. She was lying alongside the fitting-out jetty. A shimmering haze above the funnel told me that at least one of her boilers was lit. There were wires and pipes all over the place. The smell of fresh paint mingled with the smell of fuel oil. The sharp rattle of riveting machines rose in a never-ending cacophony. But I could only see her as she would be, slipping quietly out of the northern mists with only the hiss of her bow wave to disturb the sea birds, and the steady throb of her propeller beating like a heart. She was quite perfect.[10]

HMS *Verbena* was commissioned in December 1940 and became the first corvette to be officered entirely by the RNVR. This was not an unmixed blessing, as Rayner discovered he was the only one with any watch-keeping experience. His junior officers had arrived straight from *King Alfred*. They were not former RNVSR yachtsmen but had been promoted via the Commission and Warrant (CW) system. They had each served nine months 'on the lower deck' but none of them could follow a compass course at sea. 'Before the war Sub-Lieutenants PM Whittaker and RFE Pettifer had been clerks in an office and Midshipman CS Edwards had been a schoolboy.'[11] Rayner phoned his friend at the Admiralty, pleading for an experienced first lieutenant, but was told 'the bag is empty'. Even the influence of Commodore Stephenson, the Terror of Tobermory, failed, so *Verbena* spent her first patrols with Rayner on the bridge virtually full time.

The complement of a Flower-class corvette was 85 but the divide between officers and men, as well as the specialisation of their functions, could mean further subdivisions into small, unhappy groups. Monsarrat's existence on *Campanula* was immeasurably improved by the arrival of RNVSR yachtsman St John Harmsworth, not just because he increased the ship's watch-keeping capacity by 25 per cent but because he was humanly congenial. The arrival of Scottish yachtsman and pre-war barrister John Oswald Mair Hunter (Jack) as first lieutenant had a similar effect on board *Verbena*. Unlike Lieutenant Commander Case, Denys Rayner comes across as a team-builder, always concerned to run a happy as well as an efficient ship. Hunter's arrival and personality made a crucial difference to his success.

My memories of Jack Hunter are overlaid by memories of his wonderful grin. The worse the conditions, the broader the grin. [...] As one of my brother corvette captains remarked to me rather plaintively, 'It's alright for you and your bloody Verbenas. With a barrister for a First Lieutenant any of you can get away with murder.'

This use of the collective was felt as an accolade:

The commanding officer of another ship had paid us the supreme compliment of classing us all together as Verbenas [...] The sensation of being 'one' with the 'whole' gave me a feeling of deep satisfaction – a sensation which, once I had left Verbena, I was not to recapture, until another First Lieutenant did exactly the same for me on the destroyer Highlander.[12]

During Monsarrat's time on *Campanula*, this harmony was achieved only in fiction.

The responsibilities of a commanding officer were almost unimaginably heavy. The most challenging scene in *The Cruel Sea* is when Monsarrat brings together two incompatibles: the Navy's traditional mantra 'Engage the enemy more closely' (it's always a duty to press home an attack) and the seafarers' imperative to stop and save lives. The fictional first lieutenant of HMS *Compass Rose* is sure that he has a contact – the ASDIC is pinging off an underwater object that he believes to be the U-boat that has just sunk a merchant ship. Yet the surface of the sea is filled with swimming survivors. It is the captain who must decide what action to take. Ericson drives *Compass Rose* full ahead and orders the depth charges to be fired, killing the swimmers. Only afterwards do he and his first lieutenant come to suspect that they have made a terrible mistake.

Alistair MacLean, who served 'below decks' 1941–1946, dramatised this and similar duty/humanity conflicts in his debut novel *HMS Ulysses* (1955). In life, Monsarrat's next captain, Sam Lombard-Hobson, understood such dilemmas very well and might reasonably be assumed to be the story's source. It was, however, in the Indian Ocean in 1944 that a closely comparable incident happened. On 12 February, the troopship SS *Khedive Ismail* was on its way to Colombo, Ceylon, from Kilindini, Kenya, carrying a large contingent of African troops and British military personnel, including 83 women. Early in the afternoon, she was torpedoed by the Japanese submarine *I-27*: she broke in two and sank quickly. Of the 1,511 people on board, only 208 men and six women survived. It was to become Britain's third worst mercantile disaster in WWII and the worst ever involving British servicewomen.

The escorting destroyers HMSs *Petard* and *Paladin* went on the hunt for the submarine and eventually sank her, though their depth-charging caused further casualties among the people in the water. One of the dead was Paymaster Lieutenant Commander R Whitelaw RNVR, a Scottish yachtsman who used to sail regularly with the ebullient Scottish barrister Jack Hunter, first lieutenant of HMS *Verbena*. After the war, Hunter returned to Scotland and to legal practice but not to yachting, as his obituary explained:

> *Throughout his life, Jack made light of his distinguished war service but, in a quiet moment, he was heard to say that after the war ended, he found he had lost his taste for the sea. He had been deeply saddened by the death of his great friend, 'best man' and fellow yachtsman Bobby Whitelaw in an attack by a U-boat and couldn't bring himself to sail again. He was, however, a lifelong supporter of the RNLI.* [13]

A serviceman, Kenneth Harrop, later expressed his enduring gratitude for the commanding officer's decision not to hold back from the destruction of the Japanese submarine:

> *The captain of the* Petard *had the horrifying decision to make – should he save more of the swimmers or drop depth charges to sink the enemy marauder. Rightly or wrongly he chose the latter course and many of those thinking they were about to be rescued were blown to pieces in the devastating attack of patterned depth charges. [...] If that raider had not been disposed of in that terrible moment of decision by the* Petard *captain, my ship, and the lives of some 500 navy men, would almost certainly have fallen to that Japanese submarine. [...] I sincerely hope that when my two sons read this narrative they will realise that they owe their existence in this world to one moment in time – the moment when a terrible choice confronted a destroyer captain on a calm sea in the blazing heat of the Indian Ocean.* [14]

13

'The dark spaces of the North Sea'[1]

1941–1942: Submarine operations and clandestine North Sea crossings

In July 1941, Edward Young was ordered to join the new submarine HMS *Umpire* at her builder's yard in Chatham. Lieutenant Mervyn Wingfield, his previous commanding officer from *H28*, had already transferred. HMS *Umpire*'s first lieutenant, Peter Bannister, was energetic and easy to get along with, and the navigator, Tony Godden, was another friend from the training course. As HMS *Umpire* set out on her maiden voyage, joining a northbound convoy up the East Coast, Young and his companions had every reason to feel optimistic. When the convoy was attacked by a low-flying bomber off Aldeburgh, the submarine's first emergency dive was a confidence-boosting success. Towards nightfall, however, one of the engines failed and *Umpire* could no longer keep up. They continued heading north, then bore north-east and east as the convoy route bent round the curve of the Norfolk coast. This narrow channel, bounded by a minefield on the seaward side, was an E-boat hunting ground so no one was showing any lights. They lost touch with their escort.

At about midnight, HMS *Umpire* was on the surface, proceeding slowly up the seaward side of the channel. Navigator Tony Godden, who was officer of the watch, got a message that a southbound convoy was approaching, also on the seaward side. This was not normal. They should have been on the inland side, following the accepted rule of the road, which directed that vessels should pass each other port to port (left-hand side to left-hand side). Godden called Lieutenant Wingfield, who hurried to the bridge. Already, the large black shapes of the merchant ships were beginning to pass in a steady line outside them. Wingfield gave an order to turn away to port. He must have decided he had no choice but, according to the collision regulations, this was wrong.

Suddenly, out of the darkness came the solid shape of a 266-ton ASW trawler, the *Peter Hendricks*, heading straight for them. Through the voice pipe, Young, who was below with Peter Bannister, heard Wingfield shout 'hard-a-port!' The *Peter Hendricks* also tried to take avoiding action, turning (instinctively and correctly) to starboard. This made collision inevitable. Wingfield called 'Full astern both!' but it was too late. The trawler's heavy bows rammed the submarine hard. Young and Bannister heard 'the sickening metallic crash' as the two vessels ground together. Then the sub and the trawler disengaged and *Umpire* began to sink.

It took only 30 seconds for her to begin her plunge to the bottom. Wingfield, Godden and the two lookouts were swept overboard. Young, Bannister and the rest of the crew were trapped inside. Water was pouring in from above, although both the main hatch and the engine room hatch were closed. Young remembers that his brain seemed 'paralysed'. The area ripped open by the trawler's bows was forward in the torpedo stowage department. A submarine's interior is divided into separate sections by bulkheads and watertight doors. The further door to the damaged compartment was already shut. Whoever was trapped behind it was already dead. Had it been closed in some 'nameless act of self-sacrifice', Young wondered? Men were running from one compartment to the next as the water rose behind them. 'Shut that bloody door!' shouted the first lieutenant. Young was able to hold off obeying until everyone was through.

Still the water poured in. Well after the event, Young realised that there had been a ventilation shaft left open above the captain's bunk. If he had been thinking clearly, he could have closed the shaft and given them all vital extra time. *Umpire* had come to rest on the Sheringham Shoal, a relatively shallow area. Their highest point was about 60ft below the surface: the pressure outside would not be crushing. (Her grave these days is advertised as a beginners' dive site.) Meanwhile, the interior of the submarine continued to fill: if the water reached the batteries, the reaction would create highly poisonous chlorine gas. Young was searching for torches as the electrical circuits shorted out. He found a crew member trying to open the door into the flooded bow section: 'My pal's in there,' he was moaning, 'my pal's in there.' Young told him it was hopeless: the submarine had filled up forward and there could be no one left alive on that side of the door.[2]

There were people sheltering behind the closed door to the engine room at the other end of the ship but when Young returned after another attempt to search for torches he found the centre of the submarine deserted. Had they all escaped through the engine room hatch without realising he'd been left behind? He listened but could hear nothing beyond the monotonous, pitiless sound of pouring water. In that terrible moment, he came very near to panic.

Young did eventually escape, stripping to his underclothes and bursting out through the conning tower with three others, to swim jerkily to the surface, blindly, desperately, ears roaring, fighting for life. He became separated from his companions (who did not all survive) and there was a long, lonely swim in the darkness before he was taken aboard a motor launch and eventually arrived in Yarmouth. That evening, he was walking alone in a small grassy courtyard as rain drizzled down: 'To me the sound of the soft rain falling like a benediction on the living grass seemed inexpressibly sad and sweet, and life itself so desirable that I could not imagine ever again being dissatisfied with it. For the first time I knew the delirious joy of not being dead.'[3]

Land-based Margery Allingham, recording her unanticipated reactions to a near miss from a bomb in the autumn of 1940, had used that same word, delirious: 'As soon as it was over I was delirious with pleasure to find I had not been hurt. It was the most purely animal reaction I ever remember having.'[4]

About half of *Umpire's* crew of 32 had survived but Young's friends Peter Bannister and Tony Godden were not among them. He was humbled to learn of the calm – indeed heroic – way in which the chief engine room artificer (ERA) had organised his group into their escape suits (DESA) and had waited underwater on the hull of the submarine until he was certain everyone was out. Young was disappointed with himself. He felt he had failed to live up to the high standards of an officer. Why hadn't he realised that the water was coming in through the ventilator? Why hadn't it been him in the engine room with the men? He wondered how he could continue: he decided he must ask to be sent on an operational patrol as soon as possible.

His posting was to the S-class submarine *Sealion*, then commanded by the charismatic Ben Bryant. Bryant was 'the most famous British submarine ace to survive the war', to quote his Wikipedia entry. (It's hard not to put an emphasis on 'to survive' when 36 per cent of British submarines were lost.) Young described Bryant as being 'big enough to give you confidence in yourself by assuming you can do your job without appearing to check up on you'. He spent his first watch in a state of near panic: 'wherever I looked I imagined I saw ships suddenly close and about to hit us.'[5] The trauma of the night-time collision and sinking would never entirely leave him. Three and a half years later (April 1945), returning as a commanding officer from successful patrols in the Far East, Young was part of a slow convoy that ran into fog. As long-buried memories of the *Umpire* collision came back to haunt him, Young spent the next 40 hours almost continuously on the bridge.

Sealion and her fellow S-class submarines (1st and 2nd Group) had been in action from the first days of the war when *Sealion* herself, together with *Shark, Salmon* and *Snapper*, was called back from the Mediterranean to join their sisters in the dark spaces of the North Sea. By the early months of 1941, nine of the 12 S-class submarines had been lost or destroyed with a cost of 250 lives. *Sealion* had been bombed, hunted, depth-charged and rammed. She had achieved several enemy sinkings and been frustrated by a high number of misses.

Earlier in 1941, *Sealion* had formed part of the screen of submarines playing their part in the pursuit and destruction of the German battleship *Bismarck*. This episode was one of the defining moments of the sea war with Germany. The massive, recently completed *Bismarck* was attempting to sortie from Gotenhafen (Gydnia) in the Baltic to follow up on the success that *Scharnhorst* and *Gneisenau* had been enjoying, attacking convoys in the Atlantic. She was, however, spotted by one of a network of resistance agents in Norway and the message soon reached the Admiralty. On 21 May, ships were sent out from Scapa Flow to patrol her likely routes. Later that day, *Bismarck* encountered the elderly British battleship HMS *Hood* and sank her in just six minutes. Ludovic Kennedy wrote later, 'For most Englishmen the news of *Hood*'s death was traumatic, as though Buckingham Palace had been laid flat or the Prime Minister assassinated [...] they remembered, many of them, where they were when they heard the news'.[6] The sinking gave a special urgency to the Royal Navy's pursuit of the *Bismarck* and her companion, *Prinz Eugen*. Twenty-one-year-old Kennedy, in HMS *Tartar*, was there at the end, sharing the triumph and the horror:

> To see her now, surrounded by enemies on all sides, hopelessly outgunned and outnumbered, was not a pretty sight. She was a ship after all, perhaps the finest they had seen, and ships were their livelihood and life. As they watched the shells from the battleships and cruisers tearing into her, they thought of her crew, seamen like themselves.[7]

Tartar and her companion HMS *Mashona* suffered air attack on their way back to their base at Lough Foyle. *Mashona* was sunk. Kennedy remembered one almost-survivor, an older man who did not have the strength to hold on to the rope that was helping him to safety. Afterwards, he realised that he could have saved the man if he had jumped down, fastened the rope around him and had him hauled up. It wasn't that he thought of it and didn't do it; it was that the idea never occurred until it was too late. It was a regret that was to remain with him for many years.[8]

David Howarth, accompanying Admiral Binney on an official visit to the Faroe Islands on board the cruiser HMS *Arethusa*, was for a while in danger of meeting the *Bismarck* head on, both ships rushing towards one another at full speed in a narrow channel. He felt relieved when he heard *Bismarck* had been sighted steaming south-west on a course for Brest but he sensed the disappointment among the regular officers, most of whom had lost friends on board the *Hood*. At the end, he records that the feeling in the fleet was relief rather than triumph. From the German tactical point of view, the loss of the brand-new *Bismarck* increased the doubt in Hitler's mind as to the value of these hugely powerful, but also vulnerable, surface warships. Although *Scharnhorst* and *Gneisenau* had sunk many tons of merchant shipping in their Atlantic raids, by the summer of 1941 they and *Prinz Eugen* were all variously out of action and the *Bismarck* was gone. Her even larger sister ship, *Tirpitz*, had been completed but would never get further away from the Baltic than northern Norway. No one knew that yet.

★★★

When Edward Young joined the combat-hardened *Sealion*, she was manned exclusively by RN and RNR personnel and was about to undertake her 20th war patrol. For a slightly post-traumatic RNVR amateur to join as her new torpedo officer could have been tough. Young knew none of his new colleagues in advance but found he was accepted at once, on equal terms. This helped him put his personal problem in perspective. As well as his new commander, Ben Bryant, Young was particularly impressed with 'Skips' Marriott, the chief ERA, describing him as 'a tall saturnine submarine ERA of the old school with a highly developed sardonic sense of humour'. Months later, he discovered the rhyme '12 Little S-Boats', scrawled in Marriott's engine room register.

> *Twelve little S-boats 'go to it' like Bevin,*
> Starfish *goes a bit too far — then there were eleven.*
> *Eleven watchful S-boats doing fine and then*
> Seahorse *fails to answer — so there are ten.*
> *Ten stocky S-boats in a ragged line,*
> Sterlet *drops and stops out — leaving us nine.*
> *Nine plucky S-boats, all pursuing Fate,*
> Shark *is overtaken — now we are eight.*
> *Eight sturdy S-boats, men from Hants and Devon,*
> Salmon *now is overdue — and so the number's seven.*
> *Seven gallant S-boats, trying all their tricks,*
> Spearfish *tries a newer one — down we come to six.*
> *Six tireless S-boats fighting to survive,*
> *No reply from* Swordfish *— so we tally five.*
> *Five scrubby S-boats, patrolling close inshore,*
> Snapper *takes a short cut — now we are four.*
> *Four fearless S-boats, too far out to sea,*
> Sunfish *bombed and scrap-heaped — we are only three.*
> *Three threadbare S-boats patrolling o'er the blue,*
> *…*

Two ice-bound S-boats...

...

One lonely S-boat...

...

> *The survivors were HMS* Sealion
> *(scuttled), HMS* Seawolf *(broken up),*
> *and HMS* Sturgeon *(sold).*[9]

Young quotes this as an example of the fatalistic but far from defeatist humour that inspired most of *Sealion*'s crew. It was the best possible therapy. Young served under Lieutenant Commander Bryant, usually patrolling the Bay of Biscay area, until October 1941, when Bryant was posted to oversee the completion and working-up of the new S-boat HMS *Safari. Sealion* was ordered to Polyharnoe (now known as Polyarny), the Russian naval base down the river from the convoy destination port, Murmansk. Her duties were to stop vessels from occupied Norway supplying the German Army, and divert attention from the Allied convoys delivering military aid to Russia. Her new commanding officer was George Colvin, a career naval officer just a few years older than Young and a very different personality from Bryant. 'I grew to like him more than any other submariner I ever met,' wrote Young, simply.[10]

Their 1,500-mile voyage north from Scapa, in the teeth of a northerly gale, was a succession of mountainous seas and nights of misery. The weather eased slightly once they reached the Arctic circle, and the crew began to play card games and make models in their off-duty time. Colvin brought out his gros point tapestry, explaining that he found it 'creative, absorbing and soothing to the nerves'. The months in Polyharnoe were bleak and cold, relationships with Russian allies marked by unfriendliness and suspicion. They were glad when they were ordered home in late December 1941.

Sealion was instructed to pause for some days in the Lofoten Islands on her return voyage. In his 1952 memoir, Young does not explain that she was acting as a marker vessel for Operation *Anklet*, one of the British commando raids. Perhaps he wasn't told; perhaps it was one of those things that was better kept secret a little longer.

★★★

The commandos had been instigated immediately after the evacuation from Dunkirk and had been training hard, mainly in Scotland. The majority of volunteers for the commandos were selected from the former Independent Companies or from Territorial Units. Commandos retained their own regimental cap badges and remained on their regimental roll for pay.

Their first sorties were small, not overly successful raids against the French coast and the Channel Islands. By November 1940, when the immediate invasion threat had receded, some of the men who had been working to develop the clandestine Auxiliary Units could be recruited either into the commandos or the more irregular SOE. Quintin Riley was now stationed in Arisaig in the Scottish Highlands, where there were landing craft with which to practise. Lieutenant Commander Bill Fell was there too, along with other Norway specialists. Riley wrote to Andrew Croft, urging him to join them. 'The only way we shall beat the Germans is by offensive and for that we have got to have our own best men in the operations division [...] We shall not win the war by keeping men like you in Essex.'[11]

The first Norwegian raid on the Lofoten Islands had been Operation *Claymore* in March 1941. Men of 3 Commando, 4 Commando, Royal Engineers, a Norwegian Independent Company (under former actor and resistance leader Martin Linge), RN destroyers and troopships landed to attack the fish-oil processing plant, which was important to German production of glycerine (used for explosives). Prisoners were taken and more volunteers enlisted for the Norwegian forces in Britain. Sets of rotor wheels and code books for an Enigma machine were also seized.

Operation *Anklet* in December 1941, in which *Sealion* played her signposting role, was a second raid on the Lofoten Islands and achieved the capture of another Enigma machine. It was also a diversion for the more aggressive Operation *Archery* (the Vaagsoy and Måløy Raid), which took place at dawn the following day. This was another strike against fish-oil production and another opportunity to take prisoners, enlist volunteers and collect information. Casualties were quite high and retaliations harsh.

Later incursions were on a smaller scale or were carried out by the local resistance. The cumulative effect was to begin to convince

Hitler that the British were planning a reinvasion of Norway, a misconception that would be fostered as far as 1944, usefully diverting attention from the Normandy landings.

In February 1942, increasing anxiety about the likelihood of a full-scale British attack on Norway, plus the damage being inflicted by Allied bombing of the warships in the French Atlantic ports, persuaded Hitler and his advisers to order *Scharnhorst*, *Gneisenau* and *Prinz Eugen* to break out from Brest and make a dash up Channel home to Germany. HMS *Sealion* was there on patrol but missed the warships as they slipped through the narrow channels inside Ushant. This was effectively the last significant event for Young on board that hard-worked submarine. They returned to HMS *Forth* in Holy Loch and managed part of one final patrol before the defects that had accumulated over the submarine's thousands of miles of hard service finally put her out of action and her crew were dispersed to other boats.

★★★

David Howarth, meanwhile, had exchanged his flag lieutenant's aiguillettes for sea boots and fisherman's trousers. His new job was working with Major Leslie Mitchell of the SIS/SOE to provide accommodation, boat maintenance facilities and secure anchorage for the volunteer Norwegian crews and their fishing vessels that would establish a regular clandestine transport and communication service between Shetland and Norway. From June 1940, hundreds of boats had already crossed the northern North Sea carrying *Englandsfarere*, people escaping from the German occupation.

Units of the Norwegian armed forces were established in both Britain and Canada but there was also a need to support those who had remained behind: the patriots who were forming the Norwegian resistance movement. Weapons, money, supplies and people were to be delivered and refugees or endangered agents extricated. This operation became known as the Shetland Bus and its effect on morale in an occupied country may have been almost as significant as its practical benefits.

For the first two years of the service, these crossings were undertaken in a half-dozen of the sturdiest of the Norwegian fishing boats, mainly Møre cutters from the Ålesund area. They had to work under cover of darkness through the worst winter weather. Buffeting across 360–1,000 miles at a maximum 9 knots, often in ferocious gales, took an inevitable toll on these 50–70ft wooden vessels and their crews. Howarth established their initial base in the sheltered bay at Lunna Voe and requisitioned the big house there as headquarters. Additional accommodation was soon needed, together with ship-repair and engineering facilities and recreation for the men.

Later operations moved to Scalloway, where Howarth organised the construction of a slipway. The Norwegian crews were mainly fishermen or merchant sailors, profoundly independent, self-reliant characters. Neither Howarth nor Mitchell could order them to undertake operations: 'We could only consult the skippers and suggest how it might be done, and if they did not like it, they had to be free to say so.'[12]

Howarth could speak Norwegian, though not well enough to pass for anything other than English. His Cambridge degree was in physics and maths and his first job, before the BBC, had been designing circuits for the TV inventor John Logie Baird. It hadn't qualified him for disguising machine guns inside oil cans but when that became necessary, that was what he did. He caulked seams, applied antifouling, extracted the Norwegian sailors from trouble when they got drunk and did his utmost to obtain whatever equipment they told him they wanted. He filtered out some of the more unreasonable operational requests from London HQ and attempted to dissuade the skippers from taking extreme risks. The crews and their boats were incorporated as independent units within the Norwegian Navy but knew that if they were captured they were likely to be tortured or shot, not treated as prisoners of war. They lost 45 of their original 48 volunteers, but more came to take their places.

Howarth was deeply impressed by their courage and found it difficult to accept that he, as a naval officer, could not accompany them. He knew he would put them in greater danger, particularly if they had to escape overland. His spoken Norwegian was not fluent and he possessed too much information. 'No one was trusted to keep his secrets if the Gestapo really got to work on him and I certainly could not trust myself.'[13] His role was to do everything he could to support them and then endure the waiting until they returned – or didn't. Over the winter of 1942–1943, seven boats and 33 lives were lost. Howarth's job was made significantly easier – and the crossings safer – in October 1943 when the American Navy supplied the Shetland Bus with three fast, tough, well-armed submarine chasers, *Hitra*, *Vigra* and *Hessa*.[14] A further hundred journeys were achieved with no losses of ships or men.

By May 1945, the Shetland Bus had made 198 trips to Norway. It had transported 192 agents and 389 tons of weapons and supplies and brought out 73 agents and 373 refugees. Looking back, 40 years later, Howarth wondered whether his emollient management approach had been right: 'Was I really lacking in Officer-Like Qualities, lacking the guts to put my foot down and make unpopular decisions? I don't really think so but I suspect myself.' His final conclusion was that the operation had saved more lives than it destroyed, 'and that is the only bearable recollection one can have of a war'.[15]

14

'Mosquitoes with stings'[1]

1939–1942: Coastal Forces and the St-Nazaire Raid

The first string of fast patrol boats had been brought back to England from the Mediterranean in the late autumn of 1939. They had steamed north through the Rhône and the Saône, been towed through canals to the Seine and onwards via Paris to the Channel. There were six of them, built by the British Power Boat Company and carrying two 18in torpedoes, with three 600hp Napier engines. The other six were away in Hong Kong. But that was about all the Navy possessed then. The torpedo-bearing CMBs to which Childers had been attached in 1916, and which had raided Kronstadt so sensationally in 1919, had been forgotten and not replaced. The hundreds of WWI 80ft MLs supplied from America and driven by the young men of the RNVR had been sold as houseboats or left lying in the mud. They had patrolled, escorted, chased submarines, laid mines and attacked harbours. Yet, somehow, no one in the interwar Admiralty had considered that small high-powered vessels would be needed again. Vospers had designed some prototypes (George O'Brien Kennedy had worked on them) but there was little encouragement and no official purchases.

When, in 1938, the brilliant British designer and racing enthusiast Hubert Scott-Paine did develop a new 70ft seagoing MTB with three marinised Rolls-Royce Merlin engines, no orders came from the Admiralty. The boat went, as a patrol torpedo (PT) template, to Elco (Electric Launch Company) in America – whence it would need to be brought back, hastily. In the 1930s, British petrol engine production – and official interest – was focused on aero engines. It would take a while for the mental as well as the practical adjustments to be made. There was an additional problem when Italy entered the war on the side of Germany in June 1940 as she produced the Isotta Fraschini engines on which Vospers relied. The RAF had about a dozen high-speed rescue launches, such as those that had been ferrying Commander Clouston at Dunkirk, but they too were unprepared and underequipped when the Battle of Britain fighter pilots began dropping into the sea.

The Germans, meanwhile, had developed the 110ft diesel-engined *Schnellboote* – 'fast boats' – known to the British as E-boats. These well-armed, powerful raiders had speed, range and sea-kindly qualities that the British envied. They were round-hulled and built on aluminium frames, unlike the all-wood British vessels, which tended to return from action riddled with holes. Michael Gotelee, whose father Allan served in MGBs and MTBs, points out that this did at least make the British boats easy to repair – apply a sheet of plywood, glue and canvas and the vessel was ready to go out on patrol again. However, they were shockingly combustible. One engine room explosion in an MTB moored at HMS *Hornet* in Portsmouth blew crew members off the boat and reduced it in minutes to a blazing wreck, firing streams of shells while neighbouring boats scrambled to escape. When one of its compressed air cylinders (used to fire the torpedoes) exploded, debris was flung half a mile and a Wren working in the HMS *Hornet* office was killed. A year later, when Allan Gotelee was lying wounded in Haslar hospital, he heard the distant 'crump' as his boat, MGB *601*, exploded from the mix of gases in her fuel tanks.

When these wooden, petrol-driven vessels were hit in action, the results could be horrifying. In Peter Scott's book *The Battle of the Narrow Seas* (1945), former RNVSR member Kenneth Gemmell mentioned the emotional 'reaction' he felt after watching one of his flotilla mates sink in a raging inferno of flames – but he does not spell it out. 'We can only regret,' wrote Scott, 'that more interest was not taken in Diesels in this country during the pre-war years.'[2]

Robert Hichens felt more angry than regretful. Even before Dunkirk, his feeling of dedication was intense. Early in May 1940, he attended a small memorial service for colleagues and friends who had died in the minesweeper *Dunoon*. It was at this moment he determined to apply for transfer to the gunboats. He mourned Richard Hill, a fellow solicitor and RNVSR member who had been in his class at HMS *King Alfred*. Hill, dead at 28, would never know the joy of marriage and children. Hichens loved his family deeply but was also separating himself from them. In his diary, he explains how he found it necessary to blank off the past as a means of steeling himself 'for death at the worst or laborious days cut off from all I love at best'.[3] He pays his wife, Catherine, the compliment of assuming she will understand his need for intense narrow focus in order to act with reckless aggression. Much of his writing seems designed to explain his mindset to his young children.

Unlike the men on foreign service, those stationed around the British coast were often able to retain contact with their families. Though Hichens' home was in Cornwall, Catherine and the two boys would occasionally come to stay near the Felixstowe Coastal Forces base. He mentions being supplied with a bag of sweets by his youngest son Antony to take out on patrol.

Michael Gotelee and his mother lived for a while within earshot of the base. They could hear the flotillas roaring out on patrol in the evening, then, for Michael's mother at least, there was the long wait for sounds of return, some boats damaged, some missing. Life was less emotionally complex when they moved to live with Michael's grandparents near Surbiton. Michael has hundreds of letters written by his father to his mother during the war; their content unrevealing, eloquent merely through their quantity and continued existence.

Mollie Courtauld and her children remained at home in Essex where the children often slept in the cellar to avoid the bombs. In the summer of 1940, August finally escaped from intelligence work and eventually found a more congenial posting with Coastal Forces. Mollie seized opportunities to dash to Dover, Ramsgate, Rochester, Sheerness, Felixstowe, Glasgow, Troon and Weymouth for reunions away from home 'where life was routine dull, punctuated with moments of acute anxiety'.[4]

Robin Balfour remembered how reassuring it was, when heading north for an unsought, unwanted posting to HMS *Merlin* in Donibristle, to find the wife of one of his pre-war RCC friends travelling up on the same train to join her husband.

★★★

The first flotilla of MTBs was established at HMS *Beehive* in Felixstowe in January 1940 and was joined by the somewhat miscellaneous and 'experimental' 6th Flotilla in March. While the enemy coast was still Germany, there was little that they could do apart from act as rescue launches and trot boats. From May 1940, though, things began to change. With the enemy less than 40 miles away it was suddenly obvious that Childers' analysis was as valid as it might have been in 1903: 'What you want is boats – mosquitoes with stings – swarms of them – patrol-boats, scout-boats, torpedo-boats, intelligent irregulars manned by local men with a pretty free hand to play their own game.' This style of small boat warfare would become the quintessential arena for many of the WWII yachtsmen volunteers. Initially, however, the inadequate, unreliable equipment created difficulty for keen officers. John Cameron – an RNVSR member from the East Scottish division – describes his experience in command of an 'experimental' 40ft MTB at Dunkirk: 'My boat was experimental, possessing one propeller, no reverse gear and a turning circle of the phenomenal diameter which made manoeuvring in a confined space a matter of extreme delicacy.' The engine started by means of compressed air. It was very temperamental. 'Consequently once this thunderous piece of marine ironmongery had been set in motion we were loath to stop it.'

On the last night of the evacuation, Cameron's MTB had been towed over by the destroyer HMS *Shikari*. He had been waiting in the darkness outside the harbour in order to take off crews (or pick up survivors) from the three elderly blockships, which were to be sunk to seal the entrance when all vessels had finally left. Destroyers, minesweepers and troop transports hurried past him. 'As my little craft rocked in their troubled wakes I found myself meditating rather ruefully on the strange chance that had brought me, a settled barrister of 40, to be a witness of so stupendous a scene.'[5]

After the occupations of Holland, Belgium and France were complete, the 'other side' was scarcely more than a couple of hours' fast motoring. Once the E-boats were established in their new ports, they were easily able to attack East Coast convoys then retreat at speed. The damage was considerable. Nicholas Monsarrat, stationed in Harwich from 1942, characterised this coast as 'a mass of winking green wreck buoys' and Peter Scott described actions in the southern

UNCOMMON COURAGE

North Sea and the Channel as 'a battle in the new, wide sense of the word, which, like the battle of the Atlantic, lasted for years without pause, a battle of initiative and individuality and great dash'. He called it the Battle of the Narrow Seas.

Initially, this was a battle with very few boats and led by 'regular' RN officers. By the end of 1940 and the early months of 1941, however, many of the yachtsmen would find themselves called away from their anti-submarine patrol and minesweeping duties and redeployed to make even more direct use of their boathandling skills. Many of the newly available craft had been supplied by last-minute individual enterprise. At Brooklands in Surrey, for instance, sportscar manufacturer Noel Macklin had read an article about the lack of small boats for the Navy and was inspired to turn his garage at Cobham Fairmile into an assembly site for motor launches. Macklin had served in the RNVR during the latter part of WWI and his son Lance (b. 1919), a future racing driver, would soon volunteer for the WWII RNVR.

The Fairmile designs were kept simple and 'hard chine' (panelled rather than rounded) so the boats could be assembled in non-specialist yards. Belatedly, the Admiralty supplied the necessary capital for the company to expand. By 1940, the wooden Fairmile motor launches, gunboats and torpedo boats were being produced all over the country and abroad (especially Canada). Peter Scott reports some being produced by a pre-war piano manufacturer. Scott-Paine's personal advocacy (and money) also stimulated development of fast fighting boats in America and Canada but it was many months before supply began to match demand or suitable engines and armaments could be found.

Small by Navy standards, the Fairmile B MLs were 112ft – three or four times as long as most people's cruising yachts – and the Fairmile C Motor Gunboats were 110ft, whereas the Masbys (British Power Boat Company's MASB, 'Motor Anti-Submarine Boats'), which were converted to the first MTBs, were 70ft.

Additional MTB and ML shore bases were established as the numbers of boats and their functions expanded. These were often named for stinging insects: HMS *Wasp* was in Dover; *Mantis* in Lowestoft; *Midge* Great Yarmouth; *Cicala* in the River Dart. When my uncle, Jack Jones, joined Coastal Forces in the summer of 1941, he was posted to HMS *Forward II*, soon to be straightforwardly renamed HMS *Aggressive*.

In late October 1940, Robert Hichens was finally transferred from the minesweeper HMS *Niger* to HMS *Osprey* at Portland, where he was involved in overseeing the redevelopment of one of the British Power Boat launches from an anti-submarine vessel to a gunboat. There was a delay in sourcing suitable engines so Hichens was sent on as a training officer to the newly formed HMS *St Christopher* at Fort William in Scotland. His diary entries for the days around Christmas 1940 (reproduced in his son Antony's biography *Gunboat Command*) offer a memorable account of his dash northwards from Milford Haven to Fort William in HM *MASB 14*, cold, wet but also exhilarated. The hard-chined hulls had been designed by Hubert Scott-Paine and TE Lawrence to enable the vessel to ride up and plane on her own bow wave. In any sort of heavy sea, however, the bumping came as an unpleasant shock:

> *You see a big sea coming up ahead. You have the sickening sharp drop, followed by the sudden shock, bending your knees and making you hold on hard. All this is almost instantly followed by a shower of cold water which lands on your head as you crouch in the dustbin.*[6]

There's a horrifying anecdote of a seaman who went below into the forecabin of one of these boats during a rough passage. He fell and injured himself so he could not move: by the time he was found, he had been battered to death.

Hichens remained furious at the lack of effective provision. Two years into the war, feeling scarred by battles for equipment that were almost as hard-fought as enemy engagements, he had happened to look into a 1938 edition of *Jane's Fighting Ships*. There, he saw an advertisement for exactly the fast, rugged, torpedo boat – the E-boats – that he and his fellows were struggling to challenge in their inferior underequipped craft.

> *And here it all was laid out for us in Jane's. Come see, come buy! The Admiralty could have bought as many E-boats as they wished, and indeed were pressed to do so, but one short year before the outbreak of war. Well, well! Talk about visiting the sins of the fathers upon the children! The sins of our elders' omissions certainly pressed heavily on the fighting young. I wondered gloomily whether anybody had been*

sacked or even censured for not taking the most elementary interest in
the preparation of our country for war in the sphere of the fast surface
craft.[7]

The RN commanding officer at HMS *St Christopher* had pressed
Hichens to remain. For the next few years, *St Christopher* would be
a crucial training centre for many types of vessels in the extensive
preparations for D-Day. Hichens refused. As soon as he could, he
was back down south and taking command of the newly re-engined
MGB 64. He was the first RNVR officer to be appointed to a
fighting flotilla. The second RNVR appointment, East Coast
yachtsman Allan Gotelee, was also a solicitor. Both men were over
30, which made them old for their job, as well as being 'amateurs',
and they were aware of some initial scepticism concerning their
ability. Edward Young, who would become the first British RNVR
officer appointed to command a submarine, would not be able to
avoid noticing the disappointment on the face of his chief engineer
when he spotted the wavy lines on Young's uniform sleeve. Whereas
Young could afford to be understanding (by this time, he had his
new and beautiful submarine HMS *Storm*), Hichens, infuriated by
the inadequate weaponry on offer and battling for better equipment
and strategies, was ready to be derisive in return. 'We had discovered
the term "state-educated" to our great delight and used it invariably
when referring to our straight-striped brethren; a friendly dig at
our friends but more than a touch of bitterness when referring to
our enemies.'[8]

However genuinely many of the volunteer yachtsmen responded
to the spirit and traditions of the RN, they may have been quite
difficult to deal with on occasion. 'Temporaries' like Hichens,
Seligman, Dalzel-Job, Howarth and Nevil Shute could afford to
be impatient, independent or occasionally defiant, without risking
their longer-term future. Equally, they might find their suggestions
rejected time and again, possibly for the same reason.

Arthur Bennett, too, been sent north to HMS *St Christopher*
in midwinter. It was early in 1941 and he was in charge of a 72ft
Harbour Defence Motor Launch (HDML), which he was expecting
to take on to the Mediterranean. The commander asked him to stay,
also as a training officer.

Then he offered me a sherry and introduced me to some of the base staff.

'I take it, sir, we're allowed to use the mess when we come ashore?' I asked.

The commander turned to his chief training officer, 'That's alright, I suppose?'

'Why yes,' came the reply in a supercilious drawl. 'So long as he doesn't come too often.'[9]

Bennett soon saw that the *St Christopher's* training system was inadequate when it was needed to deal with larger numbers of people. He worked out a new system 'but it was too revolutionary and crossed too many people's bows'. It was rejected and Bennett applied again to be sent away on operational service. The Admiralty rejected this as well: 'He appears to be eminently suited to his present appointment and must stay where he is' – a reply that Bennett found ironic.

In February 1941, Hichens, now finally in possession of MGB 64, with inadequate guns but three powerful Rolls-Royce engines (sourced via Packard in the USA), was sent down Channel to Fowey for some Navy-run flotilla training. They 'thrashed about' in open waters practising the important skill of keeping station, yet Hichens soon began to consider that too much of this time was spent learning and obeying traditional flag signals, instead of developing appropriate tactics for high-speed, close-action night fighting. He was also critical of the RN officers' tendency to ruin boat engines by leaping in and roaring away when cold, instead of easing them up to full power. His personal experience driving and maintaining his own Le Mans racing car had taught him a great deal about the care as well as the best use of high-powered engines.

In action, everything could be sacrificed. Allan Gotelee sent Peter Scott an account of one engagement, fought off Brown Ridge, a favourite spot for the Felixstowe MGBs to lie in wait for E-boats. It lasted 55 minutes and ended with the British boats pursuing the Germans back to Ijmuiden.

To the lasting credit of Rolls-Royce engines, the action was fought at full throttle for the whole time, and in the middle of it, my motor mechanic crawled up to me in the dustbin and said, 'For God's sake stop, sir.' I asked why, being extremely incensed at the time, and he said, 'You have been running your engines on full throttle for so long that all the dynamos are on fire. Give me two minutes and I will pull the leads out.' This he did without turning a hair and the party continued. By the time we had finished one of my Browning guns was white hot.[10]

The men going out to sea every night on these Spitfire-engined attack vessels were living a very extraordinary life. Robert Hichens described the new high-octane existence that was achieved from later in 1941.

This feeling of utter physical and mental exhaustion has to be felt to be understood. I do not believe that the majority of people have ever experienced it. I certainly had not until I operated gunboats. The last few hours as the light makes, the tension of night station-keeping relaxed, searching the horizon for a landfall (on the East Coast always a buoy) are always the worst of all. [...] Shapes appear whenever you look on the horizon and you have to keep telling yourself 'I'm only seeing that' because after you have experienced the reality you know it is different from the images. When you are ashore and it is all over the relaxation is complete and overwhelming. You feel quite a different person, either stupidly happy over a drink or irritable and depressed, small difficulties seeming desperate and insurmountable. One's natural stability is largely gone.[11]

They drank to relax. Looking back, Michael Gotelee realised how astonishingly cheap the Navy gin had been, and how strong the whisky. One of the personal moments of illumination I experienced when reading *We Fought Them in Gunboats* (the memoir that Hichens dedicated to the RNVR and Hostilities Only crews and left unfinished at his death) was the proper context for a Coastal Forces Mark VIII cocktail.

We were all dead tired. I had slumped into a half recumbent posture on the wardroom settee and shut my eyes:
   'What will you have, sir?'
   'Oh, anything or everything, Kelly,' I replied without looking up.
   Kelly took me at my word. He picked up a gin bottle in one hand and a rum bottle in the other and poured in a liberal dose simultaneously. Then he picked up lemon squash and orange squash and applied them also together, finishing off with water.

Thus was born the flotilla's famous Mark VIII, I can recommend it as a delicious drink and a remarkable reviver.

My father, who spent the final two years of his war in HMS *Badger*, just across the river from HMS *Beehive*, used to serve this innocent-tasting concoction at his birthday party. As a young teenager it was an annual revelation to discover just how badly normally respectable adults could behave when they'd inadvertently gulped a few too many. That was in peacetime. The attitudes expressed in *We Fought Them in Gunboats* may not be comfortable reading now but ring absolutely true for that time then. This is a fighter's story, written during the actuality of battle. 'Hitch' (his radio call-sign became his nickname) told his crews:

There was no easy way out for gunboats. If we were to have success we must fight for it. I told them plainly that I intended to seek out and engage the enemy; that unless their guns continued to fire and fire straight, it would be they who were killed and not the enemy. The alternatives were success or death.[12]

His account conveys thrill, horror, insight, anger, intolerance, pity, pride and beauty. The gunboat's engines snarl and roar; the mariners' eyes sting red with wind and salt; the North Sea nights are dark and quiet until they erupt in streams of coloured tracer; curling plumes of spray; blistering oily flame; the rattle of machine guns and crump of explosive charge; an airman's half-inflated rubber dinghy, which retains only entrails and a contaminating smell. It's a book written on Benzedrine, gin and vitamin pills by a man who had everything to live for but didn't expect to survive. Peter Scott, David Cobb and others would later express in art what Hichens conveys in words:

The eager up thrust of the bows, the sweeping run lost to sight behind the sharp rising pressure wave, the far-flung arc of spray flying back from beneath the forefoot, the steadily rising plume up driven from the thrusting propellers, gleaming white and transparent in the moonlight, like some enormous fountain in a fairy story of giant land, the impermeable [sic] yet never-ending tracery of the interlacing wash, the sharp points and glints of light from the black gun barrels.[13]

Scott, who became the first historian of Coastal Forces, had joined later than Hichens and many of the other yachtsmen. He'd served his time, with increasing success, as first lieutenant on HMS *Broke* (one of the first RNVR officers to have achieved such promotion) and was hoping for a destroyer command. While he waited, he was told about the new steam gunboats that were being developed as more effective antagonists to the E-boats. They would be better armed than the MGBs, better-engined and built of metal, not wood. Scott accepted the command of SGB 9 *Grey Goose,* joined Coastal Forces and was leading his flotilla in Baie-de-la-Seine on the night of 13 April 1943 when Hichens' death was announced on the nine o'clock news. Their patrol that night was quiet and Scott had time to think about the friend he had sailed against in those peacetime days of International 14 dinghy racing. Two weeks later, he took the chance of a BBC Postscript to describe Hichens' qualities of leadership and the confidence he instilled in others. It had not all been about equipment. His self-belief had been inspirational: 'It developed the spirit which put our Coastal Forces on top whenever they met the enemy, by virtue not of their guns but of their determination.'

★★★

Neither Hitch nor Scott was present at Operation *Chariot,* the raid on St-Nazaire in March 1942. This was a Combined Ops undertaking when ML (Motor Launch) flotillas, trained at HMS *St Christopher,* would work together with commando units, also trained in north-west Scotland. St-Nazaire was an important harbour, as both a refuge and supply base for U-boats and possessing a large enough dock to accommodate the battleship *Tirpitz.* Early in 1942, when *Tirpitz* was reported ready for action, it seemed essential to try to close this potential bolthole by damaging the Normandie Dock sufficiently to render it unusable. An expendable Town-class destroyer, HMS *Campbeltown,* was disguised, adapted and filled with commandos and explosives. She was to be escorted over the shallows, rammed into the dock gates and scuttled. The commandos would leap ashore, causing as much local destruction as possible, then later (ideally when the invaders were all safely away) the explosives buried deep inside her would detonate. Her escort would be a dozen MLs, mainly under RNVR command. They had to bluff their way up the Loire, as close as possible to the harbour, before triggering its defences. They would be carrying more commandos and intending to cause additional damage and confusion. The MLs were also expected to take the destroyer's crew and the commandos away when their job was done – though this would prove seriously unrealistic. A motor torpedo boat (MTB 74) was armed to attack the dock gates. This group was led by MGB 314 and her French-speaking commanding officer Dunstan Curtis, formerly of the RNVSR. The senior naval commander was Robert Ryder (of *Tai-mo-Shan* and *Penola*) and the commandos were led by Colonel Charles Newman.

The raiders had left Falmouth in sunshine on 26 March, with an escort of fighters, two destroyers and two journalists, Gordon Holman and Edward Gillings. Everyone had made their wills and written their last letters. The weather was good as they reached out into the Atlantic almost unobserved except, possibly, by a U-boat, which was depth-charged by one of the accompanying destroyers. Later, it was felt necessary to sink two French fishing boats. Curtis, a former lawyer who'd studied at the Sorbonne, appears to have managed this with a degree of charm. He ran MGB *314* alongside, explaining, '*Je regrette, Monseiur le Patron, mais il va falloir vous embarquer et couler votre bateau.*' '*Eh bien, si c'est necessaire,*' replied the fisherman. '*Pouvons nous apporter nos biens?*' Curtis said yes and later described their strange collection of old blankets, half-cooked fish, a large fishing net and a basin of potatoes. Presumably, the fishermen and their '*biens*' were later put ashore from one of the destroyers that wasn't entering the Loire.[14]

Lieutenant Tom Boyd RNVR, commanding ML *160*, recalled the sweet smell of the countryside as they steamed up the river. He was the son of a Yorkshire trawler owner, had joined the RNVR early in 1940 and would return to the family business afterwards. Boyd had been keeping his crew busy by emptying the deck petrol tanks, fitting hand steering and laying out the medical equipment, as much to calm his own nerves as theirs. He describes how his initial nervousness wore off once they were nearing their destination. '"This is a queer do," I said to my coxswain. "It'll soon be a bloody sight queerer sir," was his answer.'

It was getting dark as they continued up the Loire. In MGB *314*, Dunstan Curtis had been provided with a ready-to-use German naval signal, seized during Operation *Archery*. When he was challenged, he was able to reply that he was proceeding up harbour in accordance with previous instructions. The RAF had mounted a diversionary air raid but by 1:30am the raiders' bluff had been called and the violent, destructive battle began. The old destroyer *Campbeltown* increased to her maximum speed as her helmsman was killed and her replacement helmsman wounded. To Lieutenant Tom Boyd, she 'looked glorious as she tore through the smoke and bursting shells and dashed straight into the lock gates'.[15] As he glanced astern, he saw 'the MLs replying very gamely to the fire from the shore and felt very sad at heart as I saw boat after boat hit and crash into flames or blow up'. The RNVSR yachtsmen EH Beart (ML *267*), TAM Collier (ML *457*) and IB Henderson (ML *306*) were among those who died that day. In all, 215 commandos became prisoners of war (including Colonel Newman) and a large number of German (and some French) people were killed, including some unfortunate Organisation Todt conscripted labourers.

The planning had been thorough. Boyd remembered feeling relief that he was so at home in the river, both as they arrived and, more importantly, when they needed to get away. River features appeared as he expected and he blessed the model that they'd studied so assiduously in the days before the operation. 'I think that model saved my life.'[16] His account is always human and emotional, laughing at the mistakes he made in the heat of the moment and repeating to himself, 'By God we're still alive!' Boyd's ML *160* achieved an extraordinary rescue of commandos and crew from the burning ML *443*, after which he thought it was time to leave. He was under heavy fire with most of his crew and passengers wounded and one engine out of action and wondered briefly about stealing a fishing boat to get them all home. There was a frightening moment on the return journey when Boyd mistook two British destroyers for enemy ships in the early morning light and threw all his charts and confidential books overboard in case of capture. ML *160* was one of only three of the 12 MLs to make it back to Falmouth, with an hour's petrol left in her tank.

Last to leave St-Nazaire was Dunstan Curtis' MGB *314*. Riddled with bullets and with almost everyone on board wounded, she had eventually to be sunk in mid-Channel, together with three more of the most severely damaged MLs. Her survivors were transferred to the destroyer HMS *Cleveland,* which came to meet them. Writing his later account for Peter Scott, Curtis describes MGB *314* as a mass of bullet holes, her dead gunner lying where he'd fallen and everyone wounded: 'Below decks there was a mass of groaning men. We could show no light down there until the shell holes had been blocked, otherwise we should have been spotted, so, to begin with, Holman and the Cox'n did their best, by the light of a dim torch, to help the wounded.'[17]

Gordon Holman was one of the journalists who'd travelled with the raiders. In his book, published the following year, Holman does not mention 'groaning men'. An official journalist was expected to produce positive reporting: if fighters are wounded, they are stoic, cheerful and gallant. He expressed his sadness, however, at the sinking of MGB *314* and the other MLs. It was, he says, 'a melancholy sight … the four heroic little vessels, abandoned and still, being shot out of the sea by our own guns.'[18] Of the 611 men who undertook the raid, 228 returned to Britain (many of them wounded), 169 were killed and 215 became prisoners of war. Holman quoted the Commander-in-Chief, Plymouth's report: 'Taking into consideration the extreme vulnerability of the coastal craft, neither the losses in men nor materials can be considered excessive for the results achieved.'[19]

15

'The very splash of the surf and the bubble of the tides'[1]

1940–1944: Crossings to Brittany

When MGB *314* was scuttled on her way home from St-Nazaire, she was less than a year old and at the end of a brief, adventurous career. She was a Fairmile C gunboat, not the most popular or numerous of their designs, therefore perhaps a little more likely to be made available for risky one-off operations. In the months before the raid, MGB *314* and Lieutenant Commander Dunstan Curtis had been running a surreptitious shuttle service to the French coast. As far as the Navy List was concerned, Curtis was attached to HMS *St Christopher*. In fact, he was working for the Special Operations Executive and Secret Intelligence Service, collecting and delivering agents across the Channel.

Back in the summer of 1940, as the Nazi invasion had swept in from the east, the coast of Brittany had become the final point from which small boats could reach England. In the shock of defeat and facing the reality of occupation, individuals and families had to make extraordinarily hard decisions and were torn by conflicting loyalties. General Charles de Gaulle, undersecretary for war, had refused to accept the Armistice with Germany and had left for London. On 18 June, he appealed to his countrymen to fight on. This was broadcast by the BBC on 22 June. Meanwhile, Madame de Gaulle and their children were believed to be in Carentec, a fishing and boatbuilding village in the department of Finistère. An RAF Walrus (an amphibious aircraft) carrying Major Hope of the SIS set out to retrieve them but was never heard from again. Months later, it was discovered to have crashed in fog. All three crew were killed. A Belgian yachtsman, also working for the SIS, and who had joined the RNVR, was next to set out in a fast motor torpedo boat from Plymouth. He arrived at Carentec on 20 June but discovered there were German troops in the village and that the de Gaulle family had left. Yvonne de Gaulle had borrowed some money, taken her family to Brest and found spaces on the last transport to leave before the town was bombed later that same day.

These were among the first of many rescue attempts undertaken by individual aircraft or small boats between Brittany and south-west England over the coming years. There were also intelligence-related trips – complex and dangerous. Several agencies in England needed current information about happenings in France: de Gaulle's Deuxième Bureau, the British SIS (MI6) and SOE were just three of them. Agents were landed, taken off, supplied, their families evacuated. Reports were collected, supplies delivered and escape routes established. The organisations were often mutually suspicious and competing with each other for available transport. When MGB *314* was made available to Captain Francis Slocum, the NID officer trying to co-ordinate these clandestine missions, she was a godsend. There was already an eclectic assortment of requisitioned fishing boats in the Helford River, refugee fishermen in Newlyn, a Free French group in Mylor Creek and the theoretical possibility of borrowing an MGB from Coastal Forces in Dartmouth. Very occasionally, a submarine might be made available.

When Edward Young had joined HMS *Sealion* in autumn 1941, one of their first tasks had been to rendezvous with a fishing vessel, identify the agent on board and collect important secret documents. Young recalled that the fishing vessel was to identify herself by letting her sails flap and sending a man up the mast. On the day of the mission, the wind had fallen light and the sails of the entire fleet were slatting lazily from side to side. Once they had finally spotted the most likely boat and night had fallen, *Sealion* surfaced and the SIS operative (Breton refugee turned RNVR officer Daniel Lomenech) went across in a collapsible canoe. He identified the agent. *Sealion* closed the fishing vessel and the handover of the documents was achieved with an exchange of Scotch and a bottle of wine to cement goodwill. Meanwhile, another boat had been observed drifting suspiciously close. Goodbyes were hurried and the submarine withdrew into the darkness.

In 1941, the RN had a direct interest in allowing something as valuable as *Sealion* to be used for intelligence activity: the two fast battlecruisers *Scharnhorst* and *Gneisenau* were still holed up in Brest, posing a major threat to convoys in the Atlantic should they emerge again. Reports from onshore agents were invaluable. Robert Alaterre, the agent carrying documents on the fishing vessel that night, was a former Embassy archivist, now working with the 'Johnny' network. This resistance group watched German shipping movements, monitored damage from the bombing raids and passed their information to London. During this period, more information was sent by paper (or even pigeon) than via wireless due to the lack of equipment and trained operators.

In October 1941, agent Joël le Tac and wireless operator Alain de Kergorlay were landed at Aber Benoît by Lieutenant Commander Gerry Holdsworth RNVR, using an RAF rescue launch and two folding canoes. That had been in October and, even then, experienced former ocean-racing and RCC yachtsman Holdsworth had considered the launch to have been at the limit of her endurance. Using folding canoes to land the agents had also been difficult as de Kergorlay had found it impossible to balance in the choppy seas and had only survived by being lashed to the canoe, which was paddled by le Tac. Then, at Christmas, le Tac had radioed London requesting pick-up for himself and three other agents. A new radio operator was needed as de Kergorlay had been arrested and his transmissions compromised.[2] It was then that MGB 314 and Dunstan Curtis were offered on loan from Combined Operations. Some St-Nazaire specialists have begun to wonder whether this helpful offer had any connection to the advance planning for Operation *Chariot*, but nothing has been proved.

The new team made their first crossing on 31 December 1941. The BBC broadcast the phrase '*Alfred de Musset est un grand poète*' to alert the waiting agents and the rendezvous took place at Île Guennoc, near Saint-Pabu, Finistère. Dinghies were able to be used instead of folding canoes, one agent was collected and a second wireless set was delivered, together with an operator, Pierre Moureaux (though he too was arrested on 2 February 1942). On 6 January, the BBC included the phrase '*Aide-toi et le Ciel t'aidera*', announcing the return of MGB 314 and Curtis to Aber Benoît. This time, their rendezvous was with a fishing boat. Seven passengers boarded, including Joël and Yves le Tac and the Jewish SIS agent Joseph Scheinmann (aka André Peulevey). All three were returned to the same area by Curtis and MGB 314 on 25 January. Both le Tac and Scheinmann were arrested within a couple of weeks of landing. They were sent to

Natzweiler-Struthof concentration camp and then Dachau. Both survived and were liberated in April 1945.

I wonder how much officers like Curtis knew about the people they were carrying and what happened to them? Probably very little. The rules in well-run intelligence organisations were rigid about limiting the casual dissemination of information. There was usually an SIS or SOE conducting officer on board, responsible for checking credentials and asking the crucial questions. In this case it was Holdsworth. Curtis' responsibility was for his ship, making the rendezvous unobserved, then facilitating the dangerous embarkations in the dark, off the rock-strewn coastline with strong tides running and the breaking surf. Later in 1942, Curtis would be awarded the DSC for his daring as he led the flotilla into St-Nazaire, bluffing their way in and shooting it out again, yet these secret night-time drop-offs to pinpoint locations on the French coast had required considerable boat-handling ability as well as extreme level-headedness.

Curtis (b. 1910) had joined the RNVSR in March 1937. He was the son of Arthur and Elizabeth Curtis – a schools' inspector and a head teacher. Curtis had a French nurse when he was small and gained the nickname 'Froggy' because of his French accent when at prep school. Later, he attended Eton, then Oxford. Afterwards, he continued his education in Vienna and at the Sorbonne and qualified as a solicitor (another lawyer!). When the journalist Gordon Holman observed him having a nap in the wardroom of MGB *314* before Operation *Chariot*, he noticed the 'small but well-stocked bookcase [...] which revealed the owner as a man of wide interests'.[3]

On 12 February, Curtis and MGB *314* returned again to Finistère (to the beach of Moulin de la Rive, 1½ miles west-south-west of Locquirec). He landed two British SOE agents and attempted to take off agents Pierre de Vomécourt and Mathilde Carré (aka 'La Chatte'). The weather that night was particularly poor – a fact that was helping the escaped German battleships that were now at the far end of the Channel and closing their home waters. MGB *314*'s dinghies capsized in the rough sea off the beach and the French agents were unable to board. Carré's luggage was soaked and she was apparently furious. Officers from the German Abwehr had been watching (one of them possibly her current lover) and the British agents Abbott and Redding were both captured (both survived.)

A fortnight later, on 25 February, Curtis and MGB *314* returned to Pointe de Bihit and collected Carré and de Vomécourt successfully. Once again, the operation was observed by the Abwehr. Mathilde 'La Chatte' (alias Victoire) was a resistance agent who had been arrested, threatened, turned against her former colleagues but then, apparently, turned back by de Vomécourt. It's unclear who she was working for when she boarded MGB *314*. Once she reached London, she was interrogated, used for a while as a double (or was it treble?) agent, then imprisoned for the rest of the war. There were no further landings in Brittany until Curtis and MGB *314* returned on 28 March, leading the flotilla in the approach to St-Nazaire.

★★★

MGB *314* had made one other crossing in the early months of 1942, which seems dubious in retrospect and was controversial at the time. From 22 June 1941, Britain and the Soviet Union had become allies. It was never an easy relationship and when Stalin asked Britain to assist with the infiltration of NKVD agents in Europe, many (of the few) people in the know were strongly opposed. Churchill and the SOE, however, were prepared to co-operate. A dozen agents were to be parachuted into France under the code name Operation *Pickaxe*.[4] When the first of them arrived – 26-year-old Szyfra Lypszyc/Anna Semenovna Ouspenskaya/'Hanna' – she was discovered to be highly nervous and with thyroid problems. Parachuting was not an option. She spoke French with a strong Russian accent, was a convinced Communist and had a suicide tablet hidden in her lipstick. She'd been given 21,000 francs, a revolver and a new identity as Jeannette Dupont. Curtis delivered her from Dartmouth to Lannion Bay, Côtes du Nord, Brittany on 10 January 1942. Her mission was to link up with other networks and pass information back, but SOE heard nothing more from her.

The scuttling of MGB *314* at the end of March 1942 was a setback for the cross-Channel couriers. *Sealion* had been withdrawn and redeployed. The Free French group in Newlyn had ceased functioning after key vessels had been lost and Gerry Holdsworth's SOE group in the Helford River had only a small RAF launch and a clutch of fishing vessels under their own command. They were, however, an adventurous, unorthodox group of yachtsmen and made the most of their talent for improvisation. A key member of the group, Francis Brooks Richards, would become the chronicler of many clandestine missions, both from south-west England to Brittany and, later, from Algiers. The first published hint of his activities comes in a paragraph from the RNVR news section of *Yachting Monthly*, January 1941: 'A narrow escape. During the intensified mining operations recently carried out round our coasts the Admiralty regrets to announce the loss of the trawler HMT *Sevra* in the command of T/Sub-Lieutenant FB Richards RNVR. There were no casualties.'[5]

Temporary Sub-Lieutenant Francis Brooks Richards (b. 1918) was 22 years old and from Southampton. He'd suffered a slipped disc as a teenager, which had excused him from school sport. Instead, he'd become interested in yacht design. In 1936, he'd designed his own 22-ton cutter and had her built by Percy Mitchell at Port Mellon, Cornwall. He'd named her *Windfall*. As he was only 18 at the time, perhaps that's what she was. In the previous year, however, Richards had been cited as the designer of another Port Mellon yacht, the 12-ton *Duquesne*, built for Cornish yachtsman WB Luard, an ocean-racing enthusiast, maritime novelist and a regular contributor to *Yachting Monthly*. He'd served as a submariner in the WWI Navy and had been invalided out with tuberculosis of the hip. It was deeply frustrating when Luard was refused a return to the service in 1939. Richards, though, a generation younger, was quickly accepted into the RNVR and sent minesweeping.

When Richards was posted to Falmouth in the autumn of 1940 and given command of HMT *Sevra*, he got in touch with Luard. The older man asked whether he might come out and perhaps write an article about the process of clearing magnetic mines. The date was 5 November 1940 and the mine they encountered at the entrance to Falmouth Harbour was acoustic, not magnetic. HMT *Sevra* was sunk and Richards was taken to hospital with a broken leg. When Luard came to visit him, he put forward an idea that they might write a paper together about the Breton fishing vessels, suggesting their potential for maintaining clandestine links between Cornwall and Brittany. Luard had already taken an educated guess at the nature of the comings and goings from nearby Mylor Creek, where 'Biffy'

Dunderdale of the SIS was using French fishing boats to support the 'Johnny' network. The ulterior motive for Luard's paper was to register his and Richards' interest in getting involved.

By an extraordinary coincidence, the accident to *Sevra* on 5 November 1940 had been observed by another keen pre-war yachtsman, Gerry Holdsworth, who was prospecting the area with much the same idea. Before the war, Holdsworth, a member of the RCC, had undertaken unofficial reconnaissance expeditions similar to August Courtauld (*Duet*) and Frank Carr (*Cariad*). Unlike them however, Holdsworth had joined the Army Intelligence Corps rather than the RNVR when war broke out. He'd been attached to Section D (the forerunner of SOE) for undercover work in Scandinavia but had been redeployed when his experience as a yachtsman had been discovered.[6]

The SOE was a very new organisation and although cross-Channel water transport was supposed to be shared between the secret services, Holdsworth was convinced that SIS and Free French needs would always be prioritised so had decided to collect a few boats exclusively for SOE use. Admiral Kitson (naval officer-in-charge, Falmouth) gave the necessary permission for the establishment of the Helford River base and Holdsworth began to accumulate vessels. He was working on the same principles laid out by Luard and Richards: choose vessels of precisely the right type to blend with local craft then undertake clandestine missions almost in full view.

The paper gained Luard a recall to service, initially as a volunteer attached to the NID and later properly paid with the rank of lieutenant commander. He was to work for Francis Slocum in the Operations Centre, facilitating SIS liaison with the RAF. Understanding the movements of fishing vessels as the Occupation forces imposed different local restrictions on which types of vessel could fish, in addition to normal seasonal variations, was a specialist job; essential if such vessels were to be used for covert meetings or if they needed to be discreetly cleared from an area in advance of some sensitive operation. Luard organised air reconnaissance and escorts for individual missions and used his yachting experience to provide the RAF with improved lifesaving equipment and tidal drift handbooks if they were shot down and needed to take to their dinghies at sea.

Richards was initially sent back to continue minesweeping but eventually managed to persuade the authorities that he wanted to transfer to 'Special Services'. In September 1941, he was posted to the Helford River, as second-in-command to Holdsworth. His first operation was as navigator in the requisitioned RAF launch. Their mission was to collect reports from the Free French 'Interallie' group via the fishing boat *Pourquoi-Pas?* The weather was good, they had 'Pierre', an experienced Breton tunny fisherman with them; they collected the package of documents and were back in the Helford River in time for breakfast.

Over the months to come, Holdsworth's group acquired an eclectic anchorage-full of vessels – including Walter Runciman's 195ft three-masted topsail schooner *Sunbeam II* as the depot ship, *Mutin*, a 60-ton yawl (ex-French Navy training ship), *Denise-Louise*, a motor long-liner from Honfleur, the *RAF 360* and two yacht dinghies.

The inclusion of *Pourquoi-Pas?*, a fishing boat from the Sibiril boatyard in Carentec, represented the first in what Richards describes as 'a remarkable series of escapes' where that family-run boatyard constructed new vessels behind a hidden panel, juggled official identification numbers and over the course of the war facilitated the departure of between 150 and 200 people on unregistered vessels. Twelve volunteer naval ratings – peacetime fishermen and yacht hands – were sent from Sparrow's Nest in Lowestoft as crew. From the NID, Ian Fleming identified a Guernsey boatman (and part-time smuggler) John Newton, who was serving in a minesweeping trawler at Scapa Flow but might be better employed closer to his home waters.

Fleming's network of contacts could be used to support other people's operations as well as his own and his Admiral's. Some of his appointees, such as Newton and the flamboyant Merlin Minshall, might buccaneer a step too far in the strange world of the SOE, but his introduction of Steven Mackenzie to Francis Slocum and the SIS was one of his most successful 'fixes'.

Mackenzie had joined the RNVR in June 1939 and had been posted as a liaison officer to Admiral Darlan's HQ in France. During Operation *Aerial*, he had worked with Patrick Whinney and Peter Cooper at Bayonne and St-Jean-de-Luz and was then directed by Fleming to the SIS. Early in 1942, he needed to assist agent Rémy (Colonel Gilbert Renault, Confrérie Notre-Dame [CND] network) by evacuating his wife and children. Mackenzie recruited Breton native Daniel Lomenech and took Luard's advice as to a suitable fishing vessel to blend with local craft. Their choice, *Le-Dinan*, was currently in use as an RN patrol vessel, therefore painted the standard grey. She was moved to the Scilly Isles, where Mackenzie and his team repainted her blue, with brown upper works, and dressed themselves as Breton fishermen. They tested the efficacy of their disguise by joining the fishing fleets in the bay of Concarneau and landing in full daylight via their ship's dinghy.

Achieving a successful rendezvous with the family proved elusive, however. It took several weeks and a number of different repaintings before they finally met a tiny open boat, *Les-Deux-Anges*, off the Glénan Islands. Edging cautiously alongside, they were able to embark Agent Rémy and his family, who had been hidden under the floorboards. Mackenzie wrote afterwards: 'I felt deeply moved by the sight we had just seen, four young children and their mother helped to safety, their smile of thanks, their obvious confidence of security in our hands.'[7] After an eventful but successful return to England, it was discovered that one of the documents Rémy had brought out was a blueprint for the coastal defences to be built along the coast of Normandy.

Regular missions were run during the next 15 months to support the Confrérie Notre-Dame. Fishing boat disguise developed even further when the yacht designer Jack Laurent Giles was asked to create a vessel for this route that would look like a fishing boat above the water line but was designed to travel at 18–20 knots, with new, powerful engines. Prosaically named MFV *2023,* she was known as *L'Angèle-Rouge* as a tribute to Steven Mackenzie's new wife, previously Francis Slocum's secretary.

Towards the end of 1942, Holdsworth and Richards left the Helford River to sail to Algiers in their disguised tunny boat *Mutin* and continue their SOE operations in support of the Allied landings in North Africa. Both the SIS and SOE fishing boat fleets were then amalgamated in the Helford River under the guidance of the Warington Smyth family of RNVR yachtsmen. Without Holdsworth's forceful personality (and antipathy for Slocum), relations between the intelligence organisations improved and, as, Bevil Warington Smyth commented later, 'It came as a source of great surprise to more than one officer […] to discover that – contrary to what they had been educated to believe – the principal enemy was Hitler and not their opposite number in the sister organisation.'[8]

This rapprochement was probably made easier as the available pool of vessels increased. The loss of MGB *314* had immediately been made good by the provision of MGB *318*, with Lieutenant Martin RNVR, a former racing car driver, in command. She became a workhorse for the organisation, continuing in the service under several different commanding officers (notably Jan McQuoid-Mason from the Canadian RNVR). The problem, however, with MGB *318* and other Fairmile Cs was that, although tough, they were also relatively slow. This was a serious drawback when long distances needed to be covered within short summer nights.

Hope was placed in a set of new fast MGBs being built by Camper & Nicholsons yard. The first, MGB *501*, was delivered in June 1942 and Dunstan Curtis given command. The following month, however, she blew up and sank. Curtis (who survived) was then poached by Fleming to lead his new intelligence commando unit and the West Country to Brittany transport service continued to rely largely on the trusty Fairmile Cs. These were now officially organised as the 15th MGB flotilla and based at HMS *Cicala* on the River Dart.

As the war continued, the needs of escaping aircrew were added to the needs of secret agents and resistance groups. Until November 1942, when Germany occupied the previously unoccupied zone, there were escape routes south across the Pyrenees. Slowly, through 1943, organisations such as the Shelburne Escape Line, in partnership with MI9 and the 'secret flotillas', gradually developed the necessary infrastructure to handle escapers – or 'parcels' as they were known – who were returning from Brittany to south-west England. Wherever they had landed in occupied France they needed to be found, hidden and passed on from one safe house to another until they finally reached collection points near the coast. Brooks Richards wrote in admiration:

> *Simple people had shown the most extraordinary courage, never hesitating spontaneously to help airmen overtaken by disaster, in spite of the risk of dire retribution [...]. This friendly attitude on the part of the population towards shot-down Allied aircrew, who had in many cases just bombed French cities or shot-up French trains, disconcerted the Germans and surprised even MI9.*[9]

A significant proportion of these airmen would have been directly engaged in bombing Brittany as the offensive continued against the U-boats in the Atlantic ports. Laura Quigley's book *South-West Secret Agents* (2014) includes a variety of previously unpublished testimonies and photographs and makes fascinating connections, such as the story of French-Canadian Dieppe escapee Lucian Dumais, who was eventually persuaded to join the Dartmouth MGBs and act as courier for other escapees using the successful Shelburne Escape Line during 1944.

As the 'parcel' numbers grew, the problem of safe transport from beach to waiting MGB became more pressing. Folding canoes and yacht dinghies were not suitable to carry either many passengers or heavy quantities of stores through the breaking waves. The Warington Smyths achieved a wonderfully neat solution by building and testing double-ended boats. Unlike conventional dinghies, these did not need to be turned round when loaded for departure; only the oarsmen needed to swivel, while there was a tiny transom at each end to take a steering oar. Cornwall's Sandy Prah beach served as a test site, then Camper & Nicholsons built these surf-boats in various sizes so they could be carried on the different gunboats' decks. Faster boats were eventually delivered and former RNVSR volunteer Peter Williams was regularly involved as commanding officer of MGB *502* (and previously MGB *325*). After the war, he returned to his career as a solicitor and became a member of Chelsea Council. Some readers of his obituary in the *Daily Telegraph* might have been surprised by these stories from his past:

In one typical operation Williams sailed at dusk from Dartmouth on February 26th 1944, heading towards Weymouth, then, once out of sight, he turned south. On reaching the Brittany coast he cut his speed to reduce noise, wash and phosphorescence, and crept through the rocks and the swirling tides to anchor within a few hundred yards of the beach. A sailor was placed on stand-by to cut the grass rope in case of emergency.

Williams then sent his surf-boat ashore with muffled oars, on a rising tide to avoid footprints, in order to land a party which included François Mitterand, the future President of France. As the boat returned loaded with five agents and a downed Allied pilot, it was able to find the MGB in the dark by a device, invented by Williams, which homed in on its Asdic transmissions. By breakfast time Williams was back in Dartmouth.

Among Williams's other passengers was Suzanne Warenghem, the agent 'Charisse', whose shapely figure provoked a sailor to mutter gallantly, 'Ici, mademoiselle,' as he helped her aboard. 'It's okay Jack,' she replied, 'I've been on one of these boats before.'[10]

To some extent, the secret flotillas were a version of normality for yachtsmen: crossing to Brittany, negotiating the problematic coastline and its tides, anchoring off, rowing ashore and returning from a beach – these were almost holiday cruise activities, except that they were undertaken in the dark (the 'no-moon' periods) and in conditions of intense secrecy, which, if broken, might cost many more lives than one's own. David Birkin (b. 1914), however, was no yachtsman. He was the grandson of a Nottingham lace manufacturer, had been educated at Harrow and Cambridge and had worked as a probation officer. Birkin had serious eye and sinus problems and had been declared unfit for any kind of military service. Nevertheless, he had joined the Navy as a telegraphist before finding his way to Slocum's operations section and an RNVR commission in 1942; thence, via a Captain OM Watts navigation course, to MGB *318* in the winter of 1942–1943, where he had to put his new knowledge into practice.

Until he tried, Birkin could never have believed that the motion of an MGB's chartroom could have been so horrible: it was like being shut in a hen coop attached to a universal joint, placed in a high-speed lift operated by a madman whose object was to make it bump at the bottom. Added to that was an occasional douching of freezing seawater.[11]

With no sea experience, no officer training, chronic ill health and extreme, debilitating seasickness, Birkin's remarkably accurate navigation and personal bravery won the respect of all who worked with him. He navigated on scores of clandestine operations to the end of the war but always with a bucket beside him. In 1943, Birkin married the actress Judy Campbell, who had inspired lasting affection with her rendition of 'A Nightingale Sang in Berkeley Square'. The first of their three children, Andrew, was born in 1945 and an extraordinary artistic dynasty was founded.[12] Not, however, a new generation of yachting enthusiasts; after his war experience, Birkin took to farming.

16

'Distracted by the multiplicity of its functions'[1]

Summer 1941–Spring 1944: Postings further afield
(Mediterranean and West Africa)

One reason that Coastal Forces became so quickly and thoroughly an RNVR preserve – and why the RNVR was used so often for irregular operations – was that the professional RN officers were needed elsewhere as the theatre of war widened. Their years of training could often be better employed within the complex technical systems of a battleship than in the hands-on management of small boats or the idiosyncratic activities of secret flotillas. In August 1941, Robert Hichens had been taken aback when his RN Senior Officer Peter Howes rang to ask him to assume command of the flotilla. Howes was being sent on a specialist signals course, and many other RN commanding officers were moved at the same time, which meant that a whole set of RNVR and RNR first lieutenants needed to assume responsibility. Hichens' brilliant leadership and tactical understanding soon demonstrated that the volunteers were more than temporary stand-ins. This was a new style of organisation, frequently more democratic and discussion-based.

The second half of 1941 and the turn of the year to 1942 saw a significant expansion of the places where people were sent to serve. On the world stage, headline events were Hitler's invasion of the Soviet Union, the worsening situation in the Mediterranean (especially Malta), then, in December, the entry of Japan into the war, precipitating a series of crises in the Far East and the crucial involvement of the USA.

For the Navy, August 1941 marked the commencement of the Arctic convoys, a series of gruelling journeys with significantly greater warship involvement than the Atlantic crossings (partly due to the lurking presence of the *Tirpitz* and other German battleships in Norwegian fjords). There was also some major redeployment to the Mediterranean. Between August and December 1941, 76,000 additional naval personnel were posted there from the UK and 50,000 more from India, Australia and New Zealand. The Mediterranean fleet still comprised battleships, aircraft carriers and cruisers as well as increasing numbers of submarines and the supporting cast of destroyers, minesweepers, minelayers, gunboats and motor launches. It had become seriously overstretched moving troops and supplies in and out of Greece and Crete as well supplying the troops in North Africa and confronting the Italians at sea. The Battle of Cape Matapan, 27–29 March 1941, has been described as 'the Royal Navy's greatest victory in a fleet encounter since Trafalgar; and as it was to prove, the last in its long history'.[2] But no one knew that then. Though the Italian warships had been forced to retire, the battle of supply lines continued, particularly as the conflict in North Africa deepened. 'The Navy will never let the Army down,' Admiral Andrew Cunningham promised.

Malta was crucial and there was also a continuing strategic struggle in the Eastern Mediterranean. Access to the Aegean affected access onwards, through the Dardanelles, the Sea of Marmara and the Bosphorous into the Black Sea. This was a route both to the Soviet Union, for the Allies, and to oil-rich Romania for the Axis. In early 1941, Bulgaria had aligned itself with the Axis; Yugoslavia and Greece had been invaded. The Balkans, on the western shore, were therefore in the Axis camp, thus making the ambiguous neutrality of Turkey, to the east, even more significant.

The NID habit of putting potentially useful people into RNVR uniform had proved particularly valuable with the appointment of Lieutenant Commander Vladimir Wolfson RNVR (Special Branch) as assistant naval attaché in Istanbul. Wolfson was a White Russian émigré, born in Kiev in 1903, who had escaped to Britain following the Revolution of 1917. He had been evacuated from Odessa on a ship of the Royal Navy, whose captain had paid for his subsequent education in Britain. He used his position to collect and pass back information to Ian Fleming and NID as well as to the SIS; to spread disinformation; facilitate clandestine missions; and eventually establish an escape line for Allied servicemen.

Adrian Seligman found himself involved in some odd adventures in Wolfson's part of the world. Seligman had joined the RNVSR immediately after the Munich crisis and had passed through his HMS *King Alfred* training with Iain Rutherford, David Kemsley and Arthur Bennett. He'd been sent, like them, to minesweeping and patrol duties in HMS *Unicorn II*, Dundee. Early in 1941, Rutherford, Kemsley and Bennett were posted on to service with Coastal Forces but from that summer, Seligman becomes hard to track within the Navy List. This may be simple information overload. In September 1939, the Navy List (established 1814) comprised a single 800-page book, updated at regular intervals through the year. By summer 1945, the service had expanded to such an extent that each issue filled three 1,200-page volumes. Although its apparent obsession with the minutiae of seniority may seem off-putting, it can also be considered as part of the habit of the sea that all movements should be logged and reported – a necessary contradiction to its vastness, and the ease with which a ship can disappear over the curve of the horizon. Wartime compilers were sensitive to the fact that the List might be read by unfriendly eyes and it's possible that an unusual delay in recording change may indicate that the individual was involved in Special Services work. In Seligman's case, it's clear that he had transferred to HMS *Nile* in Alexandria several months before he was taken off the lists for HMS *Unicorn II* at Dundee. While he clearly undertook routine duties at HMS *Nile* (such as commanding the minesweeping whaler HMS *Swona* as part of Operation *Tiger* – an important Mediterranean supply convoy), he also describes himself as being in Alexandria as part of a 'false nose' party.

After the war, Seligman published *No Stars to Guide* (1947), an account of a Special Services mission undertaken late in 1941. It began when he and a merchant navy colleague were called to see the senior officer intelligence in Alexandria and told it would be their job to move three ships, in secret, from Turkey, through the German- and Italian-dominated Aegean, to Beirut in Syria. This would be undertaken at night in areas where all ship movement after dark was prohibited; where the straits are narrow, the coastal navigation complex and only half the lighthouses would be lit. The ships would be large (a Russian ice-breaker and two tankers), with crews that might or might not understand rudimentary English.

Olinda, the tanker that would be Seligman's responsibility, would have no wireless transmission (W/T) set.

No WT! As soon as we were clear of the Dardanelles, I would be entirely on my own [...] free to choose any method of smuggling Olinda *down, which the weather or the presence of enemy patrols might suggest. I thought again of the inshore route; then my mind went back to schooner days in the South Seas and elsewhere [...] sneaking in through the reefs at Mangareva; midnight struggles among the rocks and shoals of the Galapagos Islands; forcing the pass at Hao against a strong race; feeling our way round the Nova Scotian banks in thick fog. Here was something I knew how to do.*[3]

At the outset of the mission, Seligman and his companions were plunged into the nebulously exotic atmosphere of Istanbul, 'the headquarters of all the intelligence organisations in the world, right now'.[4] His post-war account reads almost like a novel. Few people are what they seem: most are on their guard and watching one another while passing the time in futile quarrels and crowded bars. Seligman and his companions observe the wealthy Levantines, gay White Russian demi-mondaines and sour-looking Herrenvolk. Their paths cross repeatedly with Fritz Schreibel, a German agent, and also with Nadya, an enigmatic and attractive woman whose allegiance is unclear. The 'false nose' party enjoy expenses-paid living, good food and music, the sparkling Bosphorous, pine-covered hills and the first snows of winter. Then, into this detached cosmopolitan bubble, comes grim news of the sinking of the two British battleships, *Prince of Wales* and *Repulse*, in the South China Sea on 12 December 1941, in which 840 sailors died.

For me it was the most dramatic moment since the night I lay awake in the cabin of a trawler, in the North Sea, and heard Churchill's speech on the fall of France [...] For a long time that night I lay awake thinking about the news and Fritz Schreibel and wondering how events in the Indian Ocean would ultimately affect us. How big a part could our insignificant little Special Service party, with its pretentious Force W for a title ... how telling a part could it possibly play in the pattern of Total World War?[5]

Seligman and his companions continued with their mission. His responsibility, *Olinda,* was successfully disguised by the addition of a false funnel and finally made it to Beirut. In February 1946, he received a letter from the director of Navy Accounts, asking him to account for the sum of £6 17s 5d 'travelling expenses' advanced to him on 6 December 1941 by the naval attaché. Seligman was delighted to be able to send the completed manuscript of *No Stars to Guide* as his reply.

★★★

Maurice Griffiths was also posted to the Eastern Mediterranean in 1941. His destination was the Suez Canal. This 120-mile waterway crucially links the Mediterranean and the Red Sea – thence Aden, the Arabian Sea (including the oil-rich Persian Gulf), India, Singapore and the Far East, Australia, New Zealand as well as the East African coast. It is generally narrow and could easily be blocked if ships were disabled by mines. Griffiths' job was to offer up-to-date training in rendering mines safe (RMS) techniques. This was always intensely risky as the mine manufacturers were encouraged to vary their mechanisms and incorporate booby traps to kill or maim defusers.

Griffiths (who had won the George Medal for his work in the London Docks) was accompanied by an experienced diving instructor, Leading Seaman Smith from Whale Island Portsmouth, and records some lucky escapes in his later book on mine warfare. This volume, *The Hidden Menace* (1981), is a world away from Griffiths' *Magic of the Swatchways.* He was based in Ismailia, Egypt, where he was glad to discover that a couple of wooden herring drifters had found their way out from Britain. By January 1942, however, he had become ill with malaria and dysentery and needed to return home.

Yachting Monthly's general manager, Norman Clackson, was also in Egypt. He'd been posted to the armed yacht *Rosaura,* another of those WWI veterans with a history. She'd been built in 1905 as SS *Dieppe* for the Southern Railways Newhaven–Dieppe route. In WWI, she'd served as a hospital ship and a troopship then, in 1933, had been bought by politician and businessman Walter Guinness (Baron Moyne), renamed and converted to a private yacht. The

Prince of Wales and Wallis Simpson had cruised as guests on board *Rosaura*. So had Winston and Clementine Churchill. She'd been used to explore the Pacific, bringing the first live Komodo dragon back to Britain, and is commemorated in the naming of a species of Honduran gecko.

From 1939, when Clackson joined, *Rosaura* was being used as an armed boarding yacht in the Mediterranean. In February 1941, she reverted briefly to her WWI troopship role, carrying a company of the Sherwood Foresters on Operation *Abstention*, the failed invasion of Kastellorizo, off the Turkish Aegean coast. Then, less than a month later, she hit a mine off Tobruk and sank with the loss of her 12 crew. Clackson was not aboard at the time. His name continues to appear as stationed at HMS *Nile* until 1944, long after other evidence suggests he was in London, constructing double agent stories with Ewen Montagu in the NID.

★★★

In August 1941, Denys Rayner and HMS *Verbena* were withdrawn from convoy escort in the North Atlantic and despatched on the long haul south to Freetown (Sierra Leone). Rayner includes a lively description of his attempts to rig sails on *Verbena* when their fuel supplies ran low:

> *The griping spars of the boats, each 14 foot long, made two yards secured three-quarters of the way up the mast. These were fitted with slings, guys and lifts and stood out at right angles to the mast. They were capable of being trimmed to any required position. On the yard on the weather side we prepared to set the quarter-deck awning, and on the lee side yard to use the bridge awning. The forecastle awning which was triangular in shape would serve as a jib.*[6]

In fact, she slipped into harbour on her last drops and was soon at work escorting troopships full of soldiers going to join the armies in Egypt and the Far East via the Cape of Good Hope. Rayner felt elated when he heard the news of America's entry into the war and longed to be back in the Atlantic taking the offensive against the U-boats. It was frustrating to be held at Cape Town even though he successfully wheedled a sailing dinghy from the Simonstown dockyard as the ship's Christmas present.

Finally, *Verbena* was despatched across the Indian Ocean for duty escorting convoys between Trincomalee (Sri Lanka) and Bombay. Her momentary triumph of shooting down three Japanese aircraft was marred by the lasting sadness of ship losses, including their new 'chummy ship', HMS *Hollyhock*. Then, after thousands of miles without regular cleaning, *Verbena*'s boilers gave up. She lay moored in Bombay Harbour as an anti-aircraft platform, waiting for spare parts, with Rayner fretting for North Atlantic anti-submarine action. Eventually, he fell sufficiently ill to be invalided home.

In December 1942, Rayner became one of the first RNVR officers to be given command of a destroyer, HMS *Shikari*, and returned to his favourite hunting ground, the North Atlantic. He was a long-standing lieutenant commander in the regular RNVR and had for some time achieved 'Qualified' status. This, within the Navy's hierarchy, sometimes meant that he might find himself more senior than at RN officer of his own rank, which could cause hard feelings. For example, at Freetown an RN lieutenant commander had put in a complaint about Rayner, a reservist, being made senior officer of their small minesweeping group. According to Rayner, Captain (D) Robert Sherbrooke adjudicated promptly, telling the grumbler that when his ship was as efficient as *Verbena*, he might be prepared to listen.

My father also served at Freetown under Sherbrooke (soon to be hero of the Battle of the Barents Sea, 31 December 1942). The surviving collection of dockets and reports (most marked 'SECRET') in his suitcase give a clear impression of a base where people – even 'amateurs' – were encouraged to flourish on their merits. My father was working as captain's secretary in the paymaster's office, yet his enthusiasm for extra work resulted in him undertaking surveys of the harbour, intelligence gathering among the Vichy French and making expeditions upriver in a fishing boat (though these were probably more for pleasure and adventure than military reconnaissance). Reports also show Sherbrooke and his successor, Captain Henderson, recommending that he should be transferred to the 'permanent' RNVR. It seemed there was still a distinction between 'regular' officers like Rayner, who could become 'Qualified', and those like my father who had entered via the RNVSR and would always remain 'Temporary'.

I don't know whether there was a difference in pay. Ruari McLean (b. 1916), as a 'Special' RNVR officer, recorded a rumour that they were paid 6d a day more, but also stated that when this was looked into, the pay calculations were so complex that those who had been interested soon gave up the attempt to understand. August Courtauld returned his pay to help the war effort. Companies were encouraged to support their serving employees by making up their salary to the amount it would have been had they remained at work. Rowe & Pitman stockbrokers continued supplementing Ian Fleming's pay until the war's end and the BBC did the same for David Howarth. Howarth was offered a return to broadcasting but decided to remain in Shetland and become a boatbuilder.

Kenneth Jacob, stuck in his generally dull job supervising torpedo tubes to defend Thames Haven, records that his pay as an RNVR lieutenant was £1 a day plus 2/- marriage allowance. His pre-war employers made this up to the £600 p.a. that had been his salary before he was called up. As the threat of invasion receded and the Blitz ended, Jacob found his post increasingly monotonous. He repeatedly applied for transfer to an engineering branch where his vocational experience would be more use. This was regularly refused because he'd not been an engineer 'at sea', though he had been an active yachtsman.

Jacob's requests were finally heard in April 1943 when he was given several weeks' specialist training and was assigned to HMS *Barnehurst*, a 750-ton boom-defence vessel. On 8 August, *Barnehurst* joined a Gibraltar-bound convoy. At last, Jacob found himself standing watches at sea. They witnessed a sinking, survived an air attack (frustrated by the limited range of their 3in gun) and arrived in Gibraltar, ten days later, amazed at the sight of a town without blackout. There were tasks for them in Gibraltar and also Algiers, Bizerta and the island of La Madalena. Off-duty, Jacob played crib with his friend the chief engineer, drank cheap Sardinian red wine and went to the local cinema (officers 6d, ratings 2d). Ten months later, on 30 May 1944, when HMS *Barnehurst* eventually arrived back in Portsmouth, her crew expected to be given leave to see their families. Instead, they were immediately busy taking on coal and stores until, four days later, they steamed to Bembridge and joined the D–Day invasion fleet.

Eric Newell had also become bored with shore-based work. After playing his part in Operation *Aerial* (June 1940), he'd spent a brief period in the Naval Control Office in Falmouth before being sent north – again with Lieutenant Commander Beeching – to the Naval Control Office in Methil (Fife) to assist with rerouting the convoys that could no longer use the English Channel.

Newell and Beeching were unimpressed with the organisation, encountering too many previously retired WWI commanders who furnished their offices with leather armchairs and had *The Times* delivered every day. They made themselves unpopular advocating for a more streamlined system, until they were eventually transferred to the Admiralty Trade Division in London to put their suggestions into practice.

Meanwhile, Eric's wife Gladys and their young son John had been effectively homeless since 1939. The yacht *Onda*, in which they had all been living immediately before the war, had been requisitioned and they'd spent much of the intervening period trailing their possessions around, following Eric to his postings whenever it was practicable and staying in hotel rooms and rented accommodation. John (b. 1937) says: 'I counted around seventeen moves around the UK. Formal education was not a priority in those days so I absorbed a useful general natural education from talking to adults and observing life.'[7]

Gladys Newell was clearly a resourceful woman who had loved their pre-war life afloat. 'It will never be the same again,' she said when Eric was posted to Ramsgate in 1940. Her hair turned from a rich auburn to white. 'She never stopped worrying,' remembers John. Nevertheless, her husband's memoir shows her outwardly resilient and energetic, at one time moving into a larger house so she could let out rooms to overseas servicemen. Eric described once meeting a Canadian officer when he returned home on leave: 'He asked me if I was going to stay. When I told him that was what I hoped to do, he told me that the place was very comfortable and the food excellent!'[8]

When Newell was posted to the Admiralty, Gladys and John remained behind in Scotland. He tried living economically outside

London but this didn't prove practicable with his irregular hours, so he rented a room in South Kensington. As soon as the new convoy systems were embedded, Newell was keen to go back to sea. He knew he was fit to do so and others were not, but there was also a financial consideration:

> I went to see Captain Schofield RN, Director of the Admiralty Trade Division. He asked for my reason for wishing for a sea appointment; in reply I showed him my Midland Bank passbook. It showed all the figures in black when I first took up my appointment in May, by October all figures were in red, in spite of the extra allowances paid to officers appointed to the Admiralty. The only way a naval officer can save any money out of his pay is to be appointed to a seagoing ship that does not spend too much time secured alongside the dock.[9]

In January 1942, Newell was sent to HMS *Antrim*, Belfast, as a spare officer for duty with the fleet of Dance-class escort vessels. He found it a particularly hospitable port: 'It did not matter at what hour we docked, there was always an RC priest on the dock to take our lines. Having secured us alongside Pollock Dock he would ask permission to come aboard and see his boys. There were usually about eight to ten RCs among the crew of 40.'[10]

Initially, Newell undertook regular first lieutenant postings on different ships. It didn't support a lavish lifestyle for Gladys and John. 'Thank God I don't have to live in a house like that,' commented one of his new commanding officers. 'I said I quite understood his feelings but that was where I lived with my wife and son.' It wasn't long before Newell had his own command, HMS *Valse*. He did his best to ensure that she was a happy ship by taking trouble to select an excellent ship's cook, and also by installing hot showers in the focsle.

If Monsarrat had been provided with such facilities on HMS *Campanula*, would he have written *The Cruel Sea*? From February 1942, he'd been posted to the East Coast convoys on the more comfortable (though possibly less robust) Kingfisher-class corvette HMS *Guillemot*, where he was very much happier. His new commanding officer, Sam Lombard-Hobson RN, claimed to enjoy having an 'amateur' as his first lieutenant: 'I like a few amateurs around the place. It reminds you that there is an outside world, after all...'[11] After a year on the Harwich–Rosyth convoy route, however, Lombard-Hobson applied for a transfer. He was appointed to a destroyer and posted to the Mediterranean. Before he left, he recommended Monsarrat for promotion, which was eventually achieved, despite the opposition of senior officer Commander Jack Broome, who claimed that Monsarrat spent too much time in his cabin, writing.

Monsarrat followed *HM Corvette* with a second slim volume, *East Coast Corvette* (1943), within which he tried to define some of the dreams and emotions of the sailors. He was deeply impressed by their love of home: 'It is complementary to the ship as the inner centre of their world [...] This is what they are fighting for; the sure welcome, the bride, the old woman, the sprogs.'[12]

This makes it the more shocking when the servicemen arrive back in their home port to find familiar streets destroyed by bombing and the bride-to-be, or the sister, dead – a searing episode in *The Cruel Sea*. Many WWII participants had the disquieting experience of realising that their families at home might be in greater danger than they were. My father, in his brief days of home leave between Newfoundland and West Africa, commented on his surprise at discovering that all the windows of the family farmhouse in Essex had been shattered by bomb blast. David Howarth wrote of his admiration for the quiet bravery of his Home Counties parents, 'who calmly counted the hundreds of bombs that left holes in their garden and the neighbouring fields'.[13]

Denys and Elizabeth Rayner had agreed that it would be better both for her peace of mind and their children's upbringing that she should not continually uproot herself and them to try to follow Denys' different postings. Vyvyan Rayner, their post-war son, was assured by his elder sister that it hadn't helped their mother at all. Elizabeth's life became dominated by the dread of a telephone call, announcing bad news from wherever Denys happened to be. She also suffered a series of miscarriages. Was this due to stress, Vyvyan and his sister wondered later? Or was it, as Denys himself may have come to believe after the war, a side effect of the new, relatively untested, poorly positioned radar system that had been installed, with such excitement, in HMS *Verbena* and his subsequent ships? 'A huge structure resembling a gigantic pepper pot rose from the back of the bridge. It was higher than the funnel and to my eyes looked just about as un-seamanlike a contraption as could have been devised.'[14] Like every yachtsman when they discover the beauty of radar in poor visibility, Rayner was soon won over. When they ran into a gale, driving rain and fog in the Minches:

> *I thought then of our new radar. If it really did what it was supposed to do we might yet make Londonderry in time. I sent for its operator. Yes he could pick up the land. We tried it. It was wonderful. [...] Half the worry and strain of a commanding officer's life would be taken away by this wonderful invention. I even forgave it for its terrible outward appearance. In six hours we were through the narrows and heading for Londonderry river.*[15]

Was this at the cost of reduced sperm quality for those in immediate proximity? Vyvyan Rayner points to the positioning of the transmitter not only on *Verbena* but also on his father's later commands, *Shikari* and *Highlander*. Did his mother, who had conceived and borne two healthy children before the war and would have another immediately afterwards, suffer four failed pregnancies during the conflict because of the effects of the magic eye? Or was it her constant state of crippling anxiety?

★★★

Women's health pioneer Margery Spring Rice (b. 1887) hadn't wanted her youngest son Stephen to volunteer for the submarine service. He was just 19 in 1939, a gifted musician and mathematician who joined the RNVR from Cambridge. He served first in a destroyer but switched to submarines at the end of 1940. He was almost immediately sent to HMS *Medway*, the submarine depot ship in the Mediterranean. His mother, meanwhile, was running a children's nursery at Iken Hall, her home in Suffolk, and refusing to be evacuated. Before the war, Stephen and his teenage friends had made the most of the dinghy-sailing opportunities from this lovely place. In the Mediterranean, too, he sailed for pleasure whenever he was able. He had his clarinet with him, and exercised his charm and his gift for friendship. In May 1942, still only 22 years old, he became first lieutenant of the U-class submarine HMS *P.48*.

Edward Young met 'Sprice' in the Mediterranean in September 1942. 'I remember most of all his passion for music and the way he used to play *Mr Bach Goes to Town* on his clarinet, a lock of hair standing up on his brow above the flushed and ardent face.'[16] Young had been recommended for promotion when George Colvin (RN) was moved on from *Sealion* for Mediterranean service in HMS *Tigris*. His new submarine, HMS *Saracen*, was also destined for the Mediterranean, her routine task to lie in wait to attack Italian and German convoys as they attempted to supply their armies in North Africa (something of a role reversal from the U-boat attacks on Allied convoys that were taking place in the Atlantic). Young recorded that their submarines sank more than 1.3 million tons of enemy shipping between June 1940 when Italy entered the war and September 1943 when they signed an armistice. This was achieved at the cost of 41 British boats.

Even within the extraordinary world of submariners, being stationed in Malta during 1942 was unique. By the end of his five-year career, Young would have served across the globe, from the Arctic to the Far East, but wrote that there had been nothing similar to Malta. The submariners lurking in Marsumascetto Creek were short of food (though nothing like the almost-starving inhabitants) and spent much of their time hidden under acrid smoke screens while air battles raged overhead. When they sallied out on patrol, they were likely to find so many 'targets' that torpedo supplies could be exhausted in a matter of days. There was aggression and there was death. A friend of Sprice's recalled a letter written during this time in Malta:

> *There had been ten subs with him, he told me, in Valletta Harbour; eight of them were already lost. He worked therefore on the principle that every patrol would be his last, and a safe return would be an unexpected bonus. 'But it's occurred to me', he said, 'that it would be sensible to marry some nice girl. It's a pity that the marriage pension to a widow should be wasted.' 'But she might actually love you,' I suggested. 'I know' he said, 'that's the drawback to the idea.' He didn't marry—and he didn't come back.* [17]

Spring Rice's submarine *P48* was posted missing on 5 January 1943, but is now believed to have been depth-charged off Tunisia by Italian destroyers on Christmas Day 1942. Edward Young was luckier; he was already returning to the UK as the first British RNVR officer to be eligible for the commanding officer's course, the 'Perisher'. He had confidently expected that Sprice would soon be following. Less than two months later, on 18 February 1943, George Colvin's HMS *Tigris* left Malta to patrol south-west of Naples. She failed to return. It was to these two lost friends that Young would later dedicate his book.

Margery Spring Rice's brothers visited her soon after she'd heard of Stephen's death. One of them wrote in his diary that she was 'of course' admirably brave.

> *For half an hour after we arrived, she talked to us of things in general without giving a sign of her grief. After lunch we walked down to the river & along the wall to Iken Church, and the sight of the river, the boats' moorings etc. were for a moment too much for her; as she said, 'every turn of the channel & ripple of the water reminded her of him.'*[18]

Margery was left wondering about the manner of her son's death. What would it be like, she asked a doctor friend, to die from oxygen starvation? Perhaps Lothar-Günther Buchheim could have given her some insight – though it would probably be better if he didn't. Buchheim (b. 1918), a writer and art student, had been brought up by his unmarried artist mother and developed his sense of adventure canoeing with his brother in the Baltic and along the Danube to the Black Sea. He loved Italy and had written his first book there aged 19. Buchheim had volunteered for the Kriegsmarine in 1940 and was a '*Sonderführer*', a civilian within the military service. He was employed as a writer and photojournalist to tell the story of the U-boats. On 30 November 1941, he was attached to the Atlantic Type VIIC boat *U-96* when she attempted to pass through the Strait of Gibraltar to the Mediterranean conflict. *U-96* was spotted by a British aircraft, whereupon she was attacked, damaged and forced to dive. She lay submerged for several hours, then made her way back to her base in France. This is expanded by Buchheim into the stinking, suffocating, terrifying ordeal that makes the climax of his great novel, *Das Boot* (1973).

Other Atlantic U-boats had already penetrated the Mediterranean. When *U-331* encountered the 33,330-ton battleship HMS *Barham* off Sidi Barrani on 25 November 1941, she sunk her with a single torpedo in four-and-a half minutes. *Barham* blew up as she sank, and 862 men died. Quintin Riley's friend, the Reverend Launcelot Fleming RNVR, was serving on board *Barham*'s sister ship HMS *Queen Elizabeth II* and saw it happen. Later that day, prayers were broadcast over the loudspeaker so that men in every part of the ship should be able to take part. 'I wish I could describe to you the difference those prayers made,' preached Fleming later.[19]

There was no such comfort for the relatives at home. One of those who died on the *Barham* was 27-year-old Samuel Woodcock, pre-war dinghy-sailing champion at Kiel, keen amateur yacht designer and beloved only son of *Yachting Monthly*'s correspondent Percy Woodcock and his wife Ellie. They were a small family with that special closeness of living together with their boat as their home.

The news was an Admiralty secret and when, a fortnight later, we had a letter saying he was 'presumed to have lost his life' we were asked to keep it to ourselves. It was a hard blow made none the easier to bear by this ban of silence. It proved too much for Ellie, and a week later I was a widower.[20]

17

'Every inch of it must be important'[1]

September 1939–September 1942: Development of topographical intelligence and the Dieppe Raid

As Lieutenant Tom Boyd steamed up the Loire to St-Nazaire on 28 March 1942, everything had appeared 'just as he expected it' and he blessed the model they had studied in the weeks before they set out. Establishing the importance of topographical pre-planning was a major achievement of Admiral Godfrey and Ian Fleming at the NID. After Britain had been ejected from country after country during 1940 and 1941 – not just Holland, Belgium and France but also Greece and Crete, the Balkans and stretches of the North African coast – the realisation was inescapable that if they were ever to get back, it would be by amphibious means, for which detailed knowledge of coastlines and likely conditions would be essential. After the fall of Singapore in February 1942 and the lightning successes of the Japanese Army, there would be the additional, almost unthinkably difficult problem of regaining territory in the Far East. From the second half of 1941, Britain was under pressure from Stalin to open a second front to divert the German strength from their devastating incursions into Russia. Once America also entered the war, eagerness for early return to the continent of Europe increased, though not from the newly realistic Churchill and the British chiefs of staff. They had learned that 'the difficulty of transhipping and landing troops by boats from transports anchored in deep water in a safe, swift and orderly fashion on an open beach is enormous', as Childers had pointed out in 1903.[2]

Godfrey and Fleming had been quick to see the potential of aerial reconnaissance as Sydney Cotton overflew the north German ports early in September 1939 but when Fleming asked for more observations – were there submarine pens concealed on the west coast of Ireland? – there was a row with the head of the SIS Air Intelligence Branch, who accused Fleming of being 'underhand' in his attempt to 'entice' Cotton away from the RAF. Evidently, the level of sea–air partnership achieved in WWI reconnaissance was going to need some rebuilding.

From May 1940, NID began setting up the Inter-Service Topographical Department (ISTD) but used none of the yachtsmen's pre-war contributions. Instead, almost comically, the new department was led by a semi-retired Marines officer, Lieutenant-Colonel Sam Bassett (who had joined the corps due to his passion for horses), and Frederick Wells, a youthful Oxford Classics don. The only room in the Admiralty that could be made available to them, initially, was a disused lavatory and they were given little idea what they were expected to do. Bassett found Wells working on the detail of the coast of Norway: 'Is that because you speak Norwegian?' 'Oh not at all,' he said. 'I speak German, French, Latin and Greek quite well, but I don't know a word of Norwegian.'[3]

The pre-war amateur reconnaissance was apparently ignored, and Bassett seems to have been left spluttering by the official efforts. 'Only sheer incompetence could have produced a report in 1940 listing as a modern installation a battery of guns first installed in 1908 [...] If the same lack of even elementary preparedness obtained in other branches of the services, it's no wonder to me that Hitler almost defeated us.'[4] All too soon, his new department was being asked for detailed information on French beaches suitable for evacuations in small boats. Bassett summoned the confidence to tell the DNI that there was nothing in the files and he needed, therefore, to send destroyers across the Channel carrying naval surveyors and investigating parties with cameras. Godfrey swung into action and observations were made. 'Our report was not only useful in getting the British Army off the beaches of France in 1940 but in getting them back on again some four years later.'[5]

Bassett and Wells' early successes prompted the removal of their department out of the disused lavatory to a building on the Edgware Road (which proved to be directly on a bombing path) and thence, in 1941, to Manchester College Oxford and the facilities of the School of Geography. This was led by WWI soldier and Himalayan explorer Professor Kenneth Mason of Hertford College, who was keenly supportive. Initially, there were some odd appointments, such as a one-legged ex-cavalry officer who'd been transferred into the Navy by administrative error. He proved to be a skilled model maker and Bassett had no more doubts about his department. Naval charts were quite useless for amphibious operations, Mason explained to the director of intelligence at the War Office:

> *They simply tell* ships *how to stay* off *beaches. Topography, however, means drawing up a detailed picture of any area [...] We've got to find out the nature of the approaches to the beach so that we can land on it; what the beach itself consists of – what kind of mud, band, pebbles compose it – how troops can be moved inland after a landing. Then you have to know all about what is beyond that beach.*[6]

Bassett demanded, and got, Royal Engineers seconded to his team; the resources of Oxford University Press were put at his disposal; Margaret Godfrey, the DNI's wife, became an essential member and the project burgeoned. Ian Fleming, as Admiral Godfrey's personal assistant, was necessarily involved. He was an outstanding administrator: when he came to plan operations for his intelligence commandos from the second half of 1942, he would be meticulous in his gathering of relevant topographical facts – then correspondingly likely to believe that all teams needed do was to follow his blueprint. This could cause conflict, especially when the commander on the ground was fellow old Etonian Dunstan Curtis, operational leader at St-Nazaire and with the accumulated experience of undertaking clandestine missions to the enemy shore. Fleming was also interested in book collecting, typography and layout. One of his earliest innovations at the NID had been to enhance the readability of the *Weekly Intelligence Report* that was sent round the fleet. Evidently, this reached its readers. On 23 December 1941, Temporary Paymaster Lieutenant Jones, writing to the NID from HMS *Forth*, had 'the honour to submit the following photographs with reference to *Weekly Intelligence Report 80*' as he believed they would be of possible use in the preparation of reports. These were prints of beaches, bridges, harbours, land and seamarks, 'all acquired in a Baltic Cruise in August 1939'. It was the second batch of the *Naromis* photos.

At this point, I could close my file. The questions I was asking when I first looked through my father's suitcase are essentially answered. I understand why the photographs taken on *Naromis* were divided into two types and why it took so long for the second batch to be deemed of interest. I understand that providing intelligence needn't mean that you're a spy. The various chits marked 'SECRET' and messages scribbled on cypher pads were routine, they were part of my father's job as a paymaster, a more varied and interesting one than I had realised. I'm glad to see, from his service in Halifax and Freetown, that my father earned the right to borrow small boats, survey harbour defences, and see his recommendations implemented. I'm sorry (but not surprised) that he was regularly putting forward good ideas to his immediate superiors, who were increasingly willing to listen, even agree – but almost always advised him regretfully that 'Their Lordships' were unlikely to change their policy.

Because that's what my father was like when I knew him. He wasn't a big man or a hero, but he was fundamentally serious, thoughtful, observant and independent. If he considered something was wrong, or could be improved, he would write a letter to say so. (I used to feel quite sorry for the Chancellor of the Exchequer at Budget time.) He was also reliable. When I looked through *The Cruise of Naromis* with the thought of publication, I checked for accuracy and was reassured; his facts were correct. I remain Dad's child as well as his editor. I am glad to find him trustworthy. Recently, I was in correspondence with Eric Newell's son John, querying his father's assertion that HMS *Winchelsea* had been among the destroyers evacuating troops from St-Nazaire on 19 June 1940. It was a petty point but we both found it particularly satisfying to confirm that Eric, the person who had been there, was right.

Not every daughter who looks into her father's suitcase discovers that he is the man she thought he was. When Vicky Unwin opened her father Tom's battered old case, 'its locks stiff and rusty through lack of use', she began to uncover evidence of abandonment and betrayal. He wasn't Tom Unwin at all, he was Tomas Ungar, *The Boy from Boskovice* (2021). Vicky Unwin's story of her subsequent research confirms, incidentally, how useful an RNVR officer's uniform may be when trying to establish upward social mobility.

Amanda Harling's father, Lieutenant Robert Harling RNVR, was recruited by Ian Fleming: first to discuss the redesign of those *Weekly Intelligence Reports*, later to come and link between NID and the ISTD and finally to be part of 30AU (Fleming's intelligence commandos). In 1943 and 1946, Harling published two volumes of apparent war memoir, establishing a version of himself that remained unchallenged until after he was dead. There was no suitcase full of clues. Harling's friend Fiona MacCarthy, who had written his obituary, was asked to provide an entry for the *Dictionary of National Biography* and therefore checked his birth certificate. This showed that Harling's backstory was significantly different from the version told to his children and friends.

Amateur Sailor (1943) presents Harling as being orphaned in infancy and brought up by an 'Aunt Ruth' and her dairyman husband in a holiday town on the South Coast. He appears to explain that his sailing expertise also dates from that period, thanks to Aunt Ruth's understanding and the patronage of a wealthy enthusiast, 'Mr Crawshay'. In truth, Harling was the son of an Islington taxi driver and his wife. His parents were not dead. He had a brother called Stanley who was serving in the merchant navy and by 1939 he had already been married as well as in a serious long-term relationship. He was, clearly, a talented typographer, designer and journalist as well as an entertaining companion. Ruari McLean, who also joined the RNVR and worked for the ISTD, knew and admired Harling's innovative pre-war periodical *Typography*, as did Fleming. They took the facts of Harling's life from *Amateur Sailor*, as everyone else did – except, presumably, Harling's birth family, who seem to have shown immense dignity, allowing themselves to be written out of his story. Amanda Harling, who only learned of the existence of her father's family after his death, offers the touching detail that his merchant seaman brother had continued buying *The Sunday Times* every week to check if there was an article by Robert in the paper.

Many people blurred names and details when they wrote about their experiences in wartime. In his introduction to *No Stars to Guide*, Adrian Seligman writes: 'In order not to embarrass or involve my friends in this matter, I have peopled my story with a set of composite characters. But the incidents recorded all actually happened to some of us at some time or other.'[7] As a designer, Harling told Ruari McLean that 'it makes designing a lot easier if you can alter the copy as you want'.[8] Presumably this was what he was doing in these two volumes of 'memoir' – redesigning himself. The Royal Navy was an instinctively snobbish institution; in peacetime, at least, it had mattered where someone had been to school and who their parents were. There was a 'family' dimension to this, with strengths as well as weaknesses. And even in the RNVR, when Harling needed to hold his own socially among a bevy of Old Etonians and Varsity men, it was probably easier to be an orphan than the son of a taxi driver. Or perhaps he enjoyed the thrill of running a fantasy life? In the strange world of semi-espionage, which Seligman describes in *No Stars to Guide* – and in which Harling was also involved – it may have felt attractive to adopt temporary identities. One of Harling's autobiographical passages that carries absolute conviction is how deeply he resented the war as an interruption to his career as a craftsman.

> *I hated Hitler and his Huns with a quite personal hatred for this intrusion into Design, and I spelled the word with as emphatic a set of typographical characters as they ever spelled out* Lebensraum. *Actually I was, like any other craftsman, angered by being forced to leave my work. I remembered listening to Eric Gill talking in his lovely room high on the Buckinghamshire hills, just before the war. He said all this but much more succinctly and pungently [...] often whilst on watch I recalled his words and felt that most of what he said was true enough, even for a designer turned amateur sailor.*[9]

Harling's service with the RNVR gave him a unique chance to redesign his own past in a situation where almost everyone was out of their comfort zones. He's a good writer, everything in the books is thoughtful and plausible – it's only the awareness of Fiona MacCarthy's discovery, then checking across to the Navy List, that proves that his time at sea wasn't exactly as he said. In the Navy List, Harling first appears as a probationary, temporary sub-lieutenant in October 1940; he is listed as such at HMS *Caroline* (Belfast) in December; then in February 1941, he is recorded at the NID, where he remains for the rest of the war.

Harling's posthumously published memoir of Ian Fleming (2015) contains a photo of himself on a corvette on escort duty. The caption states that he 'served as navigator on several corvettes'. Winter 1940/1, the time he was serving as a newly qualified sub-lieutenant at HMS *Caroline*, was the time that many corvettes were coming into service and Denys Rayner was told that the bag for watch-keeping first lieutenants was 'empty'. If Harling was a navigator, I wonder perhaps whether he was used through those few winter months in Belfast being posted from ship to ship, as Eric Newell was later, to fill gaps as needed? He twice says he left corvettes and took the job at ISTD because he fell ill. In *Amateur Sailor* he says he had gastric flu in Ireland; in *The Steep Atlantick Stream* it was pneumonia in Canada. Although in *Ian Fleming: a Personal Memoir* he states that Fleming sought him out, extracted him from the Western Approaches and sent him to Colonel Bassett late in 1941, the Navy List dates don't support this. I can't find any evidence of Harling being on sea service after his brief period at HMS *Caroline* in December 1940.

I had a particular motive for my interest. My father's brother, Jack Jones, was a fledging pre-war yacht designer who didn't rush to join the RNVR. This may have been because his employment as an industrial designer was protected. I don't know its exact nature; I do know that he was beginning to make a name for himself as a naval architect and that this was the focus of his ambition. He was writing for *Yachting Monthly* under a variety of pseudonyms, and he very obviously didn't want to stop. Jack was also gay and may well have wondered how this aspect of his identity would be accepted. He was 24 in 1939, living with his widowed mother. I don't know how 'out' he was; homosexuality was of course illegal then.

Jack did talk about his war service afterwards – he talked of his anger that the state, so ready to accept the potential sacrifice of his life in war, should persecute him for his sexuality in peace. The issue appears invisible in almost every war memoir I've read, except in Harling's portrayal of Willoughby, the deeply attractive commanding officer of HMS *Tobias*, in *The Steep Atlantick Stream*. Willoughby mentions Robert Ardrey's play *Thunder Rock*, a huge success on the London stage in the early part of the war, starring the bisexual actor Michael Redgrave. '"I wonder whether many keepers are as queer as that chap in the play?" / "About the same percentage as queer sea captains," I offered, and in the moonlight saw him turn slightly to discover personal reference in my guess.'[10]

It's an ambiguous fragment and may mean nothing beyond a superficial discussion of unconventionality. I hoped it was intended as something more relevant to people like my uncle. In the novel, Willoughby does not survive. In life, Harling was considered flamboyantly heterosexual though with homosexual colleagues and friends. The novelist Charles Morgan, who was working in the publications department of the Admiralty at the beginning of the war, comments on the overall excellence of Harling's characterisation of Willoughby: (it has) 'the liveliness and the almost benign justice of objective portraiture in a good novel.' Presumably that's exactly what these books are – novels, masquerading as memoir. Appropriately, one of the friendships Harling did maintain 'into the distant peace' was with Fleming, whose fiction may be a wishful version of autobiography.

Harling's initial introduction to Colonel Bassett at the ISTD was straightforward, according to him: 'If Ian thinks you could be the man for the job that's good enough for me' was all that Bassett apparently said.[11] Harling was asked to use his skills in design and presentation to format the facts gathered by the ISTD into neat pocket-sized booklets that men such as the St-Nazaire raiders could carry with them on missions. Bassett does not mention either Fleming or Harling in his memoir. He presents the department as taking their instructions directly from Admiral Godfrey, who often called in, not least because his wife was there, working closely with Freddie Wells. Nicholas Rankin describes Margaret Godfrey and Wells working through one long autumn night to proofread the topographical information provided for the 1942 Operation *Torch* landings. They successfully corrected many small mistakes that might have had serious – even fatal – outcomes.

Accuracy mattered. The printing of these thousands of operational orders (as well as all 58 volumes of the Admiralty handbooks and the Navy's codes) was undertaken by OUP, under Dr John Johnson, printer to the University. Bassett's memoir describes a scene of intense outrage when the DNI apparently 'had the temerity to send a young RNVR officer down to Oxford to deal with the question of layout, pagination and titling. At once the DNI received a tersely-worded letter from Dr Johnston [sic], which brought him post-haste down to Oxford.' Bassett describes a staged dialogue between the outraged printer and his assistant, Mr Batey:

'Well, now, do you think we could produce this book that Colonel Bassett wants done? Do you think our printers could understand it? Do you consider that our proofreaders would, perhaps, make some mistakes?'

'Well sir,' said Batey. 'They've dealt with Bibles printed in every language of the world. They've dealt with rare manuscripts, with musical scores, with mathematical treatises, and with industrial and scientific material of all descriptions. All in all I think they could, sir.'

'Thank you, Mr Batey. That will be all.'

And with a nod of the head, Dr Johnston [sic] dismissed his assistant. Turning to the DNI, he said courteously: 'What do you think, Admiral? Do you think, perhaps, we could handle the Colonel's brochure?'

'Why of course, Dr Johnston, of course,' replied the DNI hastily and I've never seen a man look less comfortable. The young RNVR genius swiftly vanished from Oxford.[12]

Bassett's book spells Dr Johnson's name incorrectly throughout.

Harling's duties were varied and itinerant. They included making private reports to Fleming – on the activities of Vladimir Wolfson, for instance. In March 1943, Harling and 'Sandy' Glen, a member of the pre-war explorer group who had been recruited into the Special Branch of the RNVR, were sent to appear to be conducting a reconnaissance of beaches in Albania, Northern Greece and Yugoslavia. This was an attempt to convince the Germans that, after Operation *Torch*, the next Allied advance was likely to come in the Balkans, not Sicily. Before that, Harling had been used by Fleming to help collate the lists of targets to be acquired by his intelligence commandos.

This group, usually referred to by their final name as 30AU, was an idea lifted by Fleming from the Germans. Analysing the airborne invasion of Crete in spring 1941, he'd become aware of a privileged group of German paratroopers, led by Obersturmbannführer Otto Skorzeny, moving ahead of the rest, not to fight but to reach the British wireless station on the island and seize whatever code books and technical information they found there. Such 'pinches' had frequently been achieved fortuitously during commando raids or at the capture or sinking of an enemy vessel, which might be slow to destroy its confidential books. Fleming systematised the idea and first put it forward as a 'MOST SECRET' official proposal in March

1942. He then collected a 'shopping list' of documents and technical equipment that other departments and services would find especially helpful and used the resources of the ISTD to pinpoint their likely whereabouts. His idea was that the 'intelligence commandos' would dash to retrieve them while the fighting was going on, and before they could be damaged or destroyed. Dunstan Curtis and Quintin Riley (both former RNVSR members) were operational commanders. Harling relished his observations of Curtis' and Fleming's tense relationship. 'The two Etonians were as suspicious of each other's ambition and intentions as a pair of wary lynxes,' he wrote. 'In their conflicts each man invariably had some degree of reason on his side, but the degrees were usually right angles apart.'[13] Fleming was the senior with the authority and the detailed overview: Curtis had the cachet of leadership and risk-taking in the field.

The only operation actually joined by Fleming was Operation *Jubilee*, the disastrous Dieppe Raid in August 1942. He took no active part but was on board the destroyer HMS *Fernie*, observing. Several of the former RNVSR yachtsmen were also among those who were escorting landing craft, carrying troops and tanks ashore, providing covering fire where possible and helping with troop evacuation and the rescue of survivors. Peter Scott was there in HMS *Grey Goose*. These new steam gunboats (SGBs) were fast and well-armed, built of metal, not wood. But there were only nine of them and already, at Dieppe, one had been lost. Scott now had to make a captain's difficult decisions. There was, for instance, a moment when *Grey Goose* came under attack from a Dornier while he had been attempting to rescue a downed German pilot:

> *'Full ahead both, hard a-starboard!' The pilot waved pathetically from the water but his friends had sealed his doom. Another shell arrived within 30 or 40 yards. We made CSA smoke and zigzagged sharply at 28 knots. [...] We got off a good deal more lightly than we deserved for it was, on the face of it, not a justifiable thing for which to risk a steam gun boat.'[14]*

I honour Scott for inserting that qualifier 'on the face of it'. His 1945 book *The Battle of the Narrow Seas* is an explicit warning against the glorification of war, while celebrating the great personal bravery of those involved. Scott's navigator Sub-Lieutenant JB Henderson (a former RNVSR member) kept *Grey Goose's* log throughout the action. His account shows that Scott continued to pull German airmen out of the water. There's a memorable vignette of one prisoner, 'a likeable youth' sitting with the ship's black kitten on his lap. He is between a Norwegian pilot, who had shot down his first plane that day before being shot down himself, and his guard, who has fallen asleep. Scott records the effects of Benzedrine, moments of exhilaration, confusion, triumph and horror as well as the prosaic small details such as the need to replenish their ship's supply of blankets as their whole supply was either wet or blood-soaked.

When my uncle Jack Jones, in charge of Rescue Motor Launch (RML) *513*, made it back to Newhaven at the end of that long day, his blood (I'm told) was flowing into the vessel's speaking tube and he'd needed to be lashed to the wheel to enable him to endure the voyage. RML *513* had been last into the scene of carnage and had helped pick up 47 survivors. She had 209 holes in her wooden hull and extensive additional damage. Jack had shrapnel through his neck, damaging his left-side cranial nerves. This, together with injuries received earlier that year when on harbour defence duties, left him disabled and in pain for the rest of his life.

The comments Jack wrote on a 1975 account of the raid by the Canadian author John Mellor express his lasting bitterness at the failures of leadership and the disregard for individual life that he believed were shown in that operation. Specifically, he believed the decision not to bombard in advance was inexcusable and that sending men ashore in open landing craft under artillery and air attack, with no more defence than a Lewis gun or Oerlikon, showed 'the uncaring attitude of Naval Staff in those days'. He was angry with General Montgomery, who had acquiesced in the decision not to bombard, then left for North Africa; contemptuous of the poor quality of Combined Operations planning at that time (he conceded that it improved during 1943); and critical above all of Lord Louis Mountbatten, who, Jack thought, 'surely must, like all Commanders, carry responsibility for this balls-up'. The main victims were the 6,108 soldiers of the Second Division of the Canadian Army who had been stationed in Britain from 1940 to defend against invasion and whose first experience of action this had been. In all, 2,853 of them were killed, wounded or captured. Mellor's book, on which

Jack was scribbling his comments, goes on to detail the experiences of those who were marched away to POW camps. They were far from the cheery escape stories of my teenage reading.

The commander who was immediately scapegoated after the operation was not Mountbatten but the Canadian General Ham Roberts, who sent reserves in when it should have been clear that this was approaching manslaughter. Fleming's presence supports the theory (put forward among others by historian David O'Keefe, defending Roberts) that Dieppe was a 'pinch' raid – an urgent attempt to extract Enigma equipment and code books – therefore any level of sacrifice would be worthwhile, including the general's career and reputation.

The urgency during 1942 was due to the fact that the Enigma machines used to encode Kriegsmarine wireless communications had been changed from three-rotor to four-rotor and suddenly, from February, the cryptanalysts at Bletchley Park could no longer read the U-boat code. Shipping losses in the Atlantic spiralled upwards as the submarine tracking room and the convoy routers were denied this crucial information. Fleming's general idea for his naval intelligence commandos was that they should land with the second or third wave of attack and proceed straight to the buildings where the booty was thought to be stored. In Dieppe, this would be the local Kriegsmarine HQ. A specialist unit, led by Robert Ryder, attempted to dash ashore in the gunboat HMS *Locust* and capture the encryption equipment. Peter Cooper was on board, was mentioned in despatches and was injured. Ryder made several abortive attempts but eventually returned to the HQ ship and told Captain Hughes-Hallet that it was impossible. A fleet of ambulances was waiting at Portsmouth when the ships finally returned and surgeons were operating round the clock for the next 40 hours. Fleming joined up with an American general and a colonel of Marines and went out to dinner in the best hotel. In his report, he commented: 'it is difficult to add up the pros and cons of a bloody gallant affair.'[15]

The following month, September 1942, saw the first official action by the Special Intelligence Unit (later 30AU) in the forefront of the Operation *Torch* landings in North Africa. John Pearson, writing his biography immediately after Fleming's death (so with the advantage of interviewing many of those directly involved) says that Curtis and

Riley, the first unit commanders, were impressed by the detailed information Fleming was able to provide on Algiers – through the efforts of the ISTD, no doubt. Dunstan Curtis described Fleming's excitement – almost as if he was going to be part of the operation. He'd provided aerial photographs, maps, models: the location of the enemy headquarters and the deployment of troops on the ground.

The operation didn't run quite as it had been planned. HMS *Malcolm*, the destroyer carrying the intelligence commandos, came under fire from Admiral Darlan's Vichy French and was unable to achieve entrance into Algiers Harbour. HMS *Broke*, accompanying her, achieved a brief incursion before being forced to leave, seriously damaged. She was taken under tow but sank soon afterwards; 18 men died with her. Curtis and his team were landed instead at Sidi Ferruch on 8 November 1942. They had to extemporise, commandeering a French lorry at gunpoint and setting off to find the large white villa, which they'd been told was the Italian Naval Headquarters. Surprise was achieved: the Italians had no time to burn their files or destroy their code books. The haul, sent to Gibraltar then flown to London, included current German and Italian cyphers as well as the order of battle for the enemy fleets.

That crucial Enigma key had already been retrieved, however – by happenstance rather than planning. Just over a week earlier, on 30 October, the submarine *U-559* had been located by a British aircraft, surrounded by destroyers and sunk by depth charges. As *U-559* surfaced, three suicidally brave men from HMS *Petard* boarded and began hurling up code books and equipment that the Germans had failed to destroy. Two of them – an RN first lieutenant and an able seaman – went down in the submarine's death plunge. They were awarded George Crosses. The third, canteen assistant Tommy Brown, who was awarded the George Medal, was discovered to have lied about his age (he was only 16) and was discharged from the service.

18

'It's a dirty-looking night and I don't like this swell'[1]

1941–1944: Covert operations, intelligence centres and subterfuge

Finally, in 1942, HMS *Corinthian*, the ocean boarding vessel to which Patrick Dalzel-Job had been exiled since he returned from Norway 'disillusioned, ashamed and resentful',[2] was brought back from the South Atlantic. As she was about to leave for her new posting in the Far East, Dalzel-Job was withdrawn and given work more suited to his talents. He was posted to Coastal Forces and sent to Shetland to lead a flotilla of MTBs manned by Norwegians and crossing regularly to Norway. He was based in Lerwick and doesn't directly mention David Howarth or the Shetland Bus in his memoir, nor does Howarth mention him. It's possible that they were to some extent in competition.

Dalzel-Job had been allocated eight Fairmile D MTBs at a time when the Shetland Bus was finding it increasingly hard to operate the route with their fishing boats. He notes that SOE were casting 'covetous eyes' on his small flotilla – and may be referring to Mitchell and Howarth. He also resented the SIS habit of cancelling his operations if they were thought likely to compromise one of their secret wireless operatives, yet not giving him any useful information on which to act. There were political difficulties: while Dalzel-Job and the Norwegians in Britain were clear about their loyalty to King Haakon and his government and their eagerness for action, it was not equally straightforward within occupied Norway, where local people often had to endure savage reprisals after raids from overseas. Some Norwegians, reasonably, preferred to conserve their resistance until they saw clear prospects of success. Over the winter of 1942–1943, the Allied landings in North Africa and the Russian successes at Stalingrad began to give them hope.

Dalzel-Job's 'VP' flotilla was manned by the Royal Norwegian Navy and used aggressively. Its main function was to attack shipping in the Inner Leads (where entry channels had to be charted all over again due to the Admiralty's earlier 'negligence'), it was also used to transport commando raiding parties on operations such as the destruction of the copper pyrites mine on the island of Stord in January 1943. Unlike raids into occupied countries from the English East and South coasts, the distances across the northern North Sea were so great that the MTBs could not operate within a single night. They had to be able to hide up during the day, camouflaged in remote inlets. The risks for those taking part were high, particularly since Hitler's order of October 1942 that those engaged in commando activity would not be taken prisoner but would be interrogated and shot. This was the fate of commandos captured after the raid on the Norsk Hydro plant in November 1942. Their executioners were later found guilty of war crimes.

Though Dalzel-Job was scrupulously careful over the safety of his missions, grief over brave men who were ill-treated and killed would never leave him. Like many people, he had been especially touched by the reckless courage of Joe Godwin, the young dinghy sailor from Argentina who had travelled to England aged 20 to volunteer for the RNVR. In April 1943, after months of training and frustrated inactivity, Godwin led his own Operation *Checkmate*, a seven-man operation with canoes and a coble aiming to sink German shipping with limpet mines. It wasn't the best-conceived mission, partly due to mechanical failure (irreparable damage to the coble's propeller bearings, caused by it being left to spin disengaged on the long crossing under tow). In addition, it suffered from the lack of a Norwegian speaker as well as mistakes made by Godwin himself. Joe Godwin and his companions were all captured. They were interrogated at Grini concentration camp, then handed to the SD (the security service, Sicherheitsdienst). Five of them (including Godwin) were sent to Sachsenhausen concentration camp, where they were executed in 1945: two others to Belsen, where they also died. 'In the Armistice silence every year' Dalzel-Job remembered them, together with the Norwegian Lieutenant Alv Andresen, who had been captured with six others while attempting to continue MTB operations into the summer months. All had been interrogated, shot and their bodies taken out to sea and dumped with explosives. When the war was over, Dalzel-Job learned more about the internal atrocities and use of torture within Norway. 'I do not think we should too readily forget such things,' he wrote.[3]

Nevil Shute didn't publish a novel in 1943. He'd written *Most Secret* late in 1942, despite being fully employed with 60 men in his group at the Department of Miscellaneous Weapon Development (DMWD). He submitted it to the Admiralty, which he was bound to do as a serving officer. Permission to publish was refused. Shute was furious and threatened to resign but eventually had no choice other than to set the novel aside until the war was over. *Pied Piper* (1942) was selling well and became a successful film. His next novel, *Pastoral*, a romance set in a Bomber Command base, would also achieve popular success, though the author himself dismissed it as 'trivial'. Given that *Pastoral* was published in August 1944, perhaps 'trivial' was what was wanted then? It's sentimental and very readable, appropriate for the time. *Most Secret* is something more: it's a fine war novel − as opposed to a novel with a war setting. Shute later said that he had written it 'to perpetuate the mood of bitterness and hate that involved England in the later stages of the war'.[4] His characteristic literary device of the tangentially involved narrator works especially well as a standard of normality within brutally abnormal times. There's a moment, for instance, when the storyteller understands the nature of the newly devised substance that is to be loaded into the flame-thrower and sprayed over the crews of German patrol boats. He consults a doctor and discovers that the substance would trigger sepsis and possibly cancer. This sends him to check the Hague Convention:

> *I read it through that evening. But in those far-off days before the last war nobody had even thought about flame-warfare, so it seemed [...] There was no paragraph to say that if you hurl a jet of blazing oil against the Germans you must use clean oil. I took the Convention back to the library and went to bed, but I didn't sleep very well.*[5]

The disgusting substance has been devised by a temporary RNVR officer whose peacetime work is in the cosmetic industry. The more one thinks about Shute/Norway's twofold personality, the more he seems to symbolise the psychological adaptations people needed to make. There's a moment early in the war when Margery Allingham describes herself sitting in an ARP lecture:

> *I suddenly saw the abyss at our feet as vividly as if I had looked over the side of a house. To realise is one thing but to see is another and I saw that they were talking about a corrosive poison to be sprayed over one civilised people by what was presumed to be another. I wondered if we were all insane and so nearly squeaked aloud [...] that I felt the blood rushing into my face with embarrassment.[6]*

Allingham glances round at the intensely serious faces of her village neighbours, realises they see the danger quite as clearly as she does and wrenches her mind back to practical solutions. Nevil Shute didn't simply 'see' how horrifying these weapons were; as Nevil Norway, he had sometimes been involved in their development. He had, for instance, organised flame-thrower demonstrations, though part of his objective then had been to explain that their terrifying appearance was not proportionate to the damage done. In *Most Secret*, the purpose of the appalling weapon is not only destruction but also to raise local morale in an occupied village – as its priest explains: 'Men now go about our streets with their heads up, spitting towards the Germans, who three months ago were sullen and impotent, sinking into slavery.'[7]

This possibly explains why Shute considered that the novel should have been published. He would have known about cross-Channel operations by Coastal Forces in their MTBs and MGBs but perhaps he didn't realise how very closely the action of *Most Secret* mimicked the type of clandestine operations (e.g. repainting refugee Breton fishing vessels) that the South-West RNVR yachtsmen were actually doing. SOE/SIS operational lines were frequently blurred but there was always a fundamental dichotomy between incursions to alarm the occupiers and raise the morale of the occupied – as in *Most Secret* – and infiltrations to gather information, plant agents and collect escapees that demanded utmost invisibility and was the main preoccupation of the south-western secret flotillas.

Not all the DMWD projects were offensive. Some, like Edward Terrell's plastic armour, were protective. Nevil Norway was keenly involved in developing water distillation equipment for liferafts. Nevertheless, the area with which he was most usually associated was rocket weaponry. In the wake of the Dieppe Raid, he and his team had begun work converting landing craft to rocket launchers in order to offer effective covering fire for assault troops. It was highly risky for all concerned as the serried ranks of rockets burst away from the landing craft, propelled by flame. Several members of the DMWD teams were badly burned before they began using asbestos clothing and protective kiosks and discovered the neat solution of flooding the landing craft decks with sea water. Their work was counted a success.

> *The rocket landing craft which carried more explosive for its size than any vessel ever used for bombardment provided a terrifying and completely successful answer to the problem of destroying enemy morale at the most vital moment of a landing operation. It was regarded by many as the most valuable of all the projects on which the Wheezers and Dodgers worked and both in the Mediterranean and the Normandy assaults to come it was to prove a devastatingly effective reinforcement to allied gunfire.[8]*

★★★

In 1944–1945, Edward Terrell developed Norway's rocket technology into a new bomb (the 'Disney' bomb) of such extraordinary power that it could burst the sound barrier and penetrate 18ft-thick concrete shelters – such as those that had housed the U-boat pens and later the V2 rockets. Terrell chose to broadcast this achievement for propaganda purposes.

> *After the first successful raid on Ijmuiden it was decided to release the news that we possessed a rocket bomb capable of penetrating the sonic barrier and defeating the stoutest shelter the Germans could build. The psychological effect of such publicity on a retreating enemy who had obviously placed the greatest reliance upon these concrete forces, would be very great.[9]*

Terrell hoped it was better strategy to frighten rather than bludgeon people into surrender. He believed that the Japanese should have been warned and given a chance to capitulate before the atomic bomb was dropped: 'then our conscience might have been more clear in delivering the final blow in this way'.[10] Shute's imaginative horror as to where weapon development had led civilised humanity would finally be expressed in his apocalyptic novel *On The Beach* (1957).

Former barrister, Acting Temporary Lieutenant Commander the Hon EES Montagu, on the other hand, was often frustrated by what he wasn't – ethically – allowed to do as an officer in the NID. During 1942, he had proposed a scheme to frame a German U-boat ace by planting compromising material that would have him shot as a traitor.

After discussion my plan was turned down flat on the 'It's not cricket' principle. 'We don't assassinate people.' It was obvious casuistry to argue that we would not be shooting the German captain, the Germans would do it.

If we could have got someone to blow Hitler up surely we would have jumped at the opportunity and saved thousands of lives? Would getting someone to shoot the U-boat captain be wrong because it would save fewer lives? [...] in deciding one must bear in mind the conditions of 1942 and 1943. We were fighting for our very lives, for the preservation of freedom in the world, and damn near being beaten. I sometimes think it was right and sometimes that it was wrong.[11]

Ewen Montagu had been a machine gun instructor in WWI. He was the son of a prominent Jewish family and, like Fredman Ashe Lincoln (whose name was in Hitler's 'Black Book'), knew that he and his family would be at particular risk in the event of a Nazi invasion. After HMS *King Alfred*, his initial posting had been to the 500-ton armed yacht *Alice* for ASW duty together with another RNVSR friend, Tom Martin. In the glamorous world of pre-war regattas, *Alice* had been chartered by Harold Vanderbilt; so this posting might have sounded like a congenial way to go to war. When his legal qualifications were noticed, however, Montagu was told that he was 'not going to have a yachting holiday at the government's expense'; he was to be sent to a 'proper job' where his professional expertise would count. This turned out to be as a staff officer at HMS *Beaver*, the Humber HQ. Montagu set about systematically gathering intelligence from trawler skippers until a posting to the Admiralty in November 1940 finally dashed his hopes of going to sea. He found himself exposed to the abrasive personality of Admiral Godfrey, whom he disliked intensely but believed to be a genius. Once he had passed initial scrutiny, Montagu was appointed to head his own section within the OIC. He was to monitor all non-operational intelligence and serve as a member of the XX (Twenty) committee.

Montagu came to regard his as 'the most fascinating job of the war', though it was far from the salt breezes he'd anticipated. From 1941, he and his staff of RNVR officers and civilian women moved into room 13 of the Citadel – 'Lenin's Tomb', as it was nicknamed. This was built as a bomb-proof fortress. Instead of windows, it had openings that could be used for gun emplacements.

Our room was far too small, far too cluttered with safes, steel filing cabinets, tables, chairs etc., and especially far too low, with steel girders making it even lower. There was no fresh air [...] the only light was of course artificial. At first everyone worked in their shadows plus the shadows of the girders, but I did manage to get fluorescent lights put in which partially solved that problem in spite of the fact that in those days the tubes flickered almost continuously. There we worked long hours in conditions which would have been condemned instantly by any factories' inspector.[12]

His new job grew: 'I knew practically every secret of the war including the atom bomb, read the decyphered messages from enemy and neutral sources, and became part of the *German* spy system in this country – indeed its only regular and "reliable" source of naval intelligence!'[13] He discovered, with some surprise, that his civilian training was an ideal foundation for running complicated networks of double agents: 'We have to learn throughout our careers to put ourselves in our opponent's place and try to imagine what he will think or do based on *his* information.'[14] Reading Montagu's description of his work is more like following the production of a long-running soap opera than a court case: 'Our double agents were people whom the Germans believed to be working for them but whose movements, reports etc were controlled by us so that we could decide exactly what information the Germans received from them.'[15] He goes on to detail the agents who arrived and were picked up and turned; those already living here who were coerced or who volunteered. Then he introduces the rest of the cast: 'Besides all these, there were a great number who did not really exist at all in real life, but were imaginary people notionally recruited as sub-agents by the double agents with whom we were already working.' A saga writer would be impressed by the care taken to maintain these multiple deceptions: Montagu and his colleagues (who eventually included Norman Clackson of *Yachting Monthly*) needed to remember 'the characteristics and life-pattern of each one of a mass of completely non-existent notional sub-agents'. They needed to give good information as well as disinformation to the enemy but had to ensure that no valuable information could reach the Germans in time for them to use it.

Montagu knew that the Germans were receiving regular intelligence from occasional neutral visitors and diplomats but he also knew that his system was working. 'By 1943 we had established so much confidence in the double agents in the mind of the Germans that, where their reports differed from the reports that they got from those neutrals, our agents were always believed.' This was the year that he undertook his best-known deception, Operation *Mincemeat*, an elaborate ruse intended to mislead the Germans before Operation *Husky*, the invasion of Sicily. A body (publicly identified many years later as that of Glyndwr Michael) was given a new identity and a briefcase filled with compromising papers, and was launched off the coast of Spain in an attempt to persuade the Germans that Greece or Sardinia was the intended invasion target, not Sicily. One of the most appealing features of Montagu's book *The Man Who Never Was* (1953) is the extent to which he and his colleagues became emotionally involved in the fictional relationships they were creating around 'Major Martin'. It almost feels like fun in the middle of war. 'I doubt whether any crime has been more meticulously prepared – for it was in essence a large-scale fraud. Indeed, my first incursion into crime gave me an understanding how fascinating a criminal's life can be.'[16]

The Submarine Tracking Room, crucial nerve centre for the Battle of the Atlantic, was also housed deep in the Citadel. Its function was symbolised by a material 'plot', a vast map with markers moving across the board to signify convoys, escorts and their attackers. Qualities of empathy and involvement among the people who worked there needed to be held in check. Historian Patrick Beesly, then second-in-command to the legendary Rodger Winn, explained the need for the operatives to suppress imagination. It didn't help to visualise the terrible human and material consequences of mistaken decisions; the only way to stay sane and work effectively was to treat the Atlantic as a giant chess board. When ships were lost, they were removed from the board but it was imperative that the game went on.

Patrick Beesly (b. 1913) was an oarsman rather than a sailor. He'd been captain of the First Trinity Boat Club when at Cambridge, following in the wake of his elder brother, a gold medallist at the 1928 Amsterdam Olympics, then had continued his studies in Bonn, Vienna and Brussels. When he returned to England in June 1939 and volunteered for the RNVR, he was immediately commissioned into the Special Branch where he began working for Paymaster Commander Norman Denning RN, the creator of the OIC. Denning (b. 1904) had lost two of his elder brothers in WWI. He had joined the Navy soon after the war's end but was disqualified for an active service role because of his poor eyesight. He was an outstandingly talented supply officer and would eventually become the first non-executive officer to be appointed DNI.

However cerebral one's approach, it must have been hard to treat the submarine tracking plot consistently as a game of chess. When the First Sea Lord, Sir Dudley Pound, came down to the OIC with Norman Denning late in the evening of 4 July 1942, failed to understand Denning's careful answer to his question and issued the disastrous order that the escorts were to withdraw and ships were to scatter from Convoy PQ 17, he is unlikely to have known that the head of the Tracking Room, Commander Rodger Winn RNVR, had a brother on the convoy. Godfrey Winn was travelling as a guest on the anti-aircraft ship HMS *Pozarica* after taking a decision to leave broadcasting, journalism and the Ministry of Information and train to become a hostilities only seaman at HMS *Ganges*. The life-changing moment had arrived for him six months earlier, on the night he'd heard of the loss of HMSs *Prince of Wales* and *Repulse*. He'd been in Bolton giving a morale-boosting talk and he'd met the parents of a 19-year-old whom he remembered from a talk given to Bomber Command. They had asked him for a photograph. 'Yes of course he can have it,' Winn began, then stopped 'seeing the instant, absolute obliteration of the lamp from behind their two faces'.[17] Their son had been killed on his first operational trip. Winn realised that he could no longer write as he felt, because he would be 'spreading fear and despondency'. He decided he must learn to fight. But first he would go to sea for a 'holiday' – on PQ 17 to Archangel!

When Godfrey Winn eventually returned from the Arctic in August 1942, he had promised his shipmates from *Pozarica* that he would tell their story. He assumed an eye-witness account would be welcomed. He was called to the Admiralty, to see the First Lord, Mr AV Alexander. He allowed himself to imagine that he might be taken to the Ops Room, introduced and... Instead, he was informed that 'not one word of his story would come out'.[18] Winn was stunned and angry but had no choice other than to wait until the war's end before fulfilling his pledge.

Brothers, friends, fathers and sons were all part of the intricate seagoing network, together with those who loved them. There were women working in the Admiralty and in other operational centres (such as the 'plot' at the Western Approaches HQ in Liverpool) who tracked the progress of their husbands at sea. Beesly mentions Convoy TM 1 (January 1943) as especially painful within OIC, not only because it was a material disaster (seven out of nine tankers carrying supplies to the Mediterranean were lost), but it also had the additional personal dimension that the senior escort officer on the convoy had recently been part of their group. On this occasion, the Government Code and Cypher School (GC&CS Bletchley) had been too slow decyphering the signals that should have enabled the Tracking Room to reroute the convoy. HMS *Havelock*, leading the group, rescued 123 survivors but 111 merchant seamen died, with only two U-boats damaged.

★★★

Attitudes to rescue remained among the most ethically challenging decisions that commanding officers had to make. Edward Terrell, returning from a technical advice mission to the USA and Canada, recalled a conversation with Captain CG Illingworth of the liner *Queen Mary*, one of the 'monsters' forbidden to stop as they raced independently across the Atlantic. In October 1942, *Queen Mary*, under Illingworth's command, had sliced through and sunk the cruiser HMS *Curacoa*. "'I ordered her to go on," said Captain Illingworth, with his eyes blazing, "And left those poor devils to drown."'Terrell knew that Illingworth had acted correctly. The *Queen Mary* was carrying 11,000

American troops and would have been an immensely valuable sitting target for U-boats or bombers if she had paused. 'But this decision to leave British sailors to drown was one of the most cruel and harsh burdens ever placed on the shoulders of a sea captain by the stern necessities of war. Kindly Captain Illingworth would have to carry the memory of what he had done to the grave.'[19]

In the previous month, September 1942, Werner Hartenstein commanding U-156 torpedoed and sank the troopship *Laconia* 900 miles from Freetown. The *Laconia* was carrying almost 1,800 Italian prisoners of war, their Polish guards, British servicemen and their families. Horrified by the reality of the drowning prisoners, women and children, Hartenstein called other U-boats to come and help rescue survivors. He stayed alongside doing what he could to support the people in the lifeboats or in the water. Then he went further and put out a message welcoming any nearby source of assistance and offering truce. Time passed under the burning sun. Two Vichy warships were despatched from Dakar and Senegal, British ships nearby feared a trap: a US Liberator aircraft misunderstood the signals and began to bomb the surfaced U-boat and the lifeboats attached to her. The submarine cast off the lifeboats and dived. Admiral Dönitz, shocked by the bombing of his U-boat, issued new instructions, known as the Laconia Order:

All attemps to rescue the crews of sunken ships will cease forthwith. This probition applies equally to the picking up of men in the water and putting them on board a lifeboat, to the righting of overturned lifeboats, and to the supply of food and water. Such activities are a contradiction of the primary object of war: namely the destruction of hostile ships and their crews.[20]

In March 1943, Hartenstein and the crew of U-156 were killed by depth charges dropped from a US Catalina aircraft. Dönitz's instructions formed part of his indictment at the Nuremberg war crimes tribunal.

Balancing ethics and effectiveness was hard on land as well. In May 1944, one of Ewen Montagu's double agents (code name *Tricycle*) was advised by his German handlers to get out of London to avoid the imminent new bombing raids. Then, when the V1 bombs began falling in the following month, the Germans ordered all their agents in the London area to report the time and place of the explosions together with the damage done, and to do it as quickly as possible. This gave the XX committee a problem – and a potential opportunity. Montagu explains: 'If the agents were to be kept "alive" there was no possible way in which they could avoid obeying these orders.' But what were they to say? John Drew, one of the committee members, put forward an ingenious scheme whereby the agents would report the bombs but give the wrong times of impact. 'If a bomb fell in the central area of London the agents should report it at the same time as one which fell between 5 or 10 miles short. This, it was considered, would lead the German to believe that the shorter range-setting was the right one.' The chiefs of staff backed the scheme 'on the basis that the V1s which were not shot down were bound to fall somewhere and it was better they should fall where they would cause the least casualties and damage.' However, Churchill was away at a conference and the War Cabinet vetoed the idea, 'on the cowardly principle that no one was entitled to decide that A should die rather than B'.[21]

Montagu was furious but he was not alone. Sir Findlater Stewart from the Home Defence department took the decision to go ahead with the deception on the assumption that Churchill would support it on his return. The network of agents was duly briefed on their false reporting duties. After the war, Montagu was gratified to learn that among documents captured from the Germans was a plot showing how the range had been gradually altered, drawing further back and to the east, thus saving many lives – though not all, and at the cost of others elsewhere – in the crowded centre of London.

★★★

Fredman Ashe Lincoln was fierce in his decisions. Although the essence of his and others' work investigating mines and rendering them safe was defensive, he was quick to take any opportunity to turn aggression back against the enemy. One chance came with his investigations into the *Sperrbrecher*. These were auxiliary warships (*Vorpostenboote*) converted into large specialist mine-clearance ships. Their bows were strongly reinforced, and they were given added flotation material and a large electromagnet adjusted to detonate mines once the clearance vessel had passed safely overhead.

British intelligence picked up loose comments by German seamen in bars. This was interesting but insufficiently specific. What Lincoln and the HMS *Vernon* scientists needed to know was the precise magnetic field of the electrified coil so they could adjust their own mechanisms in order to remain undetectable. A lucky photo of a *Sperrbrecher* immediately after detonating a mine, taken by an RAF reconnaissance plane in July 1942, set the investigators on course to begin complex calculations and running experiments to determine its exact magnetic field. This took the best part of a year but when it was done, a booby trap mine was created. These were sown in every minefield where the ships were known to work. Within a fortnight, they had claimed their first kill. 'By the end of the war', writes Lincoln delightedly, 'more than 100 *Sperrbrecher* had fallen victim to the mines they had gone out to sweep.'[22] His figures may be a little high but it's generally accepted that more than 50 per cent of the vessels modified for this task were lost.

As well as his pride at his position within the Royal Navy, Lincoln was always conscious of his connection with the worldwide Jewish network. One poignant message arrived directly to HMS *Vernon*. It was the opposite of the booby traps against which he and his RMS colleagues usually needed to be alert:

> *One of my officers rendered safe a German magnetic mine which appeared to be of the usual type. When, however, the mine was opened and examined it was found it would never have operated as a mine because the whole of the internal works had been sabotaged. Furthermore, on the inside of the mine casing, the explanation appeared. Someone had drawn a shield of David (Magen David) and underneath in English had put the words, 'We are with you'.* [23]

It seemed obvious that this was the work of a Jewish slave labourer in a Nazi munitions factory. 'It was a very heartening thing for us to realise that even at the risk of their own lives these unhappy slaves were willing to save the lives of our fighters and ships.' The discovery was reported to Churchill but a decision taken not to publicise it for fear of reprisals and, as Lincoln added characteristically, 'Of course we did not want to throw away the undoubted advantage that this type of sabotage gave to us'.

19

'Would you care to join me in a little yachting?'[1]

1943–1944: Levant Schooner Flotilla, Sicily and the Salerno Landings, COPP7

Many of the yachtsmen who had volunteered so readily in the years immediately preceding the war would find their view of the sea challenged as never before: for some, it would be altered irrevocably. Most had laid up – or left – their yachts or dinghies in September 1939 and were to enjoy no more sailing until 1945. A few found unexpected opportunities when they were posted abroad and lugsails could be rigged on some of the ships' boats or whalers. Nigel Sharp has researched the ingenuity with which some people managed to get afloat on British inland waters but the invasion fear had prompted harsh immobilisation orders on rivers for all yachts that had not been requisitioned, particularly near the South or East coasts: a plank might need to be removed from below the waterline or holes bored in the hull. As far as I'm aware, the only RNVSR yachtsman to use his sailing skills directly in the cause of war was Adrian Seligman with the Levant Schooner Flotilla (joined peripherally by Martin Solomon).

After his assignment delivering the Russian tanker *Olinda* to Beirut, Seligman spent a few months on Mediterranean convoy escort duty as commanding officer of the corvette *Erica*. He left her in February 1943, just a few days before she struck a mine and was sunk. Her loss was announced on the wireless and Adrian's family assumed he was dead. His brother Madron, on active service in North Africa, wrote to an uncle: 'I immediately (only five minutes now since I heard the news) wonder what it was that Adrian aimed at in life. Perhaps nothing that he could name or realize; but unconsciously and inherently he stood for equality of all men, fairness to all men, recognition for the underdog, and freedom of spirit.' Madron described himself 'writing this letter in a candlelit tent on a hillside just above a little French-Arab village while the traffic of guns and tanks rolls past and the guns flash to the East; and this somber scene only adds bitterness to the sensations I have on hearing of Adrian's death.' He believed his brother had 'stood for originality and enterprise [...] I suppose, knowing Adrian's nature, we all expected this news eventually.'[2]

Adrian had not died but had been loaned to the SOE, assisting them in landing agents deep in the enemy-held archipelagos of the Aegean, until he found himself in the SOE headquarters in Cairo, up against an unidentified Colonel K. This colonel ordered Seligman to fit out a caique (many had been abandoned in Beirut), add a more powerful engine, guns and explosives, then take her into the Aegean and use her to attack Greek schooners flying the red-and-white German Sea Transport flag, which indicated that they were carrying stores and equipment between the islands. Seligman was to sink them, then machine-gun any survivors in the water. He refused. 'This is an order.' 'Not one I can obey, sir,' said Seligman, happening to mention the Geneva Convention.[3]

The unidentified colonel did not take this well. Seligman fled back to Alexandria and the more congenial company of Old Etonian John Campbell RN, a WWI veteran and experienced yachtsman, now stationed at HMS *Nile*. Campbell quickly contacted Humphrey Quill, a Royal Marine who was staff officer (intelligence) for the Levant and who would later take overall charge of Fleming's 30AU. A clever compromise was reached: Seligman would be sent to Beirut to collect and refurbish caiques but they would be a regular flotilla, not directly under SOE control, though they might assist their operations. The caiques would be given better engines and a modicum of armament, then used for transporting raiders in action against the German- and Italian-held islands, undertaking reconnaissance and facilitating escapes by potential soldiers or refugees. Not piracy.

Seligman collected a small fleet of single-masted caiques, with a couple of the larger schooner-rigged type and two fast well-armed MLs. Their work was mainly to be carried out in darkness, in potentially hostile waters. Although the Italian Armistice, signed on 8 September 1943, had seemed to offer Britain the chance of establishing control over some of the Dodecanese islands, particularly

Kos and Leros, fierce fighting there had ended in British defeat. The internal political situations within the islands were volatile and complex following both Italian and German occupations, unpredictable Turkish attitudes and the almost impenetrable local tensions between neighbouring communities and within families. Seligman's compilation narrative *War in the Islands* opens with a great *The Riddle of the Sands* moment when fisherman Yanni sails Seligman through white waters in a blizzard, purely for the purpose of luring hated cousin Orhan and the disguised German patrol schooner to destruction. The desperate agent whom they are on mission to supply seems no more than a convenient pretext for a knockout blow in a grim family feud.

The modest 25ft, low-freeboard, shallow-draught, single-masted caiques might pass unremarked when on passage but they also needed to be able to lay up unnoticed. Seligman was lucky to meet a fellow Old Harrovian in the wardroom bar in HMS *Martial* in Beirut. This was Maurice Green. Seligman remembers that Green wasn't especially eager to chat but his camouflage problem was so much on his mind that he persevered anyway. From the conversation came the idea of netting produced in different colours to blend with the different types of rock and vegetation, either reddish-ochre or grey and black. In some areas, a green-yellow combination might be needed. The caiques' masts were stepped in a tabernacle so could easily pivot down to lie flat along the length of the boat. The netting was then laid on top with bamboo poles and wires used as spreaders to break up the shape. A friendly pilot took reconnaissance photos of their experiments, confirming that the caiques were invisible from the air – as long as the correct nets were spread. As most of the landings took place in the dark, it was all too easy to make a mistake with net selection and not to realise until the sun was up. It was a similar system to that used by Patrick Dalzel-Job to ensure his flotilla of MTBs could lie unobserved in Norwegian waters.

Initially, Seligman chose a secluded anchorage off the coast of south-west Turkey as the flotilla HQ, then as the pattern of the war changed, they moved further north. Though Turkey was neutral, co-operation between Vladimir Wolfson in Istanbul and Noel Rees RNVR, vice-consul in Ismir – who were running an MI9 escape line – facilitated the informal use of small coves along the

Turkish coast. Recruitment was by volunteering only. The officers were young reservists aged 19–23 and the crews came from all three services. Frequently, they were the bored, the 'awkward squad' and the defaulters, and they got along together very well – once they'd learned some basic seamanship. *War in the Islands* includes a 'Pongo's account of his first attempt to bring LS5 to a halt in the deep-water anchorage at the head of the bay of Kos:

> *You ram your bowsprit into the bow of the vessel against which you propose to berth (in this case Jim Morgan's Fairmile ML 351), making a hole in it about 3" square. When this rebound has spent itself, you go 'slow ahead, hard a port', bumping and scraping your rubbing strake along your neighbour's hull, until your stern-line, which some kind fellow aboard the Fairmile has taken and made fast, brings you quietly alongside. And there you are, safe and snug.*
>
> *You then disregard in a gentlemanly manner, the wild and highly personal obscenities levelled at you by the infuriated skipper of the other vessel, appealing to his better nature with the suggestion that he fit a copper tingle over the hole and let it be generally understood that a 40mm enemy shell was responsible for the damage.[4]*

The officers and crews needed to wear some identifying badges but otherwise didn't look very 'pusser'. RN officer Roger Durnford, navigating officer on the destroyer HMS *Eclipse*, which had struck a mine off Leros, was surprised to be rescued by a fierce-looking ruffian in a Turkish fishing schooner, who spoke public school English and turned out to be Seligman.

Martin Solomon was also spotted in a caique off Leros. He was working directly for Quill and the SOE, having teamed up with the SBS officer Anders Lassen. I've tried to discover the names of the people who took responsibility for these little sailing ships, too small, it seems, to be included in the Navy Lists, but so far I've not succeeded. *War in the Islands* is compiled from 13 first-hand accounts in addition to Seligman's own. They're given under the writers' post-war occupations: the City Accountant's Tale, the Parson's Tale, the Artist's Tale, Tales from a Man of Malta, the Civil Engineer's Tales, the Surgeon's Tale, Tales from a Birmingham Businessman, the Bank Manager's Tale, the Professor's Tale, the Oxford Don's Tale, Tales from a Greek Shipping Company Director and the Insurance Company Director's Tales. Although this is rather a brilliant neo-Chaucerian way of ensuring that a collective endeavour is acknowledged (and may encourage younger people to look again at the venerable and wonder what adventures might lie hidden in their past), I'd still like to be able to pin names with confidence.

Geoffrey Kirk (the Professor's Tale) is easy to identify as he's apt to become diverted at moments of high tension by his first sight of an ancient Greek building in its natural habitat. Kirk (b. 1921) had left Cambridge aged 20 to join the Navy as a rating, then gained an RNVR commission. His contribution includes an episode that took place at the unfinished Temple of Apollo at Didyma (then the local Turkish HQ) to which he and a companion have been marched, accused of violating neutrality.

> As we proceeded the elder of the Turkish soldiers kept addressing his officer in distinctly surly tones. After a while a thoughtful Yiannis vouchsafed the cheerful news that he was trying to persuade him that we should be peremptorily disposed of – murdered in short – thus saving a long and unnecessary journey. It appeared that this gnarled-looking character was a Gallipoli veteran who had no particular liking for the British, let alone the Greeks.[5]

After a long, uncomfortable night, orders came that the British sailors were to be returned to their boat and expelled from Turkish waters. Kirk immediately asked permission to spend half an hour exploring the ruins of the temple. 'Almost everyone in sight came with me [...] My informal lecture as we went round was translated after a fashion and evidently much appreciated.' As soon as the war was over, Kirk returned to Cambridge, completed his degree, gained a fellowship and spent the rest of his career there, finally as Regius Professor of Greek (1974–1982).

The Oxford Don contributes a less reassuring Tale. He was in charge of *LS6* and a cargo of 12 Special Boat Service (SBS) commandos who were to be landed on the island of Lemnos after dark. He had slipped into a harbour on the small island of Strati to lie unobtrusively during the day. The dozen houses and the church in the small village were empty, doors left open, a few rumpled sheets still on the beds, scraps of food in the dog bowls. 'A weird, unearthly atmosphere hung over the whole village.' A small Greek caique came into the bay and landed two Orthodox priests. Behind them was a schooner, filled with *andartes*, threatening-looking characters wearing black scarves and bullet-filled bandoliers. The priests addressed him anxiously: '*kakourgi!*' (bad men) '*prostasia*' (protection). The narrator understood that the priests needed passage to Mitilini on Lesbos and promised to come back the next day, after delivering his current passengers. 'LS6 was not a large boat and we had twelve soldiers and sailors in her already.' His understanding of Greek was limited and he assumed they were warning him against the anti-British *andartes*. When he returned to Strati early the following morning to collect them, the island was once again deserted. Later, he discovered that once the Germans had withdrawn, the Communist parties were setting up People's Courts where suspected collaborators and anyone they didn't like — notably priests and schoolteachers — were being tried and usually executed.

> *I thought back to our meeting with the two priests in Strati harbour and all at once the whole episode took on a different and more ominous complexion. What if they had not been warning us that we were in danger from the Communists and had instead been pleading for protection rather than offering it? Had we unwittingly thrown two innocent and holy men to the wolves? It was a deeply disturbing thought which remains with me still.[6]*

The work of the Levant Schooner Flotilla was usually at one remove from the bitterness of civil war in the Aegean, although the inclusion of the Greek Shipping Company Director's Tale gives a native Greek experience. He was in command of a Greek Sacred Company's caique, running escapees to the Middle East, but was captured, taken on a forced march, beaten, interrogated and tried by a People's Court.

> *I am struck by the lasting effect that the sheer brutishness of the ensuing events had on me. The pain and shock of physical violence itself is difficult to recall, but the cold hatred and almost animal ferocity on the faces of our young executioners — some of them no more than sixteen and seventeen years old — is something I shall never forget.[7]*

The after-effect of perpetrating violence was witnessed by a former conscientious objector, who had volunteered for the Navy, though he was no sailor. He was eventually given command of one of the flotilla's HDMLs, from which he landed and collected SBS patrols. He recalled a conversation, late one night, with a young soldier who had returned in tears after a knife mission, haunted by the face of the lad he had killed: 'What are we all doing here, sorr... killing a few Germans, being killed ourselves and getting hundreds of Greek people shot for helping us? What's it all for, sorr? What are we doin' here?'[8] The narrator remembered that conversation as a part of the overall journey that would eventually lead him to enter the Church.

★★★

Lincoln records that 1943 'began unhappily'. He was war-weary and feeling the strain of his work and the emotional burden of losing colleagues who were killed undertaking mine investigations that he had ordered. He developed gall bladder trouble, needed an operation and then his convalescence was slow. After Pesach, Lincoln took the decision to volunteer for an attachment to Fleming's 30 Commando (previously known as the Special Intelligence Unit, later 30AU). 'If I was to go with it, I could pursue my investigation of enemy weapons by actually seizing them. This obviously was better than waiting in an Admiralty office for intelligence to filter through.'[9] His decision led him to Algiers and an initially confrontational meeting with Quintin Riley. Riley, who was in command, insisted that everyone should kneel for worship: Lincoln, who was there as an expert on mines with authority to requisition support from Riley's unit, refused. According to Lincoln, Riley flashed out: 'My God I hate all Jews.' Yet the requirements of working together made them firm friends for the rest of their lives, until at a memorial service for Quintin's father Aethelstan (a distinguished member of the Church of England's House of Laity) Lincoln was invited to share the family pew.

Lincoln landed together with 30 Commando in both Sicily (Operation *Husky*) and Salerno (Operation *Avalanche*). Humphrey Quill joined on a similarly informal basis, bringing with him Martin Solomon and other fluent Italian speakers who helped track down hidden Italian Navy documents. Though they were mainly 'sailors-in-jeeps' during these operations, the moments at sea immediately prior to the landings seem to have meant a great deal to Lincoln. Perhaps this was a little closer to the naval ideal for which he had joined? Instead of being a lone operative, he was momentarily part of a crew. He remembered standing with the colour sergeant as their assault craft approached the Italian coast in the dark hours of the morning: 'As we moved on towards the beach, the colour sergeant turned to me and said, "Is it not strange, sir, that you a Jew and me a Christian are likely to die together in the next few minutes?" However we successfully landed and charged up the beach to the hail of machine gun fire'. After a few hours' sleep in an open field, Lincoln woke to the crow of a cockerel as well as the screech of shell fire. He took his tefillin out of his haversack and observed his usual rituals.

> My devotions over, the colour sergeant crept up to me to say that he had scouted out the position roundabout and had sighted the German observations post which was clearly directing artillery fire on our position. He and I then took a couple of Bren guns out to the perimeter and were able to dispose of the German observation post with a few well directed bursts from the Brens.[10]

Lincoln was essentially working to his own agenda, though he was entitled to the unit's support. Marine Jock Finlayson spent an afternoon in the big naval mine warehouse at Trapani (western Sicily) helping Lincoln defuse German sea mines. He wrote afterwards that he himself had been constantly petrified, imagining booby traps and time-delay detonators, but that Lincoln appeared to possess ice-cold nerves.[11]

Although Riley and the other members of the unit experienced mixed fortunes over those summer months, they collected much worthwhile material, especially on the island of Capri, where they captured the chief of the German post-occupation organisation in the area, together with his codes, list of agents and complete Italian Navy cypher. On the mainland, they took Italian torpedo expert Admiral Minisini into custody, together with blueprints for some of Italy's innovative work in experimental torpedoes and midget submarines. Moving on to Bari in October brought unexpected complications as they found themselves involved with the bitter politics of Yugoslavia and unwelcome to the Partisans, led by Tito and supported by Brigadier Fitzroy Maclean. Riley had a tendency to sympathise more readily with the monarchist Chetniks, and Jim 'Sancho' Glanville, the unit's second-in-command, who had previously been vice-consul in Zagreb, was definitely unacceptable to the new regime.

For his part, Lincoln was concerned for the safety of a group of Jewish refugees hiding from Croatians in the northern Adriatic Islands. He prevailed on an RN commander with a flotilla of MGBs to evacuate them to Bari. Permits were eventually arranged for the refugees to be taken on to Palestine. In December 1943, Lincoln, Riley and the naval members of 30 Commando returned to London to reorganise once again and look ahead to the Operation *Overlord* landings planned for the following year.

If anyone had doubted the value of detailed beach reconnaissance before an attempt at an amphibious landing, Dieppe would have forced them to recant. The slits in the chalk cliffs, concealing artillery, had been missed and the size of the chert, with its disabling effect on tank track mechanisms, had not been fully taken into account. Lieutenant Nigel Clogstoun-Willmott RN, whose uncle had been badly wounded at Gallipoli, and had himself been a beachmaster at Narvik, had insisted that offshore surveys and wave-height overflights were not adequate to provide all the information needed for an amphibious operation. Now, Lord Mountbatten, as Combined Operations chief, asked for Clogstoun-Willmott's involvement in planning the North Africa landings.

Soon afterwards, Clogstoun-Willmott was given formal permission to form small units, to be known as Combined Operations Pilotage Parties (COPPs). These would usually use a combination of canoe (often folding folbots) and submarines to undertake direct surveys of beaches where landings were planned. Teams needed to be led by a trained hydrographer or highly experienced navigator – the sort of person who might otherwise be in charge of the navigation on an RN cruiser or other battleship. These valuable officers were to be risked on folding canoes, launched from submarines, on to intensively guarded enemy shores in the dark. Then they would have to swim. The navigators/ hydrographers would be supported by an experienced engineer, two or three additional Navy officers and three other servicemen, supporting with equipment, provisioning and sheer muscle. All of them needed to be commando-trained. It's perhaps not surprising that only ten such groups were formed.

Typographer Ruari McLean was the second naval member of COPP7 and an unlikely recruit. In 1938, McLean had written to Penguin Books to ask for a job. An answer had come back, signed Edward Young, production manager, saying that the writer had the only worthwhile job in the company but that McLean should come and see him anyway. Young was a few years older than McLean and was described by him as a 'charmer ... with iron determination hidden under a thick layer of velvet'.[12] When Young subsequently invited McLean to come and share a flat in Hammersmith, McLean was initially reluctant but agreed 'and entered the most hilarious period of my life'. Allen Lane, Young's boss at Penguin and a regular visitor to the flat, offered them a contract to produce a history of printing. Before they'd done more than begin the reading, the Munich crisis occurred. Young, a keen weekend sailor, began studying for his Master Mariner's certificate and McLean was persuaded to help him practise for half an hour each evening on a Morse buzzer. He wasn't invited, however, when Young and his sailing friends joined the London River Fire Brigade, so he signed up to the London Police War Reserve instead.

McLean was a pacifist and had planned to register as a conscientious objector but his parents, whom he loved, were so upset that he changed his mind and tried to join the Navy. He was rejected due to his poor eyesight. 'As I was going out of the door, I turned and said, "Does it help that I have a cousin who is a Lieutenant Commander?"'[13] It did. McLean went in as a telegraphist, spent a year as an ordinary seaman, then was sent to HMS *King Alfred* as a cadet rating. Once his OLQs had been confirmed, he was posted as a British liaison officer on a Free French submarine, where his poor eyesight wouldn't matter. When he became bored after a year of congenial but (he claimed) undemanding service (though he was awarded the Croix de Guerre), fellow typographer Robert Harling found him a job in the ISTD.

I found myself sitting in an Oxford College, working along the coast of France, preparing extremely detailed descriptions of every port and harbour, from the tiniest fishing village to, in due course, Brest and Toulon – of which I was astonished to find the Navy's intelligence and charts were extremely inadequate. We worked from every printed source, from all ground and air photographs available, and from interviews which we conducted with anyone who could be found who knew the place.[14]

The work was fascinating but McLean couldn't settle to an essentially civilian existence: 'Having taken a lot of trouble to get to sea it was embarrassing to be now working in Oxford, my hometown, wearing civilian clothes.'

Again, the sociable pre-war network of advertisers, journalists and print specialists came to his rescue. He met a friend, Temporary Acting Lieutenant Geoffrey Galwey RNVR, in the Admiralty and discovered that Galwey was discontented with his current occupation (acting as a flag lieutenant in Largs) but excited about his forthcoming post, second-in-command to Nigel Clogstoun-Willmott, recruiting and training canoeists for the COPPs. He explained to McLean that his eyesight wouldn't be a problem: 'It's all done at night and no one can see in the dark so eyesight doesn't matter.'[15]

McLean thus became part of COPP7. His group was led by Geoffrey Hall RN, a naval hydrographer who would later become his brother-in-law. In his account of their training, McLean is honest about the additional difficulties that he encountered because, unlike the RNVR officers with a yachting background, he didn't have the principles of basic seamanship or an adequate understanding of the effect of wind, tide and sea conditions on something as fragile as a canoe.

Experience taught us early that the danger of detection by the enemy was negligible compared with danger from the weather; the initiative always rested with us, as intruders, and we would be poor at our job if we ever allowed ourselves to be detected. But wind, sea and tide could be enemies with whom we had to reckon more seriously. The first COPP parties anxious to justify themselves and do the job for which they had been training, launched their canoes in weather which made success impossible and four valuable officers were drowned.[16]

McLean tells the story of a training incident in which he completely underestimated the effect of the lee of the land deceptively sheltering him and his 'beefy' commando companion. Hard as they paddled, they were swept helplessly backwards and out to sea in the wind and darkness. Finally catching on to the chain of an anchored landing craft, they climbed on deck, leaving their paddles in the canoe. When they looked back over the side, their canoe had overturned and the paddles were gone. 'Another lesson in elementary seamanship,' comments McLean.

Meanwhile, 12 of the 16 early COPPists, sent to survey the beaches of Sicily in preparation for Operation *Husky*, had not come back. The main problems were poor equipment, hurried training and missing their crucial rendezvous with the waiting submarines. In addition, beaches thought likely to be invasion targets were heavily patrolled, with perhaps one sentry every 75–100 yards. 'The results gained did not justify the losses in personnel,' commented Clogstoun-Willmott, resolving not to reduce the pace of training at all and never to accept poor-quality kit. The submarine commanders stressed how important it was that they should be fully informed of all aspects of the mission and have the chance to develop a close partnership with the landing parties.

In the later summer of 1943, COPP7, believing they too were destined for the Mediterranean, were sent to India. On 9 September, when Lincoln and Riley were already in their assault landing craft heading for Salerno, and when the British in the Aegean were deciding to reinforce Leros, COPP7 were at Chittagong preparing to reconnoitre beaches off the coast of Burma in readiness for possible amphibious landings at Akyab.

Edward Young, meanwhile, was in Scotland attached to HMS *Forth* and working up the brand-new S-class submarine *Storm* as her commanding officer. After a brief spell of duty inside the Arctic Circle, he too was sent to the Indian Ocean, arriving to join the 4th Submarine Flotilla in Trincomalee Harbour in February 1944. When not on patrol, it was a lovely place: swimming parties in warm water, picnics with the Wrens from the cypher office, dinghy sailing. Towards the end of May, however, Young had an assignment that he found especially unnerving. There was a focus on the reconnaissance of Sumatra, ahead of a possible attack to pave the way towards the recapture of Singapore. *Storm's* mission was to land a Sumatran native near the island of Pulau Weh in order for him to collect information about the Japanese naval base at Sabang. They were carrying an Army major and a naval rating who would row the agent ashore at night, return to the submarine, then row ashore three nights later to collect him.

The landing went according to plan; the collection didn't. The agent's signal was late and coming from the wrong place. Young aborted for that night and returned the next. Again, the signal felt indefinably wrong. Had the Sumatran been caught and tortured into giving away the rendezvous? After a tense exchange, the major went ashore. 'In that moment I admired him very much. He was extremely frightened, but in cold blood he was going ahead with the job he had to do, and you can't be braver than that.'[17] Young took *Storm* in as close as he dared and the major pulled away into the darkness. Time passed. The waiting grew ever more tense. The shoreline went dark. Young could see a black dot on the water – it was the dinghy returning. For a moment he hoped the operation had gone according to plan. But then the signal began to flash once again and suddenly the submarine was at the centre of crossfire from four machine guns positioned round the lower slopes beyond the shore.

Now it was Young who had needed to hold his nerve. They had run into an ambush and he had to consider his overriding duty to his ship. Could he continue to risk her by remaining on the surface? Young sent the rest of his crew below and hung on until finally the dinghy reached the submarine. They hauled the two men, retching and gasping, on deck, abandoned the dinghy and made ready to dive as the bullets whistled round them.

Later, when they had put together the major's account of his shore experience, they wondered what had happened to the Sumatran. It seemed most likely that he had been captured, tortured and forced to act as a decoy. 'The thought of his probable fate cast a gloom over our spirits for the remainder of the patrol.'[18]

Just days after Young and *Storm* returned to Trincomalee, he met McLean, his pre-war flatmate. McLean explained that his COPP 7 unit was surveying likely beaches to prepare for future amphibious invasions. He wondered whether 'I would take him with me on my next patrol, launch him in a boat off an enemy beach in Sumatra at the dead of night and recover him when he had completed his soundings. I roared with laughter and told him he could hardly have asked me at a worse moment [...] Poor Ruari was rather taken aback at my pusillanimity.'[19]

The submarine HMS *Tudor* was eventually assigned to carry COPP7 to Sumatra. It was August 1944. As she set out, she passed HMS *Storm* returning. McLean reflected:

> During the night my friend Edward Young passed close to us on his way in from patrol in his submarine Storm. If, five years previously when we were sharing a flat in Hammersmith and pursuing the peaceful profession of typography, we could have known that we would one night pass within a mile of each other in submarines in the Far East, we would have rushed down to the Black Lion with shaking hands, to have a pint.[20]

'Multitudes of seagoing lighters, carrying full loads of soldiers'[1]

April–June 1944: Exercise Tiger and Operation Neptune

Operation *Neptune*, the cross-Channel element of the June 1944 Normandy landings, required astonishing levels of detailed planning, communication, innovation, manufacturing and manpower as well as hardcore determination and courage. COPPists had risked their lives using X-craft (midget submarines) to produce detailed beach surveys. No effort was spared. When there was a suggestion of doubt over the load-bearing qualities of a specific area of Gold Beach near Ver-sur-Mer, former RNVSR member ARH Nye took a reconnaissance party across in MGB *312* on New Year's Eve 1943/4. They towed a small landing craft from which two men swam in, carrying augers to bore down into the beach. They were under the occasional beam of a lighthouse and could hear the distant sound of partying. It was a blustery night and the surveyors struggled to swim out through the waves, carrying their samples.

Exercise *Tiger* was a rehearsal that went wrong. It was a training exercise on 27/28 April 1944 involving a landing on Slapton Sands in Devon, a beach identified as similar to Utah Beach on the Contentin Peninsula. More men died during Exercise *Tiger* than would die in the Utah Beach landings on D-Day (ground, not air). There had been other such rehearsals – Nevil Shute had been an observer on an LCT during Exercise *Trousers*, a bombardment of Slapton Sands by Canadian forces earlier in April that had also been watched by generals Montgomery and Dempsey.

The first part of Exercise *Tiger* was a bombardment and an infantry assault. General Eisenhower had ordered live ammunition to be used to give his inexperienced troops a taste of real battle conditions. US

Rear-Admiral Don P Moon changed the time of the bombardment, delaying it for an hour. This message failed to reach all the assault troops, meaning that for many young men this was their last as well as their first experience of 'real' battle. Moon was a WWI veteran who had taken part in the 1942 North Africa landings. He went on to direct the Operation *Neptune* Utah landings from the destroyer USS *Bayfield*. He and his ship were then ordered to Italy in preparation for yet another amphibious assault, Operation *Dragoon*, the planned invasion of Southern France scheduled for 15 August 1944. On 5 August, however, Admiral Moon killed himself.

'Friendly fire' was not the only disaster to befall the unlucky troops on Exercise *Tiger*. The second element of the rehearsal was the arrival of a convoy of landing ship tanks (LSTs) from Plymouth. They had been instructed to take a long detour out into Lyme Bay to simulate the length of a Channel crossing. LSTs were eight large vessels (about 4,600 tons), slow and with little defensive armament. They were carrying men of the US First Combat Engineers and their vehicles. These men, who were wearing backpacks, had not been shown how to put on their life jackets correctly: many were wearing them round their waist, which tipped them upside down when they went overboard – then held them there. The English Channel was still very cold; many more men would die of hypothermia.

This convoy, T4, was escorted only by a single corvette, HMS *Azalea*. The destroyer HMS *Scimitar*, which should have been there providing speed, leadership and firepower, had been sent back to Plymouth for repairs. When Admiral Moon interviewed *Scimitar*'s commanding officer afterwards, he established that the damage to the destroyer had been above the waterline and she could still have continued to operate as convoy escort in the calm sea conditions. The commanding officer had queried his order to return to Plymouth but (as it transpired) a series of communication errors meant that no one had realised the significance of this withdrawal for the safety of the convoy and no message had reached Admiral Moon. When the destroyer HMS *Saladin* was ordered to T4's relief, she was too distant and it was already too late. Nine German E-boats, based in Cherbourg, had slipped through the Channel screen and intercepted the convoy. They had sunk or damaged four of the eight LSTs and approximately 639 lives had been lost, in addition to perhaps 300 earlier. It seems additionally shocking that exact figures are not known.

This story was first told to me by Allan Gotelee's son, Michael. He said it was an event that had continued to upset his father, long afterwards: if *Scimitar* had been there – as she could have been, despite her damage – the attack could have been repulsed and many lives saved. Initially, I misunderstood and thought Allan Gotelee had been HMS *Scimitar's* commanding officer then. In fact, his connection with the destroyer came later, when he took over her command in September 1944. In April, he was CO of the Hunt-class destroyer HMS *Goathland*, which had been converted as a headquarters ship and was supporting Force S (destined for Sword Beach). *Goathland* played a key role throughout Operation *Neptune. Scimitar's* commanding officer at the time of Exercise *Tiger* was Lieutenant Philip Archer-Shee RNVR, an experienced officer who had started his war service with Ludovic Kennedy on 'lucky' *Tartar*. No blame was attached to him.

Whatever people's private anger or regrets, there was little time to air them in late April 1944. Preparations for Exercise *Fabius* went ahead a week after *Tiger*, with practice landings taking place at Hayling Island, Littlehampton and Bracklesham Bay, as well as Slapton Sands again. The survivors from Convoy T4 had been rushed to hospital but an eyewitness report claims that the staff were instructed to treat them 'as though we're veterinarians; you will ask no questions and take no histories. There will be no discussion. Following standard procedures, anyone who talks about the casualties, regardless of their severity, will be subject to court martial. No one will be allowed to leave our perimeter until further orders.'[2] The survivors were then moved further away from the area, into Wales, and were split up to different units across Europe. The bodies of the dead were mainly interred in temporary graves, with many later moved to Madingley Cemetery near Cambridge or commemorated at Brookwood. It would be years before families knew how their sons, brothers and husbands died.

Meanwhile, there was an urgent, anxious search for ten dead men with BIGOT status – the top-ranking security clearance for people with specific knowledge of the invasion plans and the intended beaches. Had any of those corpses – or the documents they carried – been picked up by the E-boats, it could have been a *Man Who Never Was* scenario in reverse. For months, Ewen Montagu's double agents and the XX committee had been doing all they could to suggest that the actual invasion would be around the Pas-de-Calais area, or even Norway. Though Patrick Dalzel-Job had moved on from his MTB flotilla to work with the midget submarines involved with Operation *Source*, the attack on the *Tirpitz*, the Shetland-based 'VP' operations were stepped up over the winter of 1943–1944. These, together with other SOE and resistance activity in Norway, were credited with ensuring that Hitler continued to believe in the possibility of an invasion and therefore held back significant numbers of troops that might have been deployed elsewhere.

In England, an elaborate narrative was built up around a largely fictional US First Army apparently stationed in the south-east, threatening Calais. Suffolk historian and sailor Robert Simper remembers persuading his mother that they should be rowed out in a dinghy to look at the 'warship' anchored off Ramsholt Quay on the River Deben, then being fiercely waved away and threatened with a rifle. It was many years before he realised that this had been one of the 'Bigbobs' constructed from canvas and timber to simulate invasion craft as part of Operation *Quicksilver*.[3] In general, air defences against German reconnaissance planes were so effective by this period that the misinformation had to be more subtle, passed on by the network of apparent agents mingling little fragments of truth among the shimmering tissue of lies.

'Window' or 'chaff' was an actual shimmering tissue – also deceptive. Metallic strips were scattered by aircraft to confuse the enemies' radar. Both sides had discovered this technique and both had held off deploying it for fear the other would then discover and use it. By this stage of the war, however, the British felt sufficiently confident in the superiority of some of their radar devices (particularly centimetric radar, which had brought a crucial advantage to the escorts and covering aircraft in the Battle of the Atlantic) to include this within the grand overall deception. 'All radio signals can be jammed, bedeviled, and foxed by scientists who have sufficient wit and access to the complicated equipment that they need,' wrote Nevil Shute as he reflected on his convoy's trouble-free passage from the Thames to Juno Beach (Courseulles-sur-Mer) on D-Day.[4]

On this occasion, the scientist who had taken the lead was not Goodeve and the DMWD but Joan Curran, working at the Telecommunications Research Establishment.

> Perhaps the greatest success of the work of Joan Curran and her team was its use where foil was dropped with great precision by the Lancasters of 617 Squadron, to synthesise a phantom invasion force of ships in the straits of Dover on the night of 5-6 June 1944. This kept Von Runstedt and his commanders unsure of whether the brunt of the Allied assault would fall on Normandy or in the Pas de Calais.[5]

Curran (née Strothers; b. 1916) had won a scholarship to Newnham College Cambridge in 1934 and had rowed in the first women's direct Boat Race against Oxford the following year. She had gained an honours degree in Physics but could not receive it as no women were awarded degrees until 1948.

The DMWD development teams didn't include any female scientists but were learning to appreciate their WRNS staff members' qualities of reliability, conscientiousness and (occasionally) the ability to act independently. Gerald Pawle tells the story of Wren Frances Randall, a young hat-trimmer from South London, whom Nevil Norway sent on increasingly responsible missions to demonstrate the correct working of glider targets. Her promotion kept pace with her increasing self-assurance until she was despatched by the Admiralty to demonstrate the new systems in Egypt and Canada.

> So Wren Randall became Third Officer Randall and set off for Egypt. She handled the job remarkably well; returned to the DMWD for a short time; and went out to Canada. There she met a Lieutenant Commander in the Canadian Navy and married him. None of the Wheezers and Dodgers would have been really surprised if Wren Randall had finished the war as a member of the cabinet![6]

Except that there were no female Cabinet ministers during WWII. It seems a pity that Frances Randall's competence came as any sort of surprise (The Secret War author, Gerald Pawle, was an RNVR officer who served in the Mediterranean) but, viewed sociologically, one of the consistent themes in Shute's writing at this point is the difference being made to relationships and respect as servicemen and -women worked more closely together through this period. Kathleen Palmer, the female editor at *Yachting Monthly*, ran many articles and photographs showing the range of technical and engineering jobs that were being undertaken by women, as well as their administrative and communications work. The magazine had included a photograph of the first group of WRNS setting out on foreign service but didn't follow up that they had all been drowned.

In fiction, Leading Wren Janet Prentice, Shute's heroine in *Requiem for a Wren,* which is set in the spring and early summer of 1944 (though written in 1953), is a wronged and tragic figure. She possesses an innate talent for shooting, but when she steps out of her role as an Ordnance Wren (responsible for the maintenance of guns, not their use), she shoots down a Ju-99 that appears to pose an immediate danger. First there is applause, then there is doubt: could the aircraft have been carrying refugees? 'Friendly fire' disasters had been happening throughout the war but would any male offender have been spoken to like this?

> *Well I'm not going to take any disciplinary action, Leading Wren Prentice. I don't blame you for acting as you did. But remember this in future. You've not been trained for operations and you don't know operations. You have absolutely no right to fire any gun against the enemy, because in doing so you may make very serious mistakes. Remember that. That's all. You may go now.*[7]

Then, in the story, Leading Wren Prentice is punished; every source of comfort is stripped away, her fiancé, her father, even her dog. All die. The narrator, who could – should – have helped, is occupied elsewhere and Prentice finally takes the same exit as Admiral Moon. It's a bleak tale of brilliant natural talent encased in the 'wrong'-gendered body.

Maid Matelot, a memoir by post-war yachtswoman Rozelle Raynes, tells an opposite story from those pre-war yachtsmen who volunteered for the RNVSR and thus automatically became officers. Whereas RNVR trainees like Ruari McLean, newly promoted from the lower deck and sent to HMS *King Alfred* to develop his OLQs, were amazed to find themselves being treated to waitress service at meals, Rozelle Pierrepont (b. 1925) arrived in a WRNS dormitory bewildered by the challenge of making her own bed. Rozelle – Lady Rozelle – was the youngest child of Earl and Countess Manvers. (She was also their only surviving child, her elder sister and brother having both died before the age of ten.) She had longed to go to sea since she was three years old and spent the first years of the war cutting out photographs of warships and praying that the conflict would last long enough for her to take part.

Her applications to join the WRNS began when she was 15 and were finally successful in 1943 when she was 17 years old, though even Rozelle had to accept that there was no chance she could become a Boat's Crew Wren. These were highly sought-after positions, usually reserved for Admirals' daughters or young women with extensive previous experience. Nevertheless, by obdurately proving her unsuitability for anything else, she was finally drafted on to one of the first Wren Stoker courses. She was issued with bell-bottom trousers (in addition to her uniform skirt) and a knife with a marlinspike, then despatched to Portsmouth, 'a town of gaping craters and mountains of rubble' in September 1943. Her attempt to cheat the eye test section of the medical and become a deckhand at HMS *Hornet*, the Gosport MTB base commanded 'by the famous Peter Scott', failed spectacularly when she leapt into the water with the bow line several yards out, as she had only the haziest view of the jetty when not wearing her glasses.

As a Wren Stoker, posted to HMS *Abatos* (a base for the development of PLUTO, Pipe Line Under The Ocean), she and her companions were responsible for engine maintenance on an eclectic range of quite elderly small boats running errands between various bases on the Itchen and the Hamble rivers. In their off-duty periods, they learned splicing and semaphore from the coxswain, Fred, a man subject to deep fits of depression after his time in the Arctic convoys. Looking back, Rozelle realised how shallow her understanding had been then:

None of us had been deeply hit by the war at this stage [...] We had no personal knowledge of the indescribable tragedies suffered by many people during the war and were inclined to view the whole experience with the thoughtless egotism of extreme youth [...] None of us had any means of fully understanding the state of mind to which Fred was sometimes reduced.[8]

In January 1944, Rozelle, now 18, was posted to the Combined Operations base HMS *Tormentor* at Warsash. The River Hamble was filled with rows of landing craft tank (LCT), landing craft infantry (LCI) and landing craft artillery (LCA). The Wrens' half dozen boats were kept running day and night, whatever the weather conditions, fetching and carrying between these vessels and the base. Their varied cargoes, mixed haphazardly together, included 'senior officers, urgent signals, hospital cases, sacks of potatoes, barrels of rum and drunken sailors'.[9] Rozelle and her friend Margaret took turns as stoker and deckhand, maintaining the engines, keeping lookout and hanging on to ships' sides with a long boathook as men or stores were passed across. Sometimes they could be carrying as many as 70 drunken sailors back on the last Liberty boat of the night. Then it was the deckhand's job to ensure that all were delivered safely to the right ships, and none lost overboard. They were on mooring duty when the flotillas came in; shouted at when freezing cold hands made them fumble; and witnesses to frequent fights when the US troops arrived at the base 'and the fertile spirit of animosity flourished'. A posting to HMS *Squid*, an LCT repair centre, extended her worldly knowledge as the weeks of exercises and D-Day preparation passed: 'And so it went on night after night, soldiers and sailors all trying to forget that tomorrow might be their greatest day, or their last.'[10]

Unlike the sailors and airmen, 75 per cent of the US and British soldiers were conscripts; though not the Canadian Army, which was 100 per cent volunteer. Operation *Overlord*, the Allied invasion of Europe, was an operation to ensure the victory on land without which the war could not be won. Operation *Neptune*, the Navy's responsibility, was to get the Army and its equipment there and keep it supplied. Some of the soldiers now being moved into position along the South Coast of England were veterans of amphibious assaults in North Africa, Sicily, Italy; others would have troubled memories from Dieppe. Many were newly arrived across the Atlantic; the reduction in the U-boat threat from mid-1943 had been a vital factor in enabling thousands of troops and ever-increasing quantities of military and naval equipment to cross in relative safety. The vigilance of the convoy escorts remained vital.

Elsewhere, ferrying, minesweeping and patrolling meant business as usual for many of the yachtsmen volunteers. Some, like Peter Scott and Ludovic Kennedy, had been moved into liaison and planning jobs or had become sailors-in-jeeps. Others were posted far away. Those serving in destroyers and Coastal Forces were likely to find that new roles had been scripted for them, in an operation that would involve 1,212 Allied warships, 4,125 amphibious craft, 735 ancillary craft, 864 merchant ships and 200 naval aircraft.

Arthur Bennett, finally coming south from 'full, happy days' training at HMS *St Christopher* to lead a Combined Ops motor launch flotilla, admits to feeling daunted:

> *The multiplicity of types of craft was bewildering. I never did manage to comprehend all the abbreviations, but tank landing craft were known as LCT, and the smaller, boxlike LCA carried the assault troops; they were the craft we came to know best. We were too late forming up as a flotilla to take part in more than two of the exercises, but the memory of 'Fabius' will ever haunt my dreams. [...] The navigation was the least of our troubles. It was the aftermath that was so appalling, the sorting out, marshalling, carrying orders, passing signals to craft we failed to recognise. The loud hailer failed; signals became incomprehensible; we were utterly tired out and dispirited. Then came instructions to return 13 LCTs to Harbour and TURCO them, which meant reporting them, together with lists of defects, stores, requirements etc. Away we went to their anchorage. We hailed, bullied and cajoled. Some weighed anchor; others failed to respond. Eventually we set course for the Spithead Gate and the raggle-taggle procession somehow formed into line. By the time we were off Cowes we had landing craft following astern in perfect formation as far as the eye could see. Which were our thirteen I had not the faintest notion [...] We counted up to sixty-six and they were still streaming through the Gate.[11]*

The 4,125 'amphibious craft' – most of them newly built – required a large number of new officers and crew. In July 1943, as soon as Jack Jones was judged sufficiently recovered after his wounds at Dieppe, he was posted to Scotland for landing craft training. There were hundreds like him. For instance, 20-year-old Stewart Platt (b. 1923), from Leigh-on-Sea in Essex, was sent on an LCA commanding officer's course in Troon early in 1944 and loved it. 'There were the usual apocryphal stories of the dreadful accidents that had befallen some of the candidates but as far as I was concerned I loved it all – it was food and drink to me. At last I was doing something that motivated me, and I passed every test and exam with flying colours, whereas at school I had consistently poor exam marks.'[12]

Platt had been a member of the 3rd Chalkwell Bay Sea Scouts and a keen young dinghy sailor. In the last summer before the war, his father, who had served in an armed merchant cruiser in WWI, had bought a locally built 25ft yacht in which the family had a brief, enticing introduction to the joys of Thames Estuary sailing. Aged only 15 in 1939, Platt needed to finish his schooling. By the summer of 1941, aged 17, he'd found his way into the Royal Naval Patrol Service at Lowestoft, helped by a convenient error in his sign-up papers that ensured the Navy always thought he was a year older than he actually was. A year on anti-submarine patrol with T124 Scottish trawlermen on the late-Victorian steam yacht HMS *Tuscarora* provided a different type of education. Platt describes it as a 'cultural shock' but survived and made good friends.

Then, in 1943, he was sent (via HMS *Ganges*) to HMS *King Alfred*. There, he was impressed by the skill of the Navy 'in putting its own stamp on shore bases that were created out of towns, holiday camps and other unlikely venues'. It was perhaps a little oppressive: 'A catering company, Clifford's, had the contract for feeding us communally with the kind of fare you would be expected to eat as an officer and gentleman. Everywhere you were being watched to ensure you had "officer-like qualities" and it gave the feeling that incorrect handling of a knife and fork would count against you.' Platt failed to gain a direct commission into the RNVR but had already decided to volunteer for Combined Operations. He was glad to discover that his next training centre was Lochailort, north of Oban. He describes this, with evident relief, as set up 'to train officers not gentlemen'.

The course was tough and included running up the side of a mountain before breakfast, as well as assault courses tacked on to the more general training in boat handling, navigation and types of landing craft. One was taught fighting at close quarters – how to creep up behind a sentry and cut his throat silently and other such delights, which I am happy to say I never had to put into practice.[13]

Stewart Platt was a dear and much respected family friend. He was a pillar of our Essex community and never (to my observation) showed any lack of social adeptness. In fact, my brothers and I might have thought him almost overly punctilious – until a day, in France, when a group of teenage vandals seemed to threaten his lovely yacht *Celandine* (designed by Jack Jones). My youngest brother watched Stewart seize the boathook and charge the vandals with a roar, as they fled, terrified. 'I suddenly realised,' said my awestruck brother, 'that here was someone who had commanded a D-Day landing craft, aged 20.' Still, the Admiralty considered Sub-Lieutenant Platt, at 20, too young for command. He was appointed first lieutenant of a Mark 4 LCT 186ft long, built of steel and with two 500hp engines. In the last month before D-Day, the commanding officer was invalided ashore with a nervous breakdown and Platt finally achieved his promotion. 'I couldn't see anything wrong with it,' wrote Platt later. 'Nelson got his first command, a bomb-ketch, at the same age.'[14]

★★★

In his foreword to *Wavy Navy* (1950), a commemorative collection of RNVR WWII memories, Admiral of the Fleet Lord Cunningham recalled his feelings of apprehension in July 1943 when he had watched the Operation *Husky* invasion forces set off from Malta for Sicily: 'Watching them drawing out from under the lee of the land literally burying themselves, with spray flying over them in solid sheets as they plunged out to sea on their way to their assault positions, I confess I felt deeply anxious.' The weather had turned nasty, the timings were crucial, the crews unproven:

They were commanded for the most part by young officers of the RNVR, many of them new and inexperienced. Their crews were drawn from every walk of life and from every country, Dominion and colony of the British Empire. Few of them were seamen before the outbreak of war in 1939, yet to their gallant effort and staunch endurance a great measure of the

successful landing in Sicily was undoubtedly due [...] My anxieties had
proved unfounded. Thrashing out to sea with a strong wind and a heavy
sea, they pressed on relentlessly to their objectives.[15]

It had been a choppy crossing from Southampton Water for 20-year-old Platt and his companions as they headed for Gold Beach in LCT *879* on 6 June 1944. Departure had been delayed by the weather and a fresh to moderate westerly wind was still whipping up an unpleasant sea. Suddenly, through a break in the mass of landing craft and escorts, they glimpsed the fleet – a line of battleships with attendant cruisers and destroyers. 'Great battle ensigns streamed bravely from their maintops as these dark grey walls of steel ploughed relentlessly westwards [...] Here was the might of the Royal Navy going about its business.' Platt recalls, 'A miserable evening was transformed by this sight and the troops we were carrying who were feeling extremely uncomfortable as we rolled our way into the night suddenly lined the rails and broke into spontaneous cheering at this display of British seapower [...] I am sure none of us realised then that such a sight was never going to be seen again,' he added.[16]

Although, in retrospect, the significance attached to capital ships in WWII may seem disproportionate to their actual usefulness, they packed a tremendous emotional punch as well as their weight of firepower. The forces mobilised for Operation *Neptune* included three escort carriers, four battleships, 17 cruisers and two monitors with more than 200 destroyers, sloops, frigates and corvettes. Those cheered by Platt and his companions were (probably) the battleships *Warspite* and *Ramillies*, the monitor *Roberts* and the cruisers *Mauritius, Arethusa, Dragon, Danae* and *Frobisher;* destroyers *Kelvin, Saumarez, Scorpion, Scourge, Serapis, Swift, Verulam, Virago, Eglinton* and *Middleton* with two Norwegian destroyers *Stord* and *Svenner* and the Polish *Slazak*.[17]

On board Arthur Bennett's Itchenor-built ML *594*, the mood was different as they too crept towards France in the early morning. He remembers his crew as 'keyed up, tense, silent'. Then the first lieutenant came on deck, looked round, smiled. When Bennett asked why, he answered:

> *'I was just thinking, sir, of old Jerry ashore there coming out for a stretch and yawn, then suddenly catching sight of all us lot. Christ!'*

'Hundreds an' thousands of 'em,' added the Cockney signalman.
'Bet his old eyes don't half pop out,' said the coxswain.
We began to chuckle. Then we roared with laughter, prolonging that
blessed sense of relief until we clung helpless to the wings of the bridge. In
some mysterious fashion the joke spread to the guns' crews. Steel helmets
met in conclave, then tilted back in a burst of guffaws.[18]

Participant accounts collected by James Holland in *Normandy '44:*
D-Day and the Battle for France (2019) confirm the sense of total shock
experienced by the German forces. Kanonier Friedrich Wurster, still
only 21, had been in the Army for four years. He'd been part of the
invasion of France in 1940, then had been sent to serve in the Soviet
Union. He'd been wounded and returned to the Eastern Front;
wounded again and this time invalided back to France, on sentry
duty behind what he believed to be the impregnable Atlantic Wall –
Festung Europa. Wurster was based at Ver-sur-mer, at *Widerstandsnest*
(stronghold) WN 35a above the eastern end of Gold Beach. He had
been on duty until 2:00am then had turned in – until he was woken
by bombing and the offshore bombardment from the battleships.

The intensity of the naval shelling had horrified him – it had been far
worse than anything he'd confronted in Russia. Diving for cover in a
bunker he kept his head down throughout, save one glimpse when he had
seen cows in the nearby fields blown up and several even on fire. When the
firing finally stopped, he and his comrades had gingerly lifted their heads
and looked out to see the early morning sea thick with shipping of all sizes
and landing craft heading towards the coast. The shock had been total.[19]

Bennett, offshore, closing in, watched the air attack and then the
broadsides from the battleships – *Orion, Ajax, Emerald, Flores* – and
their accompanying destroyers. His section (Force G) contained
specialist gunships and flakships together with those rocket launchers
devised by Nevil Shute and his team at the DMWD. Bennett
had started playing music over his loudhailer. 'Then up went the
rockets from the rocketeers on either bow and obliterated the quiet,
unpretentious beach of le Hamel […] The uplift to morale was
tremendous for nothing could possibly survive on the beaches, so it
seemed to us.'[20] Nevil Shute, who visited neighbouring Juno Beach

a few days later in his capacity as a writer, had some idea what the effect of these rockets would have been on people like Friedrich Wurster (not to mention the unfortunate Normandy cows).

A man may be so protected in a concrete pill box or gun shelter that you cannot reach him with the flying shards of any shell or bomb. But that man is still subject to blast; he cannot escape that while he still breathes air, for blast is a shock wave of air. A number of twenty pound charges of high explosive set off outside his pillbox will not kill him, but they will make him so stunned and dizzy that for a long time, a quarter of an hour or more, he cannot control his eyes to read the range scale of his gun, cannot control his fingers to set sights, cannot hear anything, perhaps cannot stop vomiting. A man in that condition cannot fight or fire a gun until he has recovered.[21]

In those precious minutes, on Juno Beach, Shute recorded, the LCT had sailed in and grounded, attacking immediately as the infantry followed behind them. 'The Germans fought well in their concrete positions and slit trenches till they were surrounded; then they surrendered.'

On Gold Beach, it was time for the LCAs that had been led in by ML 594 to make their final run in to land. Bennett signalled 'All yours. Good luck.'

The LCAs revved up. We stopped and they came on past, the troops in good heart, squatting on their haunches, with netting over their steel helmets.
    'Aren't you coming in with us?' one of them shouted.
    We grinned and gave them a cheer. The LCAs scurried for the shore with white wakes showing up for all the world like rabbits' scuts. We watched them beach with a curious mixture of elation and anticlimax.[22]

Stewart Platt in LCT 879 was the last ship in his flotilla and found very little beach remaining. There were drowned vehicles from previous landings and numerous obstructions, part of the Atlantic Wall defences that had been reinforced under Rommel's command during the previous autumn. The westerly wind was still brisk and the vessels were being pushed to leeward. Platt had little choice but to go in hard for the final patch before he was swept on to the Pointe de Ver. This was towards the eastern end, the 'King' section, where Friedrich Wurster and his companions were confusedly manning strongpoint WN 35a.

> *Wurster now saw British tanks coming ashore and, one after another, the bunkers, casements and machine-gun and mortar-posts ahead overlooking the beach and the main coast road appeared to go silent. It was obvious they too would soon be surrounded [...] Tanks were now up ahead [...] The Atlantic Wall had been swept aside. They were soon to be overrun. They had been defeated.*[23]

Platt let his kedge anchor out astern and ran in hard. There was 'an almighty explosion forward' as he hit a mine. He could see the waters of the English Channel through a large hole in the plating of the vehicle deck and the bottom of his ship. They carried heavy timber as part of their stores so he and his crew set to work immediately to bridge the gap and get their cargo of vehicles ashore, before kedging off and setting on a long, slow journey home for repair. He was about to become part of a cross-Channel ferry service.[24]

21

'There was an outburst of shouting which soon died away'[1]

June–November 1944: The Normandy campaign and the Scheldt

Rozelle Pierrepont and her Leading Wren Ena Groves had been working non-stop in the days before the fleet set off. In the early hours of 6 June they'd been invited to settle down to a banquet of fried eggs, sausages and beans on one of the landing craft. A bang on the door brought a signalman with orders for LCT *7011* to go to the Hard for loading and be ready to sail at 6:00am. The two Wrens were leaving the vessel at 4:30am as the soldiers and their tanks began to come aboard. Rozelle recalls that it was 'her dearest wish' to be able to go with them.

Little more than four hours later, she and some of the others were called to the boats' office. Three LCAs had broken down off the Needles and they were to be sent with a tug to bring them back. 'I know that some of you would rather stow away on a ship that's bound for France, but the Navy won't allow that and this is the best I can do for you,' said Lieutenant Sherwood, their commanding officer. So they got their glimpse of the great armada. As they turned back for home with the three casualties in tow, they could watch a thousand dots disappearing over the southern horizon. 'Sometimes they merged together into one gigantic dot, or perhaps it just seemed that way because of the misty curtain that would persist in falling in front of our eyes.'[2]

Southampton Water seemed a place of empty mooring buoys and depression, though it would not be long before some vessels, such as Stewart Platt's LCT *879*, were back for repair and others were setting out. A regular pattern of convoys was soon established carrying people and supplies. Over the next month, almost a million men went to France. Three days after the initial assault, an armed merchant ship delivered several hundred German prisoners to Southampton – 'under-fed, tired and ill-looking youths'. Would Friedrich Wurster have been among them? Rozelle remembered this as the moment she became aware of 'the indescribable horror and tragedy of war'. Pathos was almost unbearable when a small black dog came down the gangway and ran to one of the prisoners before it was shut into a police van and taken away.[3]

On the other side of the Channel there was bitter fighting and loss of life. Jack Jones, like Stewart Platt, had hit one of the beach obstacles and damaged his vessel. He had delivered his soldiers, their jeeps, guns and tanks, but LCT 593 was holed and potentially sinking. He ran the landing craft as far up the beach as he could and sat it out for three days before trying to refloat. He and his crew dug slit trenches to shelter from the shelling and attempted to defend themselves with their two guns while they carried out repairs. The galley fire was kept going to provide hot food and drink. Salvage teams came to their aid but, on the second day, some of them and some of the crew were killed. On D-Day+3, LCT 593 was finally back into the water and out into the anchorage with all her pumps in action. It took longer to reconnect the power and get the engines to work and it was D-Day+5 before they were able to start their journey back to England.

Once LCT 879 had been repaired, Platt describes himself as taking her backwards and forwards until the war's end. He and his crew lived a strangely isolated existence, carrying supplies, waiting on the beach, unaware of the extent of the desperate struggle being made over the next two months to break out of the Normandy 'pocket'. He watched the Hawker Typhoon aircraft powering over without knowing that his future wife, Beryl Myatt, aged 20, had become the first female aeronautical engineer to be taken on by the company.

Work on the infrastructure that enabled this continued support had begun three hours after the first troops landed – and 18 months before. When Maurice Griffiths had returned from the Mediterranean in 1942, and recovered from illness, he found himself assigned to a new section within HMS *Vernon*: the Explosives and Demolition Department. His task had been quite the opposite of his peacetime employment of yacht agency and design. He was to identify 77 elderly ships – 22 for the US beaches, 55 for the British – purchase or requisition them, then work out how much explosive would be needed to sink them in shallow water and where, precisely, it should be applied. These were the 'corncobs' or 'gooseberries' that were to be scuttled to form breakwaters, protecting the beach anchorages. The specification was challenging: the ships had to sink quickly (within 10–12 minutes) and remain upright. Their hulls must be repairable so they could be refloated and removed later for their salvage value. The COPP beachmasters would have electronic positioning aids to help sink them exactly.

During 1943, Griffiths and his colleagues had travelled many miles to identify, survey and collect their fleet. It included merchant ships from half a dozen different nations (mainly condemned because they were coal burners so no longer welcome on convoys); Liberty ships supplied by the USA but with irreparable defects; and four elderly warships that proved particularly challenging to send down. They then undertook the individual calculations for each one. When this fleet was finally brought together before sailing to Normandy, they covered 10 miles of a Scottish loch and Griffiths recalled feeling quite emotional looking at his lines of doomed vessels. Each ship would be crewed by its own demolition team, led by an RNVR officer.[4] Though the scuttling of the ships off the US Omaha Beach was less successful, the 55 corncobs, laden with ballast and sunk off Gold Beach, provided shelter through the gale-swept winter of 1944–1945 and were eventually raised and removed without incident.

Kenneth Jacob, on the boom-defence vessel HMS *Barnehurst*, had hoped for leave to see his family after more than a year away. They had left Algiers on 29 April in a small zigzagging convoy, spent almost a week in Gibraltar waiting for a larger convoy and finally rounded the north coast of Ireland to arrive in Milford Haven on 23 May, almost out of coal and water. They were then sent on to Portsmouth, where they were told all leave had been stopped. They restocked the ship and were in the anchorage off Bembridge by 4 June.

On 6 June, they set out for France, where they were immediately put to work laying moorings and connecting floating breakwater sections to construct the Mulberry Harbour. They were still there when the north-east gale blew up on 19 June and destroyed much of the work they'd already completed. Their anchor chain parted and they spent the night steaming up and down until the weather moderated and they could begin to clear the wreckage and start repairs. Later in the month and during July, they were working on moorings for PLUTO, then finally, on 4 August, Jacob and the rest of the crew were given a long weekend's leave. Jacob's daughter, a nurse, met him in London and they hurried to Keighley for a family reunion.

Elsewhere, Arthur Bennett and ML 594 had remained on patrol duty after landing their soldiers on Gold Beach. He describes them as living 'in a dream of wonderment' as they watched the astonishing constructions taking shape. They were also very busy:

> Scrounging stores, chasing mail, picking up cases of American K-rations out of the water, A/S patrol by day, making smoke by night during each inevitable air attack, taking in landing craft to the beaches, salvaging derelicts, passing orders, escorting craft halfway across the channel, dodging the weather as best we could, dragging our anchor in the poor holding-ground, and all the time growing more and more weary and unkempt.[5]

Finally, they too were given leave and Bennett headed north to Scotland for an emotional reunion with Dorothy and three-year-old Elizabeth: 'I could hear her telling everyone, "That's my Daddy. That's my Daddy." It made everything worthwhile.' When he called on his mother in south-east London on his way back, however, he had the disquieting experience of feeling more afraid ashore than afloat. The VI bombs had started arriving from 13 June and while the XX committee's clever manipulation of their agents' reports in an attempt to reduce the impact on crowded central London may have been invisibly effective, the numbers falling on suburban areas such as Chislehurst and Lewisham were hard to ignore – though Mrs Bennett, tending her garden, was doing her best:

> Presently mother looked up and listened. 'Perhaps we'd better go in for a few moments. This one's coming over our way.'

It was low too. The engine seemed to falter. Then suddenly it cut right out and I felt myself coming out to the cold sweat. But mother was not least perturbed. 'It's gone over.' she said quietly, and we waited for the loud explosion, Lewisham way.[6]

★★★

In France, members of Fleming's intelligence commandos were alongside (or ideally ahead) of the invading forces with their shopping lists of technological material to locate and retrieve. Since their return from the Mediterranean, they had been reorganised, better equipped and their numbers increased. The basic concept remained that of RNVR intelligence gatherers (now officially designated NID 30 within the Admiralty), supported and protected in the field by Royal Marines. Together, they formed 30AU.

Patrick Dalzel-Job had joined them after becoming one of the few Royal Navy personnel to complete parachute training, hoping, as ever, for a return to Norway. When he came to London, he met former RNVSR members such as Dunstan Curtis and Quintin Riley, though yachting probably didn't feel very relevant by then. Once they arrived in Normandy, they'd be sailors-in-jeeps. Fleming's eye for talent was as sharp as ever and other special service volunteers with varied expertise were being recruited and put into RNVR uniforms. Riley's logistical skills were fully engaged to ensure that, when the unit did go into action, it would be properly equipped with transport and radios as well as with weapons and knowledge. Robert Harling worked with Margaret Priestley, getting the mass of technical and intelligence requests into usable form as lists of targets and locations.

Dalzel-Job arrived in Normandy on D-Day+4, landing on Utah Beach and pushing through the dust towards Cherbourg as part of the largest group, 'Woolforce'. The first group, 'Pikeforce', had landed on D-Day on Juno Beach and headed for the radar station at Douvres-la-Délivrande. 'Curtforce', Dunstan Curtis' group, landed on Gold Beach the following day and moved inland to investigate a local Luftwaffe HQ, before joining with Pikeforce. Riley, meanwhile, headed for the Far East to assess possible future operations there.

On Dalzel-Job's first evening, his unit had not been ordered to dig in so suffered unnecessary casualties from a butterfly bomb. He remembered the courage and stoicism of the wounded men as he crawled around attempting to help by the inadequate light of his torch. He also noted that he found it oddly enjoyable to be busy in this way. The experience prompted him to think back to the lingering and awful deaths in previous conflicts, particularly the long night of 1 July 1916 when his father had died on the Somme.

The V1 bombs had not started to fall on London, in that first week after D-Day, but they were known to be imminent. Information on the whereabouts of potential launch sites was high on 30AU's shopping lists. Dalzel-Job and two marines found their way through the bocage country to investigate one such location. It had already been abandoned when they arrived (on 13 June), though he was later told that the discovery had been of great value to 'the experts'. Dalzel-Job and his companions continued working as methodically as possible within the slow and difficult progress of the Allied forces. They reached Cherbourg late in June, together with the other 30AU groups. Fleming came out from England but relationships were not cordial. He was upset by the unit's losses for which he blamed the RM commander Colonel Woolley. Back at the Admiralty, Robert Harling, answering a question about the unit's whereabouts too casually for Fleming's taut nerves, found himself the target of 'the most explosive brainstorm I have witnessed [...] I had become involved in a sombre wartime scene in which one man's emotions, normally tightly controlled, had suddenly snapped. In an odd way, I felt that he and not myself was the victim and accordingly felt sorry for him. But not very.'[7]

Dalzel-Job's July objective was the port city of Caen, where he linked up with 21-year-old German-speaking Royal Marine Charles Wheeler. They enjoyed paddling out on a cork raft to raid a half-sunk patrol boat, then escaping under fire with a pile of technical equipment. It was a busy period, liaising with the Free French, interrogating German prisoners and, too often, witnessing unnecessary death. In one incident, Dalzel-Job and Wheeler were talking to a French civilian near Bréhal when a passing American soldier shot the man as casually, Dalzel-Job comments, 'as he would have done when hunting deer at home in the States'.[8] The man died in Wheeler's arms and he was left attempting to comfort the family while Dalzel-Job protested to the Americans. Not long afterwards, when Dalzel-Job was protecting the contents of a German control centre from looting, his new friends in the FFI (*Forces françaises de l'intérieur*) offered him the opportunity to shoot two women 'with shaven heads and swollen tear-stained faces'. He refused and pointed out the penalty for unauthorised executions. The women were led away 'howling' and he remained in his defence position, feeling sick.[9]

Other incidents brought extraordinary joy. There was an unforgettable moment in the town of Étretat on 2 September when a large crowd gathered in the town square and the mayor read an address of welcome with tears running down his cheeks. Dalzel-Job was invited to reply and found the words to express not only his deep emotion at being in France at such a moment, but also his consciousness that the true honour belonged to all those who had fought and died for France and liberty. Meanwhile, the fighting and the dying continued.

Dalzel-Job and his companions were on the trail of a new type of midget submarine (*Biber*, or 'beaver' in German) that they'd been told might be used against the shipping in the Channel. Further information suggested that these were now being returned to Germany. It was a deeply confused situation with columns of Allied and German forces crossing each other in unexpected directions. One of the midgets was finally found abandoned on the side of the road. The experience he'd gained training with the 12th Submarine Flotilla enabled Dalzel-Job to see that this could indeed have been a formidable weapon. Detailed measurements and photographs were taken, to be couriered back to the Admiralty by a marine on a motorbike.

★★★

This late stage of the conflict was a time of urgent technological innovation by German scientists and engineers and equally urgent efforts by the Allies to identify and forestall these. Mine warfare escalated. The cross-Channel invasion had been expected by the enemy even if the precise location of the landing beaches had been concealed. Maurice Griffiths wrote of the enormous numbers of additional explosives that had been laid to protect the estuaries, inlets and harbours along the coasts of Holland, Belgium and northern France. He describes 'the months-long wrestle the liberating forces had to face to clear the deadly mines and killer traps in the trail of ruins that lay all the way through France and Belgium and Holland' and pays tribute to the patience and the courage involved.[10]

Minesweepers had been the first ships in action on D-Day, clearing broad highways through the mine barrier, in the dark. A participant's account in *Wavy Navy* (entitled 'I was afraid') takes the reader through the kaleidoscope of emotions, from internal denial and escapism, through double whiskies, forced heartiness, pride at the breaking out of the battle ensign, then fighting back whimpering panic as the sweep is pulled in in the dark. 'Oh my God, oh my God. Never again, never in all my bloody life.' Pulling in the sweep was the moment of greatest danger when they could also be pulling in a mine. Usually, they could see. But not this night. Then his ship is swerving through the live mines cut by the sweepers ahead, feeling the shudder of detonations, fear settling in the stomach 'like a sickness'. He is shivering on the quarterdeck and longing for the dawn. 'A man as frightened as I was should never have come on an expedition such as this. I felt that it was a mistake on somebody's part to have sent me. I began to feel, besides fear, resentful and filled with a bitter grievance against authority in general.' This brave man, a first lieutenant and veteran of the Arctic convoys, reaches a point where all he wants to do is sit down in the darkness and cry. Finally, when they reach the coast of France at dawn, he is awed by the immensity of the occasion and realises that his part is over. 'I said "Some poor bastards will be copping it now," but I said it almost with satisfaction because for us it was over. The sun became hot and holiday-like and the sweepers withdrew and waited for fresh orders.'[11]

The catch in this account, which ends with the expectation that time would expunge the memories of 'the cold shivering fears of the past night', is that it was written with such vividness more than five years after the event. Obviously the memory had not been wiped away. Would it ever?

The mines that comprised this Channel barrage were the by now familiar mix of moored contact mines and magnetic mines that had been sown and swept, sown and swept, since the first winter of the war. Closer inshore, the beaches were defended by influence mines, magnetic and acoustic. There was a new – potentially unsweepable – type: the pressure mine or 'oyster'. Hitler's decision to order these to be brought into use, knowing that once deployed these were potentially as lethal to his own forces as the Allies, was described by Griffiths as 'the last desperate throw of a gambler'.[12] Although a lucky series of mistaken decisions ensured that oyster mines were not part of the initial barrage on 6 June, 2,000 of them were then rushed from Germany to be scattered among the invasion forces, often dropped on the anchorages by night. Lincoln was one of a number of HMS *Vernon* personnel sent to try to suggest countermeasures, such as speed reduction.

He was also puzzled by the unexplained destruction of three moored ships (*Frobisher, Iddlesleigh, Albatross*) within the apparent safety of the Mulberry Harbour. E-boats had been sighted 20 miles away. He took a boat out to measure the precise flow of the west-going tidal stream and discovered that it curved north-east off Courseulles-sur-Mer. This might be sufficient to carry some destructive weapon down on to the moored ships. When the boom-defence vessel *Barlake* – a sister ship to Kenneth Jacob's *Barnehurst* – attempted to check the anti-torpedo netting in that area, there was an explosion that killed one of her men and seriously injured others. An unfortunate proof that Lincoln's theory was right: two large, slow-running electric torpedoes had been welded together and launched into the tidal stream. He wondered how many more had been sent off almost at random to achieve these three hits. Desperate wastefulness extended to lives as well as torpedoes. Arthur Bennett, doing night-time patrols, received reports of whitish blobs slipping past on the ebb. These were discovered to be the Perspex domes of human torpedoes, launched from Dives-Houlgate to slip through the defences and attack ships in the anchorage before returning with the flood. He heard later that, of the 70 that had set out that night, fewer than ten returned.

It took until almost the end of July for the Allied troops to break out of Normandy. When Paris was reached a month later, Dunstan Curtis was there prospecting for 30AU. The heavily fortified Atlantic ports held out longer. When Brest fell at the end of September, Edward Terrell, whose 'Disney' rocket was still being trialled at Orford Ness, went to inspect the effects of the Tallboy bomb, developed by Barnes Wallis. This was the bomb that was regularly used against structures such as dams, canals and U-boat pens, and that would finally finish the *Tirpitz* in November. Terrell was appalled by the destruction in the old town, where scarcely a house remained standing, but noted that the nine Tallboys, which had struck the roof of the pens, had failed to penetrate the 16ft-thick concrete.

Thousands of prisoners of war were walking around in confusion and there were bodies of dead German soldiers lying unburied around the port area. He went to examine a U-boat apparently sunk in one of the dry docks. As the water drained away, the US soldiers began taking potshots with their pistols – until they realised it was attached to a 1,000lb mine, another booby trap.

Terrell fell ill and spent several days at Morlaix, hearing terrible stories of the atrocities committed by the Gestapo against members of the resistance, and also against hostages taken from the local population. Some of these incidents had taken place in the previous month, as the British and American forces were advancing. Later, Terrell expressed his view that 'The story of Morlaix was the story of all enslaved Europe'. He felt that the Nuremberg trials 'touched only a few of those who had ordered or committed those acts against humanity [...] Perhaps a new generation of Germans will abhor the deeds of their ancestors, but we who came face to face with the reality cannot forget.'[13]

The focus of the war was shifting eastwards. Once they had completed their detailed investigations into the German naval records left behind in Paris, 30AU were withdrawn for further reorganisation before recommencing their activity the following February when the Allied armies finally reached the Rhine. The information they'd uncovered in Paris would lead on to some significant technical targets within Germany itself. Meanwhile, Lincoln was deeply excited by connections being made with a torpedo arsenal at Houilles, a famous mushroom-growing site that had been requisitioned by the Germans in June 1940. Was this connected with the recent development of acoustic torpedoes, attracted towards a ship by the sound of its engines? On 14 June, the River-class frigate HMS *Mourne* had fallen victim to one such torpedo while on patrol duty at the western entrance to the English Channel, screening Operation *Neptune*.

There were only seven survivors from her crew of 118. (RNVSR yachtsman Lyulph Stanley was lucky to escape.)

Lincoln hurried to France with marine geophysicist Maurice Neville Hill, who had been seconded to HMS *Vernon*, and they crawled around the area collecting likely looking fragments of Bakelite, lengths of wire, aluminium trips and tiny microphones. They wheedled further fragments from the technical section of the French Navy in Paris – then almost lost the entire collection when the LST they had persuaded to take them home was hit by a torpedo on the crossing to Portsmouth. A mysterious link (probably managed via the Dutch resistance) with the Philips factory in Eindhoven gave Lincoln and his expert colleagues the final components they needed to understand the workings of this acoustic torpedo.

Victory at Le Havre on 9 September brought an end to the Normandy campaign but defeat at Arnhem on 17 September ensured that the war would continue through another winter. This set new strategic challenges as it meant there was an army to be maintained along Germany's border with Belgium. Antwerp was a key supply port but using Antwerp required control of the heavily mined River Scheldt, problematic as long as the Germans retained Walcheren Island and South Beveland. The Allies had taken Ostend on 9 September and used it as a base once some of the debris of battle had been shifted. The mobile maintenance unit that had been operating in the Mulberry Harbour at Arromanches-les-Bains moved here and the Coastal Forces bases at Felixstowe, Lowestoft and Great Yarmouth became centres of activity once again.

The German E-boats had well-defended bases at Den Helder, Ijmuiden and Rotterdam and were able to act more aggressively and effectively than they had from Le Havre. Small, fierce battles continued to rage between the E-boats, R-boats, MGBs, MTBs with frigates, trawlers, minesweepers and midget submarines also taking part. At stake was the protection of troop ferry services and new convoy routes. The Germans also needed to continue to supply their garrison at Dunkirk. One night in September, three E-boats on that run were attacked by a frigate, HMS *Stayner* (commanded by former Merseyside RNVSR member Alan Vincent Turner) and two new D-type MTBs from Lowestoft: MTB *724* (John Humphreys) and MTB *728* (Francis Thomson). Three E-boats were sunk and

60 prisoners were captured, including the E-boat ace Karl Müller, veteran of 164 sorties. Yet in the fiery confusion and the darkness, there was a moment when MTB *724* shot up MTB *728* and three of her crew were killed.[14]

Arthur Bennett was among those who assembled in the 'mine-blasted, desolate, dock basins of Ostend' in preparation for the attack on Walcheren. The dykes on the island had been breached and the central area was little more than a lagoon, yet it was heavily fortified and included Vlissingen (Flushing), which commands the entrance to the Scheldt. A fellow RNVR officer described Ostend as strangely hostile and full of spies. When they left for Walcheren on 1 November, Bennett felt certain their destination was no secret. His apprehension increased when he learned that the RAF could provide no air cover that day due to low cloud. Canadian forces were battling along the causeway from South Beveland, and the elderly battleship HMS *Warspite* and the monitors HMSs *Erebus* and *Roberts* had arrived to bombard the shore batteries. Bennett's job was to anchor ML *902* to mark the way through the minefields for the assault craft. As soon as he had done so, the German guns began to fire. ML *902* was straddled again and again, Bennett was hit by shell fragments but could only sit there helplessly until they were finally ordered to withdraw. They wasted no time pulling up their anchor: just slipped the chain and went.

'Goodbye Old Chap'[1]

November 1944–May 1945: Last postings, 30AU in Germany, VE Day

In the first week of November 1944, Denys Rayner took the 30th Escort Group to sea. Their orders were to patrol off the southern coast of Ireland 'to seek out and destroy the enemy wherever he may be found'.[2] Though the Atlantic wolf packs had now dispersed, the U-boats were operating on the trade routes closer inshore. They could use the different temperature layers created by estuaries and tidal streams to confuse sonar and could also escape detection by hiding close to wrecks. Their schnorkels enabled them to remain submerged for long periods without the need to surface to recharge batteries or replenish air. Once they were no longer working in packs, they didn't betray themselves by using their radios and some had been given new protection against detection by Britain's centimetric radar.

This was a whole new phase of warfare for which the escort groups needed to learn new techniques. They were told what convoys were due and were expected to clear the seas ahead of them and be on the spot in case of attack. They were also expected to co-operate with air patrols. Rayner felt they were barely managing to contain the threat. Their 'kills' were few and he had an uneasy feeling that the balance could quickly tip against them. German factories were still producing U-boats at an impressive rate and there was a well-founded fear that new, much faster designs, equipped with the latest torpedoes, would soon be in full production.

Rayner had a personal score to settle. A year ago, after his time on HMS *Shikari*, he'd been appointed to command a venerable but still magnificent destroyer, HMS *Warwick*. On 20 February 1944, she'd been torpedoed off Trevose Head on the Cornish coast. He'd been in company with HMS *Scimitar* (Philip Archer-Shee) and it hadn't been too long before fishing vessels also came to rescue survivors. Nevertheless, only 94 of the ship's company had been picked up; 67 had died and not all the rescued men lived. Rayner wanted to sink a U-boat in revenge. He'd refused to take survivors' leave and hurried to his next command, HMS *Highlander*. He'd spent a happy summer escorting convoys to Gibraltar but there'd been no opportunities for action. His most recent ship was the technically advanced but unhandy HMS *Pevensey Castle* and he didn't like her very much. Even so, as the senior officer of a group of four well-equipped ships in an area of known U-boat activity, he had set himself to achieve success.

The patrol didn't start well. Rayner's crew were inexperienced and his relationships with them not as confident as on previous ships. Two miles down the River Foyle, the young coxswain had needed to go to the heads and handed over the wheel to the quartermaster without informing Rayner. The quartermaster misunderstood an instruction from the pilot, turned the wrong way, and ran the destroyer's stern on the mud. No damage was done and they continued to sea. A few days later, a blip on the radar screen seemed likely to be an enemy U-boat. At first there was uncertainty, then the group swung into action together and achieved what felt like a copybook attack and kill. They smelled oil and saw air bubbles, though they found no survivors. They felt confident in claiming success. The patrol lasted two more weeks, without further incident. (Much later it was discovered that they had not destroyed a submarine.)[3]

Rayner began to experience an unfamiliar lassitude. A northerly gale was blowing as they returned to the River Foyle with the long sandspit of Magilligan Point to leeward. The steering engine failed; *Pevensey Castle* was being blown ashore as the chief engineer struggled to connect her hand-steering mechanism. It was too dangerous to accept the offer of a tow. Rayner put all the crew in lifejackets ready to abandon. Even after the disaster had been averted, Rayner found himself shivering so much he could hardly stand up. He took *Pevensey Castle* up the river and requested a tug to bring her alongside. Then he telephoned Admiral Sir Max Horton and resigned. 'The candle was burned out.'[4]

Denys Rayner's commitment to the RNVR had been total, his achievements considerable: the first volunteer reserve officer to be appointed to command a corvette; the first to command a destroyer and finally the first to be appointed senior officer of an escort group. He was a qualified officer and a commander but this final seagoing appointment had come after more than five years of effort and responsibility with never more than ten days off as periods of leave between ships. Now, the doctor prescribed three weeks' sick leave – a Christmas with his family at last. He also confirmed that Rayner was no longer fit for sea service. Rayner rang Horton again and asked him for a staff job. His nerve had gone, he explained.

Nicholas Monsarrat described himself, quite simply, as tired. 'After five ships, four-and-a-half years of sea time, more than a hundred long and short convoys, I was desperately tired. Tired sailors of thirty-five belonged, in wartime, somewhere else than on the bridge.'[5] He had spent most of 1944 'standing by' the Colony-class frigate HMS *Perim* then being built at Providence, Rhode Island. She was commissioned in March 1944, when Monsarrat had travelled out to take command, but was then plagued by faults throughout her sea trials. He brought her back in the winter, handed over command and went to work in the Admiralty at the Department of Naval Information. There, he portrays himself as lazy and dissolute, writing occasional short articles and enjoying the company of novelist John Moore (who had been flying Swordfish in the Fleet Air Arm) and John Scott Hughes, former yachting correspondent of *The Times*.

Ludovic Kennedy, who also spent time in the Admiralty Press Division, had been a spectator at the D-Day invasion, watching from HMS *Largs*, a former banana boat, now the headquarters ship for Sword Beach. It seems to have been a somewhat surreal experience, breakfasting in the wardroom among 'a hum of conversation and the clink of cutlery'; the white-coated steward offering 'porridge or cereal this morning, sir?', then going ashore to view wrecked ships and the unburied dead. *Largs* had one narrow escape from a torpedo, which missed by a few feet as she put her engines full speed astern.[6] Kennedy sat on deck in the sunshine typing his thousand words a day, none of which were ever used, then he returned to sea for two more periods of duty on destroyers. He found it strange and full of ghosts to be once again in Scapa Flow from where the Tribal-class destroyers had escorted the battleships of the Home Fleet during the first two years of the war. In the autumn/winter of 1944, his destroyer, HMS

Zebra, was new; 12 of the 16 Tribals had been lost. The ships they were now escorting across to the coast of Norway were aircraft carriers. Kennedy later wrote that he'd found it difficult not to keep telling his companions how much better it had been in 'the old days'.

Had it? His time on 'lucky' *Tartar* had come to an end after he'd witnessed the gruesome death of the *Bismarck*; the sinking of *Tartar's* 'chummy ship' HMS *Mashona*; an icy trip to the Kola inlet and the loss of another sister ship, HMS *Matabele*. He'd experienced a tense hunt for *Tirpitz* in the northern Norwegian darkness, with his hand on the torpedo levers, expecting at any moment to sight her giant silhouette. Kennedy's next posting had been to an elderly destroyer, HMS *Watchman*, on Atlantic escort duty, where it's possible he came close to nervous breakdown. His contribution to *Wavy Navy* is a brief, convincing description of a panic attack. *Watchman* had received (as so many Atlantic escorts also received in the grim days of 1942–1943) a signal from the submarine tracking room at the Admiralty: 'Estimate now about 15 U-boats in your vicinity. Expect attack after midnight.' When Kennedy had come off watch, at midnight, he had gone to his cabin and waited:

> *I knew that the one thing I must not do was to give rein to the imagination. And equally knew that I was powerless to stop it [...] I gripped the iron sides of my bunk and held on hard, my body taut as a stretched wire. I had a sudden insane desire to jump out of bed and rush to the top of the mast head. I said aloud to give myself courage, 'I must not panic'. I said it over and over again. It did not help. Another voice, equally loud and insistent, said, 'Get me out of here. Now. This minute. Before it's too late.'*[7]

A sudden and prolonged Atlantic gale that night saved HMS *Watchman;* Kennedy was probably saved by the offer of a job ashore for a year as ADC to the Governor of Newfoundland before his return to the Admiralty and then to sea service in 1944. He told his daughter Rachel how music (including hymns, though he was not a believer) had helped him through the most difficult times. In April 1945, after his time on HMS *Zebra*, he was sent to Taranto to join HMS *Wheatland* fitting out for the Far East. Her captain, Philip ('Tiny') Archer-Shee, was a friend from those earliest days. The end of the war with Japan stopped them having to go any further. Kennedy, like his first ship HMS *Tartar*, could have been nicknamed 'lucky' – in fact, his naval nickname was 'Ukkers' – the popular naval version of 'Ludo'.

My father had been sent home from West Africa at the Christmas of 1943 with glowing reports from senior officers but suffering from 'debility'. After his first proper period of home leave since 1939, he was posted locally to HMS *Badger* at Harwich. His duty there was to support the forces that formed a shield across the approach to the English coast from Ostend and Ijmuiden and also to help monitor the huge overall flow of shipping to Normandy during that 1944 summer. In his suitcase, I found a copy of the Day of Prayer on Sunday 4 June, led by King George VI, in which everyone was asked to join. On D-Day itself, Force L had assembled and sailed in part from Harwich, as well as Southend and Sheerness.

The East Coast ports were busy again from September. Peter Scott was posted to Great Yarmouth, still waiting for the destroyer commission he'd been promised for so long. Ever the achiever, he'd spent the later summer months of 1944 learning to fly and had also almost completed *The Battle of the Narrow Seas*, his 1945 history of WWII Coastal Forces. Scott may have been overconfident when he went to visit E-boat ace Karl Müller, who had been captured on 18 September 1944 in the operation led by Alan Turner and the Lowestoft MTBs. Among his many raids, Müller had commanded the E-boat flotilla that had killed more than 900 American servicemen on Exercise *Tiger*. He had, incidentally, been responsible for one of the deaths of the rarely mentioned women who were working on merchant ships. Her name was Alide Reicher. She was 53 and a stewardess on a neutral Swedish ship, torpedoed by Müller off the Cornish coast.

Scott and Müller had come into conflict at sea and it was probably good to hear the German's candid avowal that, despite the superiority of the E-boat vessels themselves, he and his colleagues agreed that the war was now lost and hoped it might be ended quickly. Assuming that Müller was imprisoned until the end of the war, Scott asked the Admiralty censor for permission to show him the manuscript of his book to check for accuracy. This was granted and Müller later sent him an appreciative letter. Unfortunately for Coastal Forces, Müller was released early in an unexpected prisoner swap. Not many weeks had passed before Scott noticed one of his better ideas from the book being used against them.

Britain's war had started at sea but was finishing on land. By mid-February 1945, Patrick Dalzel-Job and the other sailors-in-jeeps were camped in Belgium, waiting to get into Germany. Lincoln believed that he and a colleague (Lieutenant Albert Leslie Broom from Plymouth) may have been the first British naval officers to cross the Rhine, though this was with the American forces. On 7 March, the 9th Armoured Division of the US 1st Army had crossed by the Ludendorff Bridge at Remagen: British naval intelligence, meanwhile, had picked up rumours of German sea mines being delivered to the area. The crossing was highly vulnerable and Lincoln began to feel anxious about the possibility of frogmen being used to put explosives in position. He convinced his senior officer that he should be sent out to give the US soldiers the benefit of his expertise. Protective booms had already been erected by the Americans; Lincoln advised the addition of searchlights and guns and defence against explosive motorboats. He and Broom kept vigil by the river, altering the angles of lights to ensure there were no protective areas of shadow. 'I am pleased to report.' he wrote back, 'That of the three attempts made on these pontoon bridges all attempts were defeated by blowing the swimmers out of the water before they could reach their objective.'[8] Lincoln then moved on to spend a week checking precautions for General Montgomery's crossings on 23/24 March, while Broom remained behind, winning the George Medal for his achievement disarming 36 mines at a captured airfield at Melsbroek in Belgium.

Dalzel-Job had crossed the German frontier (though not the river) on 3 March and was soon in Cologne, where he was amazed to find friendliness among the inhabitants despite the destruction from Allied bombing. He retrieved a quantity of technical documents and new mine parts from the Schmidding works, then lashed a heavy machine gun to the front of his jeep before rejoining the main Allied forces for the well-named Operation *Plunder*. He was glad to have Charles Wheeler with him again as they adventured their way north-east to Bremen, where a new type of high-speed submarine was reported to be under construction at the Deschimag Shipyard.

Wheeler, who had been born in Bremen, was a brilliant interviewer and interrogator, easily eliciting the information that enabled them to reach their targets ahead of other units. He in turn attributed their unit's relative lack of casualties to Dalzel-Job's ability to buttonhole the locals and discover where the enemy were, the better to avoid them. They reached Bremen so far in advance of other troops that Dalzel-Job found himself taking the formal surrender of the city.

His account of a dash to the shipyard to gain early access and save it from shelling, running out of petrol, commandeering a bicycle (and then returning it) is quite astonishing in its understated way. It's worth a pause in reading to remember that this was the young man, fatherless, short of money and formal education, who'd lived with his mother on their largely self-built yacht until he became convinced that the Admiralty needed his amateur sailor's knowledge.

From Bremen, Dalzel-Job and his team moved on to investigate a huge mine dump at the village of Hesedorf, then further northwards between the Weser and the Elbe rivers to Bremerhaven, where he successfully took over the 2,600-ton destroyer *Z29* and her not-quite-subdued crew of 320 with a boarding party of five; then dined with her captain in the evening. 'It was scarcely a social occasion,' he comments.[9]

★★★

Like the other invading forces, 30AU units were making both exciting and grim discoveries as they pushed north and east. April 1945 was the month when Allied troops entered Buchenwald, and the Mittelwerk factory in the Hartz mountains, where the V2 rockets were made. On 19 April, David Howarth's former colleague Richard Dimbleby was the first broadcaster into Belsen and broke down several times while making his report. Initially, the BBC refused to play it, as they could not believe the scenes he had described.

The find that brought Fleming out from the Admiralty in May was the entire German Navy archive, seized by 30AU at Tambach Castle in Northern Bavaria. A book-collector's dream, it dated from the 1870 foundation of the Kaiserliche Marine by Admiral von Tirpitz and Kaiser Wilhelm II. Meanwhile, the unravelling story of Germany seemed to be returning to these late c. 19th-century roots – almost to the spot where Childers and *The Riddle of the Sands* had come in.

Adolf Hitler had named Admiral Karl Dönitz as his successor, before killing himself on 30 April. Dönitz, shocked by his appointment but desperate to do whatever he could to mitigate damage, withdrew to his own heartland, Flensburg, just north of Kiel, where he'd attended the submariners' school at Murwick. In 1945, he had prepared the order Operation *Regenbogen* (*Rainbow*) for all remaining U-boats to be scuttled rather than surrendered in the event of defeat. Now, however, with both his sons and 70 per cent of U-boat crews dead, desperately trying to buy time for German forces to escape capture by the advancing Russians, he hesitated. Many of his commanders did not: from 1 May until the final unconditional surrender signed on 8 May, 195 boats were scuttled, most of them in the Baltic ports and German North Sea coast.

The surrender of all German forces and ships in Holland, north Germany, the Frisian Islands, Schleswig-Holstein and Denmark had been signed and came into effect a few days earlier, on Saturday 5 May. This sent Dunstan Curtis with Team 10 of 30AU rushing for Kiel. Others were equally desperate to reach the city before the Russians could. The technological prize seemed immense: Kiel was a major naval construction centre but it was also the headquarters of Dr Hellmuth Walter, whose patented hydrogen peroxide propulsion method was used in rocket motors for the Messerschmitt Me 163, the V1 and V2 rockets, and the Walter V80 submarine. This offered a potential 28 knots underwater speed. Dr Walter was friendly when Curtis and his companions arrived but refused to do more than chat generally. The vital components were missing from all his machines and technical papers were unavailable.

Unsubdued military groups on the northern side of the Kiel Canal seemed likely to put up a fight and Soviet forces were only 40 miles away. There was an overwhelming sense of urgency. The Kiel port admiral, von Gerlach, phoned Dönitz, with Curtis listening, and ensured that there would be no fighting; that all the minefield maps from the Skaw eastwards should be handed over and access given to the Torpedo Versuchanstallt/research institute (TVA) at Eckernforde. On 10 May, a meeting at Flensburg with Dönitz's senior officers produced an order permitting access to all secret papers and components. On 23 May, the Flensburg Government came to an end and Dönitz was imprisoned to stand trial at Nuremberg. There, he was sentenced to ten years' imprisonment, about which he expressed great bitterness, insisting that he had fought hard but not illegally, and had no knowledge of the regime's crimes against humanity.

The partial German surrender on 5 May had brought rejoicing in Holland. Arthur Bennett, in yet another ML (*146*), was stationed in the South Beveland village of Wemeldinge, patrolling the East Scheldt. His crew had become friendly with the local families and it had sometimes been hard to remember that the enemy were still in possession of the other side of the estuary. On 5 May, 'flags flew from every house. Within an hour the Town Band assembled, their instruments green with verdigris, and the staid sober folk gave themselves up to a night of dancing, singing and cheering round the village.'[10] Antwerp on VE Day seemed rather less fun, though Bennett remembers enjoying an ice-cream crawl round the city. Then ML 146 was back at work, collecting the small landing craft from the Rhine crossings for shipment back to England. Bennett's crew gave one final party for their Dutch friends:

The mess deck was decorated with bunting, and the guests arrived in their Sunday best for a gargantuan feast. It was the children's day though. They came in party clothes, the most delightful children imaginable, and once their shyness had worn off, they tucked in as only children can. It was a tired and happy crowd that went ashore that night. Next morning, as we cast off for the last time, there were kiddies crying on the Quayside. I fancy there were several moist eyes among the crew. In fact I know there were.[11]

It was a restorative moment for Bennett, waiting around in Ramsgate, hoping not to be sent to the Far East, when he saw a Thames barge coming in under full sail to pick up a cargo of coke. 'I rejoiced to find how my pulse quickened. The war was over as far as I was concerned.'[12] People were beginning to come home, though not always immediately to civilian life. Adrian Seligman was brought back from his ruffianly existence with the Levant Schooner Flotilla to take command of the Hunt-class destroyer HMS *Cottesmore*. She had been part of the escort for *Erebus* and *Roberts* as they bombarded the German defences on Walcheren Island in November. Then, in December, she was deployed under Seligman's command for coastal convoy duty and anti-submarine patrols in the North Sea and Channel. Anxiety about the schnorkel-enabled U-boats perfecting their underwater navigation to attack convoys at their assembly and dispersal points continued through the early months of 1945. *Cottesmore* was one of the additional destroyers sent to exercise vigilance over these key areas.

Ewen Montagu, meanwhile, had plotted with Rodger Winn of the Submarine Tracking Room to lay a fictitious minefield at a point off southern Ireland where the U-boats were able to fix their position using an underwater ridge. There was no capacity available to lay a genuine minefield, so Montagu staged a series of encounters for his double agent (code name *Tate*) with characters from the fictitious supporting cast. One of Tate's fictional associates, a notional mine-laying expert, 'was a brash young man and, when they were sitting over a series of nightcaps in the flat, he was apt to get a little incautious in his conversation'. He was just one of the plot contrivances used by Montagu to enable 'Tate' to convince his German handler of the truth and position of this new hazard. Soon, Rodger Winn was receiving Ultra interceptions that showed their lie had been believed. 'That was the last of my frauds,' wrote Montagu. 'As I've so often had old lags say to me since then, "From now on I intend to go straight, M'Lord."'[13]

Nevil Shute had been taken out of uniform early as DMWD's work wound down. He was sent to Burma in January 1945 to report on the progress of the war there. Not finding the sort of direct action his employers at the Ministry of Information wanted, he returned to England in late July having written six articles, none of which were published. He had also collected unique observational material for his first post-war novel *The Chequer Board* (1947).

Edward Young finished his last patrol being depth-charged in the Lombok Strait on 3 January 1945. He was on his way back to Fremantle after a 'blank and depressing' patrol off Borneo. But that was it; they were going home and he was getting married. HMS *Storm* arrived back in Haslar Creek on 8 April 1945.

Ruari McLean had declined another tour of duty when he returned to Trincomalee after his team's successful reconnaissance of Sumatran beaches. 'It was a very beautiful country to come back to, I thought, as we looked again at the feathery palm trees, the hedges gay with scarlet hibiscus blossoms, the paddy fields green as a green flame... it was not its fault that I longed for a grey drizzle in the Woodstock Road.'[14] He too was planning to get married.

When my father had come home from Freetown, given six weeks' leave before starting his new job in Harwich, it had been the sounds of the English countryside that had begun his recovery from 'debility'.

One morning as I lay abed at Newney listening to the silence and the rooks and starlings and cows, it came to me that these things had been missing for so long as to be strangers. Cheap, common ordinaries of no par value, these sounds would have remade the world for many of the thousands of Englishmen in West Africa or the millions away from home – in India and Ascension Island, in Labrador or in the prison camps of Siam.[15]

I'm assuming (I wish I'd asked) that he would have been in Harwich when the E-boat commanders came to surrender their minefield charts. That was 13 May 1945, five days after VE Day. There had been combined service parades and thanksgiving services in all the East Coast towns earlier in the day, then ten of the HMS *Beehive* MTBs, led by their senior officer, former RNVSR yachtsman volunteer John Hodder, escorted two E-boats to berth in Felixstowe Dock. Admiral Brauning, commander of the German Navy in Holland, accompanied by two senior Korvettenkapitäns, was then taken across to Parkeston and the charts formally handed over. My father and others serving at HMS *Badger* would be employed for the next year on the clear-up.

VE Day is remembered by many as the day the lights came back on after five and a half years of blackout. Stewart Platt and his crew, then based in Poole, thought they'd been rather canny, ensuring that every visit to the naval stores had included a request for light bulbs. When the day finally arrived, they discovered they'd been quite modest: 'Every ship's generator was grinding out electricity for the most amazing display of lighting. If we thought we had been clever, you should have seen some of the others.'[16]

Rozelle Raynes (Pierrepont) remembered:

All the ships on Southampton Water were arrayed in flags and rainbow-coloured bunting and their fog horns and sirens blared incessantly, from dawn until long after midnight. By mid-morning most of the sailors were drunk and we had a hectic time delivering them to the right ships, dodging fireworks and rockets which seemed to come with us from all directions, refusing innumerable 'gulpers' of rum and avoiding the American Liberty boats which were roaring up and down Southampton Water on zig-zag courses, utterly oblivious to the Rule of the Road.[17]

Off-duty, Rozelle had begun to feel 'rather lost and bewildered' but was glad to fall in with a Yorkshire crew from LCT *1109*, with whom she spent the rest of the evening, singing, drinking and ending up, somewhat surprisingly, in church.

The months to come were hard as the Navy gradually 'withdrew into itself'. Wrens were no longer allowed to act as Boats' Crew and finally, in December 1945, Rozelle had to accept that she was to be demobbed: 'When the Commander murmured something about making himself personally responsible for seeing that I was offered an interesting job in a boat-building firm, I suddenly lost all control, and bursting into floods of tears ran blindly from his office into the Brave New World outside.'[18]

Nicholas Monsarrat had been acting duty captain at the Admiralty on the evening of VE Day. In his autobiography, he explains that this meant little more than being there to answer telephones, receive signals and decide whether or not they needed to be passed on. The Admiralty was an operational centre, there were still ships at sea, there was still the war beyond Europe. By midnight, however, when all seemed quiet inside, he could no longer resist the temptation to get a glimpse of happenings outside. 'The crescendo of noise and cheering, the blaring of horns, the fireworks (hoarded for this moment), the sounds of amateur music makers, were very hard to resist [...] on a guilty impulse I deserted my post and climbed up the devious stone pathway to the top of Admiralty Arch.' From there, he had an unsurpassable view – down The Mall to Buckingham Palace, across Trafalgar Square to Nelson's Column. The blaze of lights symbolised regained freedom and it was glorious to look down on a surging ocean of people, not the 'calm or cruel, peaceful or murderous' sea. It was a long time before he realised that he wasn't alone on Admiralty Arch. The First Sea Lord was also there – Admiral Cunningham, an almost legendary figure.

I watched him surveying the raucous happy crowds. He looked up at Nelson. Then he leant forward, his knuckles planted squarely on the parapet. The movement brought his face into the floodlights shining from below, and I saw, in one bare glistening fraction of a second, that he was crying. I returned to duty forthwith.[19]

23

'From that point our personal history is of no concern'[1]

Summer 1945 onwards: General Election, readjustment to
civilian life and a return (or not) to yachting

Monsarrat had been approached to stand as the Labour Party candidate for Winchester in the July 1945 General Election and was disappointed when he wasn't selected. Instead, he spent six months as Councillor Lieutenant Commander Monsarrat on the housing and welfare committees on Kensington Borough Council. Dunstan Curtis was adopted as the Liberal Party candidate for Eddisbury in Cheshire but lost – as did Peter Scott (Conservative, Wembley North) and Edward Terrell (Conservative, North Southwark). Fredman Ashe Lincoln stood as the Conservative candidate in Harrow East and lost the election but remained as the party candidate until he was forced to withdraw two years later, during the Lynskey Tribunal in October 1948. There had been a scandal involving a Jewish financier attempting to bribe a junior minister at the Board of Trade, which had been reported by several newspapers in an anti-Semitic way. This had been condemned by the then Attorney General Sir Hartley Shawcross, but the Conservative Party was running scared. No matter that the guilty man was a known fraudster who had narrowly escaped deportation in 1933; somehow, all Jewish people were tainted by association: 'One of the reported effects of the trial is that the Conservative Party has asked Commander Ashe Lincoln, a Jew with an excellent war record, to withdraw his candidacy in East Harrow because the Party feels that it is inadvisable to have a Jew as its candidate at the present time.'[2]

That year, 1948, had already taken Lincoln into another political minefield. He had continued in naval service until May 1946, mainly involved in Baltic mine clearance, then had returned to work at the Bar, taking silk in 1947. Unsurprisingly, he had continued to play an active part in Jewish affairs. This included being chairman of the Political Committee of the World Jewish Congress, supporting the Exodus refugees and being naval adviser (unpaid) to the State of Israel. The fact that the fledgling state had a navy in 1948 was largely due to Lincoln working closely with David Ben-Gurion. Disillusion came when he realised the extent to which a 'narrow Middle European socialist ideology' was going to exercise control over seagoing appointments.

> *Being used to the British way of life, it took some time for me to understand the extent and force of politics in Israeli affairs. In my philosophy and in British forces, the political views of an individual are his own affair and there had to be strong evidence of unfitness for his job in other respects to affect his career. Indeed I had experienced the case in which a Petty Officer who was outstandingly able but was a known communist was nevertheless given a commission and subsequent promotion. That this sort of thing was not going to happen in Israel was quickly brought home to me.[3]*

In June 1948, Lincoln had refused to relinquish his British nationality to accept a commission in the Israeli Navy. It must have been galling, in October, to be pressured to step down as a Parliamentary candidate in England because he was Jewish.

Other attitudes narrowed and hardened as the 1940s became the 1950s. Publication of the 1948 Kinsey Report brought homosexuality into public discourse and was followed, from 1951, by a policy of repression by the new Home Secretary David Maxwell Fyfe. I don't suppose that my uncle, Jack Jones, was the only ex-serviceman to feel bitterness that the state that had been so willing to accept the sacrifice of his body in times of war, should be ready to persecute him for his identity in time of peace. In 1943, Jack had met 22-year-old Derek van den Bogaerde when training at Arisaig and they had begun a relationship that was, like any other relationship at that time, sustained by letter writing and by meetings when on leave. Jack was demobbed early as the disability from his wounds worsened; Derek spent a year in the Far East. By the time he returned late in 1946, their lives had already taken different directions – Jack into yacht design, Derek (now Dirk) into films. Although they remained lifelong friends, their relationship was no longer possible. Lyulph Stanley and his partner Günther left Britain for Switzerland in the early 1950s in order to live together without fear.

The focus of Dunstan Curtis' political career soon became European rather than British. After his Parliamentary defeat in 1945, he remained the prospective Liberal Party candidate for Eddisbury until the constituency was abolished in 1950. Meanwhile, he had become deputy secretary general of the European Movement and devoted his energies to European unity and establishing the Convention on Human Rights. Journalist Jane McLoughlin, profiling him 25 years after the war's end for *The Observer* newspaper, described him as 'the incomparable Jeeves to the great men of Europe' and as 'looking like a happy schoolmaster with a distinguished past in the local cricket club' – quite a long way from his leadership in 'the greatest raid' at St-Nazaire or landing Soviet spies on the Breton shore.[4]

Peter Scott, who was also defeated, had left the Navy to fight the election. He'd been promised command of the newly built frigate *Cardigan Bay* and had expected he would then be sent to the Pacific to join the fight against Japan. When the suggestion came that he should stand for Parliament, it crystallised a personal dilemma: 'Not the Navy versus politics but the War versus my family.'[5] He knew his wartime marriage to Elizabeth Jane Howard, 13 years his junior, was in trouble. She encouraged him to take up the candidacy but left him anyway. Scott threw himself back into ornithology and painting. He was no longer interested in developing new artistic techniques. 'I wanted to paint birds exactly as I had done before, as a manifestation of my safe return.'[6] For many people, his 1946 illustrations for Paul Gallico's Dunkirk novella *The Snow Goose* (first published in 1940) would come to epitomise the miracle of the Little Ships.

David Cobb, not yet 24, had responded quite differently: for him, painting was a new venture, not a nostalgic return. He had been a 'late initiate' into the special world of MTBs and MGBs 'but as essentially a small boat man I had felt immediately at home.'[7] The vivid scenes and colours of night-time actions were imprinted on his mind and he was suffering 'from acute visual indigestion'. He knew there was no future for small boats in the peacetime Navy;

'instead I would try to draw and paint what I had learned and seen. [...] I had no cushion of private means, no training, nor any grasp of how to sell work to earn me a living [...] but as I was no longer responsible for a lot of lives and ships in action, my own survival was no worry.' Cobb felt that 'England, for all its faults, had fostered and guarded something that I felt the world could not afford to lose, I would try to illustrate that theme.'[8]

Scott had also tried to express this belief in words. His *Battle of the Narrow Seas* was written while he was still in uniform and was published in 1945 using his rank, Lieutenant Commander Peter Scott. It's a commemorative book, with many direct contributions from Coastal Forces officers, recording the 'sacrifice, the unselfish and continuing effort and the heroism of deliberate courage' (though not the 'strain, discomfort and boredom').[9] Despite heartfelt admiration and profound sincerity, Scott also insists that 'there is no glory to be got out of war that cannot be had of some greater and more creative enterprise' and that 'nothing will ever compensate us for the men we have lost'. He returned briefly to dinghy sailing, winning the 1946 Prince of Wales Cup with his pre-war sailing partner John Winter. He was involved in organising the 1948 Olympics and accepted other high-profile positions within yachting. He no longer wished to shoot wildfowl. Instead, his enduring achievements were the founding of the Severn Wildfowl Trust at Slimbridge (part-built by German prisoners of war and now the Wildfowl and Wetlands Trust) and the co-founding of WWF. He became a pioneer in the field of nature conservation and enjoyed a happy second marriage.

Nicholas Monsarrat had needed relationship repair in 1945. He and Eileen had married just days after the outbreak of war and their son had been born in September 1942. Monsarrat writes frequently and beautifully of the support given by Eileen's love through those years of escort duty and shows understanding of how hard it was for her, left with nothing to do but cope, in austere, bomb-battered Britain. When he was posted away in America, standing-by HMS *Perim,* he had become self-indulgent and unfaithful. Casual infidelity had continued during his time at the Admiralty until finally he, Eileen and Max attempted a new start together, moving to South Africa, where Monsarrat became director of the UK Information Office in Johannesburg. It was on their voyage out that he experienced repugnance for the sea:

> *I could not forget that we were sailing, peacefully at last, over ground literally strewn with dead sailors, blown up, burned to death, shredded by the sea, sucked down, drowned – the most awful word in a sailor's word book. Full fathom five thy father lies – the fathers and sons were all there, just under our keel. The sea now seemed poisoned for ever and I never touched the stuff for another seven years.*[10]

There would be no return to the pleasures of the pre-war Trearddur Bay Sailing Club – or uncomplicated family life – for Monsarrat. His brilliant 1952 novella *The Ship that Died of Shame* epitomises his sense of post-war disillusion as humans prove unworthy of their own finest hour. He never lived permanently in England again.

Denys Rayner, who had spent so long at sea and given so much, also withdrew from sailing in the first years of peace. He had enjoyed his staff posting at Fort Southwick, Portsmouth, in the last months of the war, though he couldn't get rid of the fear that the advantage could so quickly tip back to the attacking U-boats – if those high-speed Walter boats had come into production, for instance. He also enjoyed working in the gender-balanced atmosphere with the Wrens. Yet, when peace came, Rayner didn't hurry to recover *Robinetta*, who he'd laid up so carefully in August 1939. Instead, he sold her to his Wren colleague Audrey Parker and her husband and took up farming. What was initially a 25-acre holding, with Rayner undertaking additional sales-repping jobs, became a full-time 350-acre farm and a house that was regularly filled with other people: Commonwealth personnel with nowhere to spend Christmas or Easter, refugees, widows, harvest helpers, a shell-shocked major who wouldn't leave his room – and the Rayners' post-war child, Vyvyan. When Rayner was finally persuaded to write his Atlantic memoir, *Escort: The Battle of the Atlantic* (1955), he introduced it carefully:

> *I write only of ships and of men, both of whom have character and change from one generation to another. These I would try to fix in a moment of time as I knew them. I do not write of the sea, which has no personality of its own and does not change. The sea is neither cruel nor kind. It is supremely indifferent.*[11]

When Vyvyan Rayner was old enough and began to show an interest in water, it was natural for his father to build him a little dinghy, then come with him to sail it. The post-war yachting scene differed from the Corinthian adventures of the interwar period, particularly in the proportion of families who found that they wanted to sail together. The concept of the 'Cadet' dinghy (1947), specifically designed for an older and a young child, was also something quite new. Its inexpensive materials and self-build design sprang partly from post-war shortages but also from an increased democratisation of the sport – and a more conscious desire to make childhood special. There had been too many separations. Peter Cooper's daughter, Jenny Balmer, described one of her father's indelible memories being the burned sailors calling out for rescue in an oil-covered sea; the other was 'a large ship filled with children, many of them clutching teddy bears, standing in complete silence, their faces without colour or expression, on their way to Canada or the US'.[12]

The Cadet was the result of a competition organised by *Yachting World* magazine. *Yachting Monthly's* first post-war initiative was to sponsor a 16ft Sharpie, an economical, easy-to-build day boat designed by Jack Jones. This was soon being modelled by Kathleen Palmer, now publicly acknowledged as having run the magazine since 1939. Though Griffiths and Clackson took their jobs back, her name remained with theirs on the masthead. As the popularity of DIY sailing grew, national newspapers would see dinghy sponsorship as a mass-market gimmick. The *News Chronicle* sponsored the Enterprise in 1955 and the *Daily Mirror* sponsored the Mirror in 1963. O'Brien Kennedy, the young Irish designer and former CP member who hadn't been able to afford his own transport to compete in the 1938 Prince of Wales Cup, now took commissions for sailing club 'one-design' dinghies – all boats built to an identical specification, ensuring fairness. Maurice Griffiths developed the self-build market from day-boat kits to cruising yachts, making significant use of the 'new' material – marine plywood – that had enabled all those MLs and MGBs to be constructed at such speed.

Denys Rayner went even further. Once he had returned to sailing, he began putting into practice those 'factory-build' processes that had enabled British production to step up when it was needed – for the Flower-class corvettes, for instance. He'd been developing his eye for design through every vessel he'd known but now he used new materials and a mass-production approach as he founded the Westerly range of GRP yachts in 1963. Rayner was a man in touch with his democratic times but many of his former yachtsman colleagues were horrified by GRP. Vyvyan remembers he and his father being turned away from yacht clubs when they arrived in their 'plastic' yacht. There may have been a mood for social change in the country but it wasn't necessarily easy for all those who had been living as 'temporary gentlemen' to catch up into the new mindsets.

Griffiths, who in December 1944 had married a Wren officer who had no sailing experience but was keen to learn, had started writing his book *Post-War Yachting* (1946) while he was still serving at HMS *Vernon*. Naturally, the yachts and techniques he was recommending were those he knew before the war, though with a consistent reference to economy and likely new conditions (in fact, the recovery of the yacht industry was much more complex than expected). His attitude to 'the Wife', the 'little pal', is so cringe-making it can only be explained as an acute attack of honeymoon-itis. I like to think that his pre-war wife, offshore sailor 'Peter Gerard', would have put him in the scuppers with a hosepipe on him. Griffiths (still in uniform) didn't hesitate to use the success of the RNVR yachtsmen to introduce his optimistic market-making volume.

> Yacht cruises and yacht racing are not merely sports for the favoured few; the recent war years proved how valuable a body of trained yachtsmen can become to the Admiralty. Had there not been such a body of keen sailing and motor cruising men in this country in 1939, men of the RNVR who were ready and competent to man the minesweepers, the patrol services, the coastal defence craft, the MLs, the MTBs and MGBs, and above all the numerous landing craft in the assaults on the enemy's mainland, it is difficult to say how this country would have fared.[13]

It's probably reasonable to overlook the fact that in the early days of the RNVSR, Griffiths had assured *Yachting Monthly* readers that there would be no requirement for small ships in the coming aircraft-led conflict – because that's what the Admiralty experts had also been saying. More interesting to note is his next assertion that

'The value of yachting as a training ground for war as well as for defence was fully realised by our enemies'. Perhaps that victory by *Nordwind* and the Kriegsmarine in the 1939 Fastnet still rankled? Yet the German Navy's fully manned ocean-racing approach bore no resemblance at all to Griffiths' characteristic ideal of messing about the 'swatchways' in small shallow-draught cruising yachts – the Childers' ideal, which might, without chauvinism, be claimed to foster qualities of individual self-reliance and initiative, as well as the tangible skills of navigation and ship handling.

After their defeat, no German was allowed to own a yacht more than 6m. This freed the beautiful 8m- and 12m-class yachts, designed by the greats of their time, for use by the occupying British forces. Many were sailed to Britain and other Allied countries as 'Windfall' reparations. In Kiel, the British also took over the Yacht Club, whose grandeur had so impressed the crew of *Naromis* during their brief visit almost six years earlier. In the summer of 1945, Sub-Lieutenant Tom Unwin RNVR (born Tomas Ungar) met his future wife, Wren Sheila Mills, there. He probably couldn't have hoped for a better setting to establish himself in her eyes as an officer and gentleman. His true background as a Czechoslovakian refugee of Jewish ancestry, with an unacknowledged girlfriend and baby daughter abandoned in England, was a good deal more complex. His war service, at least, was genuine – since 1943 he'd served as a wireless operator and linguist with the RNVR on Arctic convoys and A/S patrols off the coast of Norway. He was in Kiel with 30AU. Meeting him in his sub-lieutenant's uniform and as part of the glamorous yachting and yacht club scene made it easy for Sheila to take him at face value, enjoy his company, and fall in love, without any awkward questions. She didn't want to return to her pre-war life. Marriage to an officer would be welcome.

Robert Harling, who had used his war memoirs *Amateur Sailor* and *The Steep Atlantick Stream* (1946) to edit his identity, also married while in his new persona. The children didn't discover the truth until after his death.

Griffiths' recommendation of yachting 'as a training ground for war' would have resonated with Childers, who had ended *The Riddle of the Sands* on almost exactly that note when he welcomed the formation of the RNVR in 1903. There would have been little enthusiasm for that approach in 1945. Most people, hurrying to discover whether the yacht they had laid in 1939 was still seaworthy, were yearning for recreation. The clearing of the beaches, rivers and coastal waters was undertaken as swiftly as possible, though the task was immense. JP Foynes states that the minesweeping force led from Harwich needed to sweep ten times as many mines (of both sides) as had been swept during the war. Many people stayed in their volunteer uniforms for another 12–18 months engaged on this task. Perhaps it was a comfort to them that the 1946 sailing season had some of the worst weather on record.

There would be some former yachtsmen, such as Monsarrat, who were repelled by the sea; some like Rayner, exhausted by it; others, like Rayner's former first lieutenant, Jack Hunter, too deeply saddened by the loss of friends to be able to return. Furthermore, many pre-war yachts had not survived. There had been a high mortality and damage rate among those that had been requisitioned; others had proved vulnerable to neglect while they were laid, or their owners' circumstances had changed. Arthur Ransome's *Selina King* was suffering from rot and he was suffering from age and hernias. Edward Stanley's *Our Boy* had been rammed by a Canadian ML in Brixham and had lost her moorings in the run-up to D-Day. Edward Terrell's *Swan* had suffered bomb damage and sunk. When Arthur and Dorothy Bennett went back to inspect their former home *June of Rochester*, they felt 'thoroughly despondent':

> *The decks were leaking, and there were large rusty stains where the water had seeped through on the settees. Drips of moisture hung in clusters from the cabin top. The flooring had given way beneath the fireplace, and the stove was rusty and falling to pieces. Of course she could be done up, but with all the time and money spent on her, she would still be a very old barge at the end of it.*[14]

They also had to consider that they had become parents during the war: 'We'd better look for a house,' they agreed.

Eric and Gladys Newell had lost *Onda* to the war effort so bought a robust pilot cutter, *Equinoxe*, and set up their family home again. Unfortunately, Eric's return to the SH Benson agency after five and a half years away was not a happy experience. The gulf between those who had remained in civilian life and those, like Newell, who had lived so differently, proved unbridgeable. In 1948, Eric, Gladys and John emigrated to Canada. This meant that they gave up being part of a happy extended family: Eric and Gladys both had to work hard to build up new businesses and John, aged ten, had to begin yet another new school. He had to learn that:

There were different value systems and slants on history. [...] Things gradually improved in the 1950s, but it was hard to be in a dollar zone with what was left of my parents' capital frozen in sterling. Our happiest time came in the 1960s when we could sail again and joined the Royal Canadian Yacht Club.[15]

Allan Gotelee, Ewen Montagu and Edward Terrell were among those who seemed to pick up their previous careers as easily as their civilian clothes. Terrell, who had walked so proudly away from his chambers in his new uniform, was now glad to return in a dark suit and find his name newly painted on the door. These were new chambers; the old ones had been destroyed by bombing (as had the *Yachting Monthly* office).

Montagu claimed to have been so horrified at the style and cut of his demob suit that he decided to use it for charades. He served 28 years as Judge Advocate of the Fleet (1945–1973).

The book designers and typographers (Edward Young, Ruari McLean and Robert Harling) helped each other find work as they settled into their new marriages, dreamed up new magazines and tried to find places to live.

Patrick Dalzel-Job organised himself some final 30AU reconnaissance work and went back to Norway, without telling his boss, Ian Fleming, his true motive. He was returning to seek out Bjørg Bangsund, who, aged 15, had left a note in *Mary Fortune's* cabin in August 1939 to tell him she loved him. Theirs was a very happy marriage. They spent time living and travelling in Canada with their only child, Iain, and finally settled on the West Coast of Scotland before Bjørg's premature death. While writing this book, I've sometimes envisaged Dalzel-Job as a WWII version of Childers' Arthur Davies (with Bjørg as Clara); others have included him on their lists of possible James Bond prototypes. According to Iain, his father's 'practised' response to this suggestion was 'I only ever loved one woman, and I'm not a drinking man'.[16]

Fleming himself had fallen in love with Jamaica at an Anglo-American intelligence summit in 1942. As his work at the Admiralty wound down, he began sketching plans for his dream house on his blotter at the Admiralty. Its name, 'Goldeneye', came from an early intelligence operation set up with Alan Hillgarth, naval attaché in Madrid, aimed at safeguarding Gibraltar should Spain join the war on the Axis side. Immediately after the war, Fleming negotiated a contract with his new employers, Kemsley newspapers, including the clause that he could live in Jamaica for two months a year. His first novel, *Casino Royale*, was written there in 1952 (and published in 1953), then another every year until his death in 1964. Though he loved the sea around the island, I can find no record that he ever went sailing. Neither does his hero. Although he enrols Bond in the RNVSR (in *Moonraker*), I fear they both remained 'green-stripers'. The early Bond novels have a quality of exuberance – holiday writing as well as holiday reading. In them, Bond revisits, as an autonomous man of action, locations that Fleming knew as an administrator, a diplomat, a journalist and a receiver of the reports of others. Fleming makes playful use of friends' names – his friend Loelia Ponsonby, Duchess of Westminster becomes Bond's Admiralty secretary 'Lil'. Nevertheless, the search for 'real life' Bond prototypes seems misguided. Looking back to Fleming's tense relationship with Dunstan Curtis within 30AU, it feels more interesting to note that, post-war, Curtis became the diplomat and Fleming the adventurer, in his fantasy.

Nevil Shute's novels can be read more straightforwardly as wartime commentary, in which Shute characteristically introduces a narrator, who might stand in for himself. When Shute returned from Burma, he and his family were living at Pond Head on Hayling Island, a large house with 6 acres of land and its own jetty. *Runagate* had survived in good condition and Shute's first post-war novel, *The Chequer Board* (1947), which criticised American racism and British post-imperial snobbery, was far more successful than he'd dared hope. But he couldn't settle in post-war Britain. He and Frances survived a shaky marital moment then joined the stream of emigrants when they moved to Australia in 1950. Of his post-war novels, *Requiem for a Wren* (1955) and *On the Beach* (1957) can be seen as part of this impressively perceptive WWII sequence. In *Requiem for a Wren*, he presents the active service members of his generation as forever marked by their experience, often fatally: 'Like some infernal monster, still venomous in death, a war can go on killing people long after it's all over.'[17] *On the Beach* plays this out globally.

Many ex-servicemen used their yachts as their means of escape from the new uncongenial way of life – and some wrote books and articles to fund it. Former SOE agent George Millar travelled through the French canals on the ketch *Truant* to the Mediterranean in 1946 and described wrecked Europe in *Isabel and the Sea* (1948). Ex-RNVR officer Ernle Bradford, who left England with his wife Janet on the Dutch boeier *Mother Goose* not long afterwards, wrote of the impossibility of settling down to the routines of post-war office life: 'Too much adrenaline had gone through our systems for them to adjust easily to the routines of nine to six [...] Of those who failed to make the adjustment, some emigrated, some took to drink and some climbed mountains.'[18]

Adrian Hayter, who had stayed too long in the jungle, seems to use yachting to court further near-death experience in his extraordinary single-handed voyages, notably in *Sheila in the Wind* (1952).

August Courtauld returned to sailing *Duet* in the same hard-driven way that came naturally to him. This was fine when he had a friend like Quintin Riley with him but might be tough for the less committed. The novelist Evelyn Waugh sent himself an urgent telegram to escape a cruise on *Duet*, and Courtauld's daughter was overheard threatening her dolls, 'If you don't behave, I'll send you on the boat.'[19]

It was easy for East and South coast yachtsmen to visit Holland, Belgium or France, see the evidence of bombed buildings and bullet-pocked walls and glimpse the aftermath of life in previously occupied countries. Edward Stanley used his new yacht *Carmela* to run food supplies to the people of Normandy as part of a relief organisation called Les Amis Volontaires de France. He crossed regularly from Portsmouth to Ouistreham then down the canal to Caen loaded with food, clothing, bedding and medical aid. The heaviest cargo he carried was about 20 tons, which made *Carmela* 'almost unmanageable'. He was deeply moved by the resilience of the French people, trying to reorder their lives in the aftermath of destruction.

It was here in Caen that the curtain which came down in my mind off Portland Bill on September 1st, 1939, was finally lifted. Perhaps it was being among Frenchmen again and hearing their language; perhaps it was the violent realisation of the new problems that peace would bring, but at all events it was here, amidst the ruin and shambles of war, that the war itself became infinitely remote, an incident, merely; and all the trends and problems which the war had done nothing to alter, but which served only to accelerate, stamped themselves on my consciousness with an almost physical violence.[20]

Stanley's personal affairs frequently seemed to be in a state of crisis. He was effectively homeless at this point, still legally married to the New York socialite Sylvia Ashley; his treasured 'hand' Parsons had definitely retired, after serving through the war as an RNR skipper, and he was experiencing bereavement at the loss of a former sailing friend, Roger Chetwode, who had died in August 1940. 'The narrow seas we knew so well / Are tears too few to shed / Each clanging bell-buoy rings its knell / For you untimely dead.'[21]

Fellow RCC member Robin Balfour summarises his situation:

The war was over. It was 1946 and I was no longer a 'temporary' gentleman. [...] I had not seen my family for 4 years. All were alive and well but I had to get them together and start up a home again. Jack Hope, my brother-in-law, had been killed in the air over France. My business was difficult and there was a vast amount of work required [...] All in all 1946 was a year of great strain and one which I would not like to repeat.[22]

The early relaunch of *Bluebird of Thorne*, the steel-hulled twin-keeled ketch he had designed himself and which had twice been rejected for requisitioning, was a great solace. Balfour retained his appetite for adventure under sail for the rest of his life. He said little to his family about his war experiences.

Many people of my generation, the sons and daughters of those WWII yachtsmen volunteers, have wondered whether our parents kept this period of their lives as it were locked in a suitcase, as a way of coping with post-traumatic stress disorder. It's not always that we didn't ask, it's often that they didn't want to tell. As Peter Cooper's daughter writes:

He probably felt he couldn't talk to us about it. It would have been out of our experience. The men he might have wanted to talk to and share experiences with were scattered all over the country when the war was over, and all of them had to put the war behind them and begin to pick up the pieces of their lives. They all had to carry on as best they could.[23]

We are inclined to assume that talking about difficult experiences or seeking counselling support are universal cures (as they may be for many people). In retrospect, it seems impossible and presumptuous to make any generalisations about how people 'should' have coped. The yachtsmen who volunteered for service with the Navy 'in case of an emergency' could have had no idea what was in store for them, how long they would have to forego their individual dreams, careers and choices, whether they – or those dreams – would survive. Whether they had been posted to depot ships, tracking rooms, minesweepers, gunboats or undercover operations, these had been six years out of the ordinary. They had required endurance, resilience, self-denial and, yes, uncommon courage.

Looking at the post-war activities of the four George Cross recipients, the mine-disposal volunteers briefly trained by John Ouvry: Jack Easton returned to his pre-war job in his family solicitor office and Harold Newgass to being a Dorset county councillor and treasurer of his local Conservative Association. John Miller moved from being assistant education officer for Northamptonshire to setting up a university in Ethiopia, working with Jomo Kenyatta in Kenya and farming in Rhodesia; Robert Selby Armitage was a member of the London Stock Exchange, lived in the village of Nettlebed where he had grown up, played golf regularly with Ian Fleming and ended his life by shooting himself, after shooting and wounding his wife. That was in 1977; was there any connection with the almost unimaginable strain of his wartime service? It's impossible to say.

In my own family, my mother, a civilian who went to work first in an armaments factory then a Foreign Office department, as well as living through the V1 bombing of London and feeling constant anxiety for her serving brothers and cousins, suffered more obviously from strain (and PTSD) than my father, held within the solid, if sometimes repressive, structure of the Navy. He might reasonably be said to have gained in self-confidence and self-knowledge – and love of his home river. *Hustler* was waiting for him.

I've lost faith in most of the things I used to have as ideals or fancies. They've dulled and don't fire me anymore. But one thing still retains its fascination – mystery if you like – and that is the Deben. [...] I know there is nothing I want more than to get back to this part of Suffolk.[24]

There was no sailing tradition in my mother's family. When she found herself in post-war Oxford, hoping that study would offer a way forward from partial breakdown, she was quickly attracted by the sight of dinghies sailing on the River Thames at Port Meadow. By 1947, she had spotted a *Yachting Monthly* advertisement for a small yacht offered for sale by a very new agency based at Waldringfield in Suffolk. There, she met my father and uncle, bought the little yacht (renamed *Snow Goose*) and began a completely unexpected way of life. My mother's and father's family backgrounds were far apart; had it not been for the six years he had served as a 'temporary' gentleman (to use Robin Balfour's phrase), I don't think they would have managed to establish a rapport, let alone begin taking *Snow Goose* to the Royal Burnham Yacht Club and entering races. They married in 1950.

There was one final significant event (for me) in those immediate post-war years. Arthur Ransome's doctors advised him that even if his splendid yacht *Selina King* could be brought back from her post-lay-up deterioration, she would be too much for him to handle. He needed to commission something new. So, as it was almost a patriotic duty to find work for newly demobbed yacht designers and for boatyards that had no more contracts from the Admiralty, *Peter Duck* was commissioned in 1945 from designer Jack Laurent Giles. She was to be built at Harry King's yard at Pin Mill on the River Orwell, ready for the 1947 season. Ten years later, when I was nearly three years old, she became our boat and has been almost ever since. The exception is the period between 1987 and 1999 when she had been sold after my father's death and went on her adventures with the Palmer family. That included a circumnavigation of Britain in 1991, during which she was nearly wrecked. I'm sure I've got that logbook, somewhere in my attic...

Endnotes

INTRODUCTION

1 GA Jones, *The Cruise of Naromis,* p.50.
2 Brian Lavery, *In Which We Served,* p.18.
3 Attributed to Mark Twain, probably apocryphal.
4 Arthur Ransome, *We Didn't Mean To Go To Sea,* p.29.
5 Peter Scott, *The Battle of the Narrow Seas,* p.xi.

CHAPTER 1

1 Erskine Childers, *The Riddle of the Sands,* p.95.
2 Erskine Childers, *The Riddle of the Sands,* p.270.
3 Erskine Childers, *The Riddle of the Sands,* p.277.
4 Erskine Childers, *The Riddle of the Sands,* p.95.
5 Maldwin Drummond, *The Riddle,* p.299.
6 Maldwin Drummond, *The Riddle,* p.297.
7 Leonard Piper, *The Tragedy of Erskine Childers,* p.106.
8 Maldwin Drummond, *The Riddle,* p.278.
9 Judith Hill, *In Search of Islands,* p.38.
10 Leonard Piper, *The Tragedy of Erskine Childers,* p.141.
11 Jim Ring, *Erskine Childers,* p.161.
12 https://skipperswar.com/tag/nsn
13 J Lennox Kerr & Wilfred Glanville, *The RNVR: a record of achievement,* p.94.
14 J Lennox Kerr & Wilfred Glanville, *The RNVR: a record of achievement,* p.97.
15 Erskine Childers, *The Riddle of the Sands,* p.118.

CHAPTER 2

1 Erskine Childers, *The Riddle of the Sands,* p.270.
2 Patrick Dalzel-Job, *From Arctic Snow to Dust of Normandy,* p.18.

3   Margery Allingham, *The Oaken Heart*, p.21.
4   Nevil Shute, *Slide Rule*, p.17.
5   Nevil Shute, *Slide Rule*, p.16.
6   Nevil Shute, *Slide Rule*, p.37.
7   Lord 'Skips' Riverdale, *A Life, a Sail, a Changing Sea*, p.10.
8   Maurice Griffiths, *Yachting on a Small Income*, p.5.
9   Lord Stanley of Alderley, *Sea Peace*, p.42.
10 Ludovic Kennedy, *Sub-Lieutenant*, p.23.
11 Ludovic Kennedy, *Sub-Lieutenant*, p.22.
12 Nicholas Monsarrat, *Life is a Four-Letter Word*, Volume 1, p.32.

CHAPTER 3

1   Erskine Childers, *The Riddle of the Sands*, p.95.
2   DA Rayner, *Escort*, p.11.
3   https://robinetta-log.blogspot.com/p/november-1937-yachting-monthly.html
4   DA Rayner, *Escort*, p.14.
5   Augustine Courtauld, *Man the Ropes*, p.24.
6   http://lintonsview.blogspot.com/2009/11/abbasubmariners-and-spying.html
7   Augustine Courtauld, *Man the Ropes*, p.102.
8   https://exeterflotilla.org.uk/history.html
9   Nicholas Wollaston, *The Man on the Ice Cap*, p.193.
10 Brian Lavery, *In Which We Served*, p.20.
11 Eric Newell, *What a Life*, p.103.
12 Eric Newell, *What a Life*, p.106.
13 Linda Parker, *Ice, Steel and Fire*, p.68.
14 Linda Parker, *Ice, Steel and Fire*, p.301.
15 Fredman Ashe Lincoln, *Secret Naval Investigator*, p.21.

CHAPTER 4

1   Erskine Childers, *The Riddle of the Sands*, p.142.
2   Adrian Seligman, *The Voyage of the* Cap Pilar, p.356.
3   Adrian Seligman, *The Voyage of the* Cap Pilar, p.353.
4   Lord Stanley of Alderley, *Sea Peace*, p.117.
5   http://api.parliament.uk/historic-hansard/commons/1938/oct/03/personal-explanation
6   Nevil Shute, *What Happened to the Corbetts?*
7   DA Rayner, *Escort*, p.18.

8   Peter Scott, *The Eye of the Wind*, p.151.
9   GA Jones, *The Cruise of Naromis*, p.17 (for text of speech see https://avalon.law.yale.edu/wwii/blbk09.asp).
10 GA Jones, *The Cruise of Naromis*, p.21.
11 Mollie Butler, *August and Rab*, p.23.
12 Mollie Butler, *August and Rab*, p.24.
13 Peter Scott, *The Eye of the Wind*, p.141.
14 Peter Scott, *The Eye of the Wind*, p.152.
15 GA Jones, *The Cruise of Naromis*, p.66.
16 *Yachting World* (1939, 8 September).
17 Ewen Montagu, *Beyond Top Secret U*, p.17.
18 Edward Terrell, *Admiralty Brief*, p.16.
19 AS Bennett, *Tide Time*, p.8.
20 Lord Stanley of Alderley, *Sea Peace*, p.138.

CHAPTER 5

1   Erskine Childers, *The Riddle of the Sands*, p.47.
2   Ludovic Kennedy, *Sub-Lieutenant*, p.27.
3   DA Rayner, *Escort*, p.19.
4   DA Rayner *Escort*, p.21.
5   DA Rayner *Escort*, p.28.
6   www.nevilshute.org
7   Letter and reply in GA Jones papers. The future VC recipients he met on HMS *Forth* were John 'Tubby' Linton, Anthony Miers, Malcolm Wanklyn, Peter Roberts.
8   Ewen Montagu, *Beyond Top Secret U*, p.17.
9   Tony Hugill, *The Hazard Mesh*, p.61.
10 George O'Brien Kennedy, *Not All At Sea!*, p.121.
11 George O'Brien Kennedy, *Not All At Sea!*, p.97.
12 Peter Scott, *The Eye of the Wind*, p.153.
13 Ludovic Kennedy, *Sub-Lieutenant*, p.27.
14 Adlard Coles, *Sailing Years*, p.101.
15 Eric Hiscock, *I Left the Navy,* p. 23.
16 AS Bennett, *Tide Time*, p.18.
17 Ewen Montagu, *Beyond Top Secret U*, p.17.
18 Iain W Rutherford, *At The Tiller*, p.165.
19 Iain W Rutherford, *At The Tiller*, p.160.
20 Ludovic Kennedy, *On My Way to the Club*, p.94.
21 Iain W Rutherford, *At The Tiller*, p.160.
22 John Miller, *Saints and Parachutes*, pp.14–15.

CHAPTER 6

1 Erskine Childers, *The Riddle of the Sands*, p.116.
2 DA Rayner, *Escort*, p.32.
3 GA Jones, *The Cruise of Naromis*, p.93.
4 Paul Lund & Harry Ludlam, *The Trawlers go to War*.
5 AS Bennett, *Tide Time*, p.20.
6 GA Jones, *The Cruise of Naromis*, p.50.
7 *Yachting Monthly* (1940, June).
8 Ludovic Kennedy, *Sub-Lieutenant*, p.31.
9 Ludovic Kennedy, *Sub-Lieutenant*, p.37.
10 Margery Allingham, *The Oaken Heart*, 158.
11 Iain W Rutherford, *At The Tiller*, pp.162, 163.
12 Iain W Rutherford, *At The Tiller*, p.165.
13 AS Bennett, *Tide Time*, p.20.
14 J Lennox Kerr & David James (eds.), *Wavy Navy*, p.219.
15 Maurice Griffiths, *Yachting Monthly* (1940, June).
16 *Yachting Monthly* (1940, June).
17 Antony Hichens, *Gunboat Command*, p.46.

CHAPTER 7

1 Erskine Childers, *The Riddle of the Sands*, p.111.
2 Fredman Ashe Lincoln, *Secret Naval Investigator*, p.26.
3 https://vandwdestroyerassociation.org.uk/HMSWestminster/
   Ouvry.htm
4 Maurice Griffiths, *The Hidden Menace*, p.84.
5 Maurice Griffiths, *The Hidden Menace*, p.84.
6 John Miller, *Saints and Parachutes*, p.57.
7 https://www.independent.co.uk/news/people/obituary-commander
   -j-g-d-ouvry-2320793.html
8 https://www.independent.co.uk/news/people/obituary-commander
   -j-g-d-ouvry-2320793.html
9 Over the following five years a further 13 RNVR officers would be
   awarded the George Cross for Rendering Mines Safe. They were
   John Bridge, Peter Danckwerts, Jack Easton, Edward Gidden, Leon
   Goldsworthy, George Goodman, George Gosse, John Miller, John
   Mould, Harold Newgass, Hugh Syme, William Taylor, Geoffrey Turner.

CHAPTER 8

1 Erskine Childers, *The Riddle of the Sands*, p.84.
2 Augustine Courtauld, *Man the Ropes*, p.106.

3   Jonathon Riley, *From Pole to Pole*, p.119.
4   *Yachting Monthly* (1940, June).
5   https://gilesnet.co.uk/glowworm/index.php?cmd=sip
6   Patrick Dalzel-Job, *From Arctic Snow to Dust of Normandy*, p.30.
7   Patrick Dalzel-Job, *From Arctic Snow to Dust of Normandy*, p.30.
8   Patrick Dalzel-Job, *From Arctic Snow to Dust of Normandy*, p.50.
9   Patrick Dalzel-Job, *From Arctic Snow to Dust of Normandy*, p.53.
10 Ludovic Kennedy, *Sub-Lieutenant*, p.62.
11 Ludovic Kennedy, *Sub-Lieutenant*, p.67.
12 Linda Parker, *Ice Steel and Fire*, p.84.
13 Captain WR Fell, *The Sea Our Shield*, p.49.
14 Captain WR Fell, *The Sea Our Shield*, p.56.
15 Captain WR Fell, *The Sea Our Shield*, p.59.
16 Linda Parker, *Ice Steel and Fire*, p.84.
17 Captain WR Fell, *The Sea Our Shield*, p.69.
18 Captain WR Fell, *The Sea Our Shield*, p.75.
19 Jonathon Riley, *From Pole to Pole*, p.132.

CHAPTER 9

1   Erskine Childers, *The Riddle of the Sands*, p.63.
2   https://www.historynet.com/world-war-11-defending-calais.html
3   https://winstonchurchill.org/resources/speeches/1940-the-finest
    -hour/we-shall-fight-on-the-beaches/
4   http://www.strangehistory.net/2011/07/14/unlikely-escape-from-calais/
5   Antony Hichens, *Gunboat Command*, p.74.
6   Antony Hichens, *Gunboat Command,* p.73.
7   Martin Mace, *The Royal Navy at Dunkirk*, p.119.
8   George Carter, *Looming Lights*, p.127.
9   http://trimilia.co.uk/dunkirk/
10 David Divine, *The Nine Days of Dunkirk*, p.14.
11 Nigel Sharp, *Troubled Waters*, p.9.
12 Russell Plummer, *The Ships that Saved an Army*, p.199.
13 David Divine, *The Nine Days of Dunkirk*, p.13.
14 Other RNVSR members of this group included PT Lovelock, H
    Leslie, JR Smellie, KW Kennett, JN Wise.
15 Hugh Sebag-Montefiore, *Dunkirk*, p.444.

CHAPTER 10

1   Erskine Childers, *The Riddle of the Sands*, p.108.
2   Russell Plummer, *The Ships That Saved an Army*, p.110.

3 http://ww2today.com/hm-ships-glorious-acasta-and-ardent-sunk
4 Peter Scott, *The Eye of the Wind*, p.154.
5 Peter Scott, *The Eye of the Wind*, p.163.
6 Kenneth Jacob, *Some Autobiographical Notes* (unpublished ms), p.27.
7 Peter Scott, *The Eye of the Wind*, p.164.
8 Kenneth Jacob, *Some Autobiographical Notes* (unpublished ms), p.27.
9 Julian Foynes, *The Battle of the East Coast*, p.175.
10 Eric Newell, *What a Life*, p.128.
11 Eric Newell, *What a Life*, p.129.
12 Eric Newell, *What a Life*, p.130.
13 Eric Newell, *What a Life*, p.134.
14 Lord Riverdale, *Nine Lives in One*, p.136.
15 Lord Riverdale, *Nine Lives in One*, p.131.
16 Peter Cooper, *Account of Party X Mission* (unpublished), p.15.
17 Nevil Shute, *Pied Piper*, p.276.
18 Nevil Shute, *Pied Piper*, p.281.

CHAPTER 11

1 Erskine Childers, *The Riddle of the Sands*, p.83.
2 Margery Allingham, *The Oaken Heart*, p.204.
3 Jonathon Riley, *From Pole to Pole*, p.136.
4 *Yachting Monthly* (1940, June).
5 Gerald Pawle, *The Secret War*, p.7.
6 Nevil Shute, *Pied Piper*, p.265.
7 Edward Terrell, *Admiralty Brief*, p.14.
8 Edward Terrell, *Admiralty Brief*, p.31.
9 David Cobb, *The Making of a War Artist*, p.14.
10 David Howarth, *Pursued by a Bear*, p.75.
11 David Howarth, *Pursued by a Bear*, p.81.
12 David Howarth, *Pursued by a Bear*, p.97.
13 David Howarth, *Pursued by a Bear*, p.120.
14 David Howarth, *Pursued by a Bear*, p.131.
15 J Lennox Kerr & David James (eds.), *Wavy Navy*, p.49.
16 Maurice Griffiths, *The Hidden Menace*, p.106.
17 John Miller, *Saints and Parachutes*, p.16.
18 John Miller, *Saints and Parachutes*, p.11.
19 John Miller, *Saints and Parachutes*, p.32.
20 John Miller, *Saints and Parachutes*, p.65.
21 Fredman Ashe Lincoln, *Odyssey of a Jewish Sailor*, p.37.
22 J Lennox Kerr & David James (eds.), *Wavy Navy*, p.56.

ENDNOTES

CHAPTER 12

1   Erskine Childers, *The Riddle of the Sands*, p.111.
2   Edward Young, *One of our Submarines*, pp.39–40.
3   Edward Young, *One of our Submarines*, p.42.
4   Nicholas Monsarrat, *Life is a Four Letter Word*, Volume 2, p.3.
5   Nicholas Monsarrat, *Three Corvettes*, p.279.
6   Nicholas Monsarrat, *Three Corvettes*.
7   Nicholas Monsarrat, *Three Corvettes*, p.27.
8   Nicholas Monsarrat, *Three Corvettes*, p.61.
9   Martin Middlebrook *Convoy*, p.38.
10 DA Rayner, *Escort*, p.52.
11 DA Rayner, *Escort*, p.66.
12 DA Rayner, *Escort*, pp.79–80.
13 https://www.heraldscotland.com/news/12403045.lord-hunter
    -distinguished-judge-keen-fisherman-and-man-of-exacting-principle
14 https://www.bbc.co.uk/history/ww2peopleswar/stories/96/
    a4436796.shtml

CHAPTER 13

1   Erskine Childers, *The Riddle of the Sands*, p.24.
2   Edward Young, *One of Our Submarines*, p.52.
3   Edward Young, *One of Our Submarines*, p.57.
4   Margery Allingham, *The Oaken Heart*, p.223.
5   Edward Young, *One of Our Submarines*, p.61.
6   Ludovic Kennedy, *Pursuit*, p.108.
7   Ludovic Kennedy, *Pursuit*, p.242.
8   The list on wrecksite.eu suggests that this man may have been Lt Cdr
    WA Elliott, aged 44.
9   Edward Young, *One of Our Submarines*, p.59.
10 Edward Young, *One of Our Submarines*, p.63.
11 Jonathon Riley, *From Pole to Pole*, p.137.
12 David Howarth, *Pursued by a Bear*, p.141.
13 David Howarth, *Pursued by a Bear*, p.142.
14 *Hitra* survives as a museum ship https://en.wikipedia.org/wiki/
    HNoMS_Hitra
15 David Howarth, *Pursued by a Bear*, p.154.

CHAPTER 14

1   Erskine Childers, *The Riddle of the Sands*, p.118.
2   Peter Scott, *The Battle of the Narrow Seas*, p.7.

3   Antony Hichens, *Gunboat Command*, p.59.
4   Mollie Butler, *August and Rab*, p.29.
5   Peter Scott, *The Battle of the Narrow Seas*, p.18.
6   Antony Hichens, *Gunboat Command*, p.115.
7   Robert Hichens, *We Fought Them in Gunboats*, p.119.
8   Robert Hichens, *We Fought Them in Gunboats*, p.55.
9   AS Bennett, *Tide Time*, p.34.
10 Peter Scott, *Battle of the Narrow Seas*, p.34.
11 Robert Hichens, *We Fought Them in Gunboats*, p.40.
12 Robert Hichens, *We Fought Them in Gunboats*, p.64.
13 Robert Hichens, *We Fought Them in Gunboats*, p.110.
14 Peter Scott, *Battle of the Narrow Seas*, p.46.
15 Peter Scott, *Battle of the Narrow Seas*, p.48.
16 Peter Scott, *Battle of the Narrow Seas*, p.56.
17 Peter Scott, *Battle of the Narrow Seas*, p.58.
18 Gordon Holman, *The Little Ships*, p.115.
19 Gordon Holman, *The Little Ships*, p.110.

CHAPTER 15

1   Gordon Holman, *The Little Ships*, p.110.
2   Much information from Pierre Tillot www.plan-sussex-1944.net/anglais/pdf/infiltrations_into_france.pdf
3   Gordon Holman, *The Little Ships*, p.91.
4   Donal O'Sullivan, 'Dealing with the Devil' Journal of Intelligence History, Volume 4 (2004, Winter).
5   *Yachting Monthly* (1941, January).
6   www.holdsworthtrust.org/gerry-holdsworth/
7   Brooks Richards, *Secret Flotillas*, Volume 1, p.134.
8   MRD Foot, *SOE*, p.96.
9   Brooks Richards, *Secret Flotillas*, Volume 1, p.237.
10 *Daily Telegraph* obituary (2004 February 4).
11 Brooks Richards, *Secret Flotillas*, Volume 1, p.172.
12 https://www.theguardian.com/lifeandstyle/2013/jan/18/jane-birkin-my-family-values

CHAPTER 16

1   Erskine Childers, *The Riddle of the Sands*, p.118.
2   Corelli Barnett, *Engage the Enemy More Closely*, p.345.
3   Adrian Seligman, *No Stars to Guide*, p.96.
4   Adrian Seligman, *No Stars to Guide*, p.61.

5   Adrian Seligman, *No Stars to Guide*, p.64.
6   DA Rayner, *Escort*, p.101.
7   John Newell, Correspondence with author.
8   Eric Newell, *What a Life* (unpublished ms), p.153.
9   Eric Newell, *What a Life* (unpublished ms), p.143.
10 Eric Newell, *What a Life*, p.148.
11 Nicholas Monsarrat, *Three Corvettes*, p.83.
12 Nicholas Monsarrat, *Three Corvettes*, p.123.
13 David Howarth, *Pursued by a Bear*, p.73.
14 DA Rayner, *Escort*, p.93.
15 DA Rayner, *Escort*, p.97.
16 Edward Young, *One of Our Submarines*, p.93.
17 Stephan Hopkinson, *Encounter.*
18 https://www.openbookpublishers.com/htmlreader/978-1-78374
    -881-5/ch7.xthml
19 Giles Hunt, *Launcelot Fleming*, p.96.
20 Percy Woodcock, *Looking Astern*, p.170.

CHAPTER 17

1   Erskine Childers, *The Riddle of the Sands*, p.154.
2   Erskine Childers, *The Riddle of the Sands*, p.272.
3   Colonel Sam Bassett, *Royal Marine*, p.146.
4   Colonel Sam Bassett, *Royal Marine*, p.157.
5   Colonel Sam Bassett, *Royal Marine*, p.157.
6   Colonel Sam Bassett, *Royal Marine*, p.166.
7   Adrian Seligman, *No Stars to Guide*, p.7.
8   Ruari McLean, *True to Type*, p.46.
9   Robert Harling, *Amateur Sailor*, p.270.
10 Robert Harling, *Steep Atlantick Stream*, p.223.
11 Robert Harling, *Ian Fleming: a personal memoir*, p.16.
12 Colonel Sam Bassett, *Royal Marine*, p.178.
13 Robert Harling, *Ian Fleming: a personal memoir*, p.14.
14 Peter Scott, *Battle of the Narrow Seas*, p.100.
15 Nicholas Rankin, *Ian Fleming's Commandos*, p.19.

CHAPTER 18

1   Erskine Childers, *The Riddle of the Sands*, p.110.
2   Patrick Dalzel-Job, *From Arctic Snow to Dust of Normandy*, p.54.
3   Patrick Dalzel-Job, *From Arctic Snow to Dust of Normandy*, p.66.
4   John Anderson, *Parallel Motion*, p.138.

5 Nevil Shute, *Most Secret,* p.205.
6 Margery Allingham, *The Oaken Heart*, p.55.
7 Nevil Shute, *Most Secret,* p.325.
8 Gerald Pawle, *The Secret War*, p.234.
9 Edward Terrell, *Admiralty Brief*, p.222.
10 Edward Terrell, *Admiralty Brief*, p.225.
11 Ewen Montagu, *Beyond Top Secret U*, p.131.
12 Ewen Montagu, *Beyond Top Secret U*, p.51.
13 Ewen Montagu, *Beyond Top Secret U*, p.30.
14 Ewen Montagu, *Beyond Top Secret U*, p.140.
15 Ewen Montagu, *Beyond Top Secret U*, p.36.
16 Ewen Montagu, *Beyond Top Secret U*, p.150.
17 Godfrey Winn, *PQ17*, p.42.
18 Godfrey Winn, *PQ17*, p.229.
19 Edward Terrell, *Admiralty Brief*, p.194.
20 Karl Doenitz, *Memoirs*, 263. Earlier versions included additional instructions '*Survivors are to be saved only if their statements are important for the boat. Be harsh. Remember that the enemy has no regard for women and children when bombing German cities!*'
21 Ewen Montagu, *Beyond Top Secret U*, p.159.
22 Fredman Ashe Lincoln, *Secret Naval Investigator*, p.146.
23 Fredman Ashe Lincoln, *Odyssey of a Jewish Sailor*, p.21.

CHAPTER 19

1 Erskine Childers, *The Riddle of the Sands*, p.258.
2 MS letter Madron Seligman to Bertie McDowell (1943, February 28) (thanks to Lincoln Seligman).
3 Adrian Seligman (ed), *War in the Islands*, p.10.
4 Adrian Seligman (ed), *War in the Islands*, p.149.
5 Adrian Seligman (ed), *War in the Islands*, p.169.
6 Adrian Seligman (ed), *War in the Islands*, p.184.
7 Adrian Seligman (ed), *War in the Islands*, p.220.
8 Adrian Seligman (ed), *War in the Islands*, p.34.
9 Fredman Ashe Lincoln, *Odyssey of a Jewish Sailor*, p.28.
10 Fredman Ashe Lincoln, *Odyssey of a Jewish Sailor*, pp.24–25.
11 Nicholas Rankin, *Ian Fleming's Commandos*, p.187.
12 Ruari McLean, *True to Type*, p.27.
13 Ruari McLean, *Half Seas Under*, p.11.
14 Ruari McLean, *True to Type*, p.27.

15 https://www.independent.co.uk/news/people/obituary-geoff -galwey-1340567.html
16 Ruari McLean, *Half Seas Under*, p.154.
17 Edward Young, *One of our Submarines*, p.246.
18 Edward Young, *One of our Submarines*, p.251.
19 Edward Young, *One of our Submarines*, p.255.
20 Ruari McLean, *Half Seas Under*, p.192.

CHAPTER 20

1 Erskine Childers, *The Riddle of the Sands*, p.258.
2 Ken Small, *The Forgotten Dead*, p.91.
3 Robert Simper, *The Lost Village of Ramsholt*, p.12.
4 Nevil Shute, 'Journey into Normandy' 1 https://www.nevilshute.org
5 Obituary for Joan Curran by Tam Dalyell https://www.independent .co.uk/arts-entertainment/obituary-joan-curran-1071704.html
6 Gerald Pawle, *The Secret War*, p.180.
7 Nevil Shute, *Requiem for a Wren*, p.101.
8 Rozelle Raynes, *Maid Matelot*, p.42.
9 Rozelle Raynes, *Maid Matelot*, p.52.
10 Rozelle Raynes, *Maid Matelot*, p.84.
11 AS Bennett, *Tide Time*, p.42.
12 Stewart Platt, *My Three Grey Mistresses*, p.32.
13 Stewart Platt, *My Three Grey Mistresses*, p.31.
14 Stewart Platt, *My Three Grey Mistresses*, p.32.
15 J Lennox Kerr & David James (eds.), *Wavy Navy*, p.7.
16 Stewart Platt, *My Three Grey Mistresses*, p.34.
17 Naval History Board, *Operation Neptune*, pp.14–15.
18 AS Bennett, *Tide Time*, p.42.
19 James Holland, *Normandy '44*, p.209.
20 AS Bennett, *Tide Time*, p.43.
21 Nevil Shute, 'Journey into Normandy' 2 https://www.nevilshute.org
22 AS Bennett, *Tide Time*, p.43.
23 James Holland, *Normandy '44*, p.210.
24 Stewart Platt, *My Three Grey Mistresses*, p.35.

CHAPTER 21

1 Erskine Childers, *The Riddle of the Sands*, p.263.
2 Rozelle Raynes, *Maid Matelot*, p.105.
3 Rozelle Raynes, *Maid Matelot*, p.109.

4   Maurice Griffiths, *The Hidden Menace*, p.129.
5   AS Bennett, *Tide Time*, p.43.
6   AS Bennett, *Tide Time*, p.46.
7   Robert Harling, *Ian Fleming: a personal memoir*, p.81.
8   Patrick Dalzel-Job, *From Arctic Snow to Dust of Normandy*, p.135.
9   Patrick Dalzel-Job, *From Arctic Snow to Dust of Normandy*, p.140.
10 Maurice Griffiths, *The Hidden Menace*, p.135.
11 J Lennox Kerr & David James (eds.), *Wavy Navy*, p.203.
12 Maurice Griffiths, *The Hidden Menace*, p.135.
13 Edward Terrell, *Admiralty Brief*, p.219.
14 JP Foynes, *The War on the East Coast 1939–1945*, p.361.

CHAPTER 22

1   Erskine Childers, *The Riddle of the Sands*, p.230.
2   DA Rayner, *Escort*.
3   U-1200, the submarine Rayner believed he had destroyed, was
    discovered in 1999 off Start Point in the English Channel, miles
    away and with no discernible reason for her loss. 53 had died with
    her but probably not at the hands of the 30th Escort Group.
4   DA Rayner, *Escort*, p.211.
5   Nicholas Monsarrat, *Life is a Four Letter word*, Volume 2, p.142.
6   Peter C Smith, *Hold the Narrow Sea*, p.223.
7   J Lennox Kerr & David James (eds.), *Wavy Navy*, p.127.
8   Fredman Ashe Lincoln, *Secret Naval Investigator*, p.200.
9   Patrick Dalzell-Job, *From Arctic Snow to Dust of Normandy*.
10 AS Bennett, *Tide Time*, p.67.
11 AS Bennett, *Tide Time*, p.68.
12 Ewen Montagu, *Beyond Top Secret U*, p.176.
13 Ewen Montagu, *Beyond Top Secret U*, p.177.
14 Ruari McLean, *Half Seas Under*, p.210.
15 GA Jones, *The Cruise of Naromis*, p.111.
16 Stewart Platt, *My Three Grey Mistresses*, p.40.
17 Rozelle Raynes, *Maid Matelot*, p.130.
18 Rozelle Raynes, *Maid Matelot*, p.149.
19 Nicholas Monsarrat, *Life is a Four Letter Word*, Volume 2, p.147.
    Admiral Cunningham's autobiography describes the same scene but
    says only that he was 'lucky to be able to dine quietly in my flat with
    my wife and my brother.' *A Sailor's Odyssey*, p.643.

CHAPTER 23

1   Erskine Childers, *The Riddle of the Sands*, p.270.
2   http://www.jta.org/1948.12/21/archive/british-jews-consider
    -imposition-of-sanctions-against-members-who-shame-community.
    In 1950 Lincoln's candidature at Willesden East ran into similar
    problems of prejudice.
3   Fredman Ashe Lincoln, *Odyssey of a Jewish Sailor*, p.71.
4   https://bookblast.com/blg/book-blast-archive-what-makes-a
    -european-jane-mcloughlin-the-observer-1971
5   Peter Scott, *The Eye of the Wind*, p.228.
6   Peter Scott, *The Eye of the Wind*, p.242.
7   David Cobb, *The Making of a War Artist*, p.16.
8   David Cobb, *The Making of a War Artist*, p.16.
9   Peter Scott, *The Battle of the Narrow Seas*, p.xi.
10 Nicholas Monsarrat, *Three Corvettes*, p.6.
11 DA Rayner, *Escort*, p.6.
12 Jenny Balmer, letter to author (2021, March 1).
13 Maurice Griffiths, *Post-War Yachting*, p.6.
14 AS Bennett, *Tide Time*, p.69.
15 John Newell, communication to author.
16 https://www.scotsman.com/news/my-fater-was-inspiration-james
    -bond-2463819
17 Nevil Shute, *Requiem for a Wren*, p.246.
18 Ernle Bradford, *The Journeying Moon*, p.21.
19 Author conversation with Kit Power.
20 Lord Stanley of Alderley, *Sea Peace*, p.149.
21 Lord Stanley of Alderley, *Sea Peace*, p.v.
22 Lord 'Skips' Riverdale, *A Life, A Sail. A Changing Sea*, p.80.
23 Jenny Balmer, Letter (2021, March 1).
24 GA Jones, *The Cruise of Naromis*, p.113.

Acknowledgements

First thanks must go to my mother for keeping my father's papers safe after his death and stowing them away in the mouse-proof suitcase in which they moved to my attic. I must also acknowledge the impact of her emotional pain as dementia took down her defences in the later years of her life and the recollections of 1939–1945, which she'd previously suppressed, often overwhelmed her. All our family, especially Francis, will know what a difficult time this was.

I realise how lucky I was, as a child, that my father was so involved with his post-war yacht agency that we children were automatically included, whether it was offering plates of Ritz crackers at office parties, hanging around boatyards, observing the effects of Mark VIII cocktails or spending time on *Peter Duck*. It meant that we met his colleagues, clients and friends, several of whom (like Maurice Griffiths, Norman Clackson, Stewart Platt and Jack Jones) were ex-RNVR. I was usually far too shy to speak to them (and they certainly wouldn't have been talking about the war) but their presence has had an influence on this book.

I'd also like to thank the sons, daughters and other relatives, who have talked to me about their RNVR fathers and gave me permission to share their memories or their published work. They are Jenny Balmer (Peter Cooper), Anthony Balfour (Robin Balfour), Mairet Rowe (David Cobb), the late Julien Courtauld (August Courtauld), Michael Gotelee (Allan Gotelee), Victoria Getty (Gerry Holdsworth), Rachel Hall (Ludovic Kennedy), Amanda Harling (Robert Harling), Hugh Matheson (Rozelle Raynes), John Newell (Eric Newell), Vicky Platt (Stewart Platt), James Skellorn (Kenneth Jacob), Vyvyan Rayner (Denys Rayner), Jonathon Riley (Quintin Riley), Dafila Scott

(Peter Scott), Lincoln Seligman (Adrian Seligman), Edwina Epstein (Edward Stanley), Carla Stanley (Edward & Lyulph Stanley), Vicky Unwin (Tom Unwin), Dee Watt (Bevil Warington Smyth). I'm also grateful to John Anderson, Jeremy Batch, John Blake, Nick Charman, John Coldstream, Dick Durham, Julian Foynes, Richard Ingrams, Elspeth Iskander, Sam Llewellyn, Hugh Matheson, David Mowlam, Claudia Myatt, William Nixon, Kit Power, Andrew Pool, Jim Ring, Mike Farquharson-Roberts, Martin Schultz, Nigel Sharp, my cousins Gwen and Rupert Shaw, Robert Simper, Philip Spender, Ian Stewart, Theo Stocker, Christopher Thornhill, Janet Vera-Sanso, Peter Willis and Richard Woodman for information and introductions.

There are some wonderful research websites: U-boat.net, wrecksite. eu, unithistories.com, navylistresearch.co.uk, naval-history.net, adls. org.uk, http://www.plan-sussex-1944.net/anglais/pdf/infiltrations_ into_france.pdf and Wikipedia. The Little Ship Club, the Cruising Association and the Royal Cruising Club have been unfailingly helpful as have my friends at *Yachting Monthly*.

In addition to the individuals and organisations listed above I'm grateful to the following publishers and agents for permission to quote from published work: Biteback Publishing, Bloomsbury Publishing, Helion and Company, Hodder & Stoughton, Lume Books, Orion Publishing, Pen and Sword Books, Thunderchild Publishing, Unicorn Publishing, United Agents LLP (on behalf of The Trustees of the Estate of the late N S Norway) and *Yachting Monthly*. I have made every effort to contact copyright owners and apologise to those who I haven't reached. Please get in touch so I can rectify this in future.

It was a memorable day when Camilla Shestopal of Shesto Literary agreed to represent the book. (I think I have her father's love of *The Riddle of the Sands* to thank for this decision.) I'd like to thank Camilla for being marvellously supportive and having a great eye for detail, as well as answering emails almost before I've sent them. Kathryn Beer and Elizabeth Multon at Adlard Coles are a delight to work with and my real hope is that some of my family and friends will enjoy reading this book as much as I've enjoyed writing it.

All that remains is to acknowledge the quiet heroism of those who volunteered to go wherever they were sent – and the bravery of those they left behind.

Bibliography

Allingham, Margery, *The Oaken Heart* (Golden Duck, 2011)

Anderson, John, *Parallel Motion* (The Paper Tiger, 2011)

Balchin, Nigel, *The Small Back Room* (The Reprint Society, 1945)

Beesly, Patrick, *Very Special Intelligence* (Sphere Books, 1978)

Barnett, Corelli, *Engage The Enemy More Closely* (Penguin, 2000)

Bender, Mike, *New History of Yachting* (Boydell & Brewer, 2017)

Bennett, AS, *Tide Time* (George Allen and Unwin, 1949)

Bassett, Colonel Sam, *Royal Marine* (Peter Davies, 1962)

Bradford, Ernle, *The Journeying Moon: Sailing into History* (Open Road, 2014)

Buchheim, Lothar-Günther, *Das Boot* (Cassell Military Paperbacks, 1999)

Butler, Mollie, *August and Rab: A Memoir* (Weidenfeld & Nicolson, 1987)

Cable, Alison & Julian, *Robinetta* (AJ & Family, 2019)

Carter, George Goldsmith, *Looming Lights* (Constable, 1945)

Childers, Erskine, *The Riddle of the Sands* (Wordsworth Classics, 1993)

Cobb, David, *The Making of a War Artist* (Conway Maritime Press, 1986)

Coldstream, John, *Dirk Bogarde: The Authorised Biography* (Orion, 2004)

Coles, K. Adlard, *Sailing Years: An Autobiography* (J. de Graff, 1981)

Courtauld, Augustine, *Man the Ropes* (Hodder & Stoughton, 1957)

Cunningham, Viscount Andrew Browne, *A Sailor's Odyssey* (Hutchinson, 1951)

Dalzel-Job, Patrick, *From Arctic Snow to Dust of Normandy* (Leo Cooper, 2005)

Divine, David, *The Nine Days of Dunkirk* (Faber, 1959)

Dönitz, Karl, *The Memoirs of Karl Dönitz* (Frontline Books, 2012)

Drummond, Maldwin, *The Riddle* (Unicorn Publishing Group, 2016)

Durham, Dick, *The Magician of the Swatchways* (IPC Magazines, 1994)

Foynes, JP, *The Battle of the East Coast (1939-1945)* (J.P. Foynes, 1994)

Fell, Captain W.R., *The Sea Our Shield* (Corgi Books, 1970)

Fleming, Ian, *Moonraker* (Pan, 1959)

Foot, M.R.D., *SOE: The Special Operations Executive 1940-1946* (Bodley Head, 2014)

Freeman, Kerin, *The Civilian Bomb Disposing Earl* (Pen and Sword Military, 2015)

Gallico, Paul, *The Snow Goose* (Michael Joseph, 1946)

Griffiths, Maurice, *Hidden Menace* (Conway Maritime Press, 1981)

Griffiths, Maurice, *Post-War Yachting* (Hutchinson's Scientific and Technical Publications, 1945)

Griffiths, Maurice, *Ten Small Yachts and Others* (Edward Arnold & Co, 1933)

Griffiths, Maurice, *The Magic of the Swatchways* (Adlard Coles, 1932)

Griffiths, Maurice, *Yachting on a Small Income* (Hutchinson & Co, 1925 revised edition 1940s)

Harling, Robert, *Amateur Sailor* (Chatto & Windus, 1944)

Harling, Robert, *Ian Fleming: A Personal Memoir* (The Robson Press, 2015)

Harling, Robert, *The Steep Atlantick Stream* (Chatto & Windus, 1946)

Hichens, Antony, *Gunboat Command* (Pen and Sword, 2007)

Hichens, Robert, *We Fought Them in Gunboats* (Michael Joseph, 1944)

Hill, Judith, *In Search of Islands* (The Collins Press, 2009)

Hiscock, Eric C., *I Left the Navy* (Edward Arnold & Co, 1945)

Holland, James, *Normandy '44: D-Day and the Battle for France* (Corgi, 2020)

Holman, Gordon, *The Little Ships* (Hodder & Stoughton, 1946)

Howarth, David, *Pursued by a Bear* (Collins, 1986)

Howarth, David, *The Shetland Bus* (Shetland Times, 1998)

Howarth, Patrick, *Undercover: The Men and Women of the S.O.E.* (Arrow, 1990)

Hugill, JAC, *The Hazard Mesh* (Faber & Faber, 2011)

Hunt, Giles, *Launcelot Fleming: A Portrait* (Canterbury Press, 2003)

Jones, George, *The Cruise of Naromis* (Golden Duck, 2017)

Kennedy, George O'Brien, *Not All At Sea!* (Morrigan Book Co, 1997)

Kennedy, Ludovic, *On My Way to the Club* (Fontana Press, 1990)

Kennedy, Ludovic, *Pursuit* (Cassell Military Paperbacks, 2001)

Kennedy, Ludovic, *Sub-Lieutenant: A Personal Record of the War at Sea* (Batsford Ltd, 1942)

Kerr, J Lennox and Glanville, Wilfred, *The R.N.V.R.: A Record of Achievement* (Harrap & Co, 1957)

Kerr, J Lennox and James David, *Wavy Navy by Some Who Served* (Harrap & Co, 1950)

Lavery, Brian, *In Which They Served* (Conway Maritime Press, 2008)

Lincoln, Fredman Ashe, *Odyssey of a Jewish Sailor* (Minerva Press, 1995)

Lincoln, Fredman Ashe, *Secret Naval Investigator* (Frontline Books, 2017)

Lombard-Hobson, Sam, *A Sailor's War* (Orbis Publishing, 1983)

Lund, Paul and Ludlum, Harry, *Trawlers Go to War* (New English Library, 1974)

Lycett, Andrew, *Ian Fleming, A Life* (Weidenfeld & Nicolson, 1995)

Mace, Martin, *The Royal Navy at Dunkirk* (Frontline Books, 2017)

MacIntyre, Ben, *Operation Mincemeat* (Bloomsbury Publishing, 2010)

McLachlan, Donald, *Room 39: Naval Intelligence in action 1939-45* (Weidenfeld & Nicolson, 1968)

Macksey, Kenneth, *Godwin's Saga* (Brassey's Defence Publications, 1987)

MacLean, Alistair, *HMS Ulysses* (Harper Collins, 2004) (First published Collins, 1955)

McLean, Ruari, *Half Seas Under* (Thomas Reed Publications, 2001)

McLean, Ruari, *True to Type: A Typographical Autobiography* (Werner Shaw, 2000)

Mellor, John, *The Dieppe Raid* (Coronet Books, 1979)

Middlebrook, Martin, *Convoy* (William Morrow and Company, 1977)

Miller, John, *Saints and Parachutes* (Constable, 1951)

Monsarrat, Nicholas, *Life is a Four-Letter Word, Volume One: Breaking In* (Pan Books, 1969) (First published Cassell, 1966)

Monsarrat, Nicholas, *Life is a Four-Letter Word, Volume Two: Breaking Out* (Cassell, 1970)

Monsarrat, Nicholas, *The Cruel Sea* (Penguin, 2009)

Monsarrat, Nicholas, *The Ship that Died of Shame* (Pan Books, 1985)

Monsarrat, Nicholas, *Three Corvettes* (Cassell Military Paperbacks, 1975)

Montagu, Ewen, *Beyond Top Secret Ultra* (Peter Davies, 1977)

Montagu, Ewen, *The Man Who Never Was* (Penguin Books, 1956)

Parker, Linda, *Ice, Steel and Fire: British Explorers in Peace and War 1921-45* (Helion & Company, 2013)

Pawle, Gerald, *The Secret War (1939-1945)* (George Harrap & Co, 1956)

Pearson, John, *The Life of Ian Fleming* (Jonathan Cape, 1966)

Piper, Leonard, *The Tragedy of Erskine Childers* (Hambledon Continuum, 2003)

Platt, Stewart, *My Three Grey Mistresses* (Atlantic Nautical Press, 2002)

Plummer, Russell, *The Ships That Saved an Army* (Patrick Stephens, 1990)

Popham, Hugh and Robin, *A Thirst for the Sea* (Stanford Maritime, 1979)

Quigley, Laura, *South-West Secret Agents* (The History Press, 2014)

Rankin, Nicholas, *Ian Fleming's Commandos* (Faber, 2011)

Rayner, DA, *Escort: The Battle of the Atlantic* (Thunderchild Publishing, 1955)

Rayner, DA, *The Crippled Tanker* (Thunderchild Publishing, 1960)

Rayner, DA, *The Enemy Below* (Thunderchild Publishing, 1956)

Raynes, Rozelle, *Maid Matelot* (Catweasel, 2004)

Richards, Brook, *Secret Flotillas* Volumes 1 & 2 (Pen and Sword, 2012)

Riley, Jonathon, *From Pole to Pole* (Anthony Rowe, 1998)

Ring, Jim, *Erskine Childers* (Faber and Faber, 2011)

Riverdale, Lord, *Nine Lives in One* (Sheffield Academic Press, 1998)

Riverdale, Lord 'Skips', *A Life, A Sail, A Changing Sea* (Hutton Press, 1995)

Rutherford, Iain W., *At the Tiller* (Blackie & Son, 1946)

Sayers, Dorothy, *Murder Must Advertise* (Victor Gollancz, 1933)

Scott, Sir Peter, *The Eye of the Wind* (Hodder & Stoughton, 1966)

Scott, Peter, *The Battle of the Narrow Seas: The History of the Light Coastal Forces in the Channel and North Sea 1939-1945* (Country Life, 1945)

Sebag-Montefiore, Hugh, *Dunkirk: Fight to the Last Man* (Penguin, 2015)

Seligman, Adrian, *The Voyage of the Cap Pilar* (Seafarer Books, 1993)

Seligman, Adrian, *No Stars to Guide* (Hodder & Stoughton, 1947)

Seligman, Adrian, *War in the Islands: Undercover Operations in the Aegean, 1942-4* (Alan Sutton, 1996)

Sharp, Nigel, *Troubled Waters: Leisure Boating and the Second World War* (Amberley Publishing, 2015)

Shute, Nevil, *Slide Rule* (Vintage Classics, 2009)

Shute, Nevil, *Landfall* (Vintage Classics, 2009)

Shute, Nevil, *Most Secret* (Vintage Classics, 2009)

Shute, Nevil, *On the Beach* (Vintage Classics, 2009)

Shute, Nevil, *Pastoral* (Vintage Classics, 2009)

Shute, Nevil, *Pied Piper* (The Reprint Society, 1943)

Shute, Nevil, *Requiem for a Wren* (Vintage Classics, 2009)

Shute, Nevil, *The Chequer Board* (Vintage Classics, 2009)

Shute, Nevil, *Whatever Happened to the Corbetts* (Vintage Classics, 2009)

Simper, Robert, *The Lost Village of Ramsholt* (Creekside, 2020)

Small, Ken, *The Forgotten Dead* (Osprey Publishing, 1988)

Smith, Peter C, *Hold the Narrow Sea* (Moorland Publishing, 1984)

Stanley of Alderley, Lord, *Sea Peace* (Peter Davies, 1955)

Simmons, Mark, *Ian Fleming's War* (The History Press, 2020)

Terrell, Edward, *Admiralty Brief* (Harrap & Co, 1958)

Thorn, Richard, *Shute: The Engineer Who Became a Prince of Storytellers* (Matador, 2017)

Unwin, Vicky, *The Boy from Boskovice: A Father's Secret Life* (Unbound, 2021)

Wilkinson, Peter and Bright Astley, Joan, *Gubbins and SOE* (Pen and Sword, 2010)

Winn, Godfrey, *P.Q. 17* (Arrow, 1966)

Wollaston, Nicholas, *The Man on the Ice Cap* (Constable, 1980)

Woodcock, Percy, *Looking Astern* (Frederick Muller, 1950)

Woodman, Richard, *Arctic Convoys 1941-1945* (John Murray, 1994)

Woodman, Richard, *The Real Cruel Sea* (John Murray, 2005)

Young, Edward, *One of Our Submarines* (Penguin, 1954)

Index